"An immensely rigorous and original book. Alth‹
displacement has been examined separately befc‒‒, ‒‒‒ ‒‒‒‒‒‒‒‒‒ ‒‒ ‒‒‒
book lies in showing how the English enclosures can be seen as a prototype
and precedent for the Amerindian and Palestinian cases through the instruments of enclosure, cartography, and law."

Salim Tamari, Senior Fellow, Institute for Palestine Studies,
and Professor of Sociology, Birzeit University

"To successfully bring together Palestinian dispossession, U.S. settler colonialism, and early modern English enclosure in one text requires both intellectual ambition and wide-ranging scholarship. While recognizing the
specificity of each site, Gary Fields' impressive and accessible work offers
original insights into the world-changing work of enclosure and dispossession, tracing the powerful political geographies of discourses of 'improvement,' and the particular technical work of law, maps, and architecture. This
is a valuable and important book."

Nicholas Blomley, Professor of Geography, Simon Fraser University

"*Enclosure* is a masterful study of how landscapes come into being, first as
imaginable claims to land, and then through technologies of force that
remake the material world to exclude and enclose those populations who are
outside of the imaginative geography of the claimants. While the book
focuses on the history of land claims and landscapes in Palestine/Israel,
Gary Fields' analysis is enriched through comparison with the processes
of claiming and enclosing lands in early modern England and North
America."

Lisa Hajjar, Professor of Sociology, University of California,
Santa Barbara

[Pakistan - an act of
geopolitical imagination]

to byelin of   power & space
book p20   marginal property

        linkage   Europeans
                    in UK
                    US Indians
                    Palestine

                enclosure in
                UK p 26

Protest
against
enclosure

                gender issues
                women harvest p99
                men drink 109, 111
                    fight

        -p126/127   "savage" have
                    no right to record

Christian - P XI   Though
justification   shall not
for taking   steal
                    (Thou shall
Amer Indian   not murder)
land:
prior p102
    113   p5, p13*
    -            American
Christianity   Indians
    P119
    P126*   Zionist
Row. Sym note
        p128   p16 Israel
                "state land
**   law"
128
Locke
P130   p18 settlements
10 acres
in
December   P41 - moral
    P13   economy

P103*
    - No enclosure / no possession
But own sense   P129

P139 Birth of American exceptionalism
    -

|P145 - How money was made
    -

P194 o Human mapping
    limitation
        *P217   214
        Hebrew mandate

Myth of
Arcadia/
land
p157
Zionist
book P40
    -
    militia
    P166
LAND
Hebrew
lawyer
;
Arab
refers to
as Pablo

p55 Revolt
Ludge
destruction

P66
Robinson
Crusoe

P67
Unitarian
dissident

Enclosure

PALESTINIAN LANDSCAPES IN
A HISTORICAL MIRROR

Gary Fields

UNIVERSITY OF CALIFORNIA PRESS

University of California Press, one of the most distinguished university presses in the United States, enriches lives around the world by advancing scholarship in the humanities, social sciences, and natural sciences. Its activities are supported by the UC Press Foundation and by philanthropic contributions from individuals and institutions. For more information, visit www.ucpress.edu.

University of California Press
Oakland, California

© 2017 by The Regents of the University of California

Library of Congress Cataloging-in-Publication Data

Names: Fields, Gary, 1954– author.
Title: Enclosure : Palestinian landscapes in a historical mirror / Gary Fields.
Description: University of California Press : Oakland, California, [2017] |
    Includes bibliographical references and index.
Identifiers: LCCN 2017002268 (print) | LCCN 2017011093 (ebook) |
    ISBN 9780520291041 (cloth : alk. paper) | ISBN 9780520291058
    (pbk. : alk. paper) | ISBN 9780520964921 (ebook)
Subjects: LCSH: Land tenure—Middle East.
Classification: LCC HD850 .F535 2017 (print) | LCC HD850 (ebook) |
    DDC 333.3/15694—dc23
LC record available at https://lccn.loc.gov/2017002268

Manufactured in the United States of America

26 25 24 23 22 21 20 19 18 17
10 9 8 7 6 5 4 3 2 1

CONTENTS

ILLUSTRATIONS

FIGURES

TABLE

PREFACE AND ACKNOWLEDGMENTS

Enclosure began as a study of the walled landscape in Occupied Palestine that I found both hypnotic and horrifying on a trip to the region in 2003–4. Although at the outset I had no plans to use the trip as the basis for a book project, by the time I returned I had sketched out some preliminary ideas to compare this walled environment with other deliberately walled and partitioned territorial spaces around the world, from Melilla and Ceuta in Morocco to San Diego/Tijuana, where I live and work. What was striking to me in these three borderlands was how walls, as a distinct element of landscape architecture, convey such overt impulses of power in preempting people from moving across territorial space based on notions of "otherness" and difference. Indeed, these walled spaces seemed to be the paragon of landscapes embodying "Power" (Mitchell 2002) and "Fear" (Tuan 2013) woven together in an otherwise paradoxical story about re-bordering in the modern world. With Palestine/Israel, Spain/Morocco, and the United States/Mexico, I had what I believed were three compelling case studies of how fear and power become materialized into walls as part of a global effort to control certain groups of people. My book would be a comparative cultural geography of such walled territorial landscapes.

As I began fieldwork on the Palestinian case and listened to Palestinian farmers and the mayors of several Palestinian towns describing the Wall and its impacts, my thinking about the project shifted. Although the Wall in Palestine was, and remains, a symbol of power, fear, and control, these voices were revealing a far more salient story about the landscape, focusing on dispossession and the transfer of land from one group of people to another. Framed in this way, Palestine's Wall, and the actors affected by it, become part of a historically long-standing narrative about rights to land—and land hunger.

There is a well-developed literature on Palestine that situates the land hunger confronting these farmers in a broader historical and theoretical context: settler colonialism. Within this paradigm is a compelling body of work that engages the issue of Palestinian dispossession from the perspective of territorial landscapes and geographical space (Abu El-Haj 2001; Yiftachel 2006; Weizman 2007; Hanafi 2009, 2013). In this fundamentally spatial approach to dispossession, land is a contested resource, the focus of conflict between two main groups, as settlers from outside confront landholders in the place of arrival and seek to take possession of land already possessed and used. Broadly speaking, this model of settler colonialism describes what has transpired in Palestine while placing Palestinian dispossession in a more historically enduring narrative of similar cases.

One obvious precedent for the pattern of Zionist settlement in Palestine is the Anglo-American colonization of North America. Indeed, the ever-combative early Zionist Ze'ev Jabotinsky, in his essay "The Iron Wall" (1923), spoke honestly about the parallels of Zionist settlement in Palestine and the efforts of English and later American colonists to seize control of Native American land. Far from critiquing the phenomenon, however, Jabotinsky proffered a sobering and cautionary tale to his fellow Zionists, warning that just as Zionist settlers shared a common cause with their Anglo-American colonial counterparts, so too would Palestinians follow in the spirit of Native Americans and resist Zionists taking their land. In other words, the figure considered the inspiration of the modern Israeli Right provided an affirmation of the parallels between settler colonialism in America and Zionist settlement of Palestine—in much the same way that anti-Zionist critics of Israel might argue.

If settler colonialism provides a trenchant explanation for the dispossession of Palestinians, in a sense this perspective is also incomplete. In his celebrated study of colonial ambitions, *Culture and Imperialism,* Edward Said observed that colonization in the first instance is a material phenomenon involving the takeover and possession of land (Said 1993, 78). At the same time, Said insisted that colonization was more than a narrow material reflex; rather, it derived from the mental universe of colonizers who reimagined the land they were about to possess as their rightful patrimony. Said referred to this discursive process of reinventing meanings about land as "imaginative geography." One of the most celebrated theoretical breakthroughs in cultural geography and a host of disciplines across the humanities and social sciences, imaginative geography is a central theoretical point of entry for *Enclosure.*

What colonists projected onto the geographical landscapes they were coveting and reinventing was land that was empty—*terra nullius:* land without owners. For English colonists, the idea of land in the New World being empty played a critically important role in the imagined geography of North America. If land in the New World was in fact already possessed by the indigenous Americans whom the English encountered, then the idea of repossessing that land posed something of a moral dilemma for the colonizers coveting such property. Although powerful monarchs conveniently found ways to contravene the commandment "Thou shalt not steal," theft was still a sin according to the Word of the Creator, and taking land belonging to someone else would certainly cast the perpetrator as sinful. Empty land, however, did not pose the same dilemma for the colonizer. For the English colonial mission in North America, it was essential to imagine the New World as a wasteland, empty and absent of owners.

How did English colonists, beginning with the Virginia Company in 1607–9, convince themselves and their patrons that the land they coveted in North America was waste land, and in the process imagine the English as the land's legitimate owners and stewards? At their disposal was an evolving common law discourse with roots in the mid-fifteenth century that framed basic principles by which "plots of the earth" could be owned much like so-called "moveable items." This discourse, which established the early foundations for rights to land as property, was exploited by the promotors of colonization in Virginia such as Robert Gray and William Strachey.

What this discourse suggested was that the right to own land as property accrued to persons using their labor to make improvements on what would otherwise be land lying empty in waste. "Improvement" through labor was thus the principle by which one earned rights to land. At the same time, this discourse provided a way of verifying empirically and visually whether a particular area of the landscape was legitimately improved and therefore possessed by an owner. Land improved and thus owned had two attributes. In the first place, it was plowed and cultivated; and second, the plowed and cultivated land was enclosed by the improver with a fence or other aboveground barrier to separate it from plots owned by other improvers, and from unimproved land surrounding it without owners that was held in common. This discourse helped to promote the practice of enclosing unimproved plots of land in England—mostly land used as a collective resource—in order to make the land more productive. In this way, enclosure and individual rights to land as property became fused together as a strategy for improving the unimproved land lying in waste in the English countryside.

By 1630, John Winthrop, the first governor of the Massachusetts Bay Colony, was using these same arguments to justify the taking of Amerindian land in New England. The "Natives in New England," he famously wrote, "inclose noe land" and have no means by which "to improve the Land." As a consequence, Winthrop insisted that the land "lay open to any that could and would improve it" (from Cronon 2003, 56). Despite pretenses to objectivity, Winthrop's observations were replete with culturally relative judgments about the meaning of "improvement" and "cultivation." Winthrop, like later English colonists, insisted that because Amerindian agricultural fields were not plowed but were established primitively with hoes, such plots did not conform to the standards of improvement practiced by the English settler and planter. In this way, cultivation and improvement were imbued with decidedly English attributes that essentially disqualified Amerindians as landowners and enabled colonizers to register claims on the land—as Winthrop had advocated.

No person articulated this fusion of enclosure, improvement, and colonization more systematically than John Locke (1690). Although Locke is often credited with devising a theory of landed property rights grounded in the improvement doctrine, this idea, as laid out in the Improvement Discourse of Common Law, pre-dated him by at least 150 years. What Locke did that *was* original was to merge ideas about entitlement of land through improvement and enclosure, and notions of colonization, into a universal system of landed property rights. By the time Locke was writing, promoters of land improvement conceived of territorial landscapes in two broad categories: either landscapes were enclosed and improved, or they were unenclosed and unimproved and thus available to be enclosed and appropriated by the enterprising improver of land. For Locke, the rational logic of gaining possession of land by improving it justified the takeover of otherwise unimproved land not only in England, but also in England's overseas colonies. In this way, the impulses reshaping the English countryside with enclosed and fenced plots of privately owned land were also reconfiguring English colonial settlement in North America with a landscape of enclosed and fenced settler homesteads. "When the English took possession of lands overseas," write Peter Linebaugh and Markus Rediker in *The Many-Headed Hyrda*, "they did so by building fences and hedges, the markers of enclosure and private property" (Linebaugh and Rediker 2012, 44).

From the enclosure of land in England and the colonial settlement of land in North America emerged spaces in the landscape with the same fundamental attribute: exclusivity. Such spaces were *owned,* and what comes with ownership is the right to exclude. In the case of land, the right to exclude involves the right to prevent access by others within a territorial space demarcated by boundary lines and defined as "mine and not yours." In the enforcement of this right to exclude, the law and the fence play complementary roles as instruments of force. The law prevents encroachment onto landed property by virtue of the "police power" embedded within it to arrest and remove trespassers. Fencing prevents encroachment onto landed property by virtue of its physical power as a material impediment to circulation and free movement across space. Both enclosure and colonial settlement drew lines—boundaries—on the landscape, and within the enclosed spaces promoters of enclosure and promoters of colonization pursued practices of exclusion enforceable through the power of the state and the law and through the power of physical barriers. In both cases, whether by means of enclosure or colonial settlement, the outcome on the landscape was the same. Enclosure and colonial settlement turned areas of the landscape into exclusionary space. In one case, the enclosed space was private individual property; in the other, the exclusionary space became white settler property.

Enclosure argues that the establishment of a Jewish landscape in Palestine is part of this same lineage of creating exclusionary spaces, a lineage inclusive of colonial settler space and traceable to the early modern enclosures in England. Surprisingly, I am not aware of anyone who has likened Palestinian dispossession to the enclosures in England in this way. What readers will discover in the pages that follow is how the discourse of improvement and landed property rights migrated from early modern England, to England's overseas colonies, and later to Palestine. This discourse enabled early Zionists—and even Israel's rulers today—to imagine the Palestinian landscape as waste land, and to justify the taking of this land not only because it was "promised" to the Jewish people by God, but also because the Zionists imagined themselves to be the most able improvers and modernizers of this territory. When Zionists from Theodor Herzl to David Ben-Gurion invoked images of a barren landscape in Palestine and described how Jewish settler-pioneers could and did redeem the land from those Palestinians who had so long neglected it, they were speaking the same language as Winthrop and other English colonists of his day. These English colonists, in turn, drew inspiration from the English common law discourse about improvement, enclosure, and rights to landed property in justifying the taking of Amerindian land. This discourse is still prevalent among

Zionists in Israel/Palestine today. In the end, *Enclosure* reveals how the making of private space, the making of white space, and the making of Jewish space on territorial landscapes all spring from the same exclusionary impulses deriving from the enclosures and the appropriation of land in England. Such impulses have enabled groups of people across time and territory to proclaim: "This is my land and not yours."

. . .

Once enclosure emerged as the central organizing concept for the book, three individuals played a decisive role in convincing me that I had a legitimate point of departure for understanding Palestinian dispossession. When I asked my friend and colleague Jim Rauch whether Palestinian dispossession and the English Enclosures might make a good comparison, he unhesitatingly responded that indeed they would, and one much better than my original notion. My first presentation of the concept was at the American Association of Geographers 2006 annual conference. Ghazi-Walid Falah was in the audience and commented that he had never encountered English Enclosure as an approach to Palestinian dispossession; he later invited me to revise and submit my paper to the journal he edited, *The Arab World Geographer,* where it appeared the following year (Fields 2007), the first official milestone in the long process that has led to this book. Curious about what Palestinians in the Occupied Territories might think of the idea, I asked Raja Shehadeh, author of the acclaimed *Palestinian Walks: Forays into a Vanishing Landscape* (2008), if he would meet with me in Ramallah to discuss it. I was accustomed to having to explain the English Enclosures, but before I could do so, Raja was telling me about one of the most famous poets of the Enclosure period, John Clare, and admitted that he had often thought about the English Enclosures when considering the situation in Occupied Palestine. These three individuals convinced me that I had a viable, if unorthodox, project.

With three intensive case studies consisting of very different literatures, *Enclosure* has consumed almost all of my time and energy during the past ten years and has gone through innumerable iterations while being read and critiqued along the way by many individuals. Readers of various drafts, in whole or in part, include Nadia Abu El-Haj, Stuart Banner, Nick Blomley, Max Edelson, Geremy Forman, Ross Frank, Lisa Hajjar, Deborah Hertz, Sabrina Joseph, Nathalie Kayadjanian, Hasan Kayali, Martha Lampland,

Peter Mancall, Andrew McCrae, Jeanette Neeson, Michael Provence, Jim Rauch, Pam Stern, Salim Tamari, and Oren Yiftachel.

Some of the most insightful critiques of the various drafts came from my colleagues in the Communication Department at UCSD. Never wavering in their support of the project, they contributed mightily to this book. These individuals include Patrick Anderson, Dan Hallin, Val Hartouni, Robert Horwitz, David Serlin, and Stefan Tanaka, all of whom played crucial roles in helping me sharpen my argument.

This book required a great deal of fieldwork, which was not possible without financial help. I am indebted above all to the Palestinian American Research Center (PARC) and its tireless executive director, Penelope Mitchell. At a relatively early stage in this project, PARC extended to me one of the most coveted fellowships in the field of Palestine studies. I cannot be more grateful for the support PARC gave me. A fellowship from the Hellman Foundation was also instrumental in helping me launch this project in the early phases. My own institution, UCSD, has been enormously supportive of this book, with the Academic Senate here funding several trips to Palestine/Israel. Finally, I received critical help at a late stage in the book from the UCSD Humanities Center, which supported me as a faculty fellow in 2013–14 and was instrumental in organizing reviews of my book-in-progress by other fellows at the Center.

My fieldwork was also made possible by a great many people on the ground in Palestine/Israel who were instrumental in helping me navigate a sometimes difficult environment. Above all, I want to thank Dr. Jad Issac, who put several of his staff from the Applied Research Institute of Jerusalem at my disposal, from setting up interviews to creating maps for this book. Early on in the project, Jamal Juma oriented me to the walled landscape in Palestine and took me in his car for an afternoon and evening all around the Jerusalem, Ramallah, and Bethlehem area, pointing out and explaining to me how the landscape had changed owing to Israeli occupation. Abdul-Latif Khaled from Jayyous hosted me numerous times, and his expertise as an agricultural hydrologist provided me with enormous insights about Palestinian agriculture and the challenges facing the Palestinian rural landowner. Dr. Awad Abu Freih, Sultan Abu Obaid, Khalil Alamour, Fadi Masamra, Haia Noch, and Michal Rotem were all extraordinarily generous in taking me for extensive tours of the Naqab/Negev and explaining the history and culture of the area. In addition, I want to thank Thaer Arafat, Iyad Burnat, Jonathan Cook, Paul Garon, Juliette George, Shmuel Groag, Abd al-Hameed Jabsche, Shareef

Omar Khaled, Mohammed Khel, Nasfat Al-Khofash, Hisham Matar, Ayed Morrar, Faraj Qadous, Hussein Al-Rimmawi, Qustandi Shamali, Fayez Tanib, Mona Tanib, Lisa Taraki, Ali Zbiedat, and others too numerous to name. Finally, I received critical help from Jeff Light, editor of the *San Diego Union Tribune.*

In addition to the tangible contributions to this project made by individuals already named, many people contributed to *Enclosure* in ways that are less specific but no less important. Christiane Passevant and Larry Portis are two such individuals who have inspired me enormously with their travels to and interest in Palestine since the early 1980s. Although I'm saddened that Larry is not able to see the end result of his influence, his spirit and that of Christiane are very much present in the book.

Once I had completed roughly two-thirds of the book, I started to look for a publisher and eventually contacted Niels Hooper at UC Press. He was intrigued from the first moment we spoke, and at his insistence I kept sending him updates of the manuscript. I am extremely grateful to Niels for his support of this project and for his tireless work in bringing it to life.

Often at the end of a long book project, there is one person whose level of help and generosity rises above all the rest. For *Enclosure,* that person is Ellen Seiter. During the last two years, as the push to finish this project grew more intense, Ellen read draft after draft, chapter after chapter—over and over again. At each step she provided invaluable suggestions for improving the text while at the same time reassuring me that the material was strong and the book important. I'll never be able to thank her enough.

Enclosure is appearing at an auspicious moment in time. The year 2017 marks fifty years since the state of Israel conquered the Palestinian West Bank and Gaza, territories that it controls to this day. Whether this situation will change soon is an open question. A celebrated inscription at the National Archives in Washington reminds us that in the study of human affairs, the past is prologue. There is indeed much to learn from the historical lineage that produced the dispossession still occurring today, including perhaps some insights for correcting past injustices and building a future with justice for all.

ONE

The Contours of Enclosure

God gave the world to men in common; but it cannot be supposed he meant it should always remain common.... As much land as a man tills, plants, improves, cultivates, and can use the product of, so much is his property. He by his labour does, as it were, enclose it from the common.

JOHN LOCKE, *Second Treatise on Civil Government* (1690)

As for the Natives ... they enclose no land.... Only the fields tended by the Native women are their property, the rest of the country lay open to any that could and would improve it. So if we leave them sufficient [land], we may lawfully take the rest.

JOHN WINTHROP, governor of Massachusetts (1629)

When we built Ariel, we never took one square inch of land from anybody. This land was empty. Show me the document that said it belonged to them [Palestinians].... They [Palestinians] don't plant! They don't do anything with the land! Look at what we've built here.

RON NAHMAN, mayor of Ariel, author interview, August 5, 2005

IT WAS DECEMBER 2003 when the impulses for this book initially took shape on a fragmented portion of the Israeli/Palestinian landscape. That year, I found my way to this embattled region with a group of educators sponsored by the organization Faculty for Israeli/Palestinian Peace (FFIPP), which had arranged an ambitious program of venues for us to visit, including places at that time still very much under siege. With a long-standing interest in the geopolitics of the area, I imagined myself primed for a rare opportunity to observe firsthand one of the world's most intractable, conflict-riven environments. Early in the trip, organizers took the group to a hilltop vista in the Palestinian East Jerusalem neighborhood of Ar-Ram, at the Jerusalem city limit, where we were able to look north into the Palestinian town of Qalandia,

FIGURE 1. The Wall at Qalandia in 2003 as seen from the East Jerusalem neighborhood of Ar-Ram. Photo by author.

situated just over the Green Line demarcating the boundary between Israel and the West Bank. The vantage point on that hilltop provided an almost perfect metaphor of the conflict, communicated through a view out onto a truly arresting geographical landscape.

Stationed along the southern perimeter of Qalandia was an elongated concrete wall, its grayish façade of vertically ribbed concrete panels sweeping aggressively across the landscape, partially concealing the building faces on the town's southern edge (fig. 1). I was familiar with the barrier because it had become something of a news story, though few images of it—even to this day—appeared in the mainstream media. While I had been to the Berlin Wall when it was still standing, I had never encountered such unmitigated power conveyed so forcefully in the built environment. During the rest of the trip, as the group witnessed similarly partitioned landscapes in Tulkarem and Abu Dis, I was continually taken aback by the intensity of these deliberately fractured environments. These landscapes are the foundation for the central theme in this book: enclosure.

From the very beginning, my impulse for this exploration of enclosure has been comparative. The landscapes I observed in the Palestinian West Bank had a compelling echo in the similarly imposing, walled borderland environment of San Diego/Tijuana, close to where I live and work. With this comparison as a starting point, my early fieldwork combined several visits to my immediate border area with a six-week immersion in Israel/Palestine, where my focus was the West Bank Wall and its impacts. On this second trip to Israel/Palestine, however, one of my interviewees would change how I understood what was occurring in the West Bank landscape. This interview was with the mayor of the Palestinian town of Qalqilya, Maa'rouf Zahran.

By 2004, Qalqilya had assumed a somewhat heroic status in the conflict after Israeli authorities encircled it with a concrete wall, giving the town a celebrated if unenviable pedigree as a modern-day ghetto. After an interview of almost two hours, the mayor asked if I could return the following day so he could drive me to certain areas of Qalqilya and point out firsthand some of the impacts the Wall had had on the life of the city. I was happy to oblige.

The next day, Mayor Zahran showed me where Israeli army bulldozers had come under cover of night to begin the massive construction of the barrier. "We were placed under curfew and could not come out of our houses, but we could hear construction work for the next three days," he said. "When they lifted the curfew and we came out to see what they had built, we were shocked." As we got out of his car and began walking alongside the Wall, the mayor became more impassioned. "Our farmers cannot get to their land," he insisted. "They have enclosed us." The word *enclosed*, evoking the economic history of England with its early modern enclosures of land, resonated in my imagination. I knew that the English enclosures had dispossessed small farmers and eradicated access to common land across the English countryside.

Reflecting on the mayor's metaphor over the next several months, I decided to abandon the work I had already done on the border environment near me, convinced that I had a more meaningful point of entry into what was occurring in Palestine than the walled borderland of San Diego/Tijuana. What I had come to perceive in the partitioned morphology of the Palestinian landscape was a different analytical referent, one with echoes of the dispossessed from a more distant historical past.

COMPARING PAST AND PRESENT

The meaning of events in the present often remains elusive to both the actors participating in them and those writing about them. Although this assessment might seem counterintuitive, perception of events in the moment suffers from two types of distortion that can compromise judgments about the present day. On the one hand, analysis of current events often succumbs to what economic historian Paul David (1991, 317) has vividly described as "presbyopia," the failure to see events clearly owing to an exaggerated sense of the present as historically unique. When framed in this way, current events become separated from a meaningful relationship to the past. The second tendency exhibits the opposite problem by insisting—naively—that history repeats itself. This approach suggests that human affairs are an ongoing narrative of repetitive occurrences, with events in the present being explainable by reference to past precedent. While the first view overstates the uniqueness of the moment, the second flattens the human story into an ongoing cyclical pattern, one that fails to heed the insight of historians from Hegel and Marx to Marc Bloch and E. H. Carr that history does not in fact repeat. Instead, history is more akin to verse. It *rhymes,* rather than repeats, thus revealing parallels in events and outcomes from different periods in the past that provide a way of seeing the world at hand.

In the spirit of this metaphor, *Enclosure* acts as a lens, focusing on past events to uncover the meaning of a phenomenon observable in the world today. While taking inspiration from the pioneers of comparative historical methodology (Ibn Khaldun 1381), it also draws insight from modern practitioners of comparative history (Skocpol 1984, 2003; Tilly 1984). Substantively, however, this study places *landscape* at the center of comparative analysis in order to tell a story about power and conflict over rights to land.

Enclosure reveals how a historically recurrent pattern of power manifested in different geographical places has shaped the fragmented and partitioned landscape visible in Palestine today. To support this claim, this study revisits the territorial landscapes of two earlier historical periods: the early modern enclosures of England and the Anglo-American colonial frontier. The fundamental question posed in the comparison of these three cases is:

> How does landscape become the site of confrontation between groups with territorial ambitions and indigenous groups seeking to protect their rights to land, and how do these encounters reshape the landscape to reflect the outcomes of power, resistance, and dispossession that emerge as a consequence?

Using historical comparison to address this question, *Enclosure* argues that the Palestinian landscape is part of an enduring narrative of reallocations in property rights in which groups with territorial ambitions gain control of land owned or used by others (Banner 2002, S360). This narrative reveals how across time and territory, groups coveting land partake of the landscape in a similar way. They use force to dispossess groups already there, justifying their ascendancy as the landscape's new sovereigns by referencing their capacity to modernize life on the land (Day 2008; LeVine 2005, 15–27).

Influenced by a discourse from early modern England about the virtues of "land improvement," such groups seeking a route to modernity come to imagine a modern order in terms of a changeover in the system of land tenure. This discourse suggested to would-be modernizers that land improvement leading to progress in the human condition was contingent on assigning individual rights of ownership to plots of ground, a departure from prevailing notions of the ground as a repository of use rights. While improving land conferred rights of ownership upon the improver, it was the ownership of land that provided incentive to those with ambition to initiate improvements in the first place. In this way, rights to land and improving land became inextricably linked on the path to modern progress.

By the early sixteenth century in England, the notion of owning land as a catalyst for improving it and a reward for the improver gathered momentum and inspired conversions of unimproved "waste" land into property. In such conversions, the improver became vested with the most basic right of property, the right of *exclusion*. Such a right, in turn, entitled the landowner to exclude nonowners from the land as trespassers.

What emerged from this discourse was a rationale for improving unimproved waste land along with a justification for creating exclusionary spaces on the English landscape. Moreover, once established in England, this discourse found its way to England's overseas colonies where it legitimized the colonial impulse to take possession of supposedly unimproved Amerindian land. Eventually this discourse migrated to more distant areas such as Palestine, where Zionists echoed the same themes about modernization and land improvement in justifying their own takeover of Palestinian land and the creation of Jewish spaces on the Palestinian landscape. Thus, the establishment of exclusionary Jewish spaces on the Palestinian landscape is part of the same lineage that converted common land in England to private property and Amerindian land to white property. All three cases reflect the same basic attribute of exclusivity established from a changeover in the system of land tenure, in which the land's new owners rationalized their takeover of territorial landscapes by insisting on their unique capabilities to modernize and improve the land.

Starting from this imagined vision, modernizers enlist three critical instruments—maps, property law, and landscape architecture—to gain control of land from existing landholders and remake life on the landscape consistent with their modernizing aims. Such transfers of land and changes in systems of landed property rights became inscribed into the land surface through the remaking of boundaries on landscapes. This practice of bounding the land defines "spaces of belonging" where people can live, work, and circulate. In reordering boundaries on the land, groups with modernizing aspirations and territorial ambitions set aside ever larger areas for themselves while diminishing and even eradicating spaces of belonging for the dispossessed. This process of overturning rights to land in which land passes from one group of landholders to another, and of remaking boundaries on the landscape to match this change in land ownership and use, is referred to in this study as the phenomenon of enclosure.

Enclosure is a practice resulting in the transfer of land from one group of people to another and the establishment of exclusionary spaces on territorial landscapes. At the same time, enclosure brings profound material changes to the land surface after the practitioners of enclosure replace the disinherited as sovereigns and stewards on the land and begin to construct an entirely different culture on the landscape. Equally far-reaching are enclosure's impacts in redistributing people to different locations. Those redrawing boundaries on the land designate the enclosed areas as spaces of belonging for the promoters of enclosure, while those displaced by enclosure are driven into ever-diminishing territorial spaces, their presence on the landscape now considered trespass subject to removal. One trenchant description of this process reveals how it resulted in the "clearing" of the landscape and the "sweeping" of people from the land (Marx 1867, 681).

Enclosure argues that the Palestinian landscape is part of this lineage of dispossession and that this lineage of establishing exclusionary territorial spaces on the land surface is traceable to the practice of overturning systems of rights to land stemming from the enclosures in early modern England. By the early seventeenth century, this pattern of dispossession and the creation of exclusionary landscapes had migrated from England to its North American colonies. And today, it is found on the landscapes of dispossession in Palestine/Israel. By drawing on historical comparison to reveal this recurrent pattern of enclosure on land, this book aims to uncover meanings in the Palestinian landscape not otherwise knowable from direct observation in the present alone.

THEORIZING LANDSCAPE

In the formal language of research, the three case studies of enclosure and dispossession in this book form a unified story focusing on the interplay of two primary variables, the independent variable of *power* and the dependent variable of *landscape*. In thus aligning power and landscape, *Enclosure* draws from the broad theoretical insight of Foucault (1984, 252) about power as a fundamentally spatial phenomenon and, conversely, the geographical notion of landscape as "power materialized" (Philo 2011, 165; Mitchell 2012, 397). *Enclosure* tracks the variation in the landscape across the three cases when dominant groups coveting territory use their power to seize control of land in an effort to modernize patterns of development in a place. In this way, *Enclosure* contributes empirical insights to one of the defining theoretical issues in human geography—how power shapes and remakes the space of territorial landscapes (Mitchell 2002). What results when power is applied to the landscape and control of land passes from one group to another is the focus of this study: enclosure landscapes.

As a theoretical concept, "landscape" has two basic attributes. In the first place, landscapes have materiality corresponding to the morphology of the land surface that is created by the interplay of the "natural" environment and human activity. In this sense, landscapes emerge from the way the land surface anchors human populations and the systems of cultivation, the patterns of economy and culture, and the architectural forms sustaining human presence (Baker 2003, 78). Such a perspective derives from the work of Carl Sauer, who viewed the landscape as a cultural phenomenon in which human activity is the agent, the natural environment the medium, and the cultural landscape the outcome (Sauer 1925, 343). From this perspective, landscapes are socially constructed territorial spaces that possess a material reality corresponding to what "the eye can comprehend at a glance" (Jackson 1984, 3).

Such morphological contours imbue landscapes with the attributes of *texts* that convey meanings about the life processes occurring on the land surface. Just as books communicate through words, landscapes communicate through the contours of land. While there is not always a directly perceivable route from the material landscape to human life processes in a place, the land surface is nevertheless a starting point for reading land as a document that reflects meanings about the society and human activity anchored to it (Widgren 2006, 57; Mitchell 2000, 113).

Landscapes also convey meanings about the societies anchored to them on the basis of viewers' interpretations of what they are observing (Said 2000; Cosgrove 2006, 50; Schein 1997, 664). Thus, the landscape is not limited to "what lies before our eyes"; it also comprises "what lies in our heads" (Meinig 1979, 34). From this perspective, landscapes are still texts, but now they are open-ended documents in which viewers imbue land surfaces with meaning.

By this process of perception, landscapes transition from reflections of society to sources of projection and imagination.

From this foundation of landscape as both material and representational, the land surface becomes understandable along a continuum (Braverman 2009a, 8–9). On one end of this continuum is the morphological concept of land in which land assumes strictly material attributes. On the other end is the subjective and representational idea of land in which human actors imagine and project meaning onto the land surface. *Enclosure* draws upon both notions in seeking to uncover the interplay of landscape and power.

Once imbued with meaning stemming from human imagination, landscapes are open to change from human action. Just as human actors reshape society according to their ideas about the world, so too do they remake the landscape in terms of how they understand and imagine it. This notion of landscape as a socially constructed outcome of human imagination and human activity is best described by a geographical concept that lies at the center of *Enclosure,* "territoriality."

Territoriality refers to the efforts of individuals or groups to shape patterns of development in a place by "asserting control over a geographic area" (Sack 1986, 19). From this premise, territoriality reserves a role for landscapes as outcomes of power and human agency (Mukerji 1997, 2). At the same time, territoriality elevates landscapes as *instruments* of power in which human action manipulates the land surface to remake the very life processes that are anchored to it (Weizman 2007).

Two sets of literature provide theoretical foundations in *Enclosure* for connecting landscape to power and building an argument about the recurrent pattern of power inscribed into territorial space to enclose and seize control of land. The first set of literature examines the role of human imagination—imaginative geography—as a source of power motivating human actions to remake landscapes. The second explores maps, law, and landscape architecture as "technologies of force" for transforming land.

Imaginative Geography

The inspiration for the first set of literature derives from Edward Said (1978, 1993, 2000), who crafted a theoretical explanation of how groups with territorial ambitions come to take possession of land belonging to others. Land hunger, Said insists, following Marx, ultimately derives from material impulses. "To colonize distant places," he writes, "to populate or depopulate them: all of this occurs on, about, or because of land" (Said 1993, 78). Yet the seizure of land, he argues, following insights from figures such as Max Weber, Antonio Gramsci, and E. P. Thompson, results from a discursive outlook on the part of actors coveting the land.[1] For Said, groups with a hunger for land essentially reimagine the landscapes they desire, elevating notions of themselves as the owners of the land they seek. Said (2000) described this process of reinventing the meaning of territorial landscapes as "imaginative geography."

As a process of refashioning the meaning of territorial landscapes, imaginative geography enables groups with land hunger to frame arguments justifying why they are entitled to take possession of the landscapes they desire. At the same time, those with land hunger do not respond mechanically to the material incentives for seizing land. Instead, these actors come to a new discursive understanding of themselves as owners of the landscapes they covet, as a prelude to seizing them. Consequently, Said's imaginative geography is a theory of human action deriving from the interplay of material impulses and human consciousness (Gregory 1995). In this sense, Said's imaginative geography is "performative." Reimagining landscapes is but a first step to acting upon them and creating the very outcomes on the land being imagined (Gregory 2004, 17–20). In this process of reimagining geography, groups with territorial ambitions refashion themselves as owners of the territory they desire by projecting themselves as masters and sovereigns of the land.

Technologies of Force

Technologies of force refer to the actual instruments used to enclose and seize control of land. Three instruments are decisive in this process of enclosure and dispossession.

The first instrument is *cartographic,* focusing on the power of maps to craft "arguments" about the territories they represent (Harley 1989). As arguments, maps convey a point of view about territory. What gives cartographic representation its power as an instrument of force is thus similar to the way arguments shape individual and collective thinking and inspire individual and collective action. Readers of texts often see the world differently as a result of arguments, and they then act to change it in accordance with what they see. Maps emerge as instruments of force and change by (re)shaping consciousness about the land among map viewers, some of whom act upon territory to bring it into conformity with the way they see it and understand it. In this way, maps become models *for* rather than models *of* what they supposedly represent (Winichakul 1994, 130). Mapmakers craft these projections about territory through certain formal techniques that include choosing where on maps to place boundary lines; giving places on maps certain names or even renaming places with new toponyms; and signaling specific meanings about territory through map titles and iconographic cartoons known as "cartouches." As artifacts of how groups seeking territory project meanings about land, maps become instruments for putting imagined visions of landscape onto the ground itself.

The second instrument used to enclose and take possession of land is *legal,* focusing on the use of the law, specifically property law, as well as courts and legislation to remake landscapes in the image of what is imagined and projected onto maps. At the core of legal power lies the state as the institution of legitimate force and domination. Groups coveting land enlist the lawmaking power of the state to reconfigure geographical landscapes according to their reimaginings, with themselves as the new owners and sovereigns on the land. In pursuit of such imagined territorial visions, groups with land hunger use the law as a weapon, reassigning the ownership status of spaces on the land and elevating themselves as the land's new dominant owners. As the latter leverage the law to transfer land possessed and used by other groups to themselves, they enlarge and reinforce spaces of exclusion and trespass for the disinherited, restricting where the dispossessed can live and circulate. At the same time, the law reinforces cultural routes to remaking landscapes when actors enlist the state to rename geographical places, thus helping to bring landscapes into conformity with the way they have been reimagined (Benvenisti 2000, 11–54). The use of law as a coercive technology to codify and legitimize the transfer of land from one group to another, and the use of law to remake the landscape itself has been aptly described as "lawfare" (Blomley 2003, 128; Comaroff 2001, 306; Harris 2004, 179; Hajjar 2017).

The final instrument is *architectural* and refers to changes in landscapes engineered by groups seeking to enclose land. Upon reimagining and overturning systems of rights to land, practitioners of enclosure anchor themselves more firmly to the landscape by rebuilding it, crafting material environments that convey their ascendancy on the land while erasing the built forms and cultural markers of groups once dominant on the land. Thus, the landscape is both an outcome and a process (Mitchell 2002, 1). This process of enlisting the landscape as an instrument of domination enables groups seeking territory to align the material landscape with the landscape they have imagined in maps and realized through the law. It is part of an offensive program to seize control of land in the making of modernity.

From these foundations, what remains an empirical question is the source for the imagined visions of coveted landscapes among groups with territorial ambitions, and the way that these groups used the technologies of force available to them for enclosing and seizing control of coveted land.

ENCLOSURE ACROSS THREE CASES

With comparison as a method, and with landscapes theorized as socially constructed outcomes of power imprinted on land, this study develops an argument about the enduring process of enclosing land as a platform for modernizing development in a place. Spearheading this process are dominant elites who lay claim to land in order to establish a territorial foundation for their modernizing aspirations. Such groups essentially reimagine themselves as sovereigns on the land they covet for their modernizing aims and enclose the landscape as the path to progress. *Enclosure* tells how the reordering of landscape became a critical part of modernity, and how the remapping of and boundary-making on landscapes conformed to the modernizing impulses and territorial ambitions of English estate owners, Anglo-American colonists, and Israeli Zionists alike.

Imagined Geographies of Improvement

What ignites the passions of groups with modernizing aims and territorial ambitions to enclose and take possession of land is an enduring discourse about the virtues of improving land. As a discourse, land improvement promoted an imagined vision of the landscape in which land lying empty could be improved and thus redeemed by those willing to work it. The latter, in turn, would be rewarded for their efforts by gaining rights to land where they invested their labor. While the early Islamic world embraced aspects of this idea (see chapter 6), land improvement has roots in sixteenth-century England. For promoters of this discourse, improved land could be identified by two attributes: it was *cultivated,* and it was *enclosed* by fences, walls, or hedges built by the cultivator (McRae 1996, 136–37). Through the practices of cultivation and enclosure, advocates of land improvement sought to remedy the waste of barren land by endowing those willing to cultivate, enclose, and improve such land with a proprietary right to it (Seed 2001, 29–40). Thus, the discourse of land improvement provided its practitioners with an imagined vision of what an improved landscape would be.

As this discourse evolved, its promoters increasingly targeted land used as a common resource as the source of the problem related to empty land (Warde 2011, 128). By the late seventeenth century, John Locke (1690) added a qualifier to this discourse, suggesting that land "poorly cultivated" was akin to land lying in waste, which he claimed not only violated the Enlightenment spirit of rationality but also contravened the laws of God for humans to subdue the earth for their subsistence. Accordingly, promoters of land improvement were reinventing both the common landscape in early modern England and the indigenous landscape in North America as empty and available for the enterprising cultivator (Horn 1994, 128–29). Similar reinventions of landscape resurfaced later in Zionist ideology, which represented the Palestinian landscape as barren and neglected (Eisenzweig 1981, 282). Grafted upon these three different historical landscapes, the discourse of land improvement beckoned to new owners.

In England, this imagined geography of improvement influenced owners of large estates to reclaim prerogatives over land used by their tenant cultivators as a common resource (Neeson 1993; Thompson 1991). Seeking to put such land under crop and satisfy a national outcry for increasing agricultural output, estates by the late seventeenth century embarked on a program of extinguishing the rights of tenants to use land collectively, mostly for common grazing—rights codified by early common law statutes and by custom. In addition, estate owners used their financial power to buy out small freeholders and run out the leases of their tenants, thereby taking possession of the non-common land on their estates (Allen 1992, 78). These repossessed lands were then consolidated into large farms and rented to large tenants who hired many of the displaced former cultivators as wage laborers. Thus, from an imagined vision of improvement emerged a "landlord's revolution" whereby estate owners seized land used by smaller cultivators and remade landscapes with common uses into a series of large-scale units of individual property (Allen 1992).

Not surprisingly, ideas about land improvement that influenced the enclosure of land in England migrated to England's North American colonies, where settlers, despite evidence to the contrary, regarded the Amerindian landscape as unimproved and without owners (Horn 1994, 128–29; Marzec

2002, 131; Cronon 2003, 130). In the colonial context, this discourse framed an imagined landscape in which Amerindians failed to use land efficiently and whose entitlement to land was thus rightly subordinated to those willing to work the land with plows, as God and reason had intended. Establishing colonial dominion on Amerindian land was thus an extension of the improvement outlook emerging ascendant in seventeenth-century England (Edwards 2005, 219, 222). By the time these colonists emerged victorious in the War of Independence, ideologues for the fledgling nation had succeeded in fusing the English colonial notion of unimproved Amerindian land with a newer idea of a teleological, if not divine, mission of settling North America and civilizing the entire continent through the colonization and improvement of Amerindian land (Ostler 2004, 12–13; Miller 2006, 130). As in England, a discourse about improving land inspired an imagined geography of Amerindian dispossession and English settlement of the Native landscape.

In Palestine, inspiration for enclosing the landscape derived from the idea of a state homeland for the Jewish people popularized by the early Zionist movement, but what made Palestine especially appealing for this project were long-standing Jewish perceptions of the area as underdeveloped, which Zionists exploited in representing themselves as modernizers destined to improve what had been left in waste (LeVine 2005, 23–24). In justifying Palestine as the ideal location for building a Jewish state, Herzl and early Zionists drew on the spirit of Locke in describing the area as poorly cultivated by Palestinian farmers, beckoning to be improved by Zionist colonization (Braverman 2009a, 76). "Our country, . . . has remained desolate," insisted Aaron David Gordon, "poorer than other civilized countries and empty—this is confirmation of our right to the land" (quoted in Zerubavel 2008, 205). In this way, Zionists invented a Palestinian geography of barren land awaiting Jewish labor to take possession of it, modernize it, and improve it (Eisenzweig 1981). From this imagined geography, Zionists found a rationale for taking control of the Palestinian landscape and refashioning it to conform to their invented notions of what it was, and what it should be.

In all three cases, improvement was the basis of an ideology justifying the seizure of land as a route to creating a modern order on the landscape. In each case, groups promoting this route were constrained by existing systems of land ownership and sovereignty. Enclosure is what afforded groups with territorial ambitions and modernizing aspirations a pathway through these constraints.

Once imbued with visions of an improved landscape, promoters of enclosure use the three basic instruments—maps, law, and landscape architecture—as technologies of force to enclose and take possession of coveted land.

In England, the use of maps for enclosing land began as part of a "cartographic revolution" in the late sixteenth century marked by the advent of a more graphic means of representing land on estates (Harvey 1993a, 15–17). Two key actor groups spearheaded this revolution: the estate owner inspired by the idea of improvement, who wanted a picture of how land on the estate could be enclosed and improved; and the surveyor/mapmaker, who provided estates with a graphic picture of how this aim could be fulfilled. From this alliance emerged estate mapping that revealed to estate owners how their various lands, encumbered with common rights and the complexities of differentiated tenures, could be remade into an improved, economically rational and propertied landscape. Cartography, in effect, provided a new way of seeing land on the manor—"knowing one's own"—that enabled estate owners to imagine how to enclose and take possession of certain lands in order to improve and profit from them (McCrae 1993).

In North America, cartography was also creating imagined visions of the landscape. Much in the same way that estate maps were suggesting to English landowners how to consolidate freeholds and tenancies and take control of common land, early English maps of North America, such as the 1616 map of New England by John Smith, projected notions of a territorial *vacuum domicilium* and an imagined Anglicized geography onto the landscapes of the New World (Harley 2001). Later, mapmakers such as Thomas Holme (in 1687), John Mitchell (in 1755), and John Melish (in 1816) extended this idea of emptiness by representing "improved" territorial landscapes in North America in which Amerindians were largely absent and orderly grids of property lines stretched unencumbered toward the west. In this way, Anglo-American maps of colonial America provided visual testimony to how Native land was reimagined as a Euro-American landscape demarcated by property boundaries and lines of colonial sovereignty (Boelhower 1988, 478).

Like estate owners in England and colonists in North America, Zionists drew upon cartographic representation to promote a national imagination about Palestine as Jewish land (Newman 2001, 239–40; Leuenberger and Schnell 2010, 807). During the 1920s and 1930s, the Zionist movement, through the Jewish National Fund (JNF), sought to popularize the idea of

Palestine as a Hebrew territorial space and to this end commissioned a series of maps representing Palestine as an area of *Jewish* settlement absent an Arab presence (Bar-Gal 2003, 139–51). In 1934, the JNF deployed one of these maps on its celebrated "Blue Box," used to collect money for the purchase of land and the promotion of Jewish settlement in Palestine. In conveying a message to its own constituents and the world at large, the map on the Blue Box carried two critical arguments about how Zionists imagined the Palestinian landscape. First, the map, through omission, concealed Palestinian geographical places, rendering Palestinians as absentees on the land where they lived. Second, with its title, *Eretz Yisrael,* the map conveyed an unmistakable message to Jews and non-Jews alike about the land of Palestine as Hebrew space and the patrimony of the Jewish people (Bar-Gal 2003, 137).

After the emergence of the state of Israel in 1948, cartographic projection of a Hebrew landscape on the territory of the new state continued, focused more decisively on toponymy as Arabic place-names were replaced with Hebrew names (Benvenisti 2000, 11–54; Cohen and Kliot 1981). The critical moment in this process occurred in 1949 when Israel's first prime minister, David Ben-Gurion, established an official "Place-Names Commission," charged with creating a Hebrew toponymy for the country's geographical features and places. The culmination of the commission's work was a Hebrew map of the territory now officially known as the State of Israel. This map marked the cartographic "hebraicization" of a landscape formerly represented by a system of place-names that reflected the once-dominant Arabic-speaking culture of Palestinians, who had become a people dispossessed (Falah 1996; Benvenisti 2000, 11–54). The new state used, and continues to use, this map with its Hebrew place-names to reinforce the idea of Jewish ascendancy on this land.

The second instrument, lawfare, played a decisive role in transcribing these cartographic visions into a set of laws for ordering rights of land ownership, use, and access on the landscape.

In England, enclosure was in the first instance a *legal* process of turning land encumbered with common uses to severalty (Whyte 2003, 9). While historically legal institutions such as common law, manor courts, and even Crown Courts had protected the rights of English tenant farmers to common land, by the mid-seventeenth century public support for enclosure as promoted by improvement writers emboldened estate owners to initiate a comprehensive legal challenge to such rights (Reid 1995, 245; Allen 1992, 95, 104). This legal revolution against rights of commons, in turn, was the prelude to remaking the English landscape when enclosure occurred through a very specific institution—acts of Parliament. Numbering in the thousands, Parliamentary Enclosure Acts provided estate owners with a final set of legal tools for extinguishing virtually all remaining common rights to land by the late eighteenth century, enabling those areas of the landscape once reserved for common uses to come under control of large estates (Allen 1992).

In the United States, lawfare as an instrument of dispossession is best exemplified by two legal landmarks of the early nineteenth century. The first was the Supreme Court decision *Johnson v. M'Intosh* (1823), one of the defining cases in American legal history which abrogated Amerindian rights to land (Banner 2005; Robertson 2005). In its decision, the Supreme Court remade Native Americans into "tenants-at-will," affirming that in the territory of the United States Amerindians did not possess rights to the land they occupied and used. The second was the Indian Removal Act (1830), signed into law by President Andrew Jackson. This law empowered the U.S. government to clear land in the East of Indian "tenants" and set this land aside for settlement by white American colonists.

In Palestine, the state of Israel that emerged victorious in the conflict with the Palestinian community invoked a series of legal measures enabling the new state to gain control of Palestinian land and reallocate it for new Jewish settlements (Forman and Kedar 2004). The decisive legal mechanism in this process was the creation of *state land* from land formerly possessed and used by Palestinians. This legal designation enabled the government of Israel to transfer almost the entire land surface of the new state into state ownership. On this legal foundation, hundreds of new Jewish settlements were built within present-day Israel, reflecting the realization of an imagined vision evolving among Jews for decades of Palestine as a Jewish territory. Moreover, this legal instrument of creating state land from Palestinian property continues to be used in Occupied Palestine as a means of transferring land from Palestinians to the Jewish state and ultimately to Jewish owners (Forman 2009).

The final instrument, landscape architecture, is the outcome of cartographic visions and legal inscriptions on the land, but it is also a technology for changing the material and symbolic character of the landscape itself.

In England, what proliferated on the landscape from enclosure was the large-scale "rent-maximizing farm" that spearheaded the transformation of the countryside into a more geometrically regularized pattern of privately owned spaces (Allen 1992). This institutionally driven architectural change, in turn, reshaped the rural landscape with untold miles of stone walls, fences, and hedgerows, built by those enclosing the land not only to demarcate their newly enlarged holdings (Rackham 1986, 190–91) but also to close rights of way and restrict access to what had been an agricultural system of open fields allowing free movement and use of certain lands as a common resource (Blomley 2007; J. Anderson 2007). Emerging from these institutional and architectural changes in the English countryside was a landscape unrecognizable compared to what it had been prior to the wholesale enclosure of land (Bermingham 1986, 9; Hoskins 1977, 178).

In the United States, what emerged as an institution of dispossession driving change on the landscape was the self-contained settler homestead, which, as improvement gained ascendancy, replaced an earlier colonial settlement pattern of nucleated villages similar to the open common field villages of England (Greven 1970, 50–53). Created from a felled tract of wilderness and demarcated by a fence, the settler homestead anchored the colonial idea of an improved and civilized landscape (Williams 1992, 53–73; Cronon 2003, 128, 159–70). In grafting this imagined vision of improvement onto the land, Anglo-American settlers inscribed the landscape with a radically linear order represented by individually owned plots of ground and "seemingly endless miles of fences." In so doing, they established a landscape of trespass marked by an ever-expanding grid of territorial spaces that were increasingly off-limits to Amerindians. As this landscape swept across the continent, it spawned another institution of dispossession that acted as a repository for the dispossessed: the Indian reservation.

In Palestine, the institution proliferating across the landscape with similar effect is the Jewish settlement. From the beginning of Zionist-inspired Jewish immigration to Palestine in the late nineteenth century, the newcomers sought to expand their presence on the Palestinian landscape by building settlements, easily distinguished by their geometrically ordered contours. After the Jewish community in Palestine—the *Yishuv*—prevailed in a conflict with the Palestinians in 1948–49 and assumed sovereignty over territory covering 78 percent of Palestine, now renamed the State of Israel, the state's new sovereigns embarked on a massive settlement-building program. Roughly seven hundred new Jewish settlements were built on land where close to five hundred Palestinian villages once existed, the former residents suffering exile and becoming refugees. In the Palestinian Territories occupied by Israel since 1967, the state has established an additional 145 Jewish settlements on land reclassified by the occupying power as Israeli state land, which in many instances belonged to Palestinian residents of villages nearby. What has transpired as land ownership has shifted from one group of people to another is a profound transformation on the landscape. Erased is the Palestinian village, and in its place is a landscape anchored and dominated by Jewish settlements. In 1947, the footprint of land ownership for Jewish settlement in Palestine amounted to roughly 8 percent of the land surface. Today, Jewish settlements and the infrastructure supporting them in both Israel and Occupied Palestine proliferate on roughly 85 percent of what was the Palestinian landscape (Halabi, Turner, and Benvenisti 1985, 4). In this transformation, a system of agrarian villages connected to a collective and cooperative system of land tenure has given way to a landscape of suburban-style communities that mark the transfer of land from one group of people to another (Yiftachel 2006; Weizman 2007).

As they expand and proliferate, the rent-maximizing farm, the settler homestead, and the Jewish settlement drive a set of anchors into the landscape that serve as the foundation for a new system of ownership and sovereignty and a different pattern of political economy and cultural expression.

"Clearing" the Landscape

One of the enduring outcomes of enclosure is demographic, related to the clearing and transfer of populations from territorial landscapes. Implemented through combinations of compulsion and force, such transfers of people evidenced two dimensions: a change in the location of populations, and a change in their social standing. Invariably, these two processes are interdependent.

In England, enclosure transferred small cultivators socially from agrarian activities on the land anchored by common rights, to activities on the land connected to their new status as *wage earners* in both agriculture and emerging rural industries. As the impacts of enclosure intensified, especially after the eighteenth century, and as many cultivators were dispossessed of land entirely, they migrated from their rural origins, reemerging in different locations as wage workers in a newly ascendant urban environment. In effect, as spaces of private individual property spread across the English landscape and as spaces of common property disappeared, cultivators once able to use land as a common resource assumed a new identity and were cleared from the landscape, driven into different geographical locales in order to earn a living.

In the United States, enclosing the landscape provided the basis for a change in the social status of Amerindians, who by the beginning of the nineteenth century had been reclassified as "tenants-at-will." This change in turn enabled the U.S. government, pressured by land-hungry settlers, to remove Indians from locations where they had existed, a policy institutionalized in the Indian Removal Act of 1830. Once uprooted legally, Amerindians were driven into more spatially confined reservations, where they assumed a new social status as discriminated-against, if not forgotten, second-class citizens.

In Palestine, enclosure forcibly transferred Palestinians from areas of present-day Israel to outlying foreign territories or into the West Bank and Gaza Strip, where they assumed a new social status as refugees. Palestinians remaining in what emerged as Israel, in turn, have been systematically dispossessed and confined to ever-shrinking territorial landscapes stemming from the expansion of Jewish settlement onto land that once belonged to them, an expansion and dispossession enabled by new property laws. Their land thus taken both by law and by the Jewish settlements that followed, Palestinians inside Israel have been transferred socially from agrarian activities into earning wages, primarily in construction, building—ironically—new Jewish towns and settlements (Shafir and Peled 2002, 112–25). In areas of Palestine under Israeli military rule, Palestinians are being dispossessed by an ever-expanding footprint of Israeli settlement-building, which makes areas of the landscape once used by Palestinians now off-limits to them. In this manner, Palestinians are physically moved into ever more confined territorial spaces, while socially they are relegated to the status of the permanently unemployed and impoverished.

Although unequal power enables dominant groups with territorial ambitions to enclose land, power is not absolute in these encounters but is woven into contingent relationships with the less powerful, setting in motion cycles of domination and resistance (Braddock and Walter 2000; Calloway 2003; Khalidi 1997). In this regard, indigenous groups are historical actors seeking to negotiate the conditions of their existence vis-à-vis those in power. Such groups, when facing enclosure that aims to dislodge them from the landscape, inevitably resist. Thus, enclosure landscapes are part of a long-standing narrative about power, resistance, and place in which both dominant and subordinate actors create outcomes on the land.

PLAN VIEW OF *ENCLOSURE*

Enclosure is a history of power and space. Its aim is to reveal the landscape outcomes when groups with modernizing aspirations and territorial ambitions use force to dislodge other groups from their land. In narrating parallel stories about power and space, *Enclosure* is unique in two fundamental ways, one methodological, the second theoretical.

Methodologically, there is no book-length work that situates the Palestinian landscape within the comparative frame developed in this study. To be sure, references to colonization and settlement exist in the literature on the Israeli/Palestinian conflict, which in turn allow comparisons to be made between the dispossession of the Palestinians and that of other colonized groups (e.g., Shafir 1996; LeVine 2005; Yiftachel 2006; Makdisi 2008; Hanafi 2009, 2013). Yet no studies link events on the Palestinian landscape to the long-standing discourse about land improvement with origins in English common law and rights to landed property.

From this comparative foundation, *Enclosure* makes two important theoretical contributions to spatial history. First, in focusing on the enduring narrative of land improvement and dispossession in England, America, and Palestine/Israel, *Enclosure* gives empirical life to one of the most important theoretical concepts in geography studies: the interplay of power and territorial space. Second, in revealing how groups with territorial ambitions come to reimagine land, the book constructs an empirical account of one of the most salient theoretical notions in cultural geography, the notion of imaginative geography, providing a potent example of how Edward Said's insight can be applied to dispossession in actual historical settings. Together, these two theoretical notions—the interplay of power and space, and the workings of imaginative geography—create the outlines of the model that runs throughout the book, a model describing the transfer of land from one group to another and the resulting physical transformation of landscapes.

In addition to method and theory, the argument in this book about the recurrent pattern of enclosure and dispossession reveals a unique set of political ramifications that remain relevant today.

Enclosure steps into a highly charged debate about the nature of the conflict in Israel/Palestine. While Israeli practitioners of enclosure in Palestine seek to deny that seizures of Palestinian land play any role in the conflict, parallels with dispossession in the English enclosures and the dispossession of Native Americans suggest otherwise. Indeed, *Enclosure* challenges the idea of the uniquely beleaguered nature of Israeli society as the motivation for the seizure and remaking of Palestinian land. Inspired by an enduring ideology of land improvement, Zionist settlers and their modern-day descendants have acted in much the same way as other groups with power toward the less powerful, when the latter become an obstacle to the territorial aims of the former. Like previous historical examples of groups with territorial ambitions and modernizing aspirations, Zionists have seized and remade territory at the expense of a group of people already on the land. There is, in effect, a parallel story about power embedded in the landscapes of the English enclosures, the Anglo-American colonial frontier, and Palestine today. All three of these cases are spatial projects, in that they revolve fundamentally around the control of land.[2] All three cases reveal actor groups inspired by visions of land improvement who reimagine and remake territory using similar instruments that allow them to enclose and take control of landscapes while elevating themselves to positions of sovereignty on the land.

These groups with power and land hunger, however, do not achieve their territorial aims uncontested in some grand teleological march. In each case, those enclosing land encounter resistance, in which the barriers they place on the landscape—fences, hedges, and walls— to seize control of territory and impede the mobility of the dispossessed come to serve as specific targets of systematic opposition. In this way, the enclosure of landscape, and resistance to enclosure are integrated in an enduring and contingent narrative shaping the contours of the modern world (Linebaugh 2010, 11).

Enclosure tells this story of domination and dispossession in three parts, focusing in turn on the English enclosures, Amerindian dispossession, and Palestinian land loss. Each part consists of two chapters: first, in chapters 2, 4, and 6, we look at previously existing patterns of landholding on the part of English commoners, Amerindians, and Palestinians; then, in chapters 3, 5, and 7, we see how estate owners, Anglo-American settlers, and Zionists, inspired by discourses of land improvement and using similar instruments of power, overturned existing systems of landholding and seized control of land, installing themselves as owners and stewards on the landscape. These chapters are broadly symmetrical in outlining the imagined geography of improvement in each case and showing how maps, the law, and landscape architecture transformed what was imagined into actual systems of dispossession. Chapter 7, dealing with the Palestinian case, is also informed by a second critical method, one that complements the historical comparison running throughout *Enclosure*. Portions of this chapter rely on what ethnographers refer to as "participant observation," in which the researcher "participates" to varying degrees in the social environment being studied (Fields 2016, 256). As a practical matter, this chapter utilizes data generated from interviews with both

Israeli and Palestinian actors. Finally, chapter 8 summarizes common themes across the three cases in supporting the claim of Palestinian dispossession as part of a recurrent pattern of reallocations in rights to land.

Although "landscape" is the focus of this study, human subjects are what animate the story told in this book about land. *Enclosure* shows how a discourse about improving land reshaped the mindset of human actors in different places and different time periods, and how this discourse, despite those differences, assumed similar attributes in the landscape. In the end, *Enclosure* is a story of how ideas act as change agents and become part of the landscape—but it is human actors who put new thinking into the land. What follows is a tour of these parallel stories about discourse, power, and land aimed at gaining insight into one of the most contested geographical landscapes of present day.

PART ONE

Land into Property

ENCLOSURE, LAND IMPROVEMENT,
AND MAKING PROPERTY ON
THE ENGLISH LANDSCAPE

As much land as a man tills, plants, improves, cultivates, and can use the product of, so much is his property. . . . He that incloses land, and has a greater plenty of the conveniences of life from ten acres, than he could have from a hundred left to nature, may truly be said to give 90 acres to mankind: for his labor now supplies him with provisions out of ten acres, which were but the product of a hundred lying in common.

> JOHN LOCKE, *The Second Treatise of Civil Government* (1690)

. . . By nineteen enclosure bills in twenty they [the poor] are injured, in some cases grossly injured. . . . The poor in these parishes may say, and with truth, *Parliament may be the tender of property; all I know is, I had a cow and an act of Parliament has taken it from me.*

> ARTHUR YOUNG, *An Inquiry into the Propriety of Applying Wastes to the Better Maintenance and Support of the Poor* (1801)

IT CAN HARDLY ESCAPE even the casual observer of the countryside in England how large portions of the landscape succumb to a broadly geometric order. From the drystone walls of Cumbria and the Yorkshire dales, to the quickthorn hedges of the Midlands, or the combination of walls, hedges, and fences in the Cotswolds, lines on the land form a dominant feature of English rural geography (Williamson 2000a, 269; Hook 2010, 74). To the uninitiated viewer, these linear patterns on the land may qualify as an otherwise

FIGURE 2. David Hockney, Garrowby Hill, Yorkshire (1998). Reproduced by permission of the David Hockney Association.

innocent representation of what is "English" about the landscape (Burden and Kohl 2006). To the discerning viewer, however, these angular contours, represented so masterfully by David Hockney in his painting of the Yorkshire Wolds (fig. 2), document a more contested story about landscape, but one largely hidden from view. Encoded in the contours of this landscape is a narrative about how land assumed the status of "property" and how the ground itself was transformed into privatized spaces—of inclusion for some, exclusion for others. This transformation in turn provided the foundation for the socioeconomic, legal, and cultural changes that remade England as a nation-state and ushered in a modern economy built upon the institutions of free markets and private property.

While the angular, subdivided spaces in Hockney's tableau speak to the emotions of the landscape tradition in painting, these spaces also resonate with a seemingly unlikely eighteenth-century authority. In one of the most enduring insights in all of economic thought, Adam Smith used the setting of a pin factory in his *Wealth of Nations* (1776) to describe an untapped world of economic expansion predicated on a seemingly counterintuitive notion: that of dividing up the work of individuals. For Smith, the "division of labor," depicted with meticulous detail in his description of the myriad operations involved in pin making, was "the greatest improvement" in human productive power (Smith 1776, 13). This improvement, he argued, would enable more goods to circulate and markets to expand, resulting in the growth of fortunes not only of individuals but of entire nations. At the same time, Smith's model of growth contained an unmistakable, if unintentional, spatial metaphor. If, as Smith theorized, the outer frontiers of the market were to expand, enabling the market to grow, then the space *within* the market would have to assume a more divided character, marked by an ever-expanding network of boundary lines separating the different tasks of work.

Though marking a pioneering advance in the still-nascent field of political economy, Smith's insight about the division of labor was more the culmination of an older discourse about "improvement," in which the idea of expansion began to converge with the metaphor of boundary-making. Nevertheless, what preoccupied these earlier purveyors of improvement was little different from what had inspired Smith: how to generate greater levels of output that would in turn lead to increases in personal and national wealth. In the centuries prior to *The Wealth of Nations,* however, improvement assumed its meaning not in the context of dividing up the labor in workshops, but rather in conjunction with the production factor most central to the premodern economy: *land*. Promoters of land improvement argued that productivity advances in agriculture depended on subdividing the landscape and assigning individual rights of ownership to these subdivided spaces. Such subdivisions of the landscape had a long-standing pedigree. The practice that converted common land to individual ownership and demarcated such land within hedges, walls, or fences was the practice of enclosure (Thirsk 1967b, 200).

Enclosing land in England was part of a long-term project of improving land by "making private property" on the English landscape (Blomley 2007). This transformation represents a decisive moment in the long-standing lineage of reallocations in property rights, in which groups with territorial ambitions gained control of land owned or used by others (Banner 2002, S360). Enclosure provided the mechanism for this redistribution of land and was the pivotal event in the agrarian history of early modern England (Allen 1992, 25).

By the early sixteenth century, enclosure had begun a long, if uneven, march toward eradicating common field farming and remaking a landscape that once boasted a large inventory of land used as a collective resource (Reed 1990, 205). What replaced this landscape was a system in which land was recast from a "bundle of rights" into a bounded "thing" able to be possessed by individuals as *property* (Blomley 2007, 2). In freeing landscapes of common uses and expanding the inventory of individually owned land, enclosure was instrumental in promoting a new agrarian order dominated by large estate farms worked by wage labor, and built on the foundation of private landed property (Allen 1992). Nevertheless, enclosure did not result from some teleological march toward a system in which land was destined to lose its attributes as a common resource. Improving land and turning it into property through enclosure was a contingent process involving diverse groups of actors deciding whether individual rights to land served them or contributed to their impoverishment.

By the thirteenth century, tenant cultivators were protesting enclosure by destroying the hedges and fences placed on common land by enclosure promoters seeking to sever it both physically and symbolically from collective uses (Dyer 2006). This pattern of "breaking property" would subsequently be duplicated in larger enclosure protests, from Kett's Rebellion in Norfolk (1549) to the Midlands Revolt (1607), and would mark numerous protests against specific enclosures well into the eighteenth century (McDonagh 2013; Whittle 2010; Hindle 2008; Neeson 1984). In the end, however, despite ongoing resistance, the landscape of common rights succumbed to an enclosed landscape of large "rent-maximizing farms," anchored to a new geography of exclusion and trespass in the countryside (Allen 1992; Blomley 2007). What follows are the tracings of how a discourse for improving land challenged a system of rights to land held in common and inspired a vision of a more profitable agrarian order. This imagined geography, in turn, became embedded in a set of legal, cartographic, and material instruments for enclosing land and creating a new system of property on the English landscape.

Early Modern English Landscapes

RIGHTS OF LAND TENURE AND
THE COMMON FIELDS

A DIVERSITY OF FIELD SYSTEMS marked by myriad variations in land-holding and tenancy is arguably the defining attribute of early modern English agriculture (Baker and Butlin 1973).[1] Although it was often said that England had been "cleft in twain" with upland sheep-farming in the north and lowland corn-growing from the Midlands to the south, pasture farming and corn-growing invariably coexisted in what was described as the "Midland system" of sheep-corn husbandry. That said, regionalism ultimately shaped proportions of pasture and arable farming (Thirsk 1967a, 2). In this way, England's agrarian geography counts at least 8–10 distinct regional field systems, all having innumerable local variations (Baker and Butlin 1973; Thirsk 1967a, 4).[2] At the same time, despite regional differentiation, cultivators in different areas confronted the same basic problems of land tenure along with technical issues of cropping and managing livestock that enabled field systems to assume a broadly similar character (Dodgshon 1980). Consequently, while early modern England presents a diverse agrarian geography, there are compelling reasons for treating the agrarian landscape as the outcome of an institutional environment that was helping fashion a national agrarian culture with a distinctly English identity by 1500 (McRae 1996, 6; Johnson 1996, 7; Dahlman 1980).

By 1300, common field farming had assumed dominance on more than 50 percent of the English landscape, the first major institutional innovation in English agriculture since Roman times and perhaps since the Bronze Age (Reed 1990, 130; Rowley 1982, 38; Faith 1997, 236). Common fields were tracts of land subject to certain collective rights of use and cooperative forms of management and were invariably "open," unencumbered by boundary markers such as hedges, walls, or fences (De Moor, Shaw-Taylor, and Warde 2002,

18–19). While common fields and open fields were not always synonymous (Kerridge 1992, 5), there were good reasons why common fields as a legal designation were open corresponding to their layout on the land (Roberts 1973, 190; Thirsk 1964). For land to come under common uses, members of the community had to have open access to it in order to exploit it as a collective resource (Blomley 2007, 5).

During the 250 years following the Norman Conquest of 1066 common field agriculture developed under conditions of demographic expansion, causing cultivators to farm land more intensively to provision the growing numbers of people (Thirsk 1964, 24). The spread of common field agriculture during this period suggests that cultivators embraced cooperation as a way of coping with the imperative for more intensive farming techniques, a move that was largely successful in provisioning the expanding population (Faith 1997, 236–37). This broadly similar response of common field farming to conditions after 1066, in turn, tended to bring farming systems into "rough conformity" with one another (Thirsk 1973, 234). Consequently, despite variations in soil, topography, and climate that gave field systems in England distinct attributes, common field farming became sufficiently generalized by 1300 to form an institution on the landscape (Dahlman 1980).

ORIGINS OF LANDHOLDING AND TENANCY

Common field agriculture evolved alongside the manorial economy, at the center of which stood the *manor,* the basic unit of landholding in the kingdom following the Norman Conquest (Allen 1992, 60). At that time, William decreed all land in England to be held by the Crown, but he parceled this Crown land to his supporters from the nobility, who assumed control of these parcels as lords of manors. What emerged from these grants of land was an agrarian economy tied to a hierarchical system of land tenure, consisting of lords who effectively owned the land on the manor and tenants who lived on the manor as the actual cultivators. In this system, any surplus the tenants produced above their subsistence needs was appropriated by the lords (Williamson and Bellamy, 1987: 32).

From the time of the Norman Conquest to the Hundred Rolls of 1279,[3] the manor assumed its ideal form based on three types of land: (1) *demesne land,* generally the best land on the manor and directly controlled by the lord; (2) *free land,* accorded a use right known as *socage,* or free tenure, in which the cultivator paid a fixed rent or performed a specified service for the lord in exchange for the right of occupancy and cultivation (Overton 2004, 31; Allen 1992, 60); and (3) *villein land*, cultivated by "unfree" or "customary" tenants who owed obligations to the lord, in the form of arbitrary payments or undefined labor services "where one cannot know in the evening the service to be rendered in the morning" and who had little legal protection from eviction (Faith 1997, 261). Although lords did extract income from free tenants in the form of fixed rents or from nonservile labor, it was villeins who provided most of the surplus appropriated by lords (Williamson and Bellamy 1987, 32). Although the distribution of these lands on different manors varied, in general demesne land accounted for roughly 33 percent of an individual manor's land holdings, free land about 25 percent, and villein land 40–50 percent. More telling was the size of these holdings: at the time of the Hundred Rolls, demesne farms averaged 165 acres, freehold farms were 16 acres, and villein farms 13 acres (Allen 1992, 60, 62–64).

The legal foundation of manorial land tenure resided in the language of the "fee" that obligated tenants to pay a portion of the produce in rent or render services to the lord in exchange for the right of occupancy and cultivation (Faith 1997, 255). As part of this compact, lords were responsible for offering certain protections as long as the tenants fulfilled their obligations as cultivators of land and payers of rent or services.

Authority for overseeing the terms of the fee was vested in a specific rule-making institution: the manor court (Faith 1997, 256; Harrison 1997, 48). Established by lords at the end of the twelfth century to counter the growing intrusion of royal courts into issues of manorial landownership and tenancy, manor courts enforced tenants' payment of rents and performance of labor services to the lord (Bailey 2002, 167–68; Bonfield 1989, 518). Surveys of the manor by court surveyors provided the instrument for compliance by recording the conditions of the various tenancies—holding size, rent, and services owed—which became memorialized in the court rolls as binding on both lord and tenant (Bailey 2002, 21–23; Bonfield 1989, 520). Yet the manor court was more than simply an instrument of domination by lords over tenants. It also functioned as an institution for self-regulation in which tenant communities adopted rules for cultivation and grazing in the common fields and, in conjunction with the lord, participated in shaping manorial customs, including conditions of tenancy (Williamson and Bellamy 1987, 43).

The ongoing efforts of cultivators to shape conditions of tenure, and the role of the Crown and royal courts in redefining rights of possession for manorial tenants, enabled the free tenant by the late thirteenth century to evolve into a de facto landed proprietor. A decisive turn in this process of peasant proprietorship occurred in 1290 with the passage by Edward I of the statute *Quia Emptores,* known as the Third Statute of Westminster (Allen 1992, 60–61). Designed to concentrate more power in the hands of the Crown, this statute followed a series of earlier legal writs that enabled free tenants not only to bequeath land to heirs but also to alienate land without consent of the lord, so that by the thirteenth century the *socage* or free tenant was essentially a full proprietor. At the same time, these intrusions of royal authority that strengthened free tenants helped lords increase obligations on villeins, thus sharpening the line between freedom and servility. Beginning in 1348, however, villeinage would also undergo profound change, and with it the system of landholding itself, owing to what was perhaps the most dramatic shock of the medieval period: the Black Death.

FROM PLAGUE TO COPYHOLD

In 1348, the Plague and the ensuing demographic collapse created conditions for a "revolution" in the system of land tenure (Allen 1992, 65). Fewer rent-paying tenants on the manor resulted in a steep decline in incomes for manorial lords, who in response sold off vacant land to surviving tenants, even villeins, enabling the latter to emerge as freeholders, with some even becoming relatively large proprietors. At the same time, cultivation of demesne land by servile villein labor also fell into disarray owing to depopulation, and as the demographic crisis persisted, landlords leased demesne land to surviving tenants, or in some cases sold portions of their demesne (Baker 1973, 201–5). This demographic situation created conditions for wholesale transformation in the system of manorial landholding and tenancy, in which villeins themselves played an active role.

Villeins who survived the Plague often took flight from their former lords and, in the absence of enforceable fugitive serf laws, moved to other manors where they were able to benefit from continuing labor shortages and renegotiate the terms of tenancy. By the late fourteenth century lords desperate to find rent-paying tenants for vacant holdings were abolishing servile labor dues for villeins. In the process, villeinage gave way to a new type of tenancy—tenancy "at will." Although villeinage had always been an at-will tenure—indeed, manor courts along with Crown and common law courts regarded villeins as tenants without recourse if they were evicted by lords even in violation of manorial customs (Allen 1992, 68)—the new at-will tenancies removed the most onerous conditions on villeins at least in the short term. Lords of manors, however, believed that they would be able to return villeins to their former status once conditions changed. Conditions did change, but not as lords expected. By the mid-fifteenth century, with labor shortages still persisting, villeins succeeded in converting their at-will tenancies to more secure forms of occupancy, thus becoming indistinguishable from free tenants. As a result, villeinage as a legal category effectively ended (Bonfield 1996, 105). The new form of essentially free tenure came to be known as *copyhold* and revolutionized occupancy on the land.

Originating in the early to mid-fourteenth century as the successor to villeinage, copyhold was an intermediate type of tenure. Though certainly not a freehold, copyhold provided tenants with a certain proprietary interest in the soil; it attained something of a legal standing insofar as it was memorialized in the form of a "copy" in manorial court rolls recording admission of the individual or family to the landholding for what was usually an annual rent or fine (Allen 1992, 67). Copyhold existed in two major forms. Copyholds of *inheritance* enabled the tenant to pass land to an heir or to sell it for a fine paid to the lord as compensation. Copyholds for *lives* provided a weaker claim, since the heir had to be readmitted to the manor court rolls, usually by paying a fine, to retain rights of possession. What made copyhold an intermediate rather than freehold tenure, however, was the fact that the tenant held such land "at the will of the lord according to the custom of the manor" (Reid 1995, 248). Indeed, the security of copyholds varied by circumstance and by manor and in some cases could be overturned. Nevertheless, as it evolved, copyhold provided a more durable anchor to the land than villeinage.

Although copyhold had legal status memorialized in manor courts, by the late fifteenth century the concept gained a more durable legal foundation as Chancery Courts began to protect copyholders by granting them an enforceable title to their land. Similarly, common law courts sometimes intervened in what were typically manor court decisions by ruling on manorial customs, including customs of tenancy, that were "unreasonable" and disadvantaged copyholders (Allen 1992, 66, 69; Reid 1995, 249). Despite the fact that common law courts did not officially "notice" and thus codify copyhold tenure until the mid-1500s, even these limited protections for copyholders contributed to revolutionizing landholding. The result was that in the years following the Plague until the early seventeenth century, most cultivators had essentially secured a proprietary interest in the land they cultivated (Allen 1992, 66).

If tenants ascended to positions of secure tenure owing to the pressures of the Plague and certain legal protections, they also became more firmly anchored to land thanks to their own initiative, in what has been termed "the peasant land market in medieval England." This market was defined as "the lands held by small-scale land-owners, . . . and the way these lands moved by mutual agreement from one land owner to another" (Harvey 1984, 1). What was unusual in this market was the participation of villeins and their ability to acquire land from free tenants and even from lords (Harvey 2010b, 2–3; Thirsk 1973, 270). While in theory land in free tenure had to be forfeited to the lord before it could be conveyed to villeins, in practice villeins were usually able to acquire such land on payment of a fine after reporting it to the manorial court, a practice that effectively broadened the meaning of free tenure (Harvey 1996b, 396). While some of this activity pre-dates the Plague years, that emergency accelerated the process that allowed customary tenants to acquire land, making them effective owners of the soil they cultivated (Harvey 1984, 332).

One of most critical impacts of copyhold and the peasant land market was a gradual process of socioeconomic differentiation in the countryside. Historically, tenants comprised four basic categories (Patriquin 2004, 203): (1) prosperous tenants with larger land holdings than their neighbors; (2) a group with land sufficient to support a family; (3) a group with insufficient land who supplemented their agricultural incomes with work on the farms of the larger peasants or through rural handicraft; and (4) landless "cottagers" often reduced to squatting at the margins of the manor. After the mid-fifteenth century, this structure shifted as numerous families from the first category who had survived the Plague acquired the land of their former neighbors (Lachmann 1987, 52–57; Thirsk 1992b, 50). As a result, prosperous tenants expanded their holdings from roughly 20 percent of cultivated land in the mid-fifteenth century to 25–33 percent by the seventeenth century (McRae 1996, 14; Blomley 2007, 2). This group, consisting of copyholders and leaseholders for lives who had acquired a proprietary interest in their land along with freeholders, as middle- to upper-middle-sized family farmers with an average farm size of 59 acres, formed the basis of the English yeomanry (Allen 1992, 72, 74). Their fortunes peaked during the seventeenth century but declined dramatically during the first half of the eighteenth when large estates bought them out or ran out their leases as the prelude to Parliamentary Enclosure (Allen 1992, 78, 85–87).

In sum, demographic change and the agency of tenants themselves elevated the fortunes of cultivators so that by the early 1500s the agrarian economy on the manor was essentially one of peasant proprietorship. On this foundation, cultivators crafted responses to the challenges of sustaining themselves and fulfilling sometimes shifting obligations to the lord. In the process they played a role in shaping the evolution of the common fields as a system of agriculture and landholding.

LANDHOLDING IN THE COMMON FIELDS

Common field agriculture combined collective and individual rights to land (H. Smith 2000). This interplay in turn assumed specific characteristics in relationship to the two basic types of land, arable and nonarable. Arable land was divided into two, three, or in some parishes four or more fields and placed under crop or left fallow to regenerate the soil, with variations in the number of fields occurring even among parishes in close proximity (Roberts 1973, 202; Neeson 1993, 106). Depending on the local topography, nonarable land consisted of meadows, woodlands, fenlands, heaths, fells, and moors and was often categorized as "waste." Despite this connotation, waste land occupied a central position in the common field system, providing many of the most important common uses and resources exploited by cultivators, most notably common grazing (Neeson 1992, 55–80).

On these two types of land, common field farming evolved into an agrarian system with three basic attributes (Thirsk 1964, 3).[4] First, the arable land of the parish, village, or township was divided into strips that were then distributed among the tenants, each of whom usually cultivated a number of strips. Second, arable land along with adjoining nonarable meadows were thrown open for common pasturing after harvest and in fallow seasons. Third, common grazing was generally present on waste land where cultivators of strips also possessed rights of *estover* and *turbary* to gather materials such as timber, peat, stone, and bracken along with rights to forage for wild foodstuffs.

In general, tenant families had a de facto proprietary interest in the strips of land in the arable fields known as *selions,* usually about one furlong (200 meters) long and 5–20 meters wide—the basic plowing unit in medieval and early modern England. Arguably, the most prominent feature of these holdings was that individual families usually did not possess single consolidated pieces of land. Instead, these strips tended to be scattered throughout the arable fields (Allen 1992, 26). Boundary markers between the strips consisted of either a drainage ditch or a grass border referred to as *baulks,* but these were at ground level and did not impede free movement across the landscape. In this way, arable fields had an open character and were thus often described as "open fields" (fig. 3).

Though maintaining individual control over their own arable strips, cultivators in common field villages engaged in certain activities cooperatively, notably plowing and harvesting (Thirsk 1964, 11). In spring, teams would start in one area of the field and plow the strips in succession until reaching the far side of the field. At the end of the season, gathering the harvest involved similar cooperative efforts. Thus, despite individual possession of selions and the individual nature of cultivating what was sown on each strip, the common fields permitted collective operations where such activities were desirable and efficient.

In addition to plowing and harvesting, the most important collective use of land was common grazing on the grasses growing on manorial waste lands, a right originating just after the Norman Conquest (Seed 2001, 31–34). Originally uninhabited ground, waste by the twelfth century referred to manorial land left uncultivated, which nevertheless assumed a critical function in English agriculture related to the development of animal power for plowing arable fields. Draft animals, whether oxen or horses, required pasture, and farmers logically turned to the grasses on nearby waste to provision these animals. Because all farmers with animals needed to feed them, and because many of these animals were performing collective functions in plowing, the adjacent uncultivated waste was shared by members of the manorial community.

These arrangements for the common use of waste land became legitimized through two critical institutions. One was the common law Statute of Merton (1235) that obligated lords to provide tenants with sufficient rights of pasture by designating certain land on the manor for common grazing (Shannon 2011, 175).[5] Although the common land was owned by the lord, tenants exercised rights to the grasses growing there for pasturing animals. Villagers in common field townships also had rights to other resources from waste, such as timber, peat, stone, and edibles such as berries, and in most cases it was permitted to hunt small game on common land. Such rights on commons, however, were not unrestricted, but were regulated through the

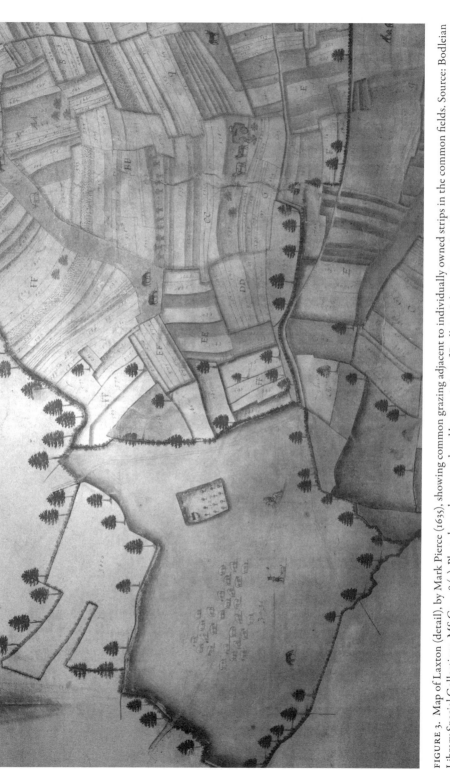

FIGURE 3. Map of Laxton (detail), by Mark Pierce (1635), showing common grazing adjacent to individually owned strips in the common fields. Source: Bodleian Library Special Collections, MS C17:48 (9). Photo by author; reproduced by permission of Bodleian Library Special Collections.

second institution, the manor court (Whyte 2009, 110; Birtles 1999, 82). Through the manor court, cultivators protected common grazing areas from overexploitation by "stinting" the number and types of animals that villagers could pasture on the commons as well as keeping outsiders from grazing on manorial land. In addition, cultivators set rules for pasturing animals on the arable land. Following the harvest, arable infields were normally thrown open for pasturing on the remaining crop stubble, while land on fields left fallow provided a source of grasses and weeds for common grazing. Such common uses on arable land required the community to make collective decisions on what was otherwise individually owned land, most notably with regard to planting and harvesting schedules.

In this way, the common field village revealed a combination of agrarian activities, some controlled individually and others organized cooperatively. Arable land used in season for cropping was individually controlled, although some of the farming practices on individually controlled land, such as plowing and harvesting, were at times undertaken collectively. This same land, however, reverted to collective grazing land for villagers following the harvest and during the fallow periods. Even certain sown areas were available for grazing, notably the pathways used by villagers to cross the fields (Neeson 1993, 95). Nonarable waste land was managed cooperatively by the village community through village bylaws or in conjunction with the lord of the manor. Cultivators with strips in the arable fields generally had rights to the cooperatively managed common land. Consequently, private and cooperative forms of landed property coexisted in common field agriculture.

Although disparaged by improvement writers as impervious to change, common field farming was more resilient as an institution, and cooperation more viable as a technology, than some of these critics suggested (Allen 2001, 43; McCloskey 1975a; Orwin 1938, 133). Cultivators in the common fields experimented with course rotations, crop choices, and cropping methods, belying what was often depicted as a system "unchanging and unbending" (De Moor, Shaw-Taylor, and Warde 2002, 17; Kerridge 1992, 67). Nevertheless, improvement promoters were unrelenting in their critique against what they perceived as the constraints on innovation posed by collective decision-making. What these authors and the public influenced by them came to embrace was the supposed superiority of exclusive individual land rights as the solution to improvement. Such a perspective would put improvement on a collision course with one of the basic institutions of early modern agrarian society, the rights of *custom*.

Where the system of land tenure and practices of common field farming came into contact, there emerged an informal set of rights known as rights of *custom* (Thompson 1991). Broadly speaking, customary rights derived from practices accepted and followed by local communities pertaining to the occupancy, uses of, and circulation on land. Reflecting local variations of common law and Crown law, rights of custom obtained legal standing by virtue of the "notice" accorded to local practices by royal and common law judges (Loux 1993, 183–84). By the sixteenth century, common law courts typically elevated custom to the status of law if the practice in question satisfied three conditions: (1) it derived from "time immemorial"; (2) it was recognized as a tradition of the community in continuous use; and (3) was deemed a reasonable practice (Loux 1993, 189; Hoyle 2011, 3). In this way, custom was the interface between law and what cultivators developed as praxis to sustain themselves in the rural environment, and the basis of common law itself (Thompson 1991, 97; Griffin 2010, 749).

Ultimately, custom was akin to law from below, its legitimacy deriving from time-honored habits of local communities on the local landscape (Loux 1993, 183). What constituted a common practice with a long-standing lineage, however, was invariably open to question, and thus what eventually emerged as customary rights codified in manor court rolls and noticed as the local law by common law and royal courts was often the outcome of conflict, where the practices of cultivators confronted the power of the lord. The establishment of customary rights was thus an open-ended and contingent process,

> a lived environment comprised of practices, inherited expectations, and rules which both determined limits to usages and disclosed possibilities.... Within this habitus all parties strove to maximize their own advantages.... The rich employed their riches and all the institutions and awe of local authority.... The peasantry and the poor employed stealth, a knowledge of every bush and by-way, and the force of numbers. It is sentimental to suppose that the poor were always losers. It is deferential to suppose that the rich and great might not act as law-breakers and predators. (Thompson 1991, 102–3)

On the common field landscape, two categories of custom prevailed. One was the custom of "easement" corresponding to occupancy (dwelling) and movement on the land; the other was the custom of commons that corresponded to the right of taking something—*profit-à-prendre*—from the lord's waste (Loux 1993, 1987). Easement custom anchored cultivators to the manorial landscape, while custom of commons enjoined their place on the land to time-honored usages in the common fields and on the common waste. With the abolition of villein tenure and the advent of copyhold, easement custom assumed a very different set of meanings for the tenant cultivator. By the mid-fifteenth century, custom of easement for the tenant cultivator became associated with the idea of proprietorship on the landscape. In effect, cultivators perceived in custom an instrument for protecting their newly acquired status as proprietors on the land. At the same time, this custom-protected right for cultivators was supplemented by customs of commons that provided cultivators with access to a range of resources on the manor, from grasses for grazing to fuel, building materials, and wild foodstuffs (Linebaugh 2008, 50).

By 1450, customary rights of easement and commons are what helped create an environment of peasant proprietorship with rights to the resources on common wastes. On the landscape itself, the most defining characteristic of custom tied to copyhold tenure and common field agriculture was the open configuration of the common fields, in general radiating outward from a nucleated village. Absent hedges, fencing, or other such barriers dividing the areas of the cultivated strips, the open landscape enabled relatively unhindered circulation on the lands of the manor across the open fields and beyond (Williamson and Bellamy 1987, 46; Crawford 2002, 46).

Affirmed in this landscape was one of the most salient rights of easement custom, the "right to roam" (Anderson 2007). This right, in turn, was imprinted onto the land in the form of footpaths, tracks, and bridleways leading to mills, churches, nearby villages, woods, or other places where villagers ventured (Anderson 2007, 381–83; Whyte 2003, 7). The outcome of this right of custom was not only a landscape of open circulation (fig. 4); the landscape was also a reflection of attitudes on the part of villagers about land ownership, in which individual rights to land coexisted with the idea of land on the manor as a resource for the community (Williamson and Bellamy 1987, 46).

Nevertheless, the custom of copyhold tied to common rights was vulnerable to challenge from manorial lords reluctant to forfeit their prerogatives as landowners. During the latter half of the fifteenth century, as the population failed to recover completely from the Plague, lords hoping to overcome declining revenues exploited a burgeoning trade in woolen cloth by turning arable fields to sheep pasturage, thus engineering the first great wave of early modern enclosure (Allen 1992, 30; Campbell 1990, 106). In this effort, lords

FIGURE 4. Map of Laxton (detail), by Mark Pierce (1635), revealing at least three footpaths through the fields. Source: Bodleian Library Special Collections, MS C17:48 (9). Photo by author; reproduced by permission of Bodleian Library Special Collections.

targeted the customary rights of copyhold. Although copyhold tenure had become common practice by the mid-1400s, it had not obtained notice from common law courts until a century later (Loux 1993, 190). Manorial lords exploited this legal ambiguity in turning out their copyhold tenants. What resulted from these evictions were depopulations of common field villages, in which new areas of trespass pertaining to occupancy multiplied and became inscribed on the landscape

EARLY ENCLOSURE

Enclosure has a long history on the English landscape and is in some ways as old as farming itself (Thirsk 1967b, 201). Nevertheless, the landlord-initiated enclosures of 1450 and other subsequent waves of enclosure by force were different from the "piecemeal" enclosures that characterized much of this older history. Although referring to myriad practices that recast the control and use of common land, piecemeal enclosure was essentially a negotiated process in which the parties involved came to an agreement (Yelling 1977, 71; Neeson 1993, 187). These agreements, in turn, were of two basic types.

The first type of piecemeal enclosure involved the exchange of arable strips or the amalgamation of land through purchase. Such exchanges were intended to overcome the disadvantages of scattered holdings or to create larger, more efficient farms. Invariably, this practice of consolidating land-holdings piecemeal by agreement was akin to *engrossing* land.

By contrast, some piecemeal enclosures were also agreements for creating private uses on otherwise common land, whether arable or waste. This second type of agreement could turn portions of common fields into private "closes" that were used by farmers with larger flocks, who relinquished their common pasture rights as compensation to the community for their now-private grazing rights (Neeson 1993, 104). Similarly, farmers might take portions of common waste for individual rights of pasture or grain-growing, again with some measure of compensation going to the community. This second type of piecemeal enclosure, where a private use right replaced a collective one, did have some effect on common field farming, since it shifted land with common uses and collective oversight by the community into the inventory of land for individual use (Neeson 1993, 101). Broadly speaking, however, piecemeal enclosure, despite at times removing land from common uses, did not threaten the overall system of common field farming or common rights

(Thirsk 1967b, 201; Yelling 1977, 6). In fact, piecemeal enclosure enabled the common field system to assume more innovative and dynamic attributes, in which common fields coexisted with a "proto-enclosed" landscape (Neeson 1993, 105).

By contrast, the landlord-initiated enclosures that began in the 1450s were marked by the use of force in eliminating common rights and security of tenure that tenants had come to understand as rights of custom. The enclosure of Stretton Baskerville (Warwickshire), as recounted in a Crown Commission Report on Depopulation in 1517, typifies this model. There the large landowner, Henry Smith, "willfully caused" cottages and dwellings of tenants to be demolished in converting 640 acres of arable land to pasture. In the process, "12 ploughs that were employed in the cultivation of those lands are withdrawn and 80 persons, ... were compelled to depart tearfully against their will. Since then they have remained idle and thus they lead a miserable existence, and indeed they die wretched" (quoted in Allen 1992, 37).

In evicting tenants and converting land to pasture, landlords took advantage of contradictory aims in the 1235 common law Statute of Merton, which protected the rights of tenants to sufficient pasture but empowered landlords to enclose land without tenant consent (Shannon 2011, 175). Remade into pasture, enclosed land regained value based on the low costs per acre of sheep farming and the power of lords to rent such land at old rates (Baker 1973, 210; Campbell 1990, 108). In addition, lords managed to seize control of common waste in an effort to transform non-income-generating land on the manor into a rent-paying asset for pasture farming (Thirsk 1967b, 200–201). In this way, conversions to pasture reversed certain gains of tenure secured by customary tenants immediately preceding and following the Black Death.

Owing to these impacts, enclosure assumed an enduring set of cultural meanings for tenant cultivators, focusing on the themes of dispossession, impoverishment, depopulation, migration, and even dearth. These associations, in turn, emerged as the basis for opposition to subsequent waves of enclosure after the first wave subsided in the early sixteenth century. While appeals to rights of custom motivated much of the early critique of enclosure, a related source of inspiration for opposition to enclosure derived from the egalitarian impulses of Christianity. From this source, alongside custom, emerged the idea that economic life should be based on a moral code of fairness in which cultivators were entitled to a place on the landscape and the right to earn a living by farming the land. Such expectations culminated in the idea of the moral economy.

With roots in the fourteenth century (Sharp 2000, 33–34), the moral economy was an imagined economic order built on the notions of customary rights and equanimity in which all persons, regardless of status, were entitled to a minimum standard of living. For advocates of moral economics, what corrupted the economy of fairness was a behavior condemned in certain Christian quarters as sinful, the behavior of covetousness (McRae 1996, 23). In order to rid economic life of this sin, moral economics prescribed a code of conduct in which landlords were forbidden to acquire land cultivated by tenants, while tenants were not to covet the holdings of other cultivators. At the same time, landlords were precluded from profiteering excessively at the expense of those paying rent and cultivating the land (Bending and McRae 2003, 4–5). In this way, the moral economy protected tenants from the expansionary aspirations of the "great possessioners" as well as from covetous neighbors on the basis of Christian egalitarianism, in which acquisition at the expense of others was considered a breach of faith (McRae 1996, 18, 23–57).

Moral economics contained an implicit critique of enclosures initiated by landowners in the mid-fifteenth century. Evictions stemming from these enclosures violated the most basic core value of the moral economy regarding the sin of covetousness. Additionally, by abrogating duly won customary rights of occupancy on the land, eviction enclosures undermined the rights of tenants to secure a minimum standard of living. Thus, by violating rights of custom, enclosure mocked moral economics by impoverishing entire communities and forcing tenants from impoverished villages to migrate in search of subsistence elsewhere. Even engrossment by prosperous tenants did not escape negative association, in that it, too, much like enclosure, reflected the sin of individuals to gain more at the expense of others.

These early enclosures registered opposition not only from defenders of custom and moral economics but also from the Crown. Beginning with Henry VII, the Tudors sought to limit enclosure and protect tenants from evictions through legislation and Crown courts (Allen 1992, 71). In 1489, a general statute was enacted seeking to prevent the "pylling doun of tounes" and the destruction of cultivation by providing that all houses with twenty acres of land be preserved for the maintenance of tillage (Thirsk 1967b, 214). Similarly, during the 1490s some evicted copyholders obtained favorable rulings from common law courts in recovering their land at least for the duration of their leases (Allen 1992, 71). Another measure enacted in 1516 at the insistence of the Crown reaffirmed the statute of 1489 in aiming to stem the conversion of arable land to pasture by insisting on payment to the State of half the profits of the conversion (Thirsk 1967b, 215–16). Finally, in 1517 the chancellor of England, Cardinal Wolsey, appointed a commission to report on villages depopulated since 1488 and the amount of land in tillage converted to pasture. The commission forced offenders to appear in Chancery Court and undo enclosures made since 1485 unless they could prove that the enclosures were for the common good (Reid 1995, 254).

In addition to the Crown, opposition to enclosure derived from reform writers during this period, the most prominent being Sir Thomas More. In *Utopia* (1516), More authored what was arguably the most uncompromising denunciation of enclosure ever published in England (McRae 1996, 23–24). Written in Latin, *Utopia* was aimed initially at a rarefied group of humanist scholars, but in 1551 the book was translated into English and from its extended readership assumed a more prominent role in a broader critique of agrarian change. In forceful metaphors More, in the voice of the character Hythlodaeus, writes of communities devoured by sheep farming and the enclosures that evicted small farmers and turned arable land to pasture. Sheep "so myke and tame," wrote More,

> become so greate devowerers, ... they consume destroy and devoure hole fields howses and cities ... [they] leave no grounde for tillage: they inclose all in pastures: they throw downe houses: they plucke downe townes, and leave nothing.... Each greedy individual preys on his native land like a malignant growth, absorbing field after field, and enclosing thousands of acres with a single fence. Result—hundreds of farmers evicted. (quoted in McRae 1996, 23)

Arguably, the most important source of opposition to the evictions and loss of commons was the very commoners affected by enclosures (McDonagh 2013). The sixteenth century was a critical period of transition when land was assuming a new status as property and the landscape was being inscribed with very differently configured spaces of access and exclusion stemming from enclosure. While users of the commons had enlisted the Crown and the courts in seeking redress from those aspects of enclosure that dislodged them from the land, they also employed direct action throughout the 1500s to protect their rights, often in the aftermath of an unfavorable legal or administrative ruling.

Undoubtedly, the best-known practice of resistance to enclosure was hedge-breaking, in which commoners destroyed the barriers erected by landholders to keep them from trespassing on enclosed land. Commoners also resorted to poaching resources from the commons—wood and peat for fuel, wild food-stuffs and wild game, and above all pasturage for their animals—that they were prohibited from accessing following enclosure (McDonagh 2013.

Although enclosure generated formidable opposition, the practice had capable defenders. By the early sixteenth century, after landowners had enclosed land and rented the enclosed area at levels above what the land yielded in tillage (Allen 1992, 48), enclosure assumed an alternate meaning. Land let at higher rents compelled tenants, whether pasture or arable-land farmers, to generate greater levels of output in order to meet the higher rental payments. In this way, enclosure was more than an instrument of covetousness and individual greed. By enabling landowners to raise rents and forcing tenants to farm more efficiently, enclosure was conceived by its defenders as a catalyst for increasing agrarian productivity and promoting the common good. Such arguments took on a new resonance beginning in the sixteenth century when the common good became fused with a new outlook: land improvement.

THREE

From Land Reimagined to Landscapes Remade

THE DISCOURSE OF IMPROVEMENT AND ENCLOSING THE COMMON FIELDS

AFTER THE EVICTION ENCLOSURES OF 1450–1525 subsided, a pioneering group of agrarian writers began to promote ideas about a more innovative agricultural system to a public of landowners in a vocabulary never before seen in English agrarian literature (Thirsk 1985, 534). Beginning with Fitzherbert (1523), these authors elevated a singular if simplistic-sounding paean for ameliorating the problems of husbandry: land improvement. As this discourse evolved, writers such as John Norden (1607a,b) and Walter Blith (1652) did not frame the improvement dilemma only in terms of farming techniques. Rather, they assailed what they believed were the institutional and cultural impediments to an improved agrarian order.

Their targets were threefold. First was the system of rights procured through *custom* that secured tenant cultivators to their landholdings and provided them access to common land. For these writers, custom preempted improvement-minded individuals from implementing innovations that would augment farm yields. Second was the system of beliefs that provided support for customary rights in the form of an idealized economic order known as the *moral economy*. Inspired by the egalitarian impulses in Christianity, moral economics held that the place of tenant cultivators on the land and their right to subsistence were part of a compact of fairness that precluded lords from coveting what belonged to their tenants and regarded the accumulation of land and riches as sinful. Improvement writers, by contrast, argued that, far from sinful, coveting land and profiting from it was precisely what was needed to establish an improved agrarian order. Finally, improvement writers insisted that common field farming stood as the primary impediment to a more productive agrarian system, being resistant to innovation. What they proposed as the route to improvement, therefore, was the conversion of common fields and common waste into severalty by enclosing land.

While the technology of print broadened the impact of improvement writers—multiple editions of their works appeared in the sixteenth and seventeenth centuries—these authors, often gentlemen-farmers themselves, circulated socially among the same landed elites they were trying to influence. In some cases, the experiments of improvement-driven landowners actually influenced improvement writers. Thus, improvement authors emerged as agents of change not only by encouraging the use of new farming techniques, but also by publicizing experiments already in play (Thirsk 1985, 533–39). "I did by proof find that action and discourse went hand in hand together," wrote the seventeenth-century agrarian writer Gervase Markham, commenting on the interplay of improvement ideas and real-world innovation on the land itself (quoted in Thirsk 1985, 536). In this way, improvement writers were acting as change agents by advocating for agrarian improvement and by documenting best farming practices. Through the power of print, and through the social familiarity of authors and audience, improvement texts gained a readership with landowners who absorbed their lessons while reimagining and remaking the landscape.

What emerged from this environment of ideas and action was a dramatic shift in the collective imagination, in which land anchored to a system of custom, moral economics, and common rights lost credibility in favor of land as *property* for profitable gain (McRae 1996, 168). Securing a property right in land was thus a pathway for improving and profiting from it—and the means for realizing this imagined geography of property and profitability was to enclose the land. In this way, enclosure enabled a landscape of boundaries and severalty, demarcated by hedges, walls, and fences, to replace a landscape of openness supporting a system of customary rights to the commons (Johnson 1996, 13, 71).

By the early seventeenth century, improvement writers conceived of landscapes in two broad categories: landscapes were either improved, or they were unimproved and empty and thus available to be enclosed and appropriated by the enterprising improver of land (Warde 2011, 128). This division of the landscape, in turn, inspired those in possession of unimproved land but influenced by improvement writing to reassess what an improved landscape might be. By universalizing the idea of improved and unimproved land, improvement writers could justify the takeover and remaking of supposedly empty, unimproved landscapes. As a practical matter, this project targeted copyhold users of common land, whose status on the landscape was progressively weakened by legal decisions during the seventeenth and eighteenth centuries that constituted a legal revolution in favor of individual landed property rights (Reid 1995; Thompson 1992).

Nevertheless, the idea of land improvement tied to enclosure did not go unchallenged. A formidable defense of common rights and a vibrant opposition to enclosure in the tradition of Thomas More emerged, especially in the eighteenth century. On the one hand, this culture of resistance was visible in cultural texts such as popular ballads, songs, and poems, many of which express undisguised antipathy for those enclosing land and nostalgia for a way of life threatened by the loss of commons (Ganev 2004). On the other, the long-standing tradition of direct action against enclosure by commoners themselves—fence breaking and pulling down hedges—did not dissipate but continued into the period of parliamentary enclosure (Neeson 1982).

IMPROVEMENT AND REIMAGINING THE LANDSCAPE

When landlords initiated enclosures in the mid-fifteenth century to regain lost incomes, they exploited the contradictory signals in the common law Statute of Merton that affirmed the right of tenants to "sufficient" land on the manor for grazing but vested the lord with the right to enclose part of his waste land without tenant consent. Thus, Edward Coke, in *The Second Part of the Institutes of the Laws of England* (1642, 87–88), referred to Merton as the Statute of Approvements, where "approvement" was an appropriation of wasteland through enclosure by landlords that left sufficient common land for tenants (Shannon 2011, 176). After the eviction enclosures subsided, however, approvement as a legal basis for enclosure gave way to "improvement," which justified enclosing land in an entirely new idiom (Shannon 2011, 178). Where approvement was a legal process for appropriating land, improvement referred to an economic process for profiting from land through "artful husbandry" (Edwards 2006, 17).

This shift in the meaning of improvement, from a legal process for alienating land to an economic process for profiting from land, is traceable to the mid-sixteenth century, by which time improvement had assumed three specific meanings. As documented in the *Oxford English Dictionary*, to "improve" meant, first, "to turn land to profit"; second, "to enclose and cultivate (waste land)"; and third, "to make land more valuable or better by such means" (i.e., enclosing and cultivating). Land that was improved was thus enclosed and brought under individual ownership; it was cultivated more efficiently; and it had an enhanced value for the owner in terms of rent (McRae 1996, 136–37). In this way, improvement brought together the economics of innovative farming and the legality of individual appropriation (Edwards 2006, 17).

Improvement as Discourse: Fitzherbert

The initial stirrings of this outlook regarding improvement found expression in John Fitzherbert's *Boke of Husbandrye* (1523) and the companion *Boke of Surveying and Improvement,* published in the same year (McRae 1996, 137–43). Targeting estate owners in both works, Fitzherbert aimed to make the landowner aware of what needed improving in order to set the estate in good order, from knowing the plow and when to sow different crops, to techniques of fertilizing known as marling and the use of water meadows to control irrigation. Where Fitzherbert was a pioneer was in his understanding of land as an economic asset (Warde 2011, 130). In his book on surveying, Fitzherbert wrote that the integrity of the estate was upheld by its "rentes, issues, revenewes, and profytes," which had to increase if the estate was to prosper (quoted in McRae 1996, 173). Improvement, he insisted, created higher yields on the land, justifying higher rents and generating more income for the landowner. Fitzherbert was also the first agrarian writer to signal, if tentatively, how the enterprising landowner could improve land by enclosing it, thereby adding to the land's rents, revenues, and profits (McRae 1996, 173).

For Fitzherbert, enclosure compelled the landlord to acquire a new type of knowledge focusing on the visibly measurable aspects of landholdings and tenancies on his estate. Fitzherbert signaled this new type of knowledge in his book on surveying when he instructs his readers on "Howe to Make a Townshippe Worth 20 Marke a yere worthe 20 .xx. li. [pounds]" (McRae 1996, 173). In order to remake the township into something more profitable, Fitzherbert insists on transforming what is common into an individual property right in land. Such a project, however, required the lord to utilize knowledge from surveys to "count the fields and their acreages, discover which are subject to common rights and what their value is" (quoted in Thirsk 1992, 24). For Fitzherbert, the physical layout of land is what enabled the landowner to understand more thoroughly its potential as a financial asset and thus improve it (McRae 1996, 172–73). It "is necessary to knowen," he writes, howe all of these maners, lordshippes, landes and tenements should be extended, surveyed, butted, bounded and valued in every parte; ... may the lorde of the saeed maners, lordshippes, and tenements, have perfite knowledge where the lande lyeth, what every parcell is worth, who is his freeholders, copye holders, customarye tenaunt, or tenaunt at his wyll. (quoted in D. Smith 2008, 44)

The appearance of Fitzherbert's *Bokes* and subsequent sixteenth-century husbandry manuals marked a watershed in the evolution of a discourse that influenced landowners to improve their land (Thirsk 1985, 534). He was arguably the first to emphasize the role of landowning as an economic activity while promoting the connection between improving, enclosing, and surveying land as a path to profit. Before the end of 1500s, Fitzherbert's *Boke of Husbandrye* appeared in seventeen editions. The extensive library of Henry, Lord Stafford, for example, contained two copies of Fitzherbert's *Boke of Husbandrye* (McCrae 1992, 39). Similarly, his *Boke of Surveying* appeared in eleven editions from 1523 to 1567 (McRae 1996, 172). Other works on land improvement during that century reflected similar patterns of diffusion in the inventories of numerous private libraries. One such work was Thomas Tusser's *A Hundreth Goode Pointes of Husbandrie* (1557), which by 1573 had expanded to five hundred points and by 1638 had appeared in twenty-three editions, making it one of the largest-selling books during the reign of Elizabeth (Bending and McRae 2003, 124). Collectively, these writers publicized best agrarian practices, motivating landowners into using land differently while framing a vision of an improved way to organize the landscape (Thirsk 1985, 534).

Seeing *Improvement: Estate Maps and "Knowing One's Own"*

Despite Fitzherbert's breakthrough on surveying, it was not until the late sixteenth century that land measurement emerged for representing, enclosing, and improving land, and only in the early seventeenth century did surveys tied to mapping become a more established practice of estate management. Although surveys had been in use during the medieval period, they were typically written terriers, or rent-rolls, specifying the names of tenants, what they held, by what tenure, and the annual rents or fines (Harvey 1996a, 41). The change in surveying to a more measurable art, and the convergence of surveying and mapping with enclosure, are traceable through the history of a particular artifact: the estate map.

At the outset of Elizabeth's reign in 1558 the estate map was uncommon, but by the close of her rule in 1603 estate mapping had become well established for representing land and landlord/tenant relations on the manor (Eden 1983, 68; Bruckner and Poole 2002, 619). Nevertheless, by the mid-sixteenth century the notion of surveying tied to measuring and mapping had become sufficiently widespread to be documented in the *Oxford English Dictionary*. The *OED* noted use of the verb "to survey" already in 1550, defining it as an act of measuring "to determine the form, extent, and situation of a tract of ground or any portion of the earth's surface by linear and angular measurements so as to construct a map, plan, or detailed description of it," while a "surveyor" denoted a person involved in measuring land (McRae 1996, 171).

Several treatises on surveying subsequent to Fitzherbert mark this transition documented in the *OED*. The earliest was Richard Benese's *Maner of Measurying* (1537), which, unlike Fitzherbert's text, focused on instructing surveyors in the calculation of boundaries on land (Smith 2008, 44). Published in five editions from 1537 to 1565, Benese's text also signaled the importance of mapping what had been surveyed (Skelton 1970, 81; Turner 1991, 313). The first treatise to link estate surveying more explicitly to mapping, however, appeared in 1582; in it, Edward Worsop emphasized the role of mathematics for "true platting" (mapping) to convey what had been measured (Harvey 1993a, 83; Edwards 2006, 25). Worsop was part of a new generation of surveyors influenced by empiricist notions of an objectively knowable and geographically measureable world that, supplemented by the advent of instrumentation, could be rendered accurately by employing principles of mathematics and geometry in the representation of space (Edney 1993, 55; Cormack 1997, 15–16; Bennett 1991, 348).

From this convergence emerged a revolution in cartography in England by the last quarter of the sixteenth century marked by a more widespread awareness of land as bounded space that was mathematically measurable (Harvey 1993, 15; Klein 2001, 5, 52). While the estate map played a central role in this mapping revolution, what drove the ascendancy of cartography in this period was empire-building, with the Crown emerging as the center of a new structure of patronage for cartographic representation (Buisseret 1992). In seeking to plant colonies as well as defend the realm, the Crown developed a need for accurately measured knowledge of territory; this in turn spawned demand for maps of a different type: maps drawn to scale (Harvey 1993b). Although inspired by interstate rivalry, maps drawn to scale were more or less transferable to the domain of large landowners, who began to appreciate the advantages of knowing their lands as measurable and bounded territorial spaces.

The emergence of large landowners as patrons of the scale-drawn estate map, however, occurred at least in part because of the close connections they enjoyed with government ministers—who, imbued with visions of colonization and the map consciousness that accompanied it, were also themselves often great landowners. Arguably, the figure who best personifies this fluid social world of elite English society where government and landed interests converged is William Cecil, First Lord Burghley. A longtime advisor to Elizabeth, Burghley was a large landowner with an extensive map collection, attesting to his professional and personal patronage of cartography and his understanding of the benefits of mapping at the level of the estate (Barber 1992, 59). By the late sixteenth century, therefore, alongside government as patron of cartography was the estate owner, who was now prepared to act as patron for scale representations of his lands (Harvey 1993b, 43). Such patronage enabled estate mapping to flourish and a cartographic imagination of manorial landscapes to gain a new foothold (Barber 1992, 59).

Among practitioners, the mapmaker most decisive in promoting this newly ascendant environment of map consciousness was Christopher Saxton, best known for producing a series of scale-drawn county maps that he bound together in his celebrated *Atlas of the Counties of England and Wales* (1579). While the *Atlas* reflected the highest-quality collection of maps produced at that time in England, Saxton's importance to mapping land lies in the roughly fifty estate maps that he produced over his career (Harvey 1996a, 35). Saxton's county maps thus stand as precursors to late-sixteenth-century estate maps, in that both focused on the representation of land drawn to scale from surveys (Harvey 1993b, 45).

Saxton played a pivotal role in framing the principles that would become part of estate mapping, but it was Ralph Agas who emerged as arguably the most accomplished early maker of estate maps. A capable writer on the subject of estate mapping, Agas was the coproducer of the first estate map drawn to scale, in 1575, but his fame as a mapmaker comes from one of the greatest masterpieces of early estate mapping, his 1581 depiction of Lord Cheny's estate at Toddington, Bedfordshire (Barber 2005, 55). The Toddington map, consisting of twenty sheets each measuring roughly one square meter, reveals in extraordinary detail the layout of the common fields in which copyholders and freeholders intermingled in cultivating their long thin strips (fig. 5).

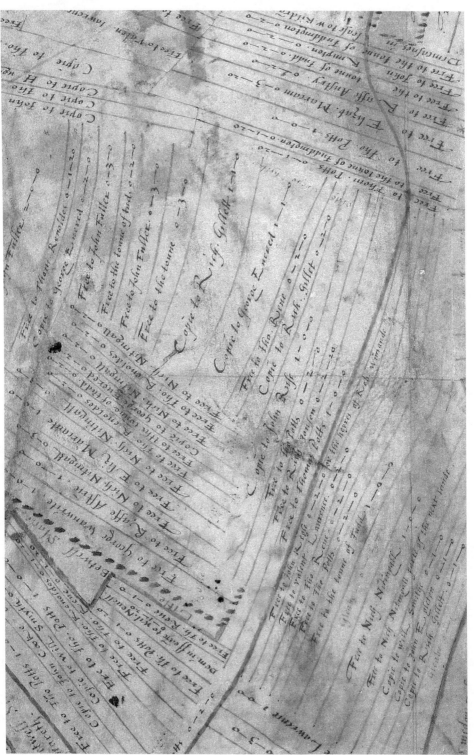

FIGURE 5. Map of the Estate of Toddington, Bedfordshire (detail), by Ralph Agas (1581). The strips in this detail reveal copyhold tenants and freeholders intermin-

In his twenty-page pamphlet "A Preparative to Platting of Landes and Tenements for Surveigh" (1596), Agas emphasized to estate owners the economic advantages of surveying their properties (Delano-Smith and Kain 1999, 117; Harvey 1996a, 43). A map presents every parcel of land in a way that text cannot match, he wrote, echoing Fitzherbert. For enclosing land, the advantages of graphic representation were obvious: "if you will sever any fielde or cloase into two or more parcels: the Scale will readily bewray how many perches, & feet shall perform the same, and where may be the rediest cut" (quoted in Harvey 1996a, 43). In this way, Agas provided a sixteenth-century affirmation of cartography's emergence as a catalyst for landowners to imagine a more profitable estate.

Even as the estate map enabled landowners to see opportunities for improvement in terms of the configuration of tenancies and freehold properties, it also conveyed symbolic meanings about estate owners themselves and about land ownership at a time when the idea of land as property was just evolving. Estate maps projected these symbolic meanings through representations such as the mapmaker's compass and the lord's coat of arms. The compass emphasized the objectively measurable nature of the land depicted in the map, while the coat of arms communicated the status of that land as the estate owner's property. In this way, the estate map conveyed a mathematically objective and rational foundation for the ownership status of the estate owner, thus subtly affirming the landowner's power and prerogatives (Klein 2001, 54–59).

As mapping expanded the vision of landowners to see opportunities for improving land, the surveyor/mapmaker became more recognizable as an agent of enclosing estate owners, perceived by wary tenants as the "Quartermaster" helping landlords to visualize reordered rights of copyhold and thereby revoke rights to commons (Harley 1988, 285; McRae 1996, 170). In this way, cartography embodied an emerging conflict pitting promoters of improvement and enclosure against those facing loss of common rights, higher rents, and even displacement. This conflict assumed literary form in *The Surveyor's Dialogue* of John Norden (1607).

John Norden and the Cartography of Conflict

From the sixteenth century onward, enclosure advocates confronted copyholders and their rights to common land as obstacles to an improved landscape (Reid 1995, 245). Although numerous copyholders had been evicted during the enclosures of 1450–1525, others had maintained and even consolidated their rights in the common fields (Allen 1992, 76, 98). Nevertheless, copyhold tenants were always vulnerable to displacement because their tenancies were still in the legal sense at will. For proponents of improvement, the challenge was how to dislodge this group from positions of proprietorship and separate them from the practices of common field farming.

In pursuit of this aim, improvement advocates focused on waste land as the impediment to an improved agrarian order and justified enclosure of waste by means of a new set of cultural representations of the commons. Where waste was once associated with legitimate common uses, by the 1600s improvement writers were assigning it the pejorative meaning of land that was empty: *terra nullius*. If the common landscape was empty, its copyhold users were recast in much the same way, as the inhabitants of empty landscapes—as was by now also occurring in other parts of the British overseas empire. Much like the Amerindians of North America, commoners were recast as "savages" (Hoyle 2011, 17). Although this characterization had appeared already in the late 1500s to describe fenland commoners, the association of commoners and savagery became more prevalent in improvement discourse during the following century. By the seventeenth century, improvement and enclosure were central in a type of "culture war" over the meaning of common land (Brace 1998, 47). John Norden emerged as a critical voice in this cultural conflict.

One of the premier surveyors of his era, Norden was also a seasoned writer on land improvement who aimed to convince estate owners of the advantages of surveying and mapping (Kitchen 1997, 52). His *Surveyor's Dialogue* (1607), representing conversations between a surveyor and a tenant farmer, reveals an author aware of the competing arguments and potential conflict between principles of custom and the imperatives of improvement.[1] In the voice of the tenant, Norden writes, "I along with many poor tenants have good cause to speak against the [survey] profession" (Norden 1607a, 3–4). Fearful of the knowledge that surveying gives lords to know their lands and "rack their tenants to a higher rent," the tenant remarks how the surveyor is "the cause that men loose their land" and the reason for the abridgment of long-standing customs and liberties on manors. The surveyor retorts, however, that custom, not surveying, has immiserated farmers: "If thou look into the mirror of history you will see in your ancestors and in the ancient custom rolls of the manor a true picture of servitude" (1607b, 38). Thus disputing the tenant's picture of a better life from customs of the past, the surveyor avers that "measuring and plotting" provide the lord with knowledge of "what he hath," enabling lord and tenant alike to prosper from a well-run manor.

Norden was also keenly aware of the power in knowledge and argued forcefully about the merits of knowing land through graphic representation rather than direct experience. In making this argument, Norden understood that graphic knowledge of the landscape favored the estate owner, while direct experience of the land—"knowledge of every bush and by-way"—was often used by tenants as a tool to defend their customary rights (Thompson 1992, 103). To the farmer's question "Is not the Field it selfe a goodly Map for the Lord to looke upon, better than a painted paper?" Norden's surveyor replies that a plat is superior, and in this way critiques the knowledge that traditionally helped tenants preserve custom in favor of knowledge that shifted power to the lord. This conversion of land into a cartographic abstraction proved a critical turning point for the improvement-driven landowner "to know one's own" (McRae 1993). Norden reveals how this transition was occurring in the minds of dissenting actors while promoting the very practice of surveying that was giving rise to this dissent (Sullivan 1998, 43).

Norden himself encountered tenant resistance to surveyors, noting how in undertaking a survey of tenancies at one estate it was not possible to proceed, because of the hundred tenants, "not 30 appeared" (quoted in Netzloff 2010, xvii). More significantly, Norden anticipated the strident characterizations of later improvement authors, noting that users of common land suffer from "idleness, beggary, atheism and consequently all disobedience to God and King . . . and infect the commonwealth with the most dangerous leprosies" (quoted in Hoyle 2011, 17). Such antipathy takes on new meaning against the backdrop of the Midland Revolt of 1607, the largest ever against enclosure in England. Norden knew of this event but omitted any reference to it in his *Dialogue* because the revolt and its aftermath suggested that the tenant indeed suffered severely from improvement and enclosure (Netzloff 2010, xxxv).

Occurring in May-June 1607, the revolt at its height counted one thousand protesters voicing resistance to enclosure and conversion of arable land to pasture in several Midland common-field villages (Hindle 2006; Hindle 2008, 21–25). As reported by Gilbert Talbot, Seventh Earl of Shrewsbury, protesters in several of these villages destroyed the enclosure hedges and fences erected by landlords who, during the 1590s, had consolidated the lands there, most notably Thomas Tresham from Northamptonshire. A militia organized by these landowners killed 40–50 protesters in 1607, while others were arrested and several executed in public hangings. At trial, those arrested provided a stark contrast to the picture of improvement provided by Norden's surveyor; rather than painting a rosy picture, the protesters depicted enclosure as a sin of covetousness by which their lands were seized to create sheep-walks, as Thomas More had decried. One village at the center of the revolt, Haselbech, reflected this broad theme of land consolidation and conversion to pastureland in an exceptional map (fig. 6) that reveals the consolidation of village lands among a small group of local landowners (Martin 1983, 184). What the revolt and its aftermath suggested about improvement was thus very different from what Norden had argued. Far from enabling landlord and tenant to prosper together, as Norden had written, land improvement enriched the landholder at the tenant's expense.

Enclosure in the National Interest: Improvement from Blith to the Hartlib Circle

In the aftermath of the Midland Revolt, a Crown-appointed commission investigating the events found that over 27,000 acres had been illegally enclosed, resulting in the destruction of 350 farms and the eviction of 1,500 people in eighteen villages. Despite this finding, Crown policy on enclosure began to change—and not in tenants' favor (Reid 1995, 249–51). No longer was the monarchy intent on ensuring protection from eviction as it had been during the Tudor years. Following the revolt, instead, the Privy Council recommended that enclosures be left intact so that "the gentleman not be hindered in his desire [for] improvement" (quoted in Thirsk 1967b, 236). In 1618, the government appointed a commission to grant exemptions from earlier anti-enclosure statutes on the rationale that these earlier laws had to be mitigated "according to present times and occasions" (quoted in Reid 1995, 258). Six years later, Chief Justice Edward Coke denounced these earlier anti-enclosure statutes, and Parliament repealed them, revealing the extent to which improvement and enclosure were converging with the outlook and interests of powerful state actors (Thirsk 1967b, 236). No longer simply seen as a prescription for individual farmers to secure higher rents and greater productivity from their land, as the seventeenth century evolved improvement and enclosure came to be viewed as projects promoting the greatest good for the greatest number. Alongside this convergence of improvement, enclosure, and nation was a theme that had appeared in Norden but assumed a far more strident tone as the century progressed: an ambivalence and even hostility to common land and its users (Warde 2011, 127). The key figure in this transition was Walter Blith (Thirsk 1983, 307).

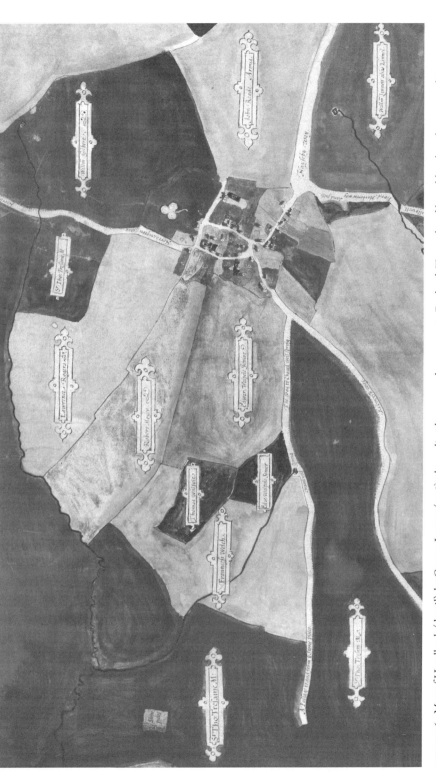

FIGURE 6. Map of Haselbech (detail), by George Levens (1598), the earliest known enclosure map in England. The enclosed large blocs have been turned into pasture farming, with the names of the new owners indicated on the map. Source: Northamptonshire Record Office, Map 561. Photo by author; reproduced by permission of Northamptonshire Record Office.

A medium-sized yeoman farmer from Leicestershire, Blith assumed a key post in Cromwell's army as a surveyor of confiscated royalist estates in Bedfordshire, Cambridgeshire, Huntingdonshire, and Norfolk. This experience gave Blith insight into agrarian conditions over a large area of central England, which he used in producing his celebrated work *The English Improver* (1649). Three years later he expanded the book to twice its original size with the new title *The English Improver Improved* (Thirsk 1985, 307). Arguably the most significant feature of Blith's book, however, and one that differentiated it from the works of previous agrarian writers, was his explicit and recurrent use of the term *improvement,* beginning with the title itself, to characterize the practice of artful husbandry.

Blith opens his work by insisting that improvement could be part of a plan for upgrading the entire nation—and not just England: "All sorts of lands," he writes, "of what nature or quality soever they be, . . . will admit of a very large improvement" (Blith 1652, 1, 17). At the same time, he argued that the primary impediments to improving land were human "prejudices"—systems of belief rooted in "ignorance" that caused agricultural landscapes to languish (Blith 1652, 5–6). For Blith, the prejudices that constrained individuals in their outlook and thinking derived from one source: *custom.*

In Blith's view, "slavish custome" to old forms of husbandry was contrary to reason, ingenuity, and the will of God (Blith 1652, 7). He singled out for special condemnation small cultivators, whom he described as "mouldy old leavened husbandmen," wedded to custom and adverse to "every new invention," who prefer toiling in common fields in perpetual drudgery because they perceive in improvement something that undermines their way of life. These individuals "have been accustomed to such a course of husbandry as they will practice and no other" and oppose improvement by referring to how well their fathers lived on the land (quoted in Outhwaite 1986, 15; Blith 1652, 72).

To remedy this pathology, Blith proffered a spirited defense of individual landed property rights and enclosure of the commons, which would supplant those wedded to old ideas and replace them with forward-looking improvers. Sounding one of the most frequent themes made by improvers about the advantages of individual property rights for agrarian innovation, Blith, in one of the introductory epistles to the book, writes that "where all men's lands lie intermixed in common fields, the ingenuous are disabled to improving theirs." He laments that anywhere from one-third to one-half of the land in common field villages was not under crop but in "wast landes." If "ingenuity" and "enclosure" were applied to this waste, Blith prophesies, more bountiful harvests would ensue than if the land were left common (Blith 1652, 81). While he concedes that some enclosures might harm tenants, the productivity enhancements from enclosure, when "one acre is made worth three" held in common, would, he insists, offset any negative impacts, enabling benefits to extend from lord to tenant and even the cottager (Blith 1652, 74; Thirsk 1983, 308, 312). Even more importantly, making private landed property through enclosure would create the type of new individual with the sentiment and mentality critical for improving land: "And were every man's part proportioned out to himself and layd severall, it would so quicken and incline his spirits, that he would be greedy in searching out all opportunities of Improvement, whatever the land. . . . A Monarch of one acre will advance more profit out of it, than he that hath his share in a hundred acres in common" (Blith 1652, 86).

In condemning older agrarian attitudes as obstacles to improvement, Blith gave voice to an increasingly aggressive cultural indictment against common land and customary rights (Brace 1998, 48). At the same time, becoming more firmly embedded in the improvement discourse that Blith was helping shape was a "mental mapping" of common field landscapes that beckoned to be upgraded by the industrious improver (Warde 2011, 142). In this way, landscapes inscribed with customary rights assumed a new identity among improvement writers as affronts to the common good. The mission of improvement was to civilize such landscapes. For this mission, Blith and other improvement writers had a steadfast ally in the celebrated writer and publisher Samuel Hartlib.

Gathered around Hartlib were some of England's most influential writers, expounding on subjects from economics and religion to science and agriculture (Thirsk 1985, 547). Blith was part of this influential circle, in which authors, landowners, and the otherwise well-connected met and circulated. By the time Blith was writing, improvement had attained far greater currency than in the sixteenth century, owing to the influence of Hartlib and his associates. Moreover, with his contacts in Parliament, Hartlib was able to broaden the improvement discourse beyond husbandry into a national conversation about the well-being of England itself (Edwards 2006, 20; Raylor 1992, 91–92). As a result, the discourse of improvement converged with the more broadly conceived imperative of promoting the common good. Hartlib himself was far from neutral in his assessment of how to enhance the economic well-being of the nation and improve society. "There are fewest poor where there are fewest commons," he said (quoted in Thirsk 1984, 228). In this way, enclosing the commons, far from a pursuit of individual self-interest, emerged as a project of national regeneration.

Two works written at roughly the same time as Blith's *Improver Improved* reflect this spirit of improvement, enclosure, and the commonweal. In *Bread for the Poor and Advancement of the English Nation Promised by Enclosure of the Wastes and Common Grounds of England* (1653), Adam Moore argues passionately that England's downtrodden will find prosperity as well as moral purpose from the conversion of waste land into enclosed, individually owned parcels of land, and that England itself will benefit from the redistribution of waste to private owners. "The principal and onely means to ripen the fruit of new hopes is *Enclosure* and distribution of Lands to new owners," he writes. Once waste lands are enclosed, the poor gain from the efforts of newly created private landowners who are able to remove the inefficiencies on the land and set the poor to work. Consequently, instead of "begging, filching, robbing, roguing," the poor are put to "diking, hedging, setting, sowing, reaping, gleaning, mowing, making hay." Such activities, Moore insists, represent "bread for the poor," in an expanding commonwealth where the less fortunate are transformed into a productive resource (Moore 1653, 30; McRae 1996, 167).

The other work, by Cressy Dymock, reveals an unusual spatial approach to improving land. In *A Discoverie for Division or Setting Out Land* (1653), penned as a letter to Hartlib, Dymock projects an ideal form for an improved and enclosed landscape. Emphasizing the importance of the common good, Dymock observes that "too much of England" has been left "as waste grounds, Commons, Mores, Heaths, Fens, Marishes and the like, . . . all capable of very great improvement" (Dymock 1653, 3). Such lands, he insists, are constrained by "want of enclosure" and the mixing of persons, land uses, and animals in the same area. As a remedy, he suggests inscribing the landscape with geometrically configured boundaries at two scales: that of the rationally ordered individual manor and, more crucially, the larger expanse of multiple improved, enclosed individual manors consisting of "great farms" of 100 acres and lesser farms of 25 acres. According to Dymock, this geometrically ordered landscape would enhance the productivity and value of the individual estate by 50 percent (Dymock 1653, 11, 22). In this sense, Dymock was a visionary. With its rectilinear contours, Dymock's proposed manorial landscape anticipated the preferences of the eighteenth century for enclosed, geometrically ordered spaces that had become so strongly associated with landscapes improved (Crawford 2002).

As improvement rallied to the status of a national concern by the mid-seventeenth century, the landowner who enclosed land in order to improve it could claim inspiration from feelings of benevolence, not covetousness. In this way, the discourse was evolving into a universalizing theory of entitlement to land in which rights to landed property were converging with ideas about improvement, enclosure, and the national interest (Warde 2011, 146). Moreover, the idea of owning land was also part of newly ascendant Enlightenment thinking about the role of landed property as a foundation for the rational organization of society. The individual who best personified this trend was John Locke.

Improvement as Property: Locke

Although Locke is rightly considered a seminal theorist of property rights, themes in his labor- and improvement-driven theory of entitlement to land had circulated among earlier improvement writers as well as promoters of England's colonial ventures (Edwards 2006, 16). Locke himself was an administrator for the Carolina territory, and his approach to landed property rights derives at least in part from his involvement in the colonial affairs of British North America (Edwards 2011). Reflecting this influence, Locke builds his argument about rights to land from the juxtaposition of two metaphorical protagonists: the "wild *Indian*" from America, "who knows no inclosure" and thus has no property in land, and the English planter, who cultivates land in enclosed fields.

At the dawn of humanity, Locke observes, land was common, and in an oft-quoted passage he likens this condition of universal common land to Amerindian society when "all the World was America" (Locke 1690, 301).[2] Nevertheless, if "God gave the world to men in common; it cannot be supposed he meant it should always remain common." Following natural law, Locked insisted that God gave land to "the Industrious . . . and Labour was to be his title to it." The industrious improved what God gave to humans by putting *labor* into the earth. By commanding humans to subdue and cultivate the earth, God was thus the authority for appropriation; in this way, "subduing or cultivating the Earth, and having Dominion, we see. are joyned together. The one gave title to the other" (Locke 1690, 291–92).

According to Locke, land improved through labor had two attributes: it was *cultivated*, and it was *enclosed*. "As *much* land as a Man tills, plants, improves, cultivates, . . . so much is his *Property*. He, by his labour does, as it were, inclose it from the commons." For Locke, labor thus employed "introduces private possessions." By enclosing land and cultivating the earth in the enclosed area, the individual draws a boundary on an otherwise open landscape and with this boundary creates what lies at the core of property: the idea of exclusion expressed as "mine" and "yours" (Locke 1690, 290–92).

Nevertheless, Locke admits to limits on the appropriation of land. Where land is already enclosed and cultivated, appropriation normally cannot take place (though there are exceptions). Where land is owned but neglected—left to spoil—it can pass into the possession of an improver willing to put labor into that land (Locke 1690, 295).

Again relying on natural law, Locke makes an additional qualification in his improvement-driven notion of the right to land that enables him to favor certain types of cultivation over others and ultimately to justify the colonization of Amerindian land, despite its being cultivated. God gave humans the gift of reason, he insists, "to make use of it to the best advantage of life and convenience," suggesting that there are superior and inferior ways of cultivating the earth. Locke uses this notion to broaden the definition of waste land where a right of property can be created. Although Locke refers to waste as "land that is left wholly to Nature, that hath no improvement of Pasturage, Tillage, or Planting," he also insists that "the provisions serving to support human life, produced by one acre of inclosed and cultivated land, . . . are ten times more than those which are yielded by an acre of land of equal richnesse lying waste in common" (Locke 1690, 294). What he suggests in this notion of common waste is twofold: first, those who work land more intensively have a higher claim to it, and second, land cultivated less intensively, despite being under crop, may in fact be waste. In this way, while Locke defined waste land as the antithesis of land enclosed and cultivated, he could now argue that land *poorly cultivated* was akin to waste. For Locke, the imperatives of reason and commandments from God for humans to subdue the earth "to the best advantage of life" provided rights of possession to those who cultivated land most productively (Armitage 2000, 97). Cultivated but poorly, the Amerindian landscape enabled Locke to expand on the notion of empty land and develop a general theory of landed property rights applicable to England's colonies and the wastes of the English countryside itself (Edwards 2005, 232; Armitage 2004, 617).

More systematically than anyone before him, Locke enjoined owning land with enclosing it and improving it. At the same time, Locke made an additional argument that justified a more aggressive role for the state in promoting land improvement and the enclosure of land. One of Locke's central claims in the *Second Treatise* was that government, as the embodiment of order and civil society, had a role in protecting the rights of individuals to landed property. Consequently, if improvement was part of the national interest, as improvement writers were arguing, and if the enclosure and private appropriation of land were the routes to improvement, as those same writers likewise insisted, then the state as protector of landed property rights had a responsibility to help improve and enclose land.

After the revolution of 1688, enclosure benefited from an increasing number of parliamentary acts and court decisions in both common law and Crown courts that weakened copyhold tenancy and opened common waste to more systematic appropriation for improvement. This more expansive involvement of the state and the judiciary in improvement resulted in the final phase of enclosure, in which virtually all remaining common land, along with the small yeoman farmer, was systematically eliminated and the landscape turned to subdivided spaces of severalty. This phase was parliamentary enclosure.

LANDSCAPES REMADE: PARLIAMENTARY ENCLOSURE

Parliamentary enclosure marked a decisive turn in the system of English landholding. In this transformation, estate owners used power and coercion to buy out land-owning yeomen, run out the leases of copyholders, and concentrate their landholdings (Allen 1992, 14, 85–104). Common field farming came to an end as estates expanded their ownership onto common wastes in order to generate income from what had been a non-income-producing asset. The result of this "landlords' revolution" was the gradual dispossession of the smallholder dependent on rights to common land (Allen 1992; Neeson 1993, 223).

With the disappearance of the yeoman farmer and small tenant commoner, a new agrarian institution came on the scene, pioneered by the great estates: the rent-maximizing farm (Allen 1992). Spawned from the consolidation in land ownership and the reallocation of common land into severalty, these large-scale farms were leased by estate owners to profit-driven tenants. The latter, in turn, employed wage laborers to create a system of capitalist agriculture on the landscape.

Although debate persists on the amount of land enclosed prior to the eighteenth century,[3] we know that parliamentary acts accounted for 21–25 percent of agricultural land enclosed in England. Before the 1700, enclosures resulted from agreements between proprietors or from rights of lordship, as was the case with the eviction enclosures. By contrast, parliamentary enclosure did not require the consent of all proprietors to enclose the land in a parish or village. Instead, a bill for enclosing a village or parish could proceed with the owner(s) of 75–80 percent of the land in the area willing to enclose. Enclosure by act thus favored large landowners, who may have lacked support for enclosing land but were able to use their ownership stake to overrule a majority of owners in the parish or village. In this sense, the conclusion of Donald McCloskey still resonates: parliamentary enclosure, he writes, "added broad powers of compulsion to the tools already available for dismantling the open field system" (McCloskey 1975, 125).

Also distinguishing the period of parliamentary enclosure were shifts in the discourse that promoted and justified it. Admittedly, the debate about enclosure dating from the time of Thomas More never disappeared, but the tone and content of the debate changed. In the seventeenth century, improvement promoters critiqued common land and commoners as impediments to a more productive agriculture but were reluctant to admit that enclosing and improving land had adverse impacts on the smallholder or that enclosure might force small cultivators to work as wage earners for someone else. By the mid-eighteenth century, enclosure defenders were willing to promote the practice even if it caused economic ruin to small users of commons or forced them into wage dependence (Neeson 1993, 19).

Complementing this argument about "freeing" the user of common land for wage work was a more strident public critique of commoners per se and the need to discipline them as laborers in the new economic order (Snell 1985, 170). Enclosure provided such leverage by taking away activities that enabled commoners to survive on the land without the need to work for wages (Neeson 1993, 29). Absent alternatives to wage work, commoners would face the sanctions of unemployment, real or threatened.

By the eighteenth century, such sentiments about wage labor as voiced by improvement promoters began to merge with an evolving ideology about the advantages of free markets. While Smith had crafted a formidable argument regarding the virtuous interplay of markets and the division of labor, the dilemma facing market advocates was how to recruit wage earners in sufficient numbers for the specialized work in factories that was needed for market growth and national prosperity. Such a project required measures restricting the sorts of activities in the countryside that had provided commoners with incomes outside the wage system. Thus, the creation of markets was as much a demographic and territorial project as it was an economic one, involving the transfer of individuals into new activities and their relocation to places of factory work.

Part of what drove the urgency among improvement writers were the demographic changes in eighteenth-century England when the country broke free of the checks on population growth described by Thomas Malthus in his *Essay on the Principle of Population* (first published in 1798). During this period, England exhibited an unprecedented increase in population numbers, expanding from 5 million to 8.6 million overall, while the urban population exploded from 13 percent of the total in 1700 to 24 percent by 1801 (Wrigley 1989, 170, 177). Provisioning this burgeoning population, especially the non-food-producing urban population, intensified public concern about the need for productivity enhancements in agriculture (Tarlow 2007). Agrarian improvement and enclosure seemed an ideal response to the need for creating a larger food supply and absorbing those potentially displaced as wage earners on the newly enclosed farms.

Finally, as demographic transformation elevated land improvement to a national imperative, and as improvement writers of the period promoted enclosure as the route to land improvement, a profound shift occurred in public perceptions about the nature of territorial space itself. These writers reinforced an evolving set of public preference for closed, contained, and partitioned spaces associated with enclosed landscapes. By the mid-eighteenth century, improvement writers had incorporated notions of space more explicitly into arguments about the irrational and unproductive nature of landscapes that were unbounded and thus akin to being empty, in contrast to the ordered and partitioned environment of enclosure. As a result, the idea of subdivided spaces seized the imagination of the eighteenth-century public. This preference for partitioned spaces, in turn, became part of the revolutionary transformation of the English landscape, characterized most prominently by the linear contours of hedges, walls, and fences (Crawford 2002, 5–64).

Landscapes Improved and the Public Sphere

By the early 1700s, the desirability of improved landscapes had become part of a national discourse (Tarlow 2007, 13, 17). One metric of the expanding visibility of improvement in the public sphere was the increase in the number of books published with the word "improvement" in the title. What was a modest output of such books during the early seventeenth century rose to unprecedented levels during the period of parliamentary enclosure (Tarlow 2007, 15).

One of the most visible early indicators of this trajectory can be gleaned from arguably the greatest classic of eighteenth-century English literature, *Robinson Crusoe* (1719), which went through four editions in its first year. In his novel, Daniel Defoe created a binary world of unimproved land that Crusoe brings into the world of improvement, cultivation, and civilization. During his twenty-eight years on the island, Crusoe spends his time appropriating a savage landscape by enclosing and fencing his arable fields, building enclosures for his cattle and goats, and enclosing his place of habitation. As Crusoe labors, more of the island succumbs to his enclosures and less is given to the unimproved and uncivilized wilds (Smit-Marais 2011, 107).

Ultimately, Crusoe is performing acts of improvement and appropriation in the spirit of Locke, fencing and creating contained spaces and taking possession of land where he has put his labor to make enclosures. "To think that this was all my own," he muses. "I was lord of the whole manor . . . as completely as any lord of a manor in *England*" (Defoe 1719, 80). Defoe's island is a metaphor of eighteenth-century England, where unenclosed, open land beckons to those with the vision to take possession of what needs improvement. Defoe affirms as much in his *Tour of Great Britain* (1723), in which he is constantly juxtaposing barren, neglected, and poorly cultivated lands to those given over to improvement and enclosure.

If Defoe's island presented enclosure as the remedy to improving England, unenclosed common field farming and common rights still had defenders who also framed their appeals by reference to the national interest. In 1732, the farmer John Cowper argued in an essay about enclosure that the practice was contrary to the national interest (Neeson 1993, 21). Open and common field villages, he insisted, were the sources of grain for the nation, which enclosure compromised by turning arable grain fields into pasture. Where there were enclosures, noted Cowper, there were depopulated villages and people without work. Cowper admitted to knowing "of no set of Men that toil and labour so hard as the smaller famers and freeholders, none of who are more industrious to increase the product of the Earth; none who are more serviceable to the Commonwealth," and concluded: "If we continue to enclose, it must end in the ruin of the Kingdom" (Cowper 1732, 18, 23).

Others, such as Thomas Andrews in his *Enquiry into the Miseries of the Poor* (1738), sharpened the enclosure critique by comparing the opulence of the rich to the industriousness of the small farmer. Enclosure was what caused the greatest injury to the user of common pasture rights, Andrews insisted, noting that a poor man's cottage by the side of a common where he can keep a cow is "as much to him as an ornamented and stately palace is to a rich person" (Andrews 1738, 39). For the Northampton clergyman Stephen Addington, the small tenant was a resource that the country could ill afford to lose. "Strip the small farms of the benefit of the commons," he wrote, "and they are all at one stroke leveled to the ground" (quoted in Neeson 1993, 15).

Undoubtedly the most influential of these enclosure critics was the Unitarian minister Dr. Richard Price, whose *Observations on Reversionary Payments* (1771) ran to six editions. Price argued that enclosure concentrated wealth and wrought misery on small farmers, who he insisted were unable to compete with large farms and thus sold out, becoming day laborers. Moreover, by turning arable fields into pasture, by impoverishing the common farmer, and by depopulating common field villages, enclosure diminished, rather than augmented, the supply of food and was thus contrary to the national interest. According to Price, the common fields and common rights should be encouraged, not eliminated, if the nation was to secure sufficient grain and prosper (Neeson 1993, 24–25).

Defenders of enclosure had equally formidable claims on representing the national interest, but shifted the focus to a new issue: farm size. By the early 1700s, improvement advocates insisted on the superiority of large farms over smaller ones. Large farms, they argued, were more productive and had higher yields because they were able to exploit economies of scale through more capital-intensive methods of farming that small farmers could not afford (Allen 1992, 4, 78). By 1727, Edward Laurence, a pioneering writer on farm size whom Cowper later scorned, was affirming the advantages of turning numerous small farms into single "great ones" while pondering how best to achieve this goal (Beckett, 1983, 313). Tenants "who rent but small Farms," wrote Laurence, "have generally speaking but little Substance wherewith to make any expensive Improvements" (Laurence 1727, 4). Although he admitted that small tenants could be "turn'd out" and their land consolidated through enclosure to make larger farming units, Laurence was reticent to admit the virtue of dispossessing the small cultivator, because "it would raise too great an *Odium* to turn poor Families into the wide World by uniting Farms all at once." Instead, he proffered a provocative recommendation: "Tis much more reasonable and popular to be content to stay till such Farms fall into Death, before the Tenant is either raid'd or turn'd out" (Laurence 1727, 4).

Whether large farms *were* more efficient and productive remains a debated issue in enclosure historiography, but apart from defenders of common field farming and common rights, public perception in the eighteenth century accepted large-scale agriculture as the key to a more productive agrarian system, and the enclosure of commons as the way to create large farms (Tarlow 2007, 39, 42). Landowners themselves believed that the productivity gains of scale economies accrued back to them as increases in rent. While numerous voices favored large-scale farming, there is no better representative of this outlook than the agrarian writer and publicist, as well as secretary to the Board of Agriculture, Arthur Young.

Enclosure, Great Farms, and Common Fields

A tireless promoter of agrarian innovation, Arthur Young made large-scale agriculture a primary theme in his vision for land improvement. Convinced that productivity advances in agriculture derived from scale economies, he argued that only large farms could generate sufficient capital for the technical innovations he was promoting (Allen 1992, 4). Young also insisted that the large farms so essential to his vision for agrarian improvement could be created from enclosing and engrossing land. By consolidating scattered holdings into one compact farming unit, enclosure enabled the farmer to overcome one of the most formidable impediments to improvement: the fragmented, small-scale plots of land scattered on the common field landscape (fig. 7) (Mingay 1975, 102). For Young, enclosure tied to "great farms" was the seedbed of all agricultural improvement (Young 1774, 155).

In promoting large farms, Young was influenced by the French physiocrat François Quesnay, who argued in 1756 that large-scale farming yielded greater surpluses over costs and thus exhibited higher productivity than *petite* agriculture (Allen 1992, 4). Two decades later, Adam Smith was equally insistent on the negative role of small agriculture. In his chapter in the *Wealth of Nations* on "The Rent of Land," Smith applauded the "diminution in the number of cottagers and other small occupiers of land," an event that he claimed "has been a forerunner of improvement and better cultivation" (A. Smith 1776, 243).

Young's similar view of small farmers as impediments to improvement is a constant theme in his various *Tours* of the farming regions of England

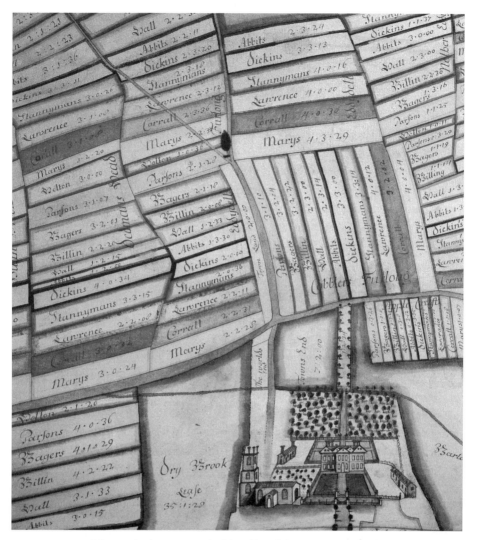

FIGURE 7. Map of the Parish of Ecton, Hertfordshire (detail), by Thomas Holmes (1703). The scattered holdings of individual farmers—Parsons, Marys, Dickens, Abbits, etc.—illustrate what Young saw as the disadvantages of scattered holding in the common fields. The largely open common field parish was eventually enclosed in 1759 by parliamentary act. Source: Northamptonshire Record Office, Map 2115. Photo by author; reproduced by permission of Northamptonshire Record Office.

published in the *Annals of Agriculture*. Improvement, Young argues, is a costly proposition, viable only for the largest farmers. "How, in the name of common sense," he asks readers of his *Political Arithmetic*, could "improvements be wrought by little or even moderate farmers!" (Young 1774, 155). Although admitting that he had once conceived of small farms as "very susceptible of good cultivation," Young wrote that what he had had seen in his travels in France "lessened my good opinion of them" (Young 1792, 407).

His views of farming in Norfolk, Lincoln, and Oxfordshire typify how he conceived of the relationship between enclosure, farm size, common fields, and land improvement. Commenting on the improvement of husbandry in Norfolk, Young writes: "Great farms have been the soul of Norfolk culture: split them into [small] tenures ... [and] you will find nothing but beggars and weeds" (Young 1771, 161–62). At the same time, Young expressed undisguised antipathy for the small cultivator who depended on common rights. Such farmers, Young insisted, were conservative in their methods of husbandry, indifferent to change, and obstacles to progress and the national interest. "I know nothing better calculated to fill a country with barbarians ready for any mischief," Young wrote of Lincolnshire, "than extensive commons" (Young 1799, 438). By contrast, large farmers on enclosed farms were progressive, open to increasing output with new methods (Mingay 1975, 103, 112). Young reserved some of his sharpest criticism for small farmers and common fields in his *General View of the Agriculture of Oxfordshire* (1809), writing that in Oxfordshire two contrasting visions of farming had come into contact. On one side were small cultivators dependent on common rights and impervious to new methods of cultivation, whom Young likens to the "Goths and Vandals of the open fields." On the other side was "the civilization of enclosures" personified by farmers motivated by improvement and innovation, who are "as much changed as their husbandry—new men in point of knowledge and ideas" (Young 1809, 35, 269). For Young, the pathway to improvement was clear: "Before any new ideas can become generally rooted," he wrote, "the old open field school must die off" (Young 1809, 36).

Young's characterization of the common fields also reflected aspects of the debate about the impacts of enclosure. In contrast to defenders of common field farming, Young argued in his *Political Arithmetic* (1774) that enclosure, far from impoverishing the commoner and depopulating villages, created employment for rural villagers. The quantity of labor in common field areas, he argued, "is not comparable to that of enclosures." Winter hedging and ditching and building of new roads in the enclosed villages, he claims, has no counterpart in common field areas. Moreover, the "vile course" of common field farming—fallow, wheat, and spring corn, with three ploughings at best—did not come close to matching the same land enclosed, "tilled four, five or six times by midsummer, then sown with turnips hand-hoed twice, and then drawn by hand and carted to stalls for beasts. . . . What a scarcity of employment in one case, what a variety in the other!" (Young 1774, 148, 72).

In his writings, Young often engages enclosure critics directly, such as Richard Price and similar writers, who, according to Young, "assure us we should throw down our hedges and waste one third of our farm in a barren fallow" and who confine themselves to criticizing "the enclosures which have converted arable to grass." For Young, these enclosure critics failed to grasp the significance of the reverse approach: reclaiming common waste for conversion to arable cultivation. "What say they to those who have changed grass to arable?" Young asks sarcastically (Young 1774, 149–50). All of these improvements, he argues, create new employment opportunities.

For Young, enclosure was central to a virtuous circle of scale economies, productivity advances, and augmentations in rent. High rents, Young argued, encouraged farmers to be more productive in order to afford the higher payments. Farms with low rents, by contrast, were "occupied by none but slovenly poor," and "in no part of England where rents are low is there good husbandry." For this reason, rent increases were not simply a transfer payment from farmer to landlord; rather, they were a "*creation* of fresh income" because when rents were high, the tenant had to be more diligent or face poverty. Indeed, Young insisted, leasing agricultural land at high rates was a civic responsibility benefiting the entire nation: "There is no evil more pernicious to the public than great families, through a false magnificence, letting their estates be rented at low rates. . . . Landlords who through a false pride will not raise [rents] when they might easily, do an inconceivable prejudice to their country. I will venture to assert that the man who doubles his rental, benefits the state more than himself" (Young 1770, 495–96).

For Young, enclosure was crucial to this feedback loop of rent increases and higher productivity because enclosing land solved the productivity problem of scattered plots in common fields. According to Young, larger, more efficient farms commanded more rent by overcoming the inefficiencies of scattered holdings, which in turn led to higher yields. In this way, enclosure, larger farm sizes, and higher rents coexisted in a virtuous world of agricultural improvement. Nowhere did Young state this more emphatically than in his *Political Arithmetic:*

What say they to the sands of Norfolk, Suffolk and Nottinghamshire which yield corn and mutton and beef from *the force of* ENCLOSURE *alone?* What say they to the wolds of York and Lincoln, which from barren heaths, at 1s. per acre, are by ENCLOSURE *alone* rendered profitable farms? Ask Sir Cecil Wray . . . if without ENCLOSURE he could advance his heaths from 1s. to 20s. an acre. What say they to the vast tracts in the peak of Derby which by ENCLOSURE *alone* are changed from black regions of ling to fertile fields covered with cattle? What say they to the improvement of moors in northern counties, where ENCLOSURES *alone* have made those countries smile with culture which before were dreary as night?

How, in the name of common sense, were such improvements to be wrought by little or even moderate farmers! . . . It is to GREAT FARMERS you owe these. Without GREAT FARMS you never would have seen these improvements. (Young 1774, 150–55; emphasis in original)

Whether enclosure, as Young insisted, produced this virtuous circle of farm enlargement, productivity gains, and rent increases was—and remains—debatable. How landowners understood this relationship between farm size, enclosure, and rent, however, and how they acted in choosing to enclose land is more certain. Owing to the influence of improvement ideas alongside their own experience, landowners believed that enclosure enabled them to enlarge their farms and that enclosed farmland was more valuable, allowing them to raise rents. This relationship between enclosure and the higher rents on enclosed farmland is what land improvement meant to them (Allen 2001, 63). Such a relationship was even acknowledged in literary representations. "I gradually inclosed all my farms," explains Mathew Bramble, one of the characters in Tobias Smollet's popular novel *Humphrey Clinker* (1771), "and made such improvements that my estate now yields clear twelve hundred pounds a year" (Smollet 1771, 218).

While Young was arguably the most strident defender of enclosure and large farms among agrarian writers as well as large landowners, his views did not go unchallenged. His most ardent and unrelenting critic, William Marshall, observed as early as the 1770s that a variety of mostly middle-sized farms of roughly 200–300 acres generated the greatest benefits for the community (Beckett 1983, 319). By the time of his most famous work, *On the Landed Property of England* (1804), Marshall had not altered his basic view, although he did admit that large farms were favored by "men of public spirit," while small farms were reserved for "minor gentlemen, the clergy and other professional men, tradesmen and others in middle life, who live in towns" (Marshall 1804, 139; Beckett 1983, 319). Nevertheless, Marshall insisted that farms in excess of 500 acres could not be managed efficiently, whereas from farms of 100–300 acres "the community receives the greatest proportion of the common necessaries of life" (Marshall 1804, 139). Marshall, in short, was unwilling to concede the superiority of large farms in all circumstances.

Very different from both Young and Marshall were the views of Nathaniel Kent in his celebrated *Hints to Gentlemen of Landed Property* (1775; 2nd ed. 1793) (Horn 1982, 5). A successful land agent and advisor to large landed proprietors, Kent believed that the upper limit for a farm should be 160 acres and that farms with holdings of 30–80 acres should outnumber those of larger size. The small farmer, Kent argued, was an industrious farmer. Because of the small size of his holdings, he "seizes all minute advantages, cultivates every obscure corner," and, owing to the limits of his farm, cultivates with "greater proportion" (Kent 1793, 227). What also differentiated Kent from Marshall and the as yet unreformed Young during this time was his concern with the welfare of the poor laborer. Estates were "of no value without hands to cultivate them," Kent argued, whereas "the labourer is one of the most valuable members of society: without him the richest soil is not worth own-ing" (Kent 1793, 241). Kent's ideas about farm size were thus situated within the larger debate of that time over the issue of poverty and the situation of the laboring poor (Horn 1982, 6).

By 1794, such debates had motivated the president of the Board of Agriculture, John Sinclair, to reconcile the differing views among his own reporters on farm size, assigning Thomas Robertson to summarize the ver-dict. According to Robertson, "The small farm is found to be attended with insufficient capital, with puny enclosures down to two acres and wretched husbandry; the poor farmer is always a bad one . . . a small farm is not worth the attention of any man of ingenuity and property" (quoted in Beckett 1983, 320). Arguably, the most aggressive attack against small cultivators and users of common rights came from Sinclair himself, who likened the common economy to a primitive age. In 1803, inspired by the Napoleonic wars and the spirit of colonial conquest, he wrote of improvement as a type of military campaign: "We have begun another campaign against the foreign enemies of the country. . . . Why should we not attempt a campaign against our great domestic foe, . . . let us not be satisfied with the liberation of Egypt, or the subjugation of Malta, but let us subdue Finchley Common; let us conquer Hounslow Heath; let us compel Epping Forest to submit to the yoke of improvement" (quoted in Neeson 1993, 31).

Enclosure as "Legal Revolution"

If the landlord's revolution consisted of using enclosure to create "great farms," as Young and other improvement writers advocated, part of what made this concentration in landownership possible was a transformation in the legal environment of landed property. This "legal revolution" eroded the foundations of copyhold tenure and rights to common land while elevating the notion of absolute individual rights to landed property (Reid 1995). Although this legal revolution reached full force only in the late 1700s, the initial stirrings are traceable to a series of treatises on common law written much earlier that posed the vexing question of how land itself could become property.

What had emerged as perhaps an anomaly in the common law was the fact that in the period from roughly 1290 to 1490, common lawyers—as well as lay writers—did not use the term *property* to describe land (Seipp 1994, 67, 86). Although as early as the mid-twelfth century the fledgling English common law did seemingly have a concept of *propriatas* for land that was held in lordship or freehold, by the year 1290 the idea of land as property had dropped from common law discourse. Instead, from 1290 until 1490 English common law restricted property to two basic categories, goods and animals. During this two-hundred-year period, common law judges referred to land by reference to a different concept: the concept of *rights*. Rather than being a material object that could be possessed, land was akin to "bundles of rights" corresponding to conditions of occupancy and use. Defining such rights, in turn, constituted one of the central tasks of late medieval common law courts. Only after the early sixteenth century did the common law begin to formulate a universal concept of property that permitted land to become an object capable of being possessed, or in turn alienated by the possessor (Seipp 1994, 32–39).

Arguably the key text in this evolving association of land with property was Christopher St. German's *Doctor and Student* (1523), written at the same time as Fitzherbert's pioneering texts. In this treatise, St. German inquired into the universal foundations of property that enabled every man to "knowe his owne thynge" (quoted in Aylmer 1980, 87). Of central concern to St. German was the question of how land might assume the status of a possession. One of the criteria noted by St. German that enabled possessions such as goods and animals to function as property was their status as bounded objects. As such, goods and animals were amenable to what is arguably the most basic principle of property—the principle of exclusion, expressed in Latin as *meum* (mine) and *tuum* (yours). The puzzle for St. German was how to transform land into a bounded object that could be delineated by the same notion of exclusion understood in the terms *mine* and *yours* (Seipp 1994, 74–77).

What St. German suggested as a legal remedy to solve this puzzle and so raise land to the status of property was the already-existing agrarian practice of enclosure (Seipp 1994, 77). Once enclosed, one piece of land was distinguishable from another piece of land in an otherwise open field. In this way, St. German uncovered in the idea of an enclosed plot of ground a mechanism for making land into a bounded object, thereby resolving the legal dilemma of how land could be possessed like other bounded things. Through enclosure, land became property.

Although St. German provided a conceptual basis for land to belong to an individual, common land and common rights still prevailed on the landscape in the early 1500s, embedded in a variety of legal institutions, agrarian practices, and rights of custom. Nevertheless, the duality of the commons—land where tenants exercised customary rights, though ultimately under the rights of lordship—was always a source of legal instability and was exploited by lords in conflicts with tenant cultivators (Everitt 2000, 217; Faith 1997, 208–9). In short, two different ideas about rights to landed property coexisted in the early sixteenth century and beyond, one based in the tradition of custom and rights of the commons, the other an evolving notion of land as a bounded object able to be possessed and thus willed, sold, and probated much like other possessions. As these two notions evolved, however, it was land as property that would emerge ascendant. And influencing this outcome was the logic of improvement, which tied a more productive agriculture to individual rights in land.

Even by the early 1600s, improvement writers were elevating the virtues of private landed property rights and denouncing commons as impediments to a more productive agrarian system. By the close of the century, Locke was not only claiming that rights to land in common represented an inferior type of tenure compared to land enclosed and made several; he also argued that land unenclosed and unimproved should be subjected to enclosure and improvement. By the mid-eighteenth century, the superiority of individual property in land was seemingly beyond debate. For Young, a "single principle" actuated the human spirit: "if you give property in land you will create the industry that shall improve it" (quoted in Crawford 2002, 39). Moreover, discourse about land improvement and enclosure of the commons was converging with the imperatives, both economic and moral, of creating a disciplined labor force. To deprive the poor of access to the benefits of common waste "must no doubt, at first view sound harsh," admitted John Clark of Herefordshire in his *Agriculture of the County of Hereford* (1794). Commoners, however, "were hurtful to society by holding forth a temptation to idleness," while farmers in Herefordshire "are often at a loss for laborers." For Clark, "the inclosure of the wastes would increase the number of hands for labour by removing the means of subsisting in idleness" (Clark 1794a, 27, 29).

Not surprisingly, the dogma about individual rights to land contained in improvement writing was helping shape notions about land law itself. Even as early as 1607, following the Midland Revolt, the Crown and Parliament under the influence of improvement thinking had essentially terminated their earlier commitment to regulating the conversion of common land into individual property through enclosure as had been done by the Tudors during much of the sixteenth century. Such political shifts, in turn, were having impacts in the field of law, as reflected in the sentiments of Chief Justice Edward Coke, who (as mentioned above) denounced earlier anti-enclosure legislation (Thirsk 1967b, 236). In this way, improvement writers, defending severalty through enclosure as the route to a more productive agrarian system, were influencing the two sectors of early modern English society most responsible for legal decisions regarding landed property rights: politicians and legal practitioners themselves. As a result, the rights of small proprietors anchored to the landscape through copyhold reached a high point by the early seventeenth century, declining thereafter (Allen 1992, 72). Only in the aftermath of the revolution of 1688 did the legal revolution in landed property rights become more visible and changes in the law converge more completely with the discourse and practices of land improvement and enclosure. This legal revolution, in turn, assumed two primary forms, one consisting of legislation passed by Parliament, the other residing in the activity of judges and lawyers themselves.

Three types of legislation are particularly noteworthy during this period with respect to landed property rights and the eighteenth-century legal revolution. The first and most important marker of this legal revolution consisted of the roughly 5,265 parliamentary enclosure acts themselves. This mechanism enabled individuals to enclose land without the consent of all parties who owned, occupied, or used the land in question by enfranchising individuals not by voice but by the extent of ownership. The second category consisted of "estate acts," numbering roughly 3,500, which intervened into what had been rules of "strict settlement" in the disposition of landed property. Estate acts changed these rules by eliminating restrictions on the uses to which landed property could be alienated in the sale, mortgage, leasing, and probate of land (Bogart and Richardson 2011, 243). Together, estate acts and parliamentary enclosure acts were the most numerous legislative actions of Parliament affirming the critical role of landed property rights in the post-revolutionary period (Bogart and Richardson, 2010, 2).

The third type of parliamentary legislation was different, aimed at creating a landscape of individual property by eradicating custom and common rights and by disciplining the users of common land to respect the new landed property regime. Arguably, the most noteworthy piece of this legislation was the Black Act (1723), which converted a number of traditional common use rights into capital offenses, some even punishable by execution (Thompson 1975). This legislation was aimed at those who tore down enclosure fences and continued to hunt game, forage for food and fuel, and gather building material on what was once common land. Influenced by the arguments about the virtues of enclosure, legislators who passed this act sought to reverse rights of common, charging violators not only as trespassers but in terms of criminal offense. Consequently, the Black Act did not simply reflect the preference of the landed class and its political allies in Parliament for individual landed property rights; rather, it represented a vision of rights to land based on exclusionary notions of enclosure while criminalizing an alternative vision based on rights of common (Thompson 1975, 261).

The other aspect of this legal revolution focused on practitioners of law itself. During the eighteenth century, "one legal decision after another signaled that lawyers had become converted to the notions of absolute property ownership, and . . . abhorred the messy complexities of coincident use right" (Thompson 1975, 241). While improvement writers ever since the sixteenth century had steadily embraced the advantages of individual rights to land over the rights of common, it was now the legal environment that aimed to codify the imperatives of improvement and the superiority of private rights to land over land as a collective resource (Thompson 1991, 162). Undoubtedly, the legal artifact that best reflected this trend of the law coming to the defense of private property rights was the "great gleaning case" adjudicated in the Court of Common Pleas known as *Steel v. Houghton et Uxor* (1788).

Gleaning was the time-honored custom of collecting crop stubble that remained after the harvest. During the eighteenth century, gleaning became an issue on enclosed farmland where tenants had formerly exercised gleaning rights. The defendant, Mary Houghton was apprehended for gleaning in a field owned by James Steel, a large landowner, who sued Houghton for trespass and damages. Lord Loughborough and two other judges on the four-judge panel argued that gleaning was not a universal common right and that the practice "was inconsistent with the nature of property" (quoted in King 1992, 3). The ruling went on to state: "No person, has, at common law, a right to glean in the harvest field. Neither have the poor of a parish legally settled any such right" (quoted in King 1992, 7).

Though not an isolated case, *Steel* was precedent-setting (King 1992, 1–2). Along with a similar case brought two years earlier, *Worlledge v. Manning*, the case of *Steel v. Houghton* was part of a new legal environment that not only made the right of gleaning into a legal question for the first time, but also pronounced definitively on that right (King 1992, 5). Consequently, despite continued resistance by commoners to the eradication of custom and common rights, by the late eighteenth century rights to individual landed property promoted by improvement and enclosure advocates now had legal precedent over rights of custom. In this regard, one need not necessarily agree with Karl Marx's observation that "the law itself becomes the instrument of theft of people's land" to admit that the legal environment played a vital role in helping spread individual rights to landed property across the English landscape (Marx 1867, 677–78; Blomley 2007). Far from a mechanical adjustment of the legal superstructure to the material practice of enclosure and land improvement, the law evolved as an instrument of force in empowering those who aspired to improve and enclose land with a legal mechanism to accomplish same (Thompson 1975, 261).

Mechanisms of Enclosure by Act

Parliamentary enclosure institutionalized a process for establishing severalty on the landscape and represented the ascendancy of large-scale agrarian land ownership on the English countryside. Enclosure by act enabled one or more landowners in an area to petition Parliament for the right to enclose land and replace common rights with individual rights to landed property. This process formalized what was once a more informal process of enclosing land by agreement (which would nevertheless be registered in chancery court). Yet in certain cases parliamentary enclosure resembled the enclosure by force associated with the evictions of 1450–1525. Enclosure by act thus had elements of both consent and force and came to prevail when the means of enclosure by agreement or by force were exhausted, causing landowners to turn to legislation to fulfill their aims (Beckett 1984, 17; Yelling 1977, 8). In the parish of Tottington (Norfolk), for example, the largest landholder, Thomas de Grey, sought to enclose the unenclosed portions of the parish through agreement in 1771, but when some of the landowners rejected his plan, he sought and obtained a parliamentary decree in 1774 and proceeded with the enclosure (J. Gregory 2005, 70). Thus, parliamentary enclosure can be understood as another tool for recasting the system of common field farming.

The mechanism for parliamentary enclosure was a petition submitted by one or more landowners in a township, village, or parish that had as its primary element a plan to subdivide and reallocate the land of the area in question. Commissioners were chosen by major landed interests in the parish, including the church, to oversee this subdivision, which involved as well the creation of new roads, tracks, and footpaths. Their primary responsibility, however, was to reallocate land in allotments to the various interests, including tenants with common rights, corresponding to what each possessed prior to the enclosure. For this task they employed a number of ancillary personnel, the most important of whom were surveyors.[4] The primary elements in the process of reallocating land were (1) the removal of common rights and reallocation of those rights to individual owners; and (2) the assignment to the new owners of specifications for hedging, fencing, or placing walls around the newly demarcated individual landed property (Whyte 2003, 9). These allotments were conceived as largely rectilinear blocks. Surrounded by hedges, fences, and walls, these reallocations of landed property imbued the landscape with a more geometrically regular form.

One of the most revealing elements of parliamentary enclosure, attesting to the influence of improvement as a public discourse, was the preamble of the petitions requesting passage of an Enclosure Bill, in which the landowners framed their reasons for desiring enclosure. Invariably the justifications focused on the constraints to land improvement posed by common fields (Turner 1980, 95). Typical was the preamble to a 1792 enclosure petition from Turkdean (Gloucestershire) that speaks of the area's "open and commonable lands" lying "intermixed, and dispersed in small parcels" and "incapable of any considerable improvement." The preamble continues that "if the same land were divided, and specific Parts or shares thereof allotted to and amongst the said Proprietors in Severalty, ... great advantages would arise to the Parties concerned (quoted in Turner 1980, 217). Repeated in over five thousand parliamentary enclosure acts, these "great advantages" brought the remaining inventory of common land into the expanding inventory of land in severalty and essentially destroyed the agrarian system of the small independent family farmer (Neeson 1993, 223). This replacement of the system of small agrarian proprietors with large-scale estate farms worked by wage labor constituted a revolution in the structure of landholding (Allen 1992, 78–104).

The process of turning land once common to severalty through parliamentary act incurred costs for the landowners enclosing the land. There were two basic costs associated with enclosure by act, one public, shared by all landowners in the enclosed area, the other borne by landholders individually (Whyte 2006a, 97). The public costs included the fees for preparing and presenting the enclosure bill to Parliament, expenses paid to various public officials for implementing the legislation—commissioners, surveyors and mapmakers, lawyers, clerks, etc.—and the costs of new roads and other rights of way to compensate for routes of access recast by enclosure (Turner 1984a, 53). The individual costs accruing to landholders focused on one element in particular—the walling, hedging, and fencing of land allotments awarded to enclosure recipients—and generally amounted to two-thirds of the total enclosure costs (Whyte 2006a, 97; Turner 1984a, 55; Clark 1998, 100).

For enclosure to be feasible, landowners had to offset these expenses; thus the decision to enclose was an investment decision driven by perceptions about costs and returns (Turner 1984a, 36–52). Contemporary comment from enclosure promoters such as Young, and even from enclosure critics, left little doubt about what landowners could expect from the impacts of enclosure in terms of revenue. Enclosed land, it was said, rented at double and sometimes triple the value of land left in common.

Such decisions, however, were not always the exclusive outcome of so-called rational choice. There were also "demonstration effects" of enclosure, in which a successful eradication of common rights in an area influenced nearby proprietors (Turner 1980, 100–105). In addition, larger macroeconomic forces, most notably the unique pattern of population growth in eighteenth-century England, entered the calculus of costs and benefits by creating incentives for landowners to seek new land and cultivate it in severalty in order to exploit market demand for increased food production. Finally, there were ideological factors connected to the ongoing influence of improvement writers and pamphleteers extolling the benefits of enclosure, as evidenced in the preambles to petitions for enclosure bills. In the end, while projection of costs and returns was paramount, landowners' decisions to enclose included other factors.

Under the influence of rational calculation, broader economic and demographic forces, other examples of enclosures around them, and the ongoing discourse of improvement itself, eighteenth-century estate owners developed a hunger for land. All of the various indicators—economic, demographic, and ideological—suggested to large landowners that engrossing their holdings would provide a path to greater returns. As a consequence, this group embarked on an ambitious program of seizing control of the remaining common field lands and common waste. In pursuit of this aim, estates complemented the formal mechanisms of enclosure by act with a second, almost equally formidable instrument. Developed as a financial innovation by the second half of the seventeenth century, and used extensively during the early eighteenth, the long-term mortgage enabled estate owners to enlarge their holdings by buying up small freeholds and heritable copyholds on a broad scale (Allen 1992, 103–4). In addition, estate owners added a related practice to enclosure by act and the long-term mortgage, one that had long been part of their prerogative as landowners but during the 1700s came into more widespread use. During this period, large landowners simply ran out the leases of copyhold for lives, effectively evicting the tenants, amalgamating the land, and leasing it to large tenants who created large-scale farms (Allen 1992, 78). Despite the formal differences between these instruments, parliamentary enclosure, the long-term mortgage, and the termination of copyhold tenancy can be understood as complementary mechanisms for the same basic process. Together these instruments were mobilized by large estates responding to a hunger for land while colonizing those portions of the landscape not under their control.

The Landlord's Revolution

The results of engrossment and consolidation were striking. While in the seventeenth century the average farm size in the South Midlands, for example, increased only slightly from the previous century, to 65 acres, between 1700 and 1800 average farm size more than doubled, to 145 acres (Allen 1992, 79). At the same time, family farms—that is, farms of less than 100 acres using family labor—declined in number by almost 60 percent, and in total acreage from 67.7 percent of total land area to 15.2 percent (Allen 1992, 83). For England as whole, in 1688 independent family-owned farms occupied at least 33 percent of total farmland. By the end of the 1700s that figure had dropped to roughly 10–14 percent. Thus the eighteenth century underwent not just a change in the structure of landholding, but a revolutionary transformation (Allen 1992, 85).

This revolution in landholding is perhaps best reflected in the examples of two villages. The first, the village of Wytham in Berkshire, illustrates the process by which large estates bought up copyholds and consolidated farmland. The second, the village of West Haddon in Northamptonshire, illustrates the effects of parliamentary enclosure on the land. The latter also illustrates why villagers were motivated to oppose enclosure and how protest itself provides an indicator of what was occurring on the landscape.

The village and manor of Wytham, Berkshire (since 1974 part of Oxfordshire), was the property of the earl of Abingdon.[5] The manor was surveyed in 1728 and again in 1814, just before it was enclosed. The survey of 1728 reveals a village of independent family farms, of which eighteen of twenty-two (82 percent) were copyholds, with the remaining four held at-will. Fully 90 percent of the farmland was in copyhold tenure. Most copyholders (ten, or 56 percent) possessed between 15 and 30 acres, the average size being 25 acres; none exceeded 100 acres. The average size of the four farms let at-will was roughly 10 acres, bringing the average size of all the independent family farms on the Wytham Manor in 1728 to 23 acres.

By 1814 the manor survey depicts a revolutionary transformation. In the first place, no copyhold tenancies existed any longer: all tenancies were now at-will. There were also fewer farms, the twenty-two farms of 1728 having shrunk in number to just eight by 1814. Whereas no farm was over 100 acres in 1728, by 1814 only two farms accounted for 419 of the 597 acres of arable land (70 percent) on the manor. In turn, the average farm size had increased by 300 percent, to 75 acres.

Also striking is the absence of commons and waste land in the later survey. In 1728, these types of land occupied 364 acres; by 1814, they had disappeared, replaced by "pasture." Since there were no longer any copyhold tenants, only the lord of the manor, the earl of Abingdon, had rights to graze animals on what was designated as pastureland; this meant that the manor was de facto enclosed by 1814, two years before it was formally enclosed by act. Thus, regardless of whether writers such as Young were correct in ascribing productivity advances to large-scale farms, the large-scale farm was for better or worse extending its presence on the landscape.

The second example, West Haddon, was a village of six hundred, with many smallholders dependent on common rights. There, in January 1764, landowners, after three attempts, succeeded in bringing an enclosure bill to the House of Commons.[6] Opponents filed a counterpetition, claiming that enclosing the fields of the village would be "very injurious to the Petitioners" and "the ruin of many, especially the poorer sort of the said Parish." Most of this opposition came from smallholder farmers and traders and artisans with small holdings, along with small cottagers. During the debate, smallholders such as Robert Earle, owner of nine acres in West Haddon, argued that it was "a very wicked thing to inclose"; smallholder David Cox insisted the enclosure "would tend to ruin ye nation"; William Page conceded that his small holding would probably be improved by the enclosure, but he himself "had no money to spare to inclose with."

Support for enclosure came from twenty-six men and women who owned 1,200 acres, amounting to 60 percent of the land in the parish. Among owners, of the eleven with holdings of more than 45 acres, ten were in favor of enclosure, with only one opposed. Among the smallest owners, those with 2–9 acres, six favored enclosure and eighteen were opposed. A similar pattern prevailed among tenants.

Of the four tenants who rented more than 45 acres, three favored enclosure and one remained opposed. By contrast, of tenants with less than 17 acres, only four were in favor, with eighteen opposed. Thus, a clear difference emerged between large and small owners or tenants in terms of support for or opposition to enclosure. Despite opposition, the enclosure bill passed in April 1764—but that was not the end of the affair

In 1765, as allotments of land were redistributed and landowners were preparing to enclose their newly consolidated holdings, a group of villagers took action to defend what they perceived as a threat to their rights from the bill. Their target, as in enclosure protests throughout the ages, was the fencing for the enclosure. "We hear from West Haddon," reported the *Northampton Mercury* of July 29, 1765, "that on Thursday and Friday last, a great number of people . . . pulled up and burnt the fences designed for inclosure of that field" (quoted in Neeson 1993, 191–92). Protesters, seemingly aware of the consequences of the enclosure, were motivated to stop what they perceived as being contrary to their interests.

The changing demography and social structure of the village just prior to (1761) and immediately following (1765) enclosure provides a compelling picture of the anticipated impacts. Both before and after enclosure, the structure of landownership in West Haddon was a pyramid—but the shape of this pyramid changed (Table 1). Following the enclosure, owners of less than

TABLE 1 Number of landowners prior to and after enclosure in West Haddon

Year	Acreage				
	< 25 acres	26–100	100–150	150 +	Total
1761	36 owners	7	3	1	57
1765	26 owners	14	3	4	47

SOURCE: Neeson (1993: 205).

25 acres declined in number from thirty-six to twenty-six families. At the same time, the largest landowners with over 150 acres increased in number from one family to four. Prior to the enclosure, the lord of the manor, Thomas Whitfield, owned 262 acres. After enclosure his heir, John Whitfield, owned 600 acres, a full 25 percent of the parish, with another six families owning over 100 acres each, making for a substantial group of great farmers. Of equal significance, ten small landowners vanished from the record. Consequently, in West Haddon parliamentary enclosure caused land to shift to the largest landowners, decreasing the number of small owners and altering the social structure of the village.

What occurred in these two townships reveals something of the broader social transformations occurring throughout England during the period of parliamentary enclosure.[7] Despite variations over time and by region, parliamentary enclosure consolidated an estate system of agriculture marked by a new type of farmer—the rack-rent tenant—and employing wage workers on a new type of agrarian institution—the rent-maximizing farm. Where entire parishes were enclosed, and where multiple parishes in a district succumbed to enclosure, by the opening years of the nineteenth century the small family farm of less than 50 acres had basically disappeared (Broad 1999, 329–30). Although some areas, such as the northern Uplands, did not experience the same levels of decline in small ownership (Whyte 2006b), most of England paralleled the Midlands experience, with the amount of land remaining in the hands of small owner occupiers declining to 11–14 percent (Mingay 1968, 15). Parliamentary enclosure essentially completed the transfer of land from common ownership to severalty, elevating the share owned by the largest landowners and shrinking the share of the smallest.

Surprisingly, it was Arthur Young in his later years who revised many of his earlier views on enclosure, offering evidence on the practice's effects on the smallholder. In 1813, for example, Young wrote that "it is for the advantage of the greatest and most opulent proprietors that a Bill is presented and [a Parliamentary Act] passed" (Young 1813, 117). Although his views must be read with some caution (Shaw-Taylor 2001), Young had little reason to reverse his earlier convictions about enclosure without strong evidence.

In his 1801 *Inquiry into the Propriety of Applying Wastes to the Better Maintenance and Support of the Poor,* Young stated that although he had no objection to enclosure, in his own observations of thirty-seven enclosures he found only twelve that did *not* injure the poor. Those poor once able to keep cows on commons in these parishes, he wrote, "could keep them no longer after the enclosure" (Young 1801, 19). Young then remarked that enclosure, "instead of giving property to the poor, or preserving it," meant that "the very contrary effect has taken place."

For Young, the reason for this "contrary effect" of enclosure derived from the meager lands allotted to smallholders by enclosure commissioners and from the termination of their common rights. As evidence, Young related his conversation with one commissioner in particular, a Mr. Forster of Norwich, who described twenty enclosures in which had he been involved, conceding that "he had been an accessory to injuring two thousand poor people at the rate of 20 families per parish" (Young 1801, 20). From this information Young concluded that among the poor, "most who have allotments, have not more than one acre, which being insufficient for the man's cow, both cow and land are usually sold to the opulent farmers" (Young 1801, 20). He therefore argued that any allotment made to a commoner with a cow should be sufficiently large as to enable the commoner to keep the cow "through the summer and winter maintenance of it" (Young 1801, 26).

Young returned to this theme even more forcefully in his *General View of the Agriculture of Lincolnshire* (1813), arguing that in an enclosure the smallholder "may as well have *nothing* allotted to him" because the large owner, receiving first choice on allotments, "renders the holding of the small farmer untenable." Thus "the small owner *must* SELL *his* property to his rich and opulent adjoining neighbor" (Young 1813, 117). Arguably, Young's most searing indictment of enclosure was contained in his *Inquiry into . . . Wastes* (1801), where he noted that the poor were concerned with the facts of their existence, not with abstract debates occurring in the legislature. And "the fact is," wrote Young,

> by nineteen enclosure bills in twenty they [the poor] are injured, in some grossly injured . . . and yet enclosures go on by commissioners, who dissipate

the poor people's cows. . . . What is it to the poor man to be told that the Houses of Parliament are extremely tender of property while the father is forced to sell his cow and his land. . . . The poor in these parishes may say, and with truth, *Parliament may be tender of property; all I know is, I had a cow, and an act of Parliament has taken it from me.* And thousands may make this speech with truth. (Young 1801, 42–43)

Young's "eulogy to the cow" has a clear economic meaning (Humphries 1990, 24–31). In Young's account, the cottager able to graze a cow on the commons could reap returns from the products of the cow's milk at roughly the value of the wage that a rural laborer might earn in the late eighteenth century in agriculture or rural handicraft. Having lost the possibility of keeping a cow due to enclosure and the elimination of common grazing rights, the cottager became economically compromised and often collapsed.

What Young was describing was a new landscape taking shape throughout England, a landscape of private spaces that preempted trespass on what was once common land (Williamson 2000, 114). This landscape embodied a new propertied order that closed access to resources—grass for cows, fuel for heating, dietary supplements of wild game and plants. At the same time, this landscape was the foundation of an economic environment in which those dependent on the commons either went to work for wages or simply disappeared.

From Discourse to Landscape: Improvement on the Ground

By 1800 improvement had rendered a physical landscape virtually unrecognizable in contrast with 1600 (Darby 1973, 303). As common fields and common waste receded, a more widespread pattern of bounded spaces emerged on the land with the advance of parliamentary enclosure (Williamson 2000, 114; Crawford 2002, 37–64). The most visible aspect of this change was the subdivision of once vast and unbroken common fields into geometrically regularized plots of land (Hoskins 1977, 187). Everything had changed with enclosure, proclaimed Thomas Batchelor in his poem "The Progress of Agriculture" (1804): "To distant fields no more the peasants roam . . . hawthorn fences, stretch'd from side to side / contiguous pastures, meadows, fields divide" (quoted in Williamson 1992, 267).

This change in the physical contours of the landscape was especially visible in the primary institution of agrarian society, the manorial estate. While in the sixteenth century manorial estates were essentially collections of rights, tenancies, and incomes, by the mid-1700s estates had become rent-seeking blocks of enclosed, privately owned land where landlords and large-scale tenants jointly developed a system of agriculture driven by profit-making and wage labor (Williamson 2011, 28; Allen 1992). As agrarian improvement gathered momentum, these enclosed spaces spread across the landscape during the eighteenth century and dominated extensive tracts of the English countryside (Williamson 2011, 29). Proliferating on the landscape, these regularized spaces communicated the superiority of enclosure and landed property rights as preconditions of a prosperous agrarian society. In this way, the discourse of improvement had become materialized on the surface of the land (Johnson 1996, 77).

Alongside these socioeconomic and visual transformations on the land there arose a new set of aesthetic preferences among the public for bounded territorial landscapes (Crawford 2002, 12). Promoted by improvement writers, enclosed and bounded landscapes were associated with productivity enhancements. Even the language of the late eighteenth century testifies to this aesthetic, in which the word *improvement* was associated widely with enclosure, both as something virtuous (Williamson 2000, 114). At the same time, public sentiment now considered wide tracts of open land unbroken by any type of boundary to be disorienting, even offensive as the representation of an unimproved and empty landscape (Barrell 1972, 32). Here, Adam Smith's division of labor—the "greatest of improvements"—provided a powerful metaphor of this ascendant aesthetic in which boundary-making and productivity enhancements were the mutually reinforcing attributes of a virtuous feedback loop. In this regard, the authors of the *General View of Agriculture in Hampshire* (1794) are revealing. "We are sorry to observe such immense tracts of open heath," they write, which "reminds the traveler of uncivilized nations, where nature pursues her own course, without the assistance of human art" (quoted in Barrell 1972, 94). The earlier writing of Young sounds similar themes. "All the country [of Norfolk] from Holkham to Houghton was a wild sheep walk before the spirit of improvement seized the inhabitants," Young writes in contrasting the once wild and unimproved landscape of earlier years with the enclosed and virtuous landscape in the present. Now, "instead of boundless wilds and uncultivated wastes inhabited by scarce anything but sheep, the country is all cut up into enclosures, cultivated in a most husbandlike manner, well peopled, and yielding an hundred times the produce that it did in its former state" (Young 1768, 21–22).

For Young and other improvement promoters, the beauty of the enclosed landscape lay in what was its most expressive visual and material symbol: the hedgerow (Barrell 1972, 75; Williamson 1992). While the hedge—and its variants, the wall and the fence—was not new, what was novel in the eighteenth century was the speed at which the landscape became inscribed with these markers of landed property (Williamson 1992, 264). After 1760, during the six-decade rule of George III, enclosure in its parliamentary guise produced the greatest areal change on the land in the shortest comparable time span, resulting in what is known as a "Georgian landscape" (Turner 1980, 16). Its most visible manifestations were the untold miles of hedges, fences, and walls that cut a distinctly linear geometry into the remaining open landscape of the English countryside (Rackham 1986, 190–191; Williamson and Bellamy 1987, 107). As common land was brought under the control of individual owners, and as landed property spread across the countryside, the landscape reflected the subdivided and exclusionary meaning of this reality via the material artifacts of the hedgerow, fence, and wall. Thus the hedge emerged as an evocative symbol conveying meanings about a new propertied order on the land through its physical attributes as a marker of boundaries and exclusionary space (Williamson 1992, 268).

At the same time, while the hedge communicated symbolic meanings about landed property, it performed a more material function by preventing trespass and enforcing the most basic attribute of individual property, the right of exclusion. In order for land to become property, individuals had to be enlisted to respect the lines demarcating exclusionary territorial space. In practice, this meant that individuals had to circulate in certain ways so as not to transgress the lines where the rights of ownership for one became trespass for another (Blomley 2007, 4). Hedges, fences, and walls helped fulfill this abstract function by acting as barriers. disciplining those who roamed unimpeded across once-common and open land. In this way, the hedge, wall, and fence fortified and materialized "a new set of controversial discourses around land and property rights, and aimed to prevent the forms of physical movement associated with the commoning economy" (Blomley 2007, 5). These barriers, in effect, aided the principal function of enclosure: the closing of the countryside (Neeson 1993, 4–5). Paradoxically, the visible and material nature of the hedge also made it susceptible to the "breaking and leveling" of enclosure protestors (Blomley 2007, 1).

If the hedgerow was the principal means of materializing enclosure and reconfiguring lines of ownership on the landscape, a second element of enclosure, the road, transformed the landscape in a similarly rectilinear and geometric way. In the common field parish, the system of roads, tracks, and pathways was primarily for circulation within and across the fields and the common land of the parish itself. Such routes of circulation were invariably configured according to the topography of the landscape and were often punctuated with frequent bends and curves (Hoskins 1977, 200). With enclosure, commissioners and landowners remade roads into systems of straight lines consistent with the aesthetic sensibilities of contained spaces and cartography. Such was the case in the parish of Tottington, Norfolk, where mapping played a critical role in crafting an imagined geography of improvement.

In Tottington, Thomas de Grey, the largest landholder, obtained an act of Parliament in 1774 allowing him to enclose the entire parish, after waging an earlier and unsuccessful attempt to enclose it piecemeal.[8] During the previous decade, de Grey had lamented that the parish, much of which was common heath, was constrained by numerous customs practiced on heath land, such as common grazing and rights of turbary for the cutting of turves and gorse for fuel (Gregory 2005, 70–71). Among the changes sought by de Grey from the Enclosure Act was the subdivision of the heath, so as to remove the rights of access that enabled such customary practices. Consequently, in the enclosure bill, de Grey indicated his aim of terminating the right to cut fuel on the heath by inserting language such that the "custom heretofore enjoyed" would now "by virtue of this act be subject to regulation" (Gregory 2005, 76). To curtail free access on and across the heaths, de Grey further sought to remove the system of intersecting tracks that enabled such access by replacing it with a system of straight roadways that would bisect and subdivide the heaths.

In pursuit of this aim, de Grey commissioned Henry Keymer to produce a map of the parish prior to the passage of the act, which de Grey used as a working document to plot his proposed changes (Gregory 2005, 70). Part of de Grey's imagined geography of improvement is visible in a critical addendum to Keymer's map, in the form of a bold line sketched by de Grey himself indicating his plans for bisecting the heath with a new road (fig. 8). In this example, a line on a map became a powerful symbol of what was arguably the most profound transformation of enclosure, the elimination of rights to land as a common resource and the replacement of such rights with a system of individual rights to land as property. De Grey's line also conveyed the elimination of another right of the common field landscape: "the right to roam" across the land. In this way, through lines on maps, lines of mine and yours conceived through law, and lines demarcated by hedges, fences, and walls,

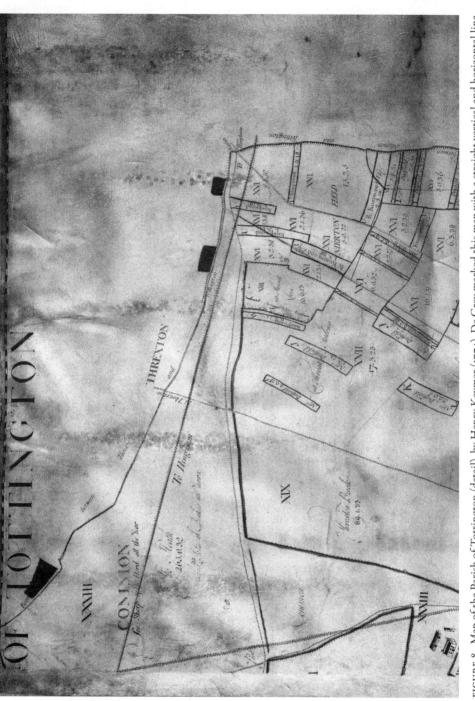

FIGURE 8. Map of the Parish of Tottington (detail), by Henry Keymer (1774). De Grey marked this map with a straight vertical and horizontal line showing his plan for a new road cutting across the common heath. Source: Norfolk Record Office WLS XVII/4. Photo taken by author and reproduced

enclosure had created a different system of rights to land that was now part of the landscape.

. . .

From modest beginnings in the early sixteenth century, the discourse of improvement emerged fully formed on the landscape by the beginning of the nineteenth century, recognizable still today in the painting of the Yorkshire Wolds by Hockney (fig. 2). The meanings inscribed on the landscape are clear. Where there once was land used as a common resource, now there were spaces of individually owned property. What was once open space had become bounded. Where there once was free access and the "right to roam," now there was trespass and closure. What initially was only imagined had become part of the landscape.

PART TWO

A Landscape of Lines

COLONIZATION AND ERADICATION
OF AMERINDIAN LANDSCAPES

These Sauages haue no particular propertie in any part or parcel
of that countrey, but only a generall residencies theire, as wild
beasts haue in the forrest, . . . so that if the whole lande should
bee taken from them, there is not a man that can complaine of
any particular wrong done.

ROBERT GRAY (1609)

What is this you call property? It cannot be the Earth for the
land is our Mother nourishing all her children, beasts, birds, fish,
and all men. The woods, the streams, everything on it belongs
to everybody and is for the use of all. How can one man say it
belongs only to him?

ATTRIBUTED TO MASSASOIT (1630)

What good man would prefer a country covered with forests
and ranged by a few thousand savages to our extensive Republic,
studded with cities, towns and prosperous farms, embellished
with all the improvements which art can devise.

ANDREW JACKSON, *annual speech to Congress* (1830)

FROM A WINDOW SEAT ON an airplane flying over the present-day United
States, on a summer day when flight conditions admit to vistas unobstructed
by clouds, even the most unassuming viewer can hardly fail to notice the vast
expanses of geometrical linearity on the land below (fig. 9). Despite forming
one of the distinctive features of the American landscape, this rectangular
patchwork jars our sensibilities as something "unnatural" compared to

FIGURE 9. The grid landscape, near Garden City, Kansas (2015). Photo by author.

landscapes idealized in our collective imagination from the distant past. In these imagined reconstructions of past environments, the "landscape" has a pristine character, existing in a stable, unchanging relationship with ecologically benevolent Native Americans who harbored little pretension of seeking mastery over their environment. This idealization of place and people, however, is no more than romanticized myth (Doolittle 2000, 3; Denevan 1992b, 369–70). Such mischaracterizations give the landscape, along with Native society itself, a timeless quality in which historical development begins only with those who would impose the linear order on the land (Fixico 1996, 32). Whether deliberate or unintentional, this idealized picture omits how the people who inhabited North America before the onslaught of the grid also imposed order on the land, shaping ecological systems to enhance the subsistence potential in the environment (Denevan 1992b; Doolittle 1992, 2000; Williams 1989, 43).

Whereas settlers remade landscapes by means of sharply angular boundaries and visibly enclosed spaces that signaled *possession,* Amerindians sustained themselves on landscapes remade by more mobile and less intrusive boundaries, marking not possession but *use.* To be sure, rights of circulation and trespass were imprinted into the indigenous landscape, but the grid landscape, by contrast, delineated ownership over plots of ground and signified a much more forcefully bounded system on the land. When these two very different ways of ordering the environment came into contact, Amerindian practices gradually succumbed to those who favored a gridded geography and with it a different system of exploitation on the landscape. From this foundation of difference, the builders of the grid gradually undermined and eventually shattered the patterns of material and cultural life that anchored Amerindian societies to the landscape. Thus were people who had little love for possessing the land as property overwhelmed by people who loved landed property above all else (Cronon 2003, 81).

Seen from the vantage of flight, the linear tracings of the grid are the relics of a struggle to settle territory and impose a different economic, legal, and cultural order on landscape. While this campaign had environmental impacts that became imprinted on the land, its deeper meaning was more foreboding and fratricidal (Blackhawk 2006, 3).

> Settlement meant land taking, and land taking meant violence.... Always [settlement] drew dark lines on the landscape whose borders were defended with bullets, blades and blood.... The history of the West is the story of how the American map came to have the boundaries it shows today. Colonization, at its most basic level, was a struggle to define boundaries on the landscape. (Cronon, Miles, and Gitlin 1992, 15)

What resulted from the imposition of the grid was the uprooting dispossession and removal of Amerindians from the places that sustained them, to make way for those with dreams of property and plenty. Ultimately, this linear landscape is a silent testament to a story of how the indigenous people of present-day America were cast to the precipice of near-extinction in an unrelenting, genocidal campaign to dispossess Native Americans and forge a system of severalty on the land (Blackhawk 2006, 3; Tomlins 2001, 316).

How did a landscape of lines demarcating privatized spaces for white settlers emerge as a dominant topographical feature over vast stretches of territory, and what is the meaning inscribed in this pattern on the land? The next two chapters address this question by focusing on how Anglo-American colonists, inspired by English ideas of land improvement and motivated by opportunities for material gain, reimagined the indigenous landscape as one of property and profit. From this imagined geography, colonists enlisted the same technologies for enclosing land that had been used in England, in an effort to gain control of Amerindian land in England's North American colonies. Using maps, property law, and built forms on the landscape itself, Anglo-American colonists encroached onto Native land and eventually enclosed indigenous Americans within a largely English system of landed property rights. In so doing, they transferred to themselves land already used by Amerindians and pushed the indigenous population into a marginal existence on tightly circumscribed reservations. As they proliferated across territory and took possession of Native lands, Anglo-American settlers imposed markers of their proprietorship, creating a landscape of fences and private rights to the ground, in the spirit of English enclosure (Linebaugh and Rediker 2012, 44). In this way land improvement and individual rights of property accruing to the improver of land became embedded in the morphology of the American landscape. In pursuing this idea, Anglo-Americans wrought an environmental revolution upon the American landscape that subjugated an entire group of people whose story resonates in the lines on the land today (Taylor 2001, 25).

FOUR

Amerindian Landscapes

SUBSISTENCE SYSTEMS, SPIRIT WORLDS, AND INDIGENOUS LAND TENURE

BY THE LATE FIFTEENTH CENTURY, on the eve of the first sustained contact between Native Americans and Europeans, indigenous communities populated virtually all areas of North America (Merchant 2007, 4).[1] Encompassing diverse cultures, languages, and economies, these communities nevertheless revealed a common approach to the challenge of securing subsistence from the environment. Wherever they existed, Amerindians engineered the environment for sustenance and survival (Williams 1989, 43). From domesticating plants and cultivating land, to burning parts of the forest floor to promote the herbaceous food stock of wild game and so enhance the hunt, to building canal networks in the Southwest for irrigating croplands, Amerindians recast the landscape for their material needs. Although Europeans routinely characterized this environment as empty wilderness, they also often established communities in proximity to Native Americans, at times securing the basic necessities of material life by exploiting the indigenous groups' own improvements to the land (Perreault 2007, 16).

From efforts to shape the environment and craft systems for subsistence emerged the baseline notions of Amerindian land tenure (Hurt 1987, 65). These basic notions were both material and spiritual, the latter focusing on a Great Spirit who had given land to people to use for subsistence (Hurt 1987, 66–67; Parker 1989, 9). As Black Hawk(1767–1838), the great chief of the Sauk nation, recounted in his autobiography, "The Great Spirit gave it [land] to his children to live upon, and cultivate as far as is necessary for their subsistence; and so long as they occupy and cultivate it, they have the right to the soil." Similar to early English notions of property as moveable, Black Hawk insisted that "land cannot be sold. . . . Nothing can be sold but such things as can be carried away" (Black Hawk 1834, 114). Thus, land, like the air and the sky, could not be possessed with a right of ownership that excluded others (Richter 2001, 54).

Alongside material and spiritual understandings, Native peoples conceived of land territorially, with the landscape akin to a spatial map with different places corresponding to different subsistence activities—cultivating, hunting, gathering, and fishing (Cronon 2003, 65). Overlaid on this map was a pattern of bounded areas where the primary units of Native society—tribes, clans, lineages, bands, and villages—held claims for occupancy on, use of, and movement across land (Sutton 1975, 23; Hurt 1987, 65). Bounded areas also corresponded to the identity of Amerindians, allowing them to define themselves as a group and differentiate themselves from others (Sutton 1975, 23; Albers and Kay 1987). This practice of bounding the landscape and assigning rights within the bounded areas to groups and individuals was a central concept in indigenous systems of rights to land.

Despite variations in the landholding unit, land for the most part was held by the collective as a common resource (Parker 1989, 16; Albers and Kay 1987, 53). At the same time, embedded in the concept of land held in common was an equally fundamental notion about land tenure. Although the boundaries in indigenous systems of rights to land established areas of access and trespass, such lines did not demarcate freehold ownership over plots of ground. Rights to land corresponded to entitlements for the use of resources on the land surface (Sutton 1975, 24). In this way, Native landscapes were bounded environments, but what existed within these bounded areas was the defining idea of Amerindian land tenure: the right to use land, otherwise known as the right of *usufruct,* a right exercised most fundamentally in securing subsistence.

AMERINDIAN SUBSISTENCE

Despite their geographical spread and socioeconomic diversity, indigenous communities had a broadly similar approach to the challenge of obtaining food from the environment. From the eastern woodlands to the grasslands of the Great Plains to the arid Southwest, different Amerindian groups survived on varying combinations of four basic activities: hunting, gathering, fishing, and agriculture (White 1983, xiv). There was a certain security in drawing sustenance from diverse sources, but the pivotal historical breakthrough that enabled these four activities to coexist as foundations of

Amerindian subsistence was the domestication of plants leading to the advent of agriculture (Wishart 1994, 234; Doolittle 2000, 23–27).[2]

As early as 1500 B.C.E., the peoples of North America had all succeeded in domesticating plants and seeds, which became the basis for Amerindian agriculture (Cordell and Smith 1996, 257). This breakthrough of encouraging the growth of certain plant species and then cultivating them enabled agriculture to emerge as a primary element of Amerindian subsistence alongside hunting, fishing, and gathering. This agricultural revolution allowed the transition to more economically complex and culturally diverse societies anchored to towns and villages (Keys 2003, 117).

In North America, these experiments with cultivated plants had three outcomes. First, from the Southwest to the Northeast, Amerindians essentially became "corn people," with corn overriding other plants as the most important cultivated foodstuff (Calloway 2003, 68–115). Second, while men helped clear fields for cultivation, it was Amerindian women who did the planting, tending, and harvesting, as well as grinding corn into flour, and thus it was women who were vested with control over rights to cultivated land (Calloway 2003, 72; Hurt 1987, 67). Finally, as corn cultivation expanded, villages emerged as the basic unit of Amerindian society, controlling the allocation of land for cultivation to family matriarchs and beginning to shape the appearance of the Amerindian landscape (fig. 10).

Two distinct pathways to corn as a prime foodstuff emerged in the subsistence economies of Native Americans, one characterizing the western United States, the other based in the Mississippi area and spreading eastward (Cordell and Smith 1996, 201ff.; Calloway 2003, 96–115). In the West, corn had assumed a decisive role in Amerindian subsistence by C.E. 200 (Cordell and Smith 1996, 210, 245). During the ninth through eleventh centuries, the Hohokam of present-day Arizona and New Mexico developed an extraordinarily sophisticated network of irrigation canals, exploiting rainwater runoff and the waters of the Salt and Gila rivers for development of a corn-based agriculture. In the Mississippi area and in the East, the shift to maize-based agriculture occurred later, in the years C.E. 400–800 (Cordell and Smith 1996, 210, 245). After 800, corn dominated cultivated food production in the region stretching from the border of Ontario to northern Florida and across the heartland of the present-day United States in the Great Lakes, Mississippi and Ohio River valleys, and into the West (Cordell and Smith 1996, 247). This geographical diversity enabled different indigenous societies to create distinct regional specializations of corn. They also raised two other primary

Their rype corne

Their greene corne

Corne newly sprong

Their sitting at meate

The place of solemne prayer

The howse wherin the Tombe of their Herounds standeth

SECOTON

A Ceremony in their prayers wth
strange gestures and songs dansing
about posts carued on the topps
lyke mens faces.

FIGURE 10. "Town of Secoton," by John White (1585–86), revealing Indian corn agriculture at three stages of cultivation: "rype corne," "greene corne," and "corne newly sprung." Source: British Museum, #1906,0509.1.7. Reproduced by permission of the Trustees of the British Museum.

food crops, beans and squash, while some cultivated sunflowers and rice, or even such nonfood crops as cotton and tobacco (Hurt 2002, 3; Doolittle 2000, 42–43, 52–53). Thus, a base crop of corn supplemented by beans and squash along with uniquely regional crops characterized the fundamentals of Amerindian agriculture.

During the period of 200–800, as the cultivation of corn came to flourish, Amerindian society developed a pivotal social and economic institution: the Amerindian village (Wishart 1994, 16). As methods of corn cultivation improved, patterns of village settlement also evolved. From 1100 to 1400, a steady process of agricultural intensification enabled more stable agriculturally based village environments to emerge in different areas of North America (Pauketat 2004, 3; Salisbury 2007, 6).

One of the most salient examples of this agrarian-driven pattern of town and village development prior to contact comes from the communities of the Mississippi and Ohio river basins, at the center of which stood the monumental city of Cahokia (Pauketat 2004, 3). By the beginning of the thirteenth century, Cahokia was the largest urban center north of Mexico, anchoring a system of settlements known collectively as the Mississippians that ran along the Mississippi River from Minnesota to the Gulf of Mexico and along the numerous tributaries of the Ohio, Arkansas, and Missouri rivers (Richter 2001, 3). Cahokia's own estimated population of 15,000–20,000 depended on a hinterland of outlying agricultural villages that provisioned the city with corn and other crops and created a nucleated pattern of town- and village-based agrarian landscapes (Calloway 2003, 99; Emerson 1997, 44, 49).

If attributes of fixity associated with agriculture and village life emerged as decisive in Native subsistence systems such as Cahokia, mobility was equally instrumental in defining how Amerindians secured their livelihood—including aspects of agriculture itself. Although cultivation gives rise to sedentarism, Native agriculture was not anchored to fixed locations but maintained a pattern of periodic relocation driven by the need to exploit more fertile soil conditions. This search for better soils, in turn, pulled villages to the locations of new croplands. Thus mobility became part of the subsistence pattern of Mississippian society, with larger fixed towns depending on networks of outlying villages that relocated periodically when soils became less fertile (Richter 2001, 57). In this way, Mississippian society combined the fixity and sedentary culture of large settlements with a system of mobile outlying agricultural villages (Galloway 1995, 34).[3]

Centuries later, one colonial observer of this mobile tendency of Amerindian agriculture and village life was Father Jean de Lamberville, who in 1682 observed how the Onondaga Iroquois relocated their principal town near present-day Syracuse: "I found on my arrival the Iroquois of this town transporting their corn, their effects, and their lodges to a situation 2 leagues from their former dwelling place, where they have been for 19 years. They made this change in order to have nearer to them the convenience of firewood and fields more fertile than those which they abandoned" (quoted in Williams 1989, 38).

Mobility was also inherent in the hunting, gathering, and fishing that supplemented the primary staples of corn, beans, and squash. These activities required extensive territorial hinterlands (Richter 2001, 57), and their mobility, in turn, was driven most fundamentally by factors of seasonality. In New England, Amerindian groups typically moved entire villages seasonally to take advantage of wooded inland hunting areas in the winter and coastal fishing locations during the summer (Williams 1989, 38). As a consequence, temporary settlements emerged to exploit the changing seasonal subsistence opportunities (Richter 2001, 57). Even communities heavily oriented toward agriculture often depended on seasonal use of hinterlands for hunting, gathering, and fishing. In short, movement was a way of exploiting the diversity of foodstuffs available in the environment to supplement cultivated crops. This included the mobile rather than fixed character of the primary unit of indigenous socioeconomic life, the Amerindian village (Cronon 2003, 54).

On the eve of contact, Amerindians had developed food economies with a broadly uniform foundation (White 1983, xiv). Domesticated cultigens anchored by maize and supplemented by beans and squashes coexisted with varying combinations of hunting, fishing, and gathering of wild foodstuffs. Atop this common foundation, however, Native food systems exhibited regional variations. Amerindians cultivated regionally specialized corn varieties and crops adapted to specific climate conditions and had access to different types of game, fish, and naturally growing wild foodstuffs. Such differentiation, in turn, shaped not only varying combinations in the overall mix of the four basic subsistence activities but also the interplay of mobility and fixity in Amerindian food economies. Despite these variations, the landscapes where Amerindians secured their material livelihood were inscribed with a fundamental principle of land tenure, the right of usufruct.

Amerindian rights of usufruct were fundamentally a collective right, with the village being the most important landholding collective in Amerindian society (Hurt 1987, 74). The basic problem confronting the Amerindian village was how to make the best use of the village landscape to meet the subsistence needs of village members (Hurt 1987, 75). In practice, this problem meant allocating access to different areas of the landscape, both immediately proximate to the village and in the hinterlands, for cultivation, hunting, fishing, and foraging. In practice, therefore, while land was conceived as a common resource of the village community, individual family lineages or households had rights of use. What was "owned" by members of the village community, in other words, was the *right* to use areas of the village landscape for growing crops, hunting game, and collecting foodstuffs from the land and water (Richter 2001, 54). Within this context, two basic concepts framed Amerindian notions of usufruct.

The first was the idea of *sovereignty*. As villages assumed the role of the most central landholding unit, sovereign use rights over a certain territorial domain became vested within the village chief—the *sachem*—who was generally chosen by a council of chiefs from different family lineages. Nevertheless, the land under sovereignty of the *sachem* was not his personal estate; rather, it was possessed similar to the way an English king owned the land of England and distributed it to his subjects (Cronon 2003, 60). Village land of the *sachem* was configured by precise boundaries, which entitled villagers to use land within the bounded area. Such delimited areas were well understood by different villages, making boundaries the basis of institutionalized relationships of mutual recognition on the landscape (Taylor 2006, 36; Albers and Kay 1987, 51). At the same time, if assigning boundaries to territorial landscapes imposed some semblance of spatial fixity onto the land, the village landscape was also inscribed with more mobile practices of boundary-making (Cronon 2003, 54–81). Because Native villages moved to exploit new subsistence potential in the environment, the areas where they exercised sovereign rights on the landscape shifted to the new location. Such shifting markers of sovereignty had to be at least tacitly accepted by other villages, or defended against counter territorial claims in the event of a dispute. In this way, boundaries, whether fixed or mobile, were part of an Amerindian landscape replete with rights of possession, access, and trespass. When the Rhode Island colonist Roger Williams wrote that "the Natives are very exact and punctuall in the bounds of their Lands belonging to this or that Prince or People," he was referring to practices of sovereignty and refuting colonists who insisted that Natives did not have a system of rights to land (quoted in Cronon 2003, 60).

Overlaid upon the sovereign and bounded territorial landscapes of villages were ties of kinship or family that often cut across different villages and gave rise to the phenomenon of "sharing the land" (Albers and Kay 1987, 54). When different Amerindian villages were related in this way, they often created territories of joint sovereignty, opening them up for use by all the villagers. In other instances, a village with sovereignty over a certain choice location, such as a waterfall, might negotiate a compact with another village for shared access to the site during fish spawning runs, owing to plentiful supplies of the resource at that particular time of year. In other words, boundaries demarcating the sovereign use rights of different villages were permeable, dependent on social ties. Yet while sharing portions of the landscape based on social ties was common, uninvited hunting by outsiders was considered trespass. In certain cases, trespass was a cause of conflict or even war. In comments on "Indian wars," the missionary David McClure observed in 1772 that Amerindian nations "have bounds affixed by custom or agreement.... To destroy the game of the territory of another nation, is in their view, as much a violation of property, as it would be deemed among us" (McClure 1792, 95). Although he was commenting on the nature of Amerindian violence, McClure essentially conceded the existence of Amerindian rights to land.

The second concept that framed the practice of usufruct had to do with the allocation of use rights among village subgroups and individual villagers. This occurred in two fundamental ways. One involved the village chief, in conjunction with the council of chiefs from representative families, distributing plots of land to family, clan, or kin groups for cultivation and allocating areas of access on the landscape to family lineages or households for other subsistence activities (Hurt 2002, 25–26). The second method prevailed largely in villages heavily dependent on agriculture. There, the eldest women of the various family lineages assigned plots for cultivation among the family networks of the village, while the sachem allocated access to the sites of other subsistence activities. In effect, the village community controlled agricultural land along with the grounds for hunting, fishing, and foraging as a collective resource (Hurt 1987, 74).

Once assigned plots for cultivation, family subgroups and individuals maintained rights of use as long as they kept the land under crop (Hurt 2002,

25). Once a plot was cleared and planted, it was removed from common ownership and placed in the possession of those who maintained it (Hurt 2002, 26). Similarly, in what was akin to the improvement of waste land, if a family or individual cleared and planted an otherwise empty field, they were entitled to claim that land for their own agricultural use (Hurt 1987, 74). If, however, a field was abandoned, it reverted to the village. When villages relocated, family or kin groups were allocated roughly equivalent plots in the new location and retained the same rights of cultivation (Saunt 1999, 41). The principle of usufruct and the assignment of this principle to subgroups also prevailed for rights to the bounty of rivers, streams, lakes, and oceans. While individuals could take foodstuffs from watery places, the setting of fishing weirs and nets in particular places was a right of use assigned to family and kin groups.

An additional factor overlaid on indigenous rights to land was seasonality. As on English common lands, where seasonality allowed land to alternate between individual and common use, seasonality on Native landscapes modified rights of use in certain places for certain types of activities. In the Northeast, the hunting of certain animals in the autumn, such as deer, was more effective as part of a collective hunting drive. In such cases, the hunting area of the village was considered common. In winter, however, when animals were less numerous, villages reverted to the setting of snares or traps by individual kin groups spread over wider areas. Each kin group would take a particular area and bait a number of traps, retaining the rights to the animals snared. Like English common field villages, Amerindian villages had systems for establishing and implementing rules for both common and individual uses as the seasons shifted. More than undifferentiated collective property, Amerindian territorial domains consisted of multiple layers of use rights that varied within and between villages and between different Amerindian groups, and fluctuated according to time of year (DuVal 2006, 7).

Many English colonists with intimate knowledge of Amerindian society conceded that Natives had clear understandings of boundaries and trespass, and tacitly, if not explicitly, acknowledged Amerindian notions of rights to land. "Each household knowth their own landes and gardens," confirmed John Smith about indigenous communities near Jamestown that he explored and mapped. "They all know their several landes and habitations and limites to fish, fowle or hunt in" (quoted in Banner 2005, 19). Pilgrim leader and Plymouth governor Edward Winslow made similar observations, reporting that Indians of New England knew their territories; when individuals endeavored to cultivate, he said, the village sachem would "giveth as much as [each] can use and set them their bounds" (quoted in Banner 2005, 20).

However, because Amerindian societies used mobility as part of their subsistence strategies and routinely changed locations, as well as altering boundaries by the season, other English colonists argued that Amerindians had no fixed attachment to territory and thus could not claim rights of property in land. Such cultural differences over the meaning of rights to land, one based on notions of mobility and use, the other based on ownership of fixed plots of ground, would eventually emerge as a primary cause of conflict between settlers and Amerindians (Richter 2001, 54).

COSMOLOGY, CARTOGRAPHY, AND LANDSCAPE

If bounding land with rights of access and trespass was tied most intimately to the material imperatives of subsistence, land was also part of broader spiritual notions about the place of Amerindians on earth and in the cosmos (Barr and Countryman 2014, 8).[4] Sacred in Amerindian cosmology was the notion of a center, or "pivot," where indigenous groups located the origins of existence essential to human life (Nabokov 1998, 250). Central to this idea is the fundamentally geographical construct of the four cardinal directions, which allow territorial space to radiate outward from the pivot (Lewis 1998a, 53). This gives a spatial dimension both to the spirit world and to material life on earth. Born of the four directions, territorial space is what anchors human life to places on the landscape and provides the foundation for cultivating crops. At the same time, the four directions and the spaces they embody enable mobility across the land for hunting, fishing, and foraging. Thus are symbolic and spiritual attributes of the cosmos connected to the terrestrial and material landscape, with land being given to humans by the Great Spirit to use for subsistence and material life—for building shelter and for cultivating, hunting, fishing, and foraging.

This cosmology and materiality of subsistence also gave rise to Native mapping practices that stood in sharp contrast to Anglo-European practices of cartography (Barr and Countryman 2014, 8). White settlers aimed to render territory cartographically through techniques of measuring and surveying, the result being representations of the land that focused on the placement of boundaries and the extent of territory. Alongside such efforts to depict landscapes with mathematical precision, Anglo-European maps created narratives about land—projections—based on imagined notions of how land could be appropriated, possessed, and brought under control (Nabokov 1998, 242). By contrast, Amerindians believed that only by engaging with features of the landscape directly could land be understood and represented. Rather than seeking to render territory as a series of measured and triangulated relationships, therefore, Amerindians represented the land as a narration about their experience of various landscape features (Barr and Countryman 2014, 8).

Such contrasts in geographical outlook between Europeans and Amerindians are apparent in the way Natives created place-names—toponyms—for geographical locations. For the most part, Amerindian place-names consist of a descriptive language referring topographical features in the landscape or how such a landscape can be put to use—the types of flora that can be gathered there, for example, or animals that can be hunted—or an event that occurred there (Pearce 1998, 159). This site-specific approach to geographical naming recasts the landscape in terms of experience. In this way, "the web of place-names on the land comprises a map that orders physical, economic and cultural information in a spatial framework which may be accessed through the combination of oral recitation and direct experience" (Pearce 1998, 160). Most importantly, such name-based practices of mapping emphasized the purpose of landscape as a provider of subsistence. "What the Indians owned—or, more precisely, what their villages gave them claim to—was not the land but the things that were on the land. . . . In nothing is this more clear than in the names they attached to their landscape. . . . The purpose of such names was to turn the landscape into a map which, if studied carefully, literally gave a village's inhabitants the information they needed to sustain themselves" (Cronon 2003, 65).

One of the most revealing examples of how Amerindians themselves perceived the difference between their notion of rights to land and the English system of landed property is encoded in a map known as the "Catawba map" (1721). Originally rendered on deerskin by a member of the Catawba confederation and presented to Francis Nicholson, colonial governor of South Carolina, the map now extant is a copy of the original (fig. 11). The endorsement in the lower left corner by the English draftsman who made the copy explains that the original was "drawn & painted on a Deerskin by an Indian Cacique and presented to Francis Nicholson, Esqr. Governour of South Carolina." An ardent collector of Native American maps, Nicholson may have solicited the map from a knowledgeable Amerindian source to find out more about rival French colonial activity in the relatively unknown interior

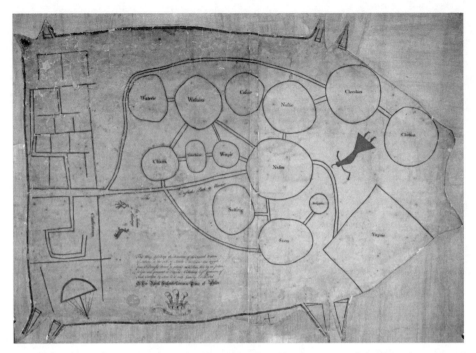

FIGURE 11. Copy of Indian map on deerskin "describing the Scituation of the Several Nations of Indians to the N.W. of South Carolina . . . " (1723), presented to Francis Nicholson, governor of South Carolina, to inform him of the Indian people of the area. Source: British Library Add. MS 4Y23. Reproduced by permission of the Trustees of the British Library.

of the Piedmont region (Lewis 1998b, 22). It is also possible that the Catawbas gifted the map to Nicholson in the hope of gaining good relations with their colonist neighbors (Warhus 1997, 77).

The map depicts three groups. In the middle are the Catawba communities, the most important of which is Nasaw, occupying a position of centrality on the map. In the upper right are two Indian tribes bordering the Catawba confederacy, the Cherokees and Chickasaws. English settlement is represented by Charlestown (Charleston) on the left side of the map and Virginia in the lower right corner. In a symbolic sense, the map depicts how the Catawbas imagined the connections between themselves and these other groups deriving from trade, alliances, and group affiliations (Edelson 2013, 41; Edelson 2012). The first set of connections links the various Catawba towns. Second are the links between the Catawba confederation and the Cherokees and Chickasaws bordering them. The final set of connections is the most compelling, involving the Catawabas and the Anglo-settler communities of Charleston and the larger colony of Virginia. Instead of a measured rendering of physical space to describe these groups, the map privileges what was important to the Catawabas, which was how different groups of people, Amerindians and settlers, were related in a symbolic sense.

By far the most striking element on the map is how the Catawba mapmaker conceived of English settlement in terms of spatial symbolism. The map actually depicts two distinct spatial—and spiritual—visions of the landscape. Both the city of Charleston and the colony of Virginia are represented in geometrically rectilinear forms, in contrast to the circular forms that represent Amerindian communities. What the map suggests is that by the early eighteenth century, when it was created, the Catawbas had come to some understanding of the fundamentally linear geometry in the pattern of English settlement and the contrast of this pattern with Amerindian life. In this sense, the map is a metaphor for two dramatically different visions of landscape promoted by two groups of people who had come into contact and from this prolonged encounter would experience vastly divergent fates.

CONTACT: EVOLVING PATTERNS OF SUBSISTENCE AND LANDHOLDING

Despite the seemingly inexorable march of colonial settlement in North America, the taking of indigenous land was far from a preordained story of unbridled colonial power leveled against hapless Amerindian victims (Hamalainen 2008, 6; Richter 2001, 7–8). Native societies participated in shaping the contact with colonists by choosing to trade with the newcomers, based on long-standing practices of exchange with other groups and traditions of reciprocity. From these exchanges, Indians secured a range of new items— wool blankets, knives, axes, metal cooking pots, and most importantly guns that enabled them to hunt and conduct war in new ways—along with another trade good, alcohol, which wreaked untold havoc on their society.

Two aspects of contact had particularly fatal impacts on indigenous society. In the first instance, Native Americans played no part. The second point of contact, more insidious and ultimately more destabilizing, involved a calamitous set of economic choices. The first had to do with microbes; the second, with markets.

From the beginning of contact, Amerindian nations were the unwitting victims of diseases carried to North America by Europeans, resulting in a well-documented series of demographic shocks to Indian societies.[5] Although Native societies had confronted crises in the past, it is unlikely they had ever experienced depletion on the scale of what occurred following contact with Europeans in the late fifteenth century. In many ways, this event was the rough equivalent of the fourteenth-century Black Death in England and Europe. Decimated by disease and depleted in numbers, Indian communities abandoned towns and villages, resettling in different areas and merging with other groups in an effort to survive in unfamiliar terrain (Trigger and Swagerty 1996, 364; Merrell 2007, 27). In these circumstances, people had to relearn the landscape, identifying the richest soils, the best areas for hunting and fishing, and where wild foodstuffs could be gathered (Merrell 2007, 30–31). Moreover, with kin networks disrupted and villages reconstituted in different locations, Native populations were forced to reinvent even the most fundamental practices of subsistence and material life—the allocation and laying out of cultivated fields, the building of shelters, and the bounding and assignment of territorial landscapes for hunting, gathering, fishing, and fowling (Merrell 2007, 31). Although some populations stabilized, recovery was uneven, with numerous Indian societies prone to periodic outbreaks of disease that continued to ravage Native communities well into the nineteenth century, leaving them weakened and ultimately compromised in their interactions with colonists (White 1983, 317).

If microbes and their attendant impacts on population overtook and weakened Indian societies overtly, markets emerged in the economic and cultural life of Amerindian society far less visibly but arguably more corrosively as an agent of change (Merrell 2007, 33). Markets entered Amerindian life through trade with colonists. Trade, however, did not inherently portend a transition to market-based forms of exchange. What occurred instead as part of the transition to more market-oriented forms of trade was a gradual but dramatic change in the relationship of Amerindians and colonists as Amerindians grew dependent on their colonial trading partners.

At the outset, Indians traded with colonists in the same way they had traded with other Indian groups—on the basis of reciprocity, which emphasized the value of goods not for accumulation but for use. The items sought by Indians—guns, knives, kettles, axes, woolen cloth—altered Native societies, but the impact of these goods as change agents was limited because Indians incorporated these items into their own established modes of life essentially as replacements for existing implements (Merrell 2007, 33; Miller and Hamel 1986, 318; White 1983, 318). Even alcohol, at least at the outset, could be substituted for other intoxicants used in Native spiritual ceremonies

(Merrell 2007, 33). What enabled the trade in items from guns and knives to cloth and kettles to become transformative was that ultimately, with the exception of firearms, Indians ceased producing those items that the trade goods had replaced. This pattern of trade created dependency as Indians came to rely on their colonial trading partners for goods that had gradually assumed the role in Native society of necessities. As one colonist familiar with the Piedmont Indians of Virginia remarked, by the 1690s the trade in muskets had made Indians "think of themselves as undrest and not fit to walk, unless they have their gun on their shoulder, and their shot-bag by their side" (quoted in Merrell 2007, 34). While such forms of exchange can be beneficial if the parties in trade seek from each other what they are incapable of producing efficiently themselves, this benign Ricardian picture of trade specialization proved illusory for Native Americans. Dependency on English colonial traders was but a first step in drawing Amerindian societies into the nexus of market-based exchange, with its subtle but in the end powerful impact as a destabilizing agent of change.

In order to sustain their desire for English goods, Native societies by the mid-eighteenth century were compelled to jettison notions of reciprocity and instead embrace a different set of incentives lying at the core of market economies: supply and demand. In the trade that developed between Indians and English, the latter originally sought two basic items from Natives, animal furs and deerskins, which later expanded to include a third item as colonists expanded westward, buffalo robes. The initial exchanges between Indians and Europeans, however, failed to satisfy the commercial demand of English and European traders for these items (White 1983, 318). Instead, colonial traders demanded pelts, skins, and robes from Indians in quantities large enough to supply growing European markets. Indians, if they wanted such trade, had to acquiesce to the terms demanded by their European counterparts for large inventories of goods. In this way, Indians were drawn into the nexus of a global market economy and became dependent on its demands and requirements.

This market-based pattern of exchange had two far-reaching impacts on Native societies. The first impact was on Indian subsistence systems. The type of hunting required to satisfy colonial demand for furs and skins represented an enormous departure from the ways in which Indians were accustomed to exploiting resources of game in the environment. Indian hunting techniques and methods of environmental management ensured that stocks of game would be replenished. Trade with colonists, however, opened up Native societies to an entirely new set of economic opportunities that compelled them to exploit local resources on a scale hitherto unknown to them. One of the most dramatic examples of this phenomenon comes from the Creek Indians.

Prior to the early eighteenth century, Creeks traded in deerskins with colonists, but after 1715 traders from South Carolina and Georgia encouraged Creeks to take on the deerskin trade on a much larger scale (Braund 1993, 40). English traders wanted the skins of whitetail deer in ever greater quantities, to satisfy a growing international market. Creeks, in turn, wanted English trade goods—guns, cloth, and also alcohol. By the 1760s, Creeks were killing enough deer to yield 800,000 pounds of deerskins annually, producing one of the southern colonies' most lucrative exports and causing this trade to become a dominant economic force in Creek society (Braund 1993, 98, 61, 25). At the same time, this trade brought about a pernicious cultural change within the Creek nation. Individual Creeks were now able to enrich themselves and came to accumulate "property and things," which resulted in more pronounced socioeconomic differentiation and eventually a civil war (Saunt 1999). Arguably the most enduring impact of the market-driven trade in deerskins, however, was the ecological destruction it wrought on subsistence systems, with the incentives it created to overhunt and deplete stocks of game. Even more insidiously, expansions in hunting tied to trade with Europeans created new rivalries between different Amerindian groups, which further exacerbated the decline in game stocks as Creeks and other groups competed to supply the colonial trade. Moreover, once stocks of game dwindled and Amerindians were no longer able to generate sufficient quantities of furs and skins to secure the English items on which they depended, they became even more susceptible to manipulation and pressure by colonists over the one resource they could still conceivably trade: land.

Endemic demographic weakness and the ever-diminishing returns from market exchange with white settlers left Amerindian society fractured and less capable of resisting the seemingly insatiable ambitions of Anglo-Americans for land. By the mid-eighteenth century, the English were able to exploit the changing balance of power by using the weakened situation of Native Americans to force "sales" of land and "treaties" in which Natives ceded territory to land-hungry colonial governments and settlers.

. . .

In engineering the environment for subsistence, Amerindian societies had a development pattern that was far from static (Fixico 1996, 32). With periods of stability punctuated by disequilibrium and transformation, this pattern emerged at least in part from responses of indigenous societies to naturally occurring changes in their environment. When local environments became less fertile, Amerindians relied on mobility to move to new locations where resources were relatively more abundant. On occasion, subsistence pressures from environmental change were intense, leading to abandonment of places such as Cahokia and the large-scale migration of Amerindian groups to new places. Faced with the challenge of securing subsistence, Amerindian societies established adaptive systems of use rights that were grafted onto territorial landscapes.

The landscapes where Native people secured their material life were configured with a dense network of boundaries demarcating areas of possession, access, and trespass along with rules for rights of use, occupancy, and circulation (Taylor 2006, 36). To English colonists such as William Johnson, British superintendent for Indian Affairs in the mid-1700s, the system of Amerindian rights to land was understandable if one took the time to examine it. "That it is a difficult matter to discover a true owner of any Lands amongst Indians is a gross error," Johnson argued in 1764, addressing the New York Assembly. "Each Nation is perfectly well acquainted with their exact original bounds, the same is again divided into due proportions for each [clan], and afterwards subdivided into shares to each family all [of] which they are most particularly acquainted, neither do they ever infringe upon one another or invade their neighbours' hunting grounds" (quoted in Taylor 2006, 36). In addition to being demarcated by boundaries of possession and use, access and trespass, Amerindian landscapes were replete with "improvements" that facilitated access to the environment's material bounties. Richard Smith, a Quaker traveling in the Susquehanna Valley of New York in 1769, marveled at Iroquois "deer fences," consisting of brush piled for hundreds of yards to funnel deer toward waiting Iroquois hunters. Far from empty wilderness, such landscapes were undeniable embodiments of improvement marked by Native possession (Taylor 2006, 35–36).

In sum, Amerindians and English were not differentiated by the presence or absence of rights to land. Rather, the two groups differed on the *meaning* of rights to land (Richter 2001, 54). Where the English elevated individual ownership of plots of ground, Amerindians vested tenure in collectives and, prior to contact, had no concept of owning and alienating pieces of the earth (Saunt 1999, 40–41; Greer 2014, 73). Where the English plotted permanent lines on maps to designate possession of plots of ground, Amerindians had a system of boundaries designating access and trespass but shifted without permanent spatial fixity. Moreover with use rights that shifted seasonally, the system of Amerindian land tenure remained opaque to most of the English, who brought with them the idea of absolute individual ownership over fixed plots of the landscape. Finally, where the English enclosed pieces of ground to designate improvement and possession and prevent trespass, Amerindians utilized open landscapes as areas of use and improvement. This notion of using enclosure to establish rights to landed property, and the absence of such markings on the Amerindian landscape, would be one a cornerstone of the English impulse to claim Amerindian land.

FIVE

Reimagining and Remaking Native Landscapes

LAND IMPROVEMENT AND TAKING AMERINDIAN LAND

BY THE TIME EUROPEANS HAD their first sustained encounters with Amerindians at the end of the fifteenth century, they already had recourse to long-standing precepts from canon law specifying the conditions under which it was licit to take land belonging to non-Christians. Asserting the right of Christian nations to wage war to regain lands lost to so-called infidels, this discourse had served the West during the Crusades of 1096–1271 to wrest control of the Holy Land from Muslims (Williams 1990, 13). Canon lawyer Sinibaldo dei Fieschi, who became Pope Innocent IV in 1243, spurred development of this discourse to look at the broader issue of relations between Christian and non-Christian societies and whether Christians had a general right to dispossess infidels (Muldoon 1979, 7–8).

Innocent conceded that papal authority could not deprive infidels of their lands without just cause, but he also accepted papal jurisdiction over infidels based on the premise in canon law of papal responsibility for the souls of all people, non-Christian as well as Christian (Muldoon 1979, 10). Thus, while Innocent's *Commentaries* conceded certain rights of infidels to their land, his work left room for alternative interpretations by subsequent canonists (Muldoon 1979, 18). By the late fifteenth century, as Portugal and Spain launched expeditions of exploration, relations between Christian nations and infidels emerged as a paramount issue alongside a new and related problem: the relations between Christian nations competing for territories where non-Christians resided. What was originally an issue involving only Christian nations' responsibilities toward infidels became more complex, with different European nations arrayed against one another in pursuing claims on territory inhabited by non-Europeans.

In seeking to resolve this issue, Europeans were forced to clarify two concepts involving territory from Roman law, one focusing on *imperium,* the other involving *dominium* (Armitage 2000, 92–99; MacMillan 2006, 6–13). Though similar, the two concepts were not identical. Imperium referred to the territorial extent of monarchical sovereignty, while dominium referred to the right to possess land within the imperial boundaries (Mancke 2002, 236). The legal dilemma confronting Christian nations seeking overseas territories inhabited by non-Christians was how to establish both sovereignty and possession in these places. Two approaches emerged from this dilemma, reflecting two culturally distinct interpretations of the legalities of empire and the rights to possess land (Seed 1992, 191ff.).

One approach was that of Spain and Portugal. These nations established claims of sovereignty and possession over territory inhabited by non-Christians through the "discovery doctrine," by which "discoverers" of places populated by infidels could claim such territories, and preempt the claims of others, on the basis of being there first (MacMillan 2006, 11). This doctrine relied on the notion that the invention of technologies needed for discovery of distant territories—maps, sailing ships, navigation—deserved compensation through patent rights (Seed 1992, 195). Such claims of discovery were accorded legal status by Pope Alexander VI in bulls issued in 1493–94 and in his oversight of the Treaty of Tordesillas (1494) dividing up the "New World" between Spain and Portugal. At the same time, however, Alexander made the taking of territory contingent on Christian nations converting native populations (Seed 1992, 188). Thus, with the rights of discovery went the responsibility of spreading Christianity to non-Christians.

By contrast, England pursued claims of sovereignty and possession in the New World on the basis of settling territory. While also promising to spread the Gospel, English promoters of colonization sought to legitimize claims to territory through practices of occupation on the landscape—the building of dwellings, the erection of fences as boundary markers, and the planting of crops (Seed 1992, 191ff.; Seed 1995, 31). Rights to land deriving from such practices, in turn, were predicated on the assumption that the land to be occupied and cultivated was not owned by anyone else. This English notion of entitlement to land based on improving it through cultivation has come to be known as the *agriculturalist* argument.

These two approaches to the dilemma of seizing land overseas reflected two culturally distinct perspectives on the legalities of empire (Seed 1992, 191ff.). One approach, emphasizing imperium, focused on rights of discovery.

The other, emphasizing dominium, focused on rights of possession of land. Ultimately, it was the latter, the agriculturalist approach of England, that reshaped the Amerindian landscape most profoundly, because England, with its notion of empire that depended on actual settlement of the land, would prevail as colonizer in North America.

IMAGINED GEOGRAPHY: ENGLISH CONCEPTS OF PROPERTY AND EMPIRE

In establishing a legal foundation for colonizing foreign territory, English jurists drew from their own common law traditions about land ownership, which elevated the idea of improving land as the basis for possessing it. In this tradition, the duty of humans as commanded by God and natural law was to subdue the earth for their subsistence and welfare. Subduing the earth, in turn, meant improving it—taking possession of pieces of ground and cultivating crops where possession was established. Extending this logic to the problems of empire and the territory of infidels, English claims made imperium and dominium a function of settling upon and cultivating the earth. Thus, English charters issued to explorers were similar in spirit to the common law. Charters gave rights of sovereignty to those who would cultivate and improve the land and thus take possession of it.

By the late fifteenth century, England had embarked on a modest program of overseas exploration compared to the more ambitious colonizers Spain and Portugal (Williams 1990, 121–22). These early overseas ventures by the English, however, did not seek an agriculturalist approach to colonization and did not result in the establishment of durable settlements in the areas explored. Instead, the charter granted by Henry VII to John Cabot and his son Sebastian in 1496 instructed the two Italian explorers commissioned by the English king to sail to lands "unknown to all Christians" and emphasized the right to claim sovereignty over lands of infidels and heathens in accordance with the doctrine of discovery (Williams 1990, 121). By the time Henry's son ascended to the throne in 1509 and became the most celebrated monarch in English history by transforming England into a Protestant nation, colonial ventures had receded to a secondary role in the affairs of the state and Crown. It was only during the latter part of the reign of Elizabeth (r. 1558–1603) that England would once again become interested in territory overseas—but now on a very different basis.

Two developments placed England on a colonial path different from its Iberian rivals. The first was the introduction of Protestantism into England (Armitage 2000, 61–99). The break with the Catholic Church allowed England to free itself from the influence of papal bulls, which had restricted Cabot in the charter granted him by the pre-Reformation monarch Henry VII. Accordingly, in her patents for New World charters, Elizabeth altered papal formulations of "authority apostolic" in favor of rights deriving from "the lawes of England" (quoted in Seed 1992, 201). Thus England developed legal foundations for imperium and dominium in the Americas that were different from papal and Iberian authority.

The second development was the advance of a domestic discourse of *improvement,* beginning with Fitzherbert (1523) and continuing throughout the sixteenth and seventeenth centuries (see chapter 3). This discourse not only sharpened arguments in English common law about landed property rights, but it also provided a legal foundation adaptable to empire, one that departed from the discovery doctrine. By 1629, when John Winthrop was extolling the virtues of Puritan colonization in New England as a special pact with God, he was also voicing arguments about why the colonists were justified in their claims to Indian land based on colonial perceptions of Indian territory as absent of owners, and thus empty, and English commitments to improving empty land—claims that paralleled concurrent arguments about rights to land in the English countryside (Edwards 2005).

From this crucible emerged a discourse of empire in the late sixteenth century that elevated notions of property rights in the English countryside as the foundation for possession of land overseas. The individual most responsible for this new idea of colonization and its promotion was the Protestant minister Richard Hakluyt. While justifying colonization as a geopolitical, economic, and even Godly venture, Hakluyt in his writings marked a decisive turn in the discourse that eventually justified expansion in North America by virtue of it being an "empty countrie."

Planting Colonies: The Vision of Hakluyt

One of the most oft-used terms appearing in early English promotions of North American colonization derives from the verb "to plant." In the *Oxford English Dictionary,* this verb has three primary definitions, all present by the early sixteenth century. The first refers to the cultivation of botanical species. The second refers to the establishment of "colonies" or "settlements," both religious and secular. The third refers to the placement of an object or thing firmly in or on the ground. These themes—cultivation, colonization, and physical occupation—would come to define the distinctly English method of conquest in the Americas.

In 1584, Richard Hakluyt, the younger of two Hakluyts with the same name, synthesized these themes in a celebrated position paper prepared for Elizabeth on the advantages of colonizing the Americas popularly known as the *Discourse of Western Planting*. Written as a confidential report to the Crown, Hakluyt's *Discourse* was the most thoroughgoing set of sixteenth-century arguments encouraging and justifying English "planting" in North America, akin to a "blueprint" for empire (Mancall 1995, 45, 129). Essentially a work of propaganda, Hakluyt expanded its core arguments in his later, copious published works promoting English expansion overseas, thus earning the distinction of being the intellectual architect of English colonization in America (Mancall 2007, 129, 139; Armitage 2000, 70).

Hakluyt divided the *Discourse* into twenty-one chapters, each making separate but overlapping arguments on the virtues of expansion into the Americas (Hakluyt 1584, 4–7). These arguments fall into three broad categories: religious, economic, and legal (Mancall 2007, 139ff.). For Hakluyt, spreading Christianity to heathens, expanding the traffic in goods, and competing with other colonizing nations to secure access to overseas territory were all part of the same enterprise (Armitage 2000, 75). *Richart Hakluyt*

Hakluyt begins his justification for colonization with an appeal to the virtues of extending the "glorious gospell of Christe" to "Idolaters" in America and reducing the multitudes of those "simple people that are in errour into the righte and perfecte waye of their saluacion." Where once the Apostle Paul in Romans 10 had called on Christians to preach to and convert infidels, now that task, according to Hakluyt, had fallen to the English Crown, which had emerged as the true "Defendours of the Faithe." Planting the seeds of faith in America, Hakluyt insisted, could be accomplished by "plantinge one or twoo Colonies of our nation vpon that fyrme [land]" among the heathen, effectively merging spiritual and territorial goals (Hakluyt 1584, 8; Mancall 2007, 139).

While Hakluyt admitted to the goal of securing colonies to convert the infidels, his real aim was to counter the expansion of Spain and promote the enlightened Christianity of English Protestantism. The Iberians, he insisted, had forfeited their claims to a moral quest in the Americas by their insatiable desire for treasure and their "monstrous cruelties" committed against "those peaceable, lowly, milde and gentle people" in the Americas (Hakluyt 1584, 52). To argue his case, Hakluyt relied on *A Short Account of the Destruction of the Indies* by the Spaniard Bartolomé de las Casas (1552; English translation 1583), who had brought the atrocities of his own countrymen to light (Mancall 2007, 150–51). Referencing las Casas, Hakluyt described torture, decapitation, hangings, and disembowelment, but whereas the Spaniard wrote that his countrymen killed twelve million West Indians, Hakluyt raised the number to fifteen million (Hakluyt 1584, 56–58). In a spirit more of self-interest than compassion, Hakluyt insisted that the time had come to try once again to colonize North America because "the people of America crye oute unto us their nexte neighboures, to comme and helpe them, . . . shake of their moste intollerable yoke . . . and bringe unto them the gladd tidings of the gospelle" (Hakluyt 1584, 52, 11).

In addition to the religious and moral justifications for colonization, Hakluyt, in an echo of the mercantilists, emphasized the role of colonies in promoting the domestic economy (Mancall 2007, 144). Colonies in the Americas, he argued, would serve as a captive market for English manufactures, providing employment in numerous industries such that "many decayed towns may be repaired." Colonies also helped solve certain social problems by providing an outlet for redistribution of undesirable populations such as criminals and the chronically unemployed. In addition, the growing colonial population would provide opportunities for more educated and skilled types of work, including "merchauntes, souldiers, capitaines, phisitions, lawyers, devines, cosmographers, hydrographers, astronomers, historigraphers." In the spirit of the later Protestant work ethic, even traditional dependents—the elderly, the lame, women, and children—would be "kepte from idleness" and thus would not be a burden "surchardginge others" (Hakluyt 1584, 28–32).

Hakluyt supplemented his spiritual and commercial arguments by providing his Crown patrons with legal justifications for colonies in the Americas, fearing that Elizabeth would be reluctant to promote colonial ventures without such arguments (Mancall 2007, 151). Much of this legal work aimed at refuting arguments made in the Alexandrine bulls. Hakluyt was intent on demonstrating why "the Queen of Englandes Title to all the West Indies . . . is more lawfull and righte then the Spaniardes or any other christian Princes" (Hakluyt 1584, 88). Surprisingly, Hakluyt argued this point by appealing to the discovery doctrine, which lay at the core of Spanish colonial claims. Turning it against Spain, Hakluyt claimed that it was the *English* who had come first to the Americas "322 yeres before Columbus," supporting his claim with a philological analysis that supposedly revealed similarities between old Welsh and English, on the one hand, and the language of Native Americans on the other:

> ... wee find that one Madock ap Owen Guyneth a prince of North Wales ... made twoo voyadges oute of Wales & discovered and planted large countries which he founde in the mayne Ocean southwestwarde of Ireland, in the yere of our lorde 1170.... And this is confirmed by the language of somme of those people that dwell vpon the continent between the Bay of Mexico and the graunde Bay of Newfounde Lande, whose language is said to agree with the welshe in divers wordes and names of places by experience of somme of our nation that have bene in those parts. By this Testimonie it appears that the ewst Indies were discovered and inhabited 322 yeres before Columbus made his firste voyage which was in the year 1492. (Hakluyt 1584, 88)

Although Hakluyt's legal reasoning for English imperium in the New World rested on a dubious reading of history, it was formidable as propaganda justifying English overseas expansion (Mancall 2007, 151). Ironically, in the period of Hakluyt's *Discourse,* such expansion exhibited little success. Despite Francis Drake's circumnavigation of the globe in 1578 and the landing of Humphrey Gilbert in Newfoundland in 1583, English colonies in the Americas did not take root. The most dramatic example of this failure was the abandonment of Roanoke in 1590 following the abortive attempt of Walter Raleigh and the Virginia Company to establish a permanent settlement there. More than fifteen years passed before England again mobilized resources for colonization under the Stuart king and successor to the Tudors, James I. In this intervening period, however, what Hakluyt suggested only obliquely in his *Discourse* as a legal justification for colonization gathered new momentum. The idea that would justify planting colonies was a country consisting of empty land.

Creating "Savage" Landscapes

In 1606, James I granted a charter to the Virginia Company that led to the establishment of Jamestown the following year. Like Roanoke, however, Jamestown encountered severe hardships—hunger, disease, factional disputes among the colonists, and conflict with the Powhatan Indians—that made continuing support from the Crown as well as the public difficult to predict (Fitzmaurice 2000, 25). In early 1609, two years after landing at

Jamestown, the Virginia Company sought help from a host of churchmen—figures such as William Crashaw, William Symonds, and Robert Gray—in promoting its venture. With Crashaw acting as a facilitator of these efforts, these men engineered the most far-reaching public campaign for colonization that had ever been waged in England (Fitzmaurice 1999, 34–35; Fitzmaurice 2000, 26).

The arguments framed by this campaign were quite different from those used by Hakluyt. While the preachers enlisted by the Virginia Company appealed to the same Christian and civic virtues of colonization as Hakluyt, they downplayed the idea of commercial gain that had in part inspired his *Discourse* (Mackenthun 1997, 194). "If there be any that came in only or principally for profit," Crashaw stated, "or any that would so come in, I wish the *latter* may neuer bee in, and the *former* out againe" (quoted in Fitzmaurice 2007a, 793). Such a renunciation of commerce did not necessarily represent rejection of the economic designs of colonization. It was only in the eighteenth century that economic interest could be expressed without reservation as part of colonial design (Fitzmaurice 2007a, 793).

Yet if the churchmen were ready to minimize the commercial rationale and glorify the missionary aspects of planting colonies, they differed from earlier colonial discourse in their willingness to confront the vexing problem that Hakluyt skirted: how to take possession of Indian land (Fitzmaurice 2003, 137–38). For the men of the Virginia Company, the Christian mission somehow had to be fused with arguments justifying English dominium in Indian country, because Christianizing the Indians required settlement on their land. As Crashaw admitted, "conversion of the heathen from the divel to God" still required "the plantation of a Church of English Christians there" (Crashaw 1610; Zakai 1992, 114).

Two divergent approaches to this dilemma characterized the churchmen's response. One, reflected by Crashaw, implied that the English could acquire Indian land lawfully by *purchasing* it. The second, represented by Gray, suggested that the English could lawfully *take* Indian land. These differing notions of what constituted a lawful approach to possessing Indian land, in turn, drew upon two distinct traditions in representing the savagery of Indians, one as benevolent and sympathetic, the other as hostile and bellicose. The benevolent tradition of Indian savagery derived from Columbus himself, who had written of the "great amity" of Native Americans, "a generous pastoral people living in childlike innocence" (quoted in Nash 1972, 201). This notion of the "good savage" was later given a more iconic visual imagery in the woodcut illustrations that accompanied Jean de Lery's descriptions in 1578 of the Tupinamba of Brazil (Rubies 2009, 120). Other early European accounts of the New World, however, including the letters of Amerigo Vespucci, depicted Native Americans as "beastlike," closer to animals than humans in appearance and behavior (Nash 1972, 199). Far more than being simple moral judgments, these perspectives on Indian savagery had profound legal ramifications in terms of what colonists believed were Indians' rights to land, and how the colonists themselves might appropriate Indian lands.

The Benevolent Savage. Among the English, Hakluyt provided initial inspiration for the Amerindian as a benevolent savage. While acknowledging their idolatrous character and admitting to the virtues of conquering the pagan and savage barbarians, Hakluyt wrote of them as a "people goodd and of a gentle and amyable nature" (quoted in Nash 1972, 202). Thus in Hakluyt, the indigenous appear not as brutes but as God's children in need of salvation to save their souls, and of English protection to save them from the depravities of Spain. A similar depiction emerged at roughly the same time by Arthur Barlowe, sent by Walter Raleigh in 1584 to scout the Outer Banks of North Carolina as a prelude to establishing the colony of Roanoke. Barlowe, who had good reason to represent the area favorably to Raleigh and his English patrons, described the Indians there as a "handsome and goodly people, . . . most gentle, loving and faithfull, void of all guile, and treason" (quoted in Horn 2005, 28).

This sympathetic if patronizing depiction of the Amerindians would receive more widespread diffusion in the first-hand observations from the colony of Roanoke written by Thomas Harriot. In his *Briefe and True Report of the New Found Land of Virginia* (1588), Harriot portrayed the Amerindians of Virginia in a tone similar to that of Hakluyt. Unlike Hakluyt, however, Harriot had direct experience of Indian society and was one of only a few English colonists to learn Indian languages. He traveled with Raleigh to Roanoke to document colonial life and the flora and fauna of Virginia, but the most compelling portion of his *Report* was the penultimate section, "Of the Nature and Manners of the People," where he provided first-hand accounts of local Amerindian society. He remarks that the local inhabitants were poor, but concedes that they had all the attributes necessary for civility; he admired their "excellencie of wit," despite their having "no such tooles, nor any crafts, sciences and artes as wee." As for their worship of "many Gods," Harriot is again the compassionate Christian when he writes that, "although it [their religion] be farre from the truth, yet beyng as it is, there is hope it may bee the easier and sooner reformed." For Harriot, such "savages" had a certain dignity as well as ingenuity, while their religious practices, though idolatrous and in error, suggested that they were ready for the true path (Hariot 1588, 36).

What enabled Harriot's *Report* to become influential was a second edition (1590) published by the Belgian printer Theodore de Bry, who added a series of engravings to the text based on John White's paintings of Algonquians (Kupperman 2000, 144). Although de Bry's engravings added subtle idealizations to White's Indian figures and places, the images, notably that of the village of Secoton (see fig. 10), remain among the most authentic records of southeastern peoples at early contact and testify to a highly organized civil society (Mancall 1995, 71–72; Kupperman 2000, 144). Printed in German, French, Latin, and English, De Bry's folio edition of Harriot's *Report* graphically depicted Amerindians—their towns, their agriculture, their religion, and daily life—in a way that belied notions of brutishness. To be sure, images of settled habitation in villages supported by agriculture had little in common with notions of beasts in woods.

Roughly twenty years after Harriot's *Report,* this tradition of depicting the savage Indian sympathetically was still apparent in a sermon delivered on February 21, 1609, by Crashaw (published in 1610), despite his aim of promoting the colonizing mission of the Virginia Company. In his sermon Crashaw asked his audience, which consisted of colonial sympathizers and skeptics alike, to consider the paramount question of whether the mission of planting colonies in America could pass the test of "lawfulness" with respect to securing Indian lands. He left no doubt as to what was lawful and what was illicit with respect to colonization and Amerindian land. "A Christian may take nothing from a heathen against his will," Crashaw stated, "but in faire and lawfull bargain," emphasizing that "we will *exchange* with them for that which *they may spare,* and wee doe neede; and they shall have that which wee may spare and they do much more neede." What they had and could spare, noted Crashaw, was "land and roome for vs to plant in," since Indian country lay "wild & inhabited of none but the beastes of the fielde and the trees that have grown there may be 1000 years" (Crashaw 1610). Crashaw insisted that colonists would not only compensate Indians fairly but also part with more than they took, because the colonists would relinquish two things in the bargain. There would be those items desired by the Indians for their bodily needs, corresponding to "civilitie," and for their spiritual needs and souls there would be "Christianity." Those items given to the Indians for civility would enable them to cultivate, thus making them richer; that which was given to enlighten their souls would be given to them for free. Crashaw's vision of colonization had practical consequences. In the end, English colonists could acquire Indian land only through legal bargain—that is, through sale and purchase (Banner 2005, 13–14).

The Contemptible Savage. Other early European accounts of the New World circulating in England depicted Amerindians far more contemptuously, not only likening them in appearance and behavior to animals but even depicting them as cannibals (Nash 1972, 199). While Vespucci's descriptions are not one-sided, sometimes depicting Indians as cruel, other times as friendly, some editions of his *Letters from America* contained two woodcut images that enduring influenced how Native Americans were perceived. One depicts a group of Tupi Indians from Brazil butchering a human body; the other shows a European about to be hit from behind and presumably also butchered and consumed. Such early sensationalist literature about cannibalism effectively underscored the impression of Indians as truly savage in the minds of Europeans (Rubies 2009, 121–23). Even accounts of the voyages to Cathay undertaken by the English explorer Martin Frobisher in the 1570s contain descriptions of Native Americans as "crafty, brutal, and loathsome half-men" with "cannibalistic instincts" (Nash 1972, 200). In this discourse, Indians were transformed from sympathetic personages needing English help to find God, as described by Hakluyt, Harriot, and Crashaw, into contemptible figures needing to submit to English planting.

By the early seventeenth century, this tradition of representing the Indian as a loathsome savage found a receptive audience among another group of church promoters of the Virginia Company, this time organized around the figure of Robert Gray. What Gray and his group added to the tradition, however, was a carefully crafted argument inspired by natural law, which gave Indian land a legal status different from what Crashaw had suggested. Instead of having to transact with Indians to secure land for planting, colonists from this new perspective could lawfully *take* Indian land.

Natural law affirmed certain rights to be universally applicable to the human condition.[1] Such rights included the right of possession, which emerged from humans pursuing their own self-preservation in a society ordained by God. Among the commandments of God to humans was the order to subdue the earth—to take possession of it for subsistence. From such commandments, human beings acquired a basic right of appropriation—of taking—in order to survive and procreate. At the same time, natural law prohibited leaving the earth to lie idle in waste. During the early modern period, these principles in natural law of possession and prohibition became part of English common law through the time-honored English practice of custom. Taking possession of land and prohibiting it from lying idle in waste thus fulfilled the laws of God and nature, and the customs of the country.

According to Gray and his followers, Amerindians showed no interest in taking possession of the land they occupied and used. By living an unsettled life in a wilderness environment left idle as waste, Indians were savages who transgressed the laws of God and nature. The promoters of the Virginia Company, however, added a critical element to this argument about Amerindian savagery and natural law that enabled them to insist upon Indian country as empty and thus unencumbered by the conventions of exchange. Indians, they argued, were not only brutish savages; Indians were beasts akin to animals.

The Reverend William Symonds of St. Saviour's Church, Southwark, London, signaled this theme in a 1609 sermon titled "Virginia: A Sermon Preached at White Chapel" when he insisted that Virginia was a "country where the people do live but like Deere in heards." More than a moral judgment, this idea, contrary to Crashaw, held that Amerindians, as beasts, had neither the legal status to bargain over land nor rights of possession on the landscape. And if Indians had no legitimate claims to the land they occupied, then Virginia became an open country available to the English for planting.

While Symonds was the first of the Virginia sermonizers to associate Amerindians with beasts, it was Gray who made this argument even more forcefully in his sermon "A Good Speed to Virginia," also in 1609 (Manahan n.d.). Gray chastises those in England reluctant to colonize lands in the Americas that were under the control of "brutish savages, which by reason of their godless ignorance and blasphemous idolatrie are worse than those beasts which are of most wilde and savage nature." Referencing the notion of just war from canon law, he asks whether it is lawful to make war on the savages of Virginia. Citing Augustine, he retorts that indeed a Christian king "may lawfully make war upon a barbarous and savage people, . . . to reclaim and reduce those savages from their barbarous kinds of life and from their brutish manners to humanity piety and honesty" (quoted in Williams 1990, 210). Thus Gray insists on the godless character of savagery as justification for the Christian mission of planting, but takes his argument in a direction similar to Symonds in likening the Indians to animals, arguing that as beasts Indians have no landed property. This association of Indians with animals enables Gray and colonists following his logic to advance territorial claims upon Indian land based on the notion that animals do not possess land. "Some affirmed, and it is likely to be true," Gray writes,

> that these Sauages haue no particular propertie in any part or parcel of that countrey, but only a generall residencies theire, as wild beasts haue in the forrest, for they range and wander vp and downe the countrey, without a law or gouernment, being led only by their owne lusts and sensualitie, there is not a meum & tuum amongst them; so that if the whole lande should bee taken from them, there is not a man that can complaine of any particular wrong done vunto him. (quoted in Mackenthun 1997, 195)

The distinction between human and beast for Gray has clear ramifications in terms of rights to land. "So man may say to himself: the earth was mine, God gave it to me . . . and yet I stay and take it not out of the hand of beasts and brutish savages, which have no interest in it, because they participate rather of the nature of beasts than men" (quoted in Fitzmaurice 2003, 142–43). For Gray, the conclusion is obvious: by constructing their lives as animals, without stable communities, without boundaries denoting possession, and without ongoing practices of cultivation, Indians have no claim on what God gave to humans to sustain—land for improvement.

The association of Indians with animals also emphasizes another legal principle for English claims to Indian land: the idea of land that is empty being available for the taking. If, as both Symonds and Gray insisted, Indians could be likened to animals, then Amerindian territory was logically uninhabited because animals had no possessory rights to land. This notion was endorsed by William Strachey, a colonist and chronicler of the early years in Jamestown. "Who will think it is an unlawful act," he wrote, "to fortefye, and strengthen our selves" in "the wast and vast uninhabited groundes" in a "world of which not one foot of a thousand do they either use or know how to turne to any benefit, and therefore lyes so great a Circuit vayne and idle before them?" (Strachey 1612, 19; Fitzmaurice 2003, 143). Such arguments about savagery and property rights—the idea that the land was empty and had no owners—provided early colonists with a legal rationale for the taking of Amerindian land.

From Savage Landscapes to Empty Land

Among promoters of the Virginia Company, the possibility of New World settlement rested on an ancient principle of Roman law that in turn had become a core element of English common law and colonial practice abroad—that of *res nullius*. In Roman law, *res nullius* referred to objects without owners that were available to be acquired by the first taker. From the end of the thirteenth century until roughly 1490, English common law had restricted what could be owned to two basic categories, goods and animals, but by the early sixteenth century common law had extended the notion of what could be owned to a new category: land (Seipp 1994, 33–39). As with acquiring goods without owners, common law targeted land that was empty—*terra nullius*—in determining rights to land as property (Seipp 1994, 88; Seed 2001, 29–40). Rather than ownerless land going to the first taker, however, common law established a condition for possession that focused on a singular idea: improvement through cultivation.

On the eve of English colonization, cultivating empty land as a condition of ownership found a powerful, if unwitting, defender in Thomas More's *Utopia* of 1516. Ironically, More's Utopians emerge as the morally justified usurpers of land left idle by Utopia's indigenous inhabitants. More's protagonists thus followed the law of nature by putting idle land to productive use (Seed 2001, 30). In denying Indians dominium on land they occupied and affirming the right of English colonists to that land, Gray, Symonds, and Strachey were restating what More had argued about the law of nature. However, these promoters of planting confronted a difficult problem in the use of agriculturalist logic to justify their designs on Indian country. Amerindians indeed cultivated the landscape, but in ways different from the English. Somehow English colonial promoters had to recast Indian land as a vacant place without owners—a *vacuum domicilium*.

English colonial promoters arrived at two solutions to their problem. First, they argued that Amerindians, by farming without plows, failed to exploit the land to the fullest that God intended.[2] Although Indians did have an agricultural presence on the landscape, the more intensive farming practices of the English gave them a superior claim to the land, which in their eyes the Indians were misusing. Colonial promoters were thus entitled to refer to the land of Indians as "waste." The second solution was to borrow a key element from the improvement discourse that by the early 1600s was already helping to divide landscapes into either unimproved or improved (Warde 2011). An improved landscape was not only land under crop, but was verifiable through the visible markers of fences, walls, and hedges. These two notions enabled promoters of colonization to deride what they regarded as *savage landscapes*—landscapes underutilized and unenclosed, without fencing.

By 1629, John Winthrop, the first governor of Massachusetts, used these elements of a savage landscape to justify the taking of Indian land. According to Winthrop, God gave the earth to the sons of Adam "to be tilled and improved by them." Natives in America, he wrote, "inclose noe land" and thus left the landscape unimproved. For Winthrop, such a landscape was without owners. His conclusion is unambiguous: "If we leave them sufficient [land] for their use," he writes, "we may lawfully take the rest" (quoted in Cronon 2003, 56).

By the early seventeenth century, English promoters of colonization in the Americas had formidable arguments to justify the taking of Indian land for planting colonies. At the same time, these arguments contained critical denials that planting colonies would result in taking Indian land (Fitzmaurice 2003, 140–46). No dispossession could take place, it was argued, because Amerindians possessed no land. This notion of ownerless land would dominate English arguments for colonization in the Americas and dispossession of indigenous peoples throughout the seventeenth century (Pagden 1995, 77; Armitage 2000, 97). The greatest heir to this line of argument about rights to land was John Locke.

Locke and the "Wild Indian"

While Locke is a seminal theorist of landed property rights, his involvement in the colonial affairs of British North America explains at least in part how he derived his views on entitlement to land.[3] Seven of the eighteen chapters of his *Second Treatise* (1690) refer to America and its Indian inhabitants, with half of these references occurring in the fifth chapter, "On Property" (Armitage 2004, 617). Colonial America was a type of "blank slate" that enabled Locke to develop a general theory of rights to land, applicable to both England and its colonies (Edwards 2005, 2011). It was this general theory that enabled Locke to resolve the vexing dilemma of Amerindian cultivation and affirm the rights of English colonists to Amerindian land.

Locke builds his argument about English rights to land in the colonies via two metaphorical protagonists: the "wild *Indian*" from America "who knows no inclosure" and the English planter who cultivates land in enclosed fields. Locke had emphasized how cultivating the earth and separating it from the commons "introduces private possessions" in land. In failing to enclose their croplands, Amerindians thus did not take possession of their cultivated fields. Perhaps more importantly, Locke adds a second qualification to the agriculturalist argument about cultivation that allows him to push the

Indian landscape deeper into the realm of *terra nullius*. Locke insists that not all labor put into the earth is equivalent. God gave humans the gift of reason, he writes, "to make use of it to the best advantage of life and convenience," suggesting that rights of possession accrue to those who cultivate the earth in the most productive way (Armitage 2000, 97). A thousand acres of land in America, Locke observes, "yield the needy and wretched inhabitants as many conveniences of life as ten acres of equally fertile land in Devonshire where the land is well cultivated" (Locke 1690, 37). The English planter in America, by contrast, in tilling the land with plows, is following the word of God. Because America, occupied by the "wild Indian," was planted unproductively without plows, it was akin to land in waste. Such differences between England and America enable Locke to qualify the notion of land where a right of property can be created by arguing that land *poorly cultivated* was akin to waste. In England, such land was being claimed for improvement. These same principles, reasoned Locke, made land in America available for improvement as well.

Although notions of property rights in land preceded Locke, his *Second Treatise* marked a pivotal moment in the evolving telos of landed property (Blomley 2007, 2). More systematically than anyone before him, Locke enjoined owning land with enclosing it, cultivating it, and improving it to the fullest. In setting out these parameters, Locke broadened the notion of emptiness while establishing the conditions for taking possession of empty land. His work was thus not only a philosophical defense of English dominium in Indian country; it represented the legal and philosophical foundations of an imagined landscape of property across North America.

CARTOGRAPHY: REINVENTING THE AMERINDIAN LANDSCAPE IN MAPS

Just as the discourse of improvement and property rights was creating an imagined geography of emptiness and rightful English dominium on the North American landscape, a parallel set of arguments was taking shape in cartographic representations. In this parallel discourse, maps emerged as instruments conveying a *vacuum domicilium* in North America and projecting an anglicized geography on that empty space (Barr and Countryman 2014, 18). In this sense, early Anglo-American maps of North America show how Anglo-American colonists imagined indigenous land, and how from such imagined visions depicted in maps they transformed an Amerindian landscape into a Euro-American territorial space (Boelhower 1988, 478).

Although these two discourses, one ideological the other cartographic, have their own internal logic and development, they are both inspired by similar notions of improvement and tend toward similar outcomes. The logic of the improvement discourse led to Anglo-American settlement of North America, the removal of Indians from the land, and the establishment of the property grid on the landscape. This same outcome of appropriation, removal, and linear organization of the land has a cartographic equivalent represented in the development of Anglo-American maps of territory in North America. This map history begins with the early-seventeenth-century maps of Virginia and New England by John Smith, and culminates in the 1816 map of the United States by John Melish.

Cartographies of Improvement, Erasure and Property

Early English maps of North America are influenced by arguments for the taking of Indian land (Clarke 1988, 471; Brückner 2006, 6–12). Years before English and later American colonists established dominance over Indians, Anglo-American maps gave promoters of colonization a vision of future control by ordering land in ways that both mirrored and projected settlement (Nobles 1993, 27–28). Three formal attributes of maps served this function of making claims upon territory: (1) the use of place-names; (2) the use of an ornament, usually referred to as a *cartouche,* to guide the narrative meaning of the map; (3) the use of lines to mark territorial boundaries.

Much as the early-seventeenth-century improvement discourse both affirmed and denied Indian rights to, and presence on, the landscape, Anglo-American maps reflected similar ambiguities. The long-term trend in English and then American maps of North America, however, is one of diminishing the Indian presence on the landscape, thereby emphasizing the power of maps as instruments causing Indians to be progressively dispossessed of their land (Harley 2001, 170). There is perhaps no better starting point for illustrating this trajectory than the maps of early English explorer John Smith, whose cartographic depictions of Virginia (1612) and New England (1616) represent two of the most important documents in North American mapmaking (Cumming 1982, 281).

Smith prepared his map of Virginia (fig. 12) for his *Description of the Country, the Commodities, People, Government, and Religion,* but it was the map that is most central in this document (MacMillan 2003, 437). Twelve

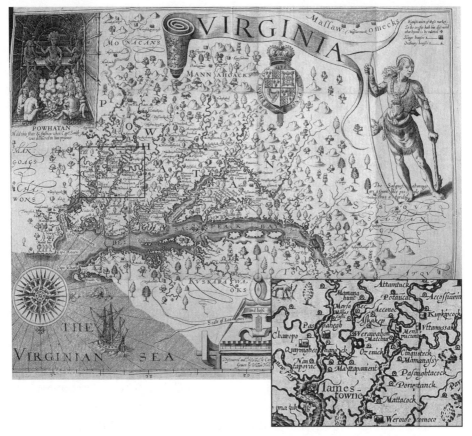

FIGURE 12. Map of Virginia, by John Smith (1612). Native American places are prominent on this map. Source: Newberry Library VAULT Ayer 150.5 .V7 S6 1612. Reproduced by permission of the Newberry Library.

editions of the map appeared between 1612 and 1624. For sixty years following its initial appearance it was the most accurate European representation of the region, and it remains a seminal document in the history of Anglo-American cartography (Library of Virginia 2007).

Several aspects of this map distinguish the territory being represented as an English possession. The title, "Virginia," appears prominently at the top. Just underneath is a royal coat of arms, while in the lower left corner is the name the "Virginian Sea" and a lone English sailing ship. At the bottom is depicted a draftsman's compass, giving the territory a certain authority as scientifically and objectively rendered, and at the base between the two compass points is a line of rectangles conveying the idea of a territory being

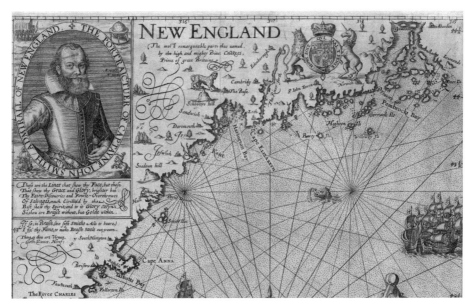

FIGURE 13. Map of New England (detail), by John Smith (1616). This version of the 1616 map was reproduced in 1624. Image courtesy of the Norman B. Leventhal Map Center at the Boston Public Library.

ordered geometrically through surveying. The inscription underneath the compass announces that this territory has been "discovered and described by Captain John Smith, 1606." The map's interior contains thirty-two English place-names, including Jamestown, Cape Henry, and Cape Charles, emphasizing an English presence on this landscape (MacMillan 2003, 438). All of these devices tell a story of a territory being appropriated and brought under English control (Blansett 2003, 71).[4]

At the same time, aspects of the map challenge such a representation. Ten Indian groups are depicted on the map along with 166 Indian villages labeled with the Indian names, knowledge that Smith obtained from the Natives themselves. There are also two dozen houses of Indian sachems, described by Smith in the text as "King's houses" (MacMillan 2003, 438). Two prominent cartouches, one in the upper left corner depicting Powhatan, the most powerful Indian ruler in the area, the other an image of a Sasquesahanough Indian much in the style of the earlier de Bry engravings, add to the visual image of Indian presence on this map. Thus, while the map strongly suggests English dominium over the territory, it does not render Indians invisible.

In some ways, Smith's map of New England (fig. 13) duplicates themes from the Virginia map. Despite knowing that the area "hath formerly beene called Norumbega," Smith used an English place-name for the title and included the royal coat of arms, denoting the territory as an English possession. The harbor also shows ships flying the British ensign, although in this case there is a fleet of eight ships instead of just one. And again, a compass imbues the territory on the map as rationally and objectively calculated.

Most striking about the New England map, however, are its differences with the earlier Virginia map. Quite distinct is the cartouche in the upper left corner, where instead of an Indian chief, Smith has placed *himself,* making reference in the inscription beneath to civilizing the savages. This change, in turn, signals what is most different in this map: the complete omission of Indian presence on the land (MacMillan 2003, 440; Harley 2001, 178–81). This removal was deliberate, as evidenced in correspondence between Smith and Britain's Prince Charles.

In 1616, Smith sent a letter to Prince Charles with the manuscript copy of his map containing Indian place-names; however, he urged the king to change the Indian names to English ones. "My humble suit is," Smith wrote, "you would please to change their Barbarous names, for such English, as Posterity may say, Prince Charles was their Godfather" (quoted in Harley 2001, 180). Charles complied and saw to it that the final engraving was altered to include only English toponyms. Renaming the landscape with English monikers is akin to planting a flag on claimed territory, a poignant example of the way English colonists reimagined the Amerindian landscape (Clarke 1988, 456). Such cartographic reinvention of the land in the image and likeness of England and rendering invisible the Indian population would become integral to English mapping of North America. Although this process was uneven—not all English maps after 1600 completely eliminated references to Indian geography—the tendency in colonial mapping was a gradual process of erasing traces of the Indian landscape and substituting a landscape English in character (Harley 2001, 179, 188, 185).

While renaming places with anglicized toponyms and emptying territory of Indian presence were critical cartographic devices helping to project an imagined English landscape onto Amerindian land, an equally important motif for representing the idea of territorial control was the crafting of lines on maps. When inscribed on maps, lines impose a certain order on the landscape, with a set of meanings focusing on boundaries. One of the best examples of territory as part of an imagined landscape of bounded spaces denoting property and improvement is a 1687 map of Pennsylvania by Thomas Holme (fig. 14).

FIGURE 14. "A Mapp of ye Improved Part of Pensilvania in America, divided into Countyes, Townships, and Lotts," by Thomas Holme (1687). Source: Library of Congress G3820 1687 H62. Retrieved from the Library of Congress, www.loc.gov/resource/g3820.ct004137/.

Holme's map is connected to one of the most ambitious settlement projects in the English colonies, the peopling of Pennsylvania under the stewardship of William Penn, who had been granted a patent over the domain in 1681 by Charles II (Klinefelter 1970, 41).[5] Penn had a vision of a colony built on religious tolerance, and as a first step toward realizing his vision he undertook an advertising campaign unprecedented in scope to lure purchasers of the lands granted to him. By 1682, Penn had sold the first 500,000 acres, but he needed a map that would reveal the configuration of the parcels to the new owners as well as potential buyers. Holme, who had been Penn's official surveyor, was commissioned to produce such a map, and after numerous delays he completed his draft sheets in the winter of 1686. The map was sent to engravers in London and was published in the *London Gazette* on January 5–9, 1687, under the title "A Map of the Improved Part of the Province of Pennsilvania."

While the facts surrounding the map's commission speak to its role in the making of a propertied landscape in Pennsylvania, its formal elements testify to the virtues of land improvement and the association of improved land with a proprietary geometric order. The very title of the map, in conjunction with the representation of the privately owned parcels, makes an unmistakable argument about the nature of improved land. Such land is, above all, property that has been configured int the 750 regularly shaped parcels and assigned owners corresponding to the 670 buyers who had answered Penn's call (Klinfelter 1970, 46).

In addition to depicting the geometrically regular character of improved land, the map contains a subtle message aimed at future buyers. For the settler contemplating a land purchase, the map projects Pennsylvania as a territory already brought safely under control—the control of property. While the map depicts forested areas absent proprietors in its western portion, no Native American presence is suggested. Juxtaposed to the propertied portion of the landscape as *terra nullius,* this area of the map therefore beckons to new buyers who will do to the land what the parcel owners in the eastern portion have already done in making improved land. In this way, the map presents a cartographically rendered narrative of property and land improvement overpowering the unimproved and unpropertied former landscape. It is an instrument calling people to settle and populate the land.

Holme adds a final argument about the virtuous nature of the colonial settlement in his cartouche of the city of Philadelphia in the upper middle of the map. In 1683, Holme had drafted a plan for the new city of Philadelphia on instructions from Penn and produced a rendition of the city as a series of rectangles, the first colonial city in America planned on a grid (Ridner 2011, 335). Together, the cartouche of urban Philadelphia with its rectilinear pattern and the geometrically regularized domains of rural Pennsylvania depicted on the rest of the map project a universal order of improvement and property ready to absorb those areas of the map still encumbered by wilderness. In this way, Holme created a map with an imagined geography of land improvement, projecting a territorial future in which individual rights of property—dominium—stand ascendant as a gridlike formation sweeping across the landscape.

Equally impressive as an example of boundaries on maps as expressions of territorial control is the 1755 "Map of the British Colonies in North America" by John Mitchell (fig. 15), another of the significant maps in the history of North American cartography (Edney 2007, 4). Seven versions of the map appeared from 1755 to 1775. In contrast to Holme's map, Mitchell's elevates the theme of sovereign control over territory by the nation-state rather than the dominium of the individual property owners. While Mitchell's map was intended to represent the threat posed by France to English territorial interests in North America, the cartographer also succeeds in projecting an argument about the nature of colonial territory and its relationship to Native American land. He does this in two ways.

First is the linearly ordered terrain, created by a series of horizontal lines that demarcate the limits of the various British colonies in the direction of the frontier with New France, seemingly continuing west indefinitely. While Mitchell has carefully rendered both textual and cartographic information on various Indian tribes and towns, those details are subordinated within the map's linear geography. Second, in the cartouche in the lower right part of the map, Mitchell provides clues about how to read these two sets of facts—Indian presence overlaid by a gridlike territory. At the top of the cartouche is an English coat of arms underneath a British flag, making clear that despite a Native presence in this territory, the land in the map is a British domain. A Native American kneels with eyes cast upward, looking reverentially at the coat of arms and the flag. A second Native gazes at the scene in the lower left corner of the cartouche, where Mitchell provides a poignant metaphor of the map's intended meaning, in the image of a small homestead surrounded by a just-visible fence (Clarke 1988, 466). The home and fence represent the westward-bound settler spearheading the movement across the landscape—and the Indians are depicted as grateful for this advance. In sum, Mitchell's map

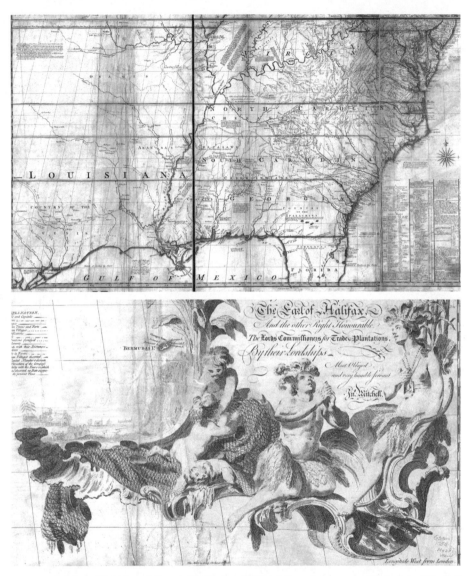

FIGURE 15. Map of British and French Dominions in North America (top, detail), by John Mitchell (1755; 3rd impression of 1st edition) and the cartouche (detail, above) with the homestead and fence. Source: Library of Congress GS 3300 1755 M5 Vault, Control No. 74693174.

is a projection about settlement and conquest (Nobles 1993, 13). Though revealing something of the Indian population, the map tells a story of a territory being remade by westward-moving settlers casting order across the landscape by means of a grid of property boundaries, representing dominium, and political boundaries, representing sovereignty.

The teleological narrative of westward settlement in Mitchell's map was also embraced by Anglo-American colonists of the period, beginning with Benjamin Franklin. In his celebrated essay on American demography from 1751, Franklin wrote about land in North America being in plentiful supply and the inevitability of the white population expanding and filling the continent (Franklin 1751; Hutson 1973, 431). Franklin was arguably the first Anglo-American to articulate what in the next century emerged more categorically as America's "manifest destiny," a divinely inspired mission for settlers to populate the continent from the Atlantic to the Pacific.[6]

After the colonists emerged victorious in forging a new nation-state independent of Britain, other Americans would articulate Franklin's vision as well, fusing the notion of an empty and available western frontier with a newer idea of a teleological, if not divinely sanctified, mission of settling North America and civilizing the continent through the practices of colonizing and improving land. By 1801 Thomas Jefferson was echoing this messianic vision, outlining how American settlers would eventually populate the continent, thereby forcing Indians to assimilate (Ostler 2004, 13). The most explicit recognition of a divine role in American colonization, however, came from John Quincy Adams, who in 1811 observed that the "whole continent of North America appeared destined by Divine Providence to be peopled by one *nation*" (Miller 2006, 130). In these assessments, Americans and their political leaders were reconceiving the landscape of North America as a westward-expanding grid, with white property owners cultivating and improving the land.

This idea deriving from Franklin had already assumed concrete cartographic representation by 1785, in the Land Ordinance passed by the newly independent nation-state. The ostensible purpose of the Ordinance was to create an orderly process for the conveyance of land lying west of the existing boundaries of the thirteen states to buyers, speculators, and small homesteaders alike. The real aim of the Ordinance, however, was to frame a blueprint for westward expansion onto Indian land. Therefore, a critical stipulation of the legislation was that any Indian title to such land in the West had to be overturned through either treaty or sale (Calloway 2003, 373; Carstensen

1988, 33). In pursuit of this expansionist aim, land west of the Appalachians was to be surveyed with the idea of establishing a rectangular grid on the landscape to make it easier to convey land to potential users. According to the Ordinance, surveyors were "to divide the said territory into townships of 6 miles square, by lines running north and south, and others crossing these at right angles." (White 1983, 12). Represented in this grid of six-mile square townships was a vision of westward-moving, orderly property rights being consciously imposed on the landscape by ordinance and survey. Within the abstract squares was an implied vision of geometric urban settlements configured from a pattern of fenced homes occupying square or rectangular lots. At the outset, the survey was confined to a relatively small corner of southeastern Ohio, and while the accuracy of the work was at times compromised, the "Plat of the Seven Ranges of Townships" (fig. 16), as it came to be called, signaled the extent to which a rectilinearly ordered landscape came to dominate how leaders and settlers in the newly emergent nation-state imagined and recast land.

Although the work of the survey was halted after the initial seven ranges had been demarcated, work resumed after 1796 to cover the remainder of the old Northwest Territory, the Southwest Territory, the Louisiana Territory, Florida, lands acquired from Mexico, and the Oregon Territory. Eventually, 69 percent of the land in the lower forty-eight states was covered by the rectangular survey system (Johnson 1976, vii). Once the idea of the rectangular survey was fully accepted and the institutions and administrative mechanisms for carrying it out were put into place, surveyors extended the straight lines of landed property in all directions, spreading the grid over the various topographical features of the landscape—prairies, foothills, mountains, deserts, and even over some shallow lakes—in an unrelenting effort to regularize the country's geography (Carstensen 1988, 31). As these lines expanded, they represented a type of solvent on the Amerindian landscape.

One of the most illustrative cartographic representations of a westward-moving destiny and a landscape emptied of Indian presence that was both a reflection of an imagined geography and an instrument for diffusing this imagined vision more widely to the public was the 1816 map of the United States created by John Melish (fig. 17).[7] Instead of transcribing the actual boundaries of the still-young republic, Melish projected the territory he imagined. "The map so constructed," wrote Melish in describing his achievement, "shows at a glance the whole extent of the territory of the United States, from sea to sea; and in tracing the probable expansion of the human

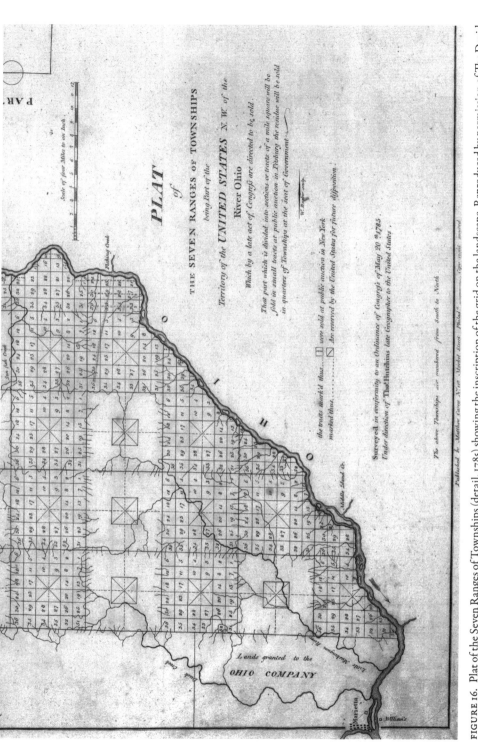

FIGURE 16. Plat of the Seven Ranges of Townships (detail, 1785) showing the inscription of the grid on the landscape. Reproduced by permission of The David Rumsey Map Collection, www.davidrumsey.com.

FIGURE 17. Map of the United States, by John Melish (1816). Reproduced by permission of The David Rumsey Map Collection, www.davidrumsey.com.

[i.e. white] race from east to west, the mind finds an agreeable resting place on its western limits."

Audaciously conceived, Melish's map echoed the spirit of destiny expressed by such luminaries as Franklin, Jefferson, and Adams. Thomas Jefferson himself sent a congratulatory letter to Melish thanking him for his achievement. This was a map of the United States not as it was, but as it would become; a territory in the imagination that minimized Native Americans in a nation stretching, as Melish predicted, from the Atlantic to the Pacific.

"LAWFARE": THE LAW AS CONVEYOR OF INDIAN LAND

Between the early seventeenth and late nineteenth centuries, virtually all of the land in the present-day United States was transferred from its former Amerindian owners and occupants to mostly English-speaking descendants of Anglo-American colonists (Banner 2005, 1). While maps had provided colonists and their political leaders with a way of seeing and projecting Amerindian land as their own, the Crown and later the American government exploited the power of lawmaking to wrest control of Indigenous land so that colonists could settle the landscape. Lawmaking, however, was far from a benign process of creating neutral systems of rights, in this case rights to land. Rather, lawmaking operated alongside overt forms of violence, orchestrated by the state as well as non-state actors, to wrest control of land from Native Americans (Blackhawk 2006). Indeed, lawmaking in and of itself, which proved so decisive in the transfer of land from Amerindians to Anglo-American settlers, is replete with violence; for ultimately, the law depends on the power of organized force to enforce its covenants (Cover 1986, 1601). Lawmaking, then, is perhaps best understood as "violence rendered legible, legal and legitimate," with the law operating as a subtle form of power backed by overtly violent forms of organized force (Comaroff and Comaroff 2006, 30). This notion of lawmaking as an instrument of power resting on undisguised forms of violence describes the process of *lawfare,* which played a decisive role in dispossessing Amerindians of their territory and creating a geography of landed property on the American landscape (Harris 2004, 179; Blomley 2003).

As an institution and set of practices for the transfer of land from Amerindians to colonists, lawmaking assumed different roles in different periods of settlement in North America (Banner 2005).[8] At the outset of English colonization, the law functioned as an instrument for the conveyance of land from Amerindians to colonial governments and colonists through purchase contracts and treaties. Whatever beliefs colonists and colonial officials may have held about the legitimacy of Indian land ownership, early colonial practice tended to favor acquisition of Amerindian land through what colonists considered lawful purchase, in a tacit acceptance of Indians as landholders. With passage of the Royal Proclamation of 1763, however, and especially after the American Revolution, this notion of Indians as landholders changed. By the late eighteenth century, American legal opinion, the successor to English law, no longer conceded Indian dominium in the territory of the United States. This shift was eventually codified in two landmark legal acts: the Supreme Court case of *Johnson v. M'Intosh* (1823), which recast Native Americans from owners of land into tenants at-will; and the Indian Removal Act (1830), which dispossessed Amerindians first in the Southeast and later in other parts of the country and relocated them in what would be the beginning of massive forced movements of Amerindian populations into the confined spaces of reservations.

In this way, the law, as an institution for transferring land from one group of people to another, had evolved. Where the law originally served as a rule-making framework for the sale of Amerindian land to colonists, by the late 1700s, and especially by the time of *Johnson,* the law had become an instrument of lawfare enabling the transfer of Amerindian land to settlers through forcible seizure. This process, whereby the law emerged as a crucial instrument in dispossessing Amerindians and transferring their land to colonists, is traceable in the trajectory of English settlement and in the changes in how English and later American settlers conceived of, and secured, Amerindian land.

Law and Early Purchases of Amerindian Land

At the outset, the practice of early English colonialism regarding land acquisition favored purchase over seizure. Despite arguments about the rightful claims of the English to Amerindian land, the Crown and colonial officials insisted that land acquired in America belonged to the English because they had purchased it lawfully from the Indians. When the Virginia Company explained in 1610 why it was lawful for them to possess Indian land, its representatives emphasized that they had purchased it from Paspehay, one of Virginia's Indian kings (Banner 2005, 20–21). The Massachusetts Bay

Company also pursued this policy, instructing its representatives that "if any of the Savages pretend Right of Inheritance to all or any Part of the land in our Patent . . . purchase their claim in order to avoid the least Scruple of Intrusion" (quoted in Kades 2001, 74). Thus, throughout the seventeenth century, from Maine to Georgia, it was the law of contract that prevailed in opening up Indian land for acquisition.

Spearheading efforts in the purchase of Indian land were three primary colonial actors: (1) colonial governments empowered by the Crown to negotiate directly with Indians for the purchase of land; (2) land speculators, who were often officials in the same colonial governments that were negotiating with Indians for land and who saw in Indian land opportunities for enormous profits; and (3) individual colonists seeking to purchase land as freehold proprietors.

Following precedent established by the Massachusetts Bay colony in 1634, colonial governments required settlers and speculators to obtain government-issued licenses for the right to buy Indian land. Invariably, however, colonial governments would purchase Indian land at the behest of speculators, who would buy back the land from the government at steep discounts in what amounted to transparent corruption. These speculators would then resell this ill-gotten land to other colonists for a huge profit. The rules aimed at limiting buyers of Indian land to those with the connections to obtain the licenses or patents from colonial or Crown officials (Robertson 2005, 7). In practice, however, the law did little to limit land purchases or constrain the transfer of land from Indians to colonists because the licenses proved relatively easy to obtain for settlers and speculators alike (Banner 2005, 27–29). What the law did accomplish was to create an ordered if corrupt process for land transactions, thereby serving as an institutional catalyst for transferring land from one group to another.

Resigned to the idea of having to purchase Indian land, colonists were nevertheless able to shape the terms of sale and buy Indian land cheap. Arguably the greatest risk to the colonial buyer of Indian land was the price, but Indian unfamiliarity with concepts of landed property rights enabled colonists to offset this risk and buy land at bargain prices. Later, as Indians acquired a more sophisticated understanding of English contracting practices as well as a better appreciation of their own land values, they were still at a disadvantage in shaping the terms of land sales. With the free population of the colonies expanding more than twelve-fold between 1700 and 1790, from 250,000 to 3.2 million, waves of colonial immigrants were soon encroaching on Indian land. Under such population pressures, Indians had less power to drive the terms of sale (Banner 2005, 83). If Indians tried to obtain what might have been a fair price and colonists refused to pay it, Indians faced the prospect of restive colonists as neighbors. Indians had to sell.

While more and more sales were conducted in an environment of settler encroachment on indigenous land, colonists were reluctant to admit their advantage in these transactions (Banner 2005, 83). To colonists, an agreement of purchase and sale was proof enough of the essential fairness of the process. "Did we do any wrong to the Indians," asked the Massachusetts minister Solomon Stoddard rhetorically in 1722, "in buying their land at a small price?" Stoddard responded that if buyer and seller agreed on the price, the transaction was fair. Indian land is "worth but little," Stoddard insisted. "It is our dwelling on it, and our Improvements," he argued, "that have made it to be of worth" (quoted in Banner 2005, 79).

Of course, the English controlled the legal framework in which these so-called contracts took place, which was another huge advantage for the colonists (Banner 2005, 82). Such control explains, at least in part, how the English were able to drive the bargains with their Indian counterparts, but the impacts of control over the legal system are even more far-reaching. For the Crown and settlers alike, the success of colonization depended precisely on the issue of securing land, and colonial institutions such as the law and the courts were established to provide the legal framework for facilitating that mission. Although Indians had recourse to colonial courts on matters of land sales, and in some cases colonial courts may have given redress to Indian plaintiffs, judges and colonial officials in general understood themselves to be accountable to English colonial subjects (Banner 2005, 82). Indians played no role in shaping this legal framework, which functioned as a legal monopoly for the colonists. There were no Indian courts in matters of land transactions, only colonial courts and English law. More importantly, the idea of conveying land in severalty was itself foreign to Indians. Over time, Indians did begin to grasp the English concept of conveying pieces of ground, but what Indians learned about English property rights did not alter the legal process for land transactions. English law and English courts were fully in control of the disposition and conveyance of Indian land.

Another reason why the English were willing buyers of Indian land was that for most of the seventeenth century they were in no position to seize by force what they might have imagined as their right to Amerindian land. At the time of King Philip's War in 1775–76, however, and certainly after 1763, the relative strength of the two sides had diverged. By the time the Americans succeeded the British as rulers of the new United States, Amerindians confronted a more aggressive colonizer, willing to use the overt power of violence along with a far more subtle legal instrument for transferring Indian land to settlers, the *treaty*.

From Purchase Contracts to Treaties

In many ways, the treaties used by American governments to secure Amerindian land after the Revolutionary War reflected continuity with practices established with the Royal Proclamation of 1763, which prohibited private purchases of such land. Instead of private individuals negotiating to purchase Indian land, the proclamation established a system of land acquisition whereby land could be conveyed solely by treaties between Indian nations and the Crown (Banner 2005, 92). The lands affected lay west of a line that ran from western New York through the middle of Georgia. The proclamation, however, had unintended consequences.

Many Anglo-American colonists, both small proprietors and land speculators, believed the regulations of the Proclamation to be unjust, if not illegal, and ignored the law, setting in motion a flourishing black market in Amerindian land west of the line. One wealthy Virginia speculator acknowledged that it was good business to buy Indian land, "notwithstanding the Proclamation that restrains it at present," and advised his agent to keep his purchases a secret because they were illegal. That speculator was George Washington (Banner 2005, 100). Such sentiments anticipated the Declaration of Independence, which lists as one of its complaints that King George III had placed "onerous" conditions on those wishing to acquire western lands. Thus, one of the impacts of the proclamation was to replace private land acquisitions through contract with an illegal black market that enjoyed the support of colonists challenging the restrictions of the law (Banner 2005, 104).

The illegal land market aside, however, the law had more enduring impacts as a rule-making framework, since most of those seeking Amerindian land followed the law (Banner 2005, 105). The period after 1763 was marked by the emergence of large land companies, whose major activity was to lobby colonial officials to buy large tracts of Indian land in the West. Such land would then be conveyed to the companies, much as in the earlier period but on a larger scale. Government officials again were invariably investors in such ventures, meaning that these officials were essentially conveying Indian land to themselves.

The Proclamation also had a more long-standing, if less visible, impact as an instrument of dispossession by undermining the idea of Indians as owners of land. In the new circumstances, title to Indian land was no longer dependent on an Indian deed. Instead, prospective land owners after 1763 derived title from the Crown or colonial governments. In observing this change, the royal governor of North Carolina, William Tyron, noted that in the new period "the Indian deed makes no part of the subject's title" (quoted in Banner 2005, 108). After 1763, in other words, the patent, grant title, or license from the Crown was not just an authorization to acquire a property right from Indians; it *was* the property right. Although the change was subtle, the fact that all land titles now derived from the Crown and colonial governments, rather than from the Indians directly, shifted the way colonists understood Indian rights to and presence on the land. Prior to 1763, when colonists purchased land directly from Indians, they understood them to be landowners. When colonists could secure land legally only through a title granted by the Crown or colonial governments, the idea of Indians as owners of land with a legitimate presence on the landscape weakened (Banner 2005, 108). As a result, the Royal Proclamation of 1763, with its notion of "treaty" rights, had a significant effect in delegitimizing Indians as owners of their land while creating a process of land transfer in which Indians had only a shadow presence.

After the Americans emerged victorious in the Revolutionary War against the British, they began to implement policies that weakened Native claims to land and affirmed the notion of Indians as tenants at-will. At the war's conclusion, in the spring of 1783, the Continental Congress sent General Phillip Schuyler to a council of the Six Nation Indians in New York to inform them of what the newly independent states intended as policy toward Indians. Schuyler wasted few words. "We are now Masters," he told the assembled Indians, "and can dispose of the lands as we think proper.... We claim the lands and property of all the white people [loyalists] and all of the Indians who fought against us" (quoted in Banner 2005, 112).

By 1790 the new government, reflecting what Schuyler had dictated to the Six Nations, had put in place a system of Indian land acquisition, codified in the Trade and Intercourse Act of 1790, that designated the federal government as the sole agent to conduct or regulate all transactions with Indian nations.[9] The major provisions of the act were contained in section 1, which prohibited any person to conduct trade with Indian tribes without a license, and especially section 4, which stipulated that "no sale of lands made by any Indians, or any nation or tribe of Indians within the United States, shall be valid to any person or persons, or to any state" (quoted in Prucha 2000, 15). Subsequent to the passage of the 1790 act were five additional statutes that together frame the outlines of the law governing Indian commerce. The most significant of these additions to the original 1790 act was passed in 1802. In the 1802 law, the provisions on conveyance of Indian land *through treaty* were more explicitly codified, in section 12, which stated that "no purchase, grant, lease, or other conveyance of lands, or of any title or claim thereto, from any Indian, or nation, or tribe of Indians, within the bounds of the United States, shall be of any validity in law or equity, unless the same be made by treaty" (quoted in Prucha 2000, 19). Thus, the 1790 act and its subsequent supplementary statutes essentially reaffirmed the spirit of the 1763 proclamation by prohibiting private purchases of Indian land and normalizing the process of Indian land acquisition within the framework of government-controlled treaties.

If the language of the act *seemed* to protect Indian nations from unscrupulous speculators and to elevate the government as a fair-minded party to the process of Indian land sales through treaty, such an interpretation would be naïve. Indeed, George Mason, one the framers of the Bill of Rights, candidly described the character of Indian land acquisition in this period while offering prescient observations about the way this practice was enclosing the Indian landscape. "We attempted, indeed, to form Treaties with the Indians, and to make Purchases. But in doing this, we conducted ourselves rather as Proprietors of the Soil than as Purchasers; and prescribed Bounds, beyond which we wou'd still suffer them to live" (quoted in Banner 2005, 147). As Mason recognized, the U.S. government was not purchasing land. It was seizing it under the legal fiction of "agreements" with Indians, thereby perfecting practices that had prevailed since the Proclamation of 1763.

Reinforcing the role of treaties as the mechanism for securing Indian land, as well as the notion of Indians as tenants at-will, was a new and complementary instrument: the "preemption right," which allowed private citizens to acquire Indian land before it entered the government inventory as public land. Preemption rights emerged after the Revolutionary War as a type of futures contract to compensate soldiers by giving them the right to own parcels of land before such parcels were actually secured by the government from Indians.[10] These rights, however—not to mention the burgeoning market that grew up around them—were not immune from controversy. There were two legal questions: (1) Did Amerindians possess rights that overrode the preemptions? and (2) Did states have the authority to issue such rights when the land in question had not yet been secured by the federal government?

The test case for these questions was *Marshall v. Clark* (1791), argued before the Virginia Supreme Court. Not only did the decision sanction preemption rights, leaving intact the power of state governments to grant Indian land to a third party, but it also contributed to a legal environment in which the preemption right was the equivalent of the fee-simple title to land, thus reaffirming Indian presence as nothing more than a type of tenancy at-will. In effect, the decision was another legal milestone in the ongoing erosion of Indian claims to land.

The issue of preemption rights was revisited in the U.S. Congress in discussions around the 1796 renewal of the Trade and Intercourse Act. During debates in the House of Representatives on a clause of the bill that would have banned surveys on land still in Indian possession, two positions emerged. James Hillhouse, a representative from Connecticut, argued that surveyors should not be allowed on Indian land before it was conveyed to the United States because the surveyor would be trespassing on land belonging to the Indians, who, Hillhouse insisted, had "the fee simple." Opposing Hillhouse was James Holland of North Carolina, who argued that Indians were not and never were the owners and that the holder of the preemption right was the land's true owner. "The Savages of these Provinces," Holland said, "when under the British Government were a conquered people, and tenants at will . . . and not tenants in possession of a fee simple estate" (quoted in Banner 2005, 166). Despite a close vote, the House upheld the legality of preemption rights. What had thus emerged from treaties, and the court decisions and legislation supporting the treaty idea, was a new status for the country's indigenous peoples: Indians were evolving into tenants on the land (Banner 2005, 176).

Law and the Cultural Road to Indians as Tenants

If treaties, courts, and lawmakers were shaping a legal environment in which Amerindians were tenants, this legal environment in turn was responding to a broader cultural discourse of antipathy toward Native Americans. Harking back to the notion of Amerindians as contemptible savages, this discourse reemphasized the indigenous as nomadic and without anchors to the soil.

The central aim of those promoting this representation, however, was to reinvent Indians by erasing them as cultivators. Such an erasure eliminated Amerindian legitimacy on the land.

One of the early signals of this erasure of Indian agriculture was a legal study, *The History of Land Titles in Massachusetts* (1801), by James Sullivan, the attorney general of Massachusetts for twenty years and governor for the last year of his life. In his book, Sullivan makes several provocative claims. For one thing, he writes that "there were no traces of agriculture in this part of North America," except on certain "soft and yielding pieces of ground" (Sullivan 1801, 22; Banner 2005, 151). While admitting to some Indian cultivation, Sullivan, much like Locke, thus dismisses Indian ownership of land by disparaging the character of Indian farming, writing that where Indians cultivated crops, the land was "carelessly tilled" and there was no evidence of any claim on the harvest. "As property is defined by Mr. Locke," Sullivan concludes, the Indians had only a "precarious and transient occupancy" that did not make them owners of land (Sullivan 1801, 23; Banner 2005, 152). At the same time, Sullivan is making more than an agriculturalist argument about Indians rights to land. His tone about "the savages" and the Indians' "barbarous state" recalls an older view of the contemptible savage associated with figures such as Robert Gray that had found its way into the work of Locke and then resurfaced in the late 1700s as part of a newer Enlightenment-inspired discourse about progress.

In this discourse, society evolved in stages from savagery to civilization. What provided the material as well as conceptual foundation for this transition was landed property. Indians having no property were thus in conflict with the forces of progress and civilization. A key text in disseminating this representation, and one that influenced subsequent understandings of Indians during the early to mid-1800s such as Sullivan's legal history, was the *History of America* (1777) by William Robertson. Already printed in an eighth edition by 1800, Robertson's *History* remained the definitive account of Native Americans into the mid-nineteenth century (Robertson 1800; Konkle 2008, 308).

Following in the spirit of Locke's "wild Indian," but with far less empathy for Native Americans than the English philosopher evinced, Robertson makes constant reference to the "savage state" of Amerindian society. With the exception of the civilizations in Mexico and Peru, Native society in every other part of America, he writes, "was nearly similar and so extremely rude that the denomination of *Savage* may be applied to all of them." Such savages, he insists, are "unacquainted with the most basic of arts for human improve-ment" while practicing an agriculture "neither extensive nor laborious." Even among the more "improved" Amerindian groups, "labour is deemed igno-minious and degrading." Perhaps most importantly, Amerindians were "strangers to property." Without well-established customs of ownership rights, Amerindian society is "unacquainted with what is the great object of laws and policy, as well as the chief motive which induced mankind to estab-lish the various arrangements of regular government." Absent property and without government, Indian society was thus the paragon of savagery in which conquest would only be the fulfillment of progress (Robertson 1810, 1:311, 1: 310, 2:6, 1:347, 2:17).

This notion of savagery and the way it came to dominate representations of Indians in the early nineteenth century is perhaps best exemplified by Hugh Henry Brackenridge in his legal commentaries titled *Law Miscellanies* (1814). A justice of the Pennsylvania Supreme Court, Brackenridge in his text reflects the ways in which the longstanding lineage of contemptible savagery and ideas about property and progress influenced a new depiction of Indians as primitive nomadic hunters, in turn erasing Indian agriculture (Konkle 2008, 309–10). Also noteworthy is the patronizing and moralistic tone in this work where he describes Indian life. The life of hunting, he writes, requires a more extensive territory than one of agriculture, while from the very circum-stances of Indians' "thin and scattered settlements"

> the powers of genius are inactive, the arts and sciences remain unknown, and man continues to be an animal differing in nothing but in shape from the beasts of prey that roam upon the mountain; the life of these is therefore not human; for it is abhorrent from the way of life which God and nature points out is the life of man.... The aborigines of this continent can therefore have but small pretense to a soil which they have never cultivated. The most they can with justice claim, is a right to those spots of ground where their wig-wams have been planted.... I would justify encroachment on the territory claimed by them, until they are reduced to smaller bounds, and under the necessity of changing their unpolished and ferocious state of life, for fixed habitations and the arts of agriculture. (Brackenridge 1814, 124–25)

Although Brackenridge concedes that negotiating for Indian land was pref-erable to taking it through warfare, he leaves little doubt about his beliefs for a final solution to the problem of Indian savagery.

In this way during the early 1800s, Indians were reinvented. Beginning with Robertson's historical work, extending through figures such as Sullivan, and culminating in Brackenridge, Indians lost their history as farmers. A new history, drawing inspiration from an early-seventeenth-century discourse on savagery, represented Indians as nomadic beasts without cultivated fields, without property. Absent property, Indians had no claim of rights to land.

In addition to figures such as Robertson, Sullivan, and Brackenridge, Indian reformers, many of them missionaries, contributed to this transformation in popular perceptions of Indians. In trying to help Indians, however, reformers and missionaries mistakenly emphasized Indian dependence on hunting, urging upon them the need to "replenish the earth and subdue it," as Locke, quoting scripture, had written. Even where missionaries encountered Indian farming, they pointed to its failings—not employing plows or horses, for example—and urged them to imitate European-style farming. In 1811 William Jenkins, a missionary to the Oneida, conceded that the tribe had made "wonderful improvements," having "ploughed up much of their open ground, and likewise cut down and cleared off timber from large tracts of land," while one of his counterparts with the Seneca remarked that the latter, following the counsel of the reformers, "have cut down the woods, made good fences, raised wheat . . . and have got oxen and cows" (quoted in Banner 2005, 154). While there were differences between Indian and white American agriculture, the chief difference was that Indian farmers were women. When reformers spoke of teaching the Indians to farm, what they meant was teaching Indian *men* to farm. Women's dominance in farming made Indian agriculture less visible to colonists.

By the early nineteenth century, other factors were reinforcing beliefs about the nonexistence of Indian agriculture, including real changes in Indian subsistence practices. Over large areas of the Great Plains, Indians had indeed transitioned to nomadic hunting cultures reliant on horses. These bison hunters were now reshaping popular images of Indian society, reinforced by the artistic renderings of figures such as George Catlin in the 1840s. In addition, expeditions such as that of Lewis and Clark were reporting about tribes with "no idea of an exclusive possession of any country" and tribes without " any idea of exclusive rights to the soil" (Banner 2005, 156). A profound transformation in the representation of the Indian had occurred since the late-sixteenth-century depictions of Indian agriculture in Secoton by Thomas Harriot.

All of these sources—Robertson's description of Native Americans, Sullivan's legal history, the activities of Indian reformers, early-nineteenth-century observations by white explorers of the West, and artistic imagery—

contributed to creating not only a popular culture of Indians but a potent legal culture as well. The more pervasive the representation of Indians as unattached nomadic hunters, and the more these were absorbed into popular consciousness, the less compelling were Indian claims to ownership of land. These cultural and legal discourses in many ways helped contribute to the politics underlying the *Johnson* decision of 1823.

Johnson v. M'Intosh

Johnson v. M'Intosh was a landmark example of the power of law to dispossess Indians and remove them from the landscape. The case came to the U.S. Supreme Court in the form of a dispute between two land development companies trying to purchase land from Indians, but Chief Justice John Marshall turned the case into a far broader issue about Indian land rights generally.[11] In rendering his opinion, Marshall drew from late-eighteenth- and early-nineteenth-century historical and legal texts, including his own work on the American Colonies culled from a number of secondary texts, which he published in five volumes in 1804 as *The Life of George Washington* (Robertston 2005, 100–102). Marshall's opinion in *Johnson* rested on many of the same historical misrepresentations about Indian land ownership that had become increasingly dominant by the late 1700s in cultural and legal discourses.

In his summation, Marshall's central claim was that Indians had possessed only a right of occupancy, not ownership, since the earliest days of English colonization and that Americans were applying this same principle as the colonies' inheritors. Marshall then added something original: a legal argument about what he insisted was British policy from the beginning, namely the "discovery doctrine." He invoked it not only to affirm European sovereignty in North America, but also as the basis for colonial dominium in denying Indian ownership of land. "On the discovery of this immense continent, the great nations of Europe were eager to appropriate to themselves so much of it as they could respectively acquire. . . . Discovery gave title to the government." In effect, Marshall was arguing that discovery not only protected the claims of Europeans against one another; it also gave the discoverer title to land, nullifying Indian property rights (Robertson 2005, 99).

Yet Marshall took the discovery doctrine to another level when he suggested the equivalence of discovery and *conquest*. "Conquest gives a title which the Courts of the conqueror cannot deny," Marshall argued. Marshall thus made two critical arguments in denying Indian dominium. First, he used the discovery doctrine to claim that Indian land had belonged to the colonizer from the beginning. This assertion, however, was contradicted by actual English colonial practice. Despite what some English colonists believed to be their right to take Indian land based on agriculturalist notions of cultivation along with cultural notions of savagery, in practice English colonists and officials alike treated Indians as owners when arranging purchases of Indian land. Marshall essentially disputed this set of historical facts and instead claimed that English discovery gave the English colonists not only sovereignty but also dominium over Indian land. In addition, he suggested that in 1823 Indians were a conquered people and that conquest entitled Americans to their land. Indians had occupancy rights, Marshall conceded, but they had no rights of the soil in terms of conveyance. Perhaps even more significantly, relations between "the discoverer and the natives" were to be regulated by the discoverer, and such rights being exclusive, "no other power could interpose between them" (quoted in Robertson 2005, 99). American courts, in short, would be responsible for regulating these issues.

In the aftermath of the *Johnson* case, Indian removal emerged as respectable public policy garnering support in Congress following vigorous lobbying by the Jackson administration. In addition to shaping the legal landscape, Marshall's opinion had an impact on the imagined landscape as well, helping to plant the notion of Indians as a defeated people.

FENCED AND BOUNDED: THE SPREAD
OF THE GRID ON THE LANDSCAPE

While the law acted as a potent instrument for transforming Amerindians into tenants and moving them to new locations, it was the economic life of settlers that gave material meaning to this legal geography of dispossession and removal. This material manifestation of dispossession emerged most forcefully from the establishment of bounded and fenced agricultural spaces on the landscape demarcating plots of property under fee-simple tenure (Lemon 1987, 80).

The most sweeping change wrought by colonists that contributed to this geography of lines and enclosed spaces was deforestation (Cronon 2003, 126). Where settlers cleared trees and established farms and towns, they set down the economic and cultural foundations of this linear geography of property. Although early colonists in New England had tended to establish nucleated villages that resembled the common field villages of England, with allotments to individual families in cleared and open fields, by the 1660s they were abandoning this settlement pattern in favor of allotments in more dispersed individual farmsteads (Greven 1974, 50–53). In these new circumstances, reordering the environment by felling trees and clearing land was essential for the household and also consistent with the evolving patterns of agrarian life in England, inspired by ideologies of improvement and individual rights of possession. For these colonists, clearing the forest and establishing cultivated fields represented the creation of civilization from uncultivated wilderness and was thus the paragon of land improvement.

For Amerindians, leveling the forest had destructive consequences. For one thing, it undermined their hunting economies, maintained through practices of controlled burning and forest management. In the spaces of felled trees where settlers set down farms, their activities of cultivating crops, pasturing animals, building roads, and ultimately establishing towns continually encroached on Indian land, creating an ever-widening landscape of territorial spaces off limits to Indians. Encroachment in turn led to dispossession, followed by repossession by settlers. A very specific material marker constructed on the landscape by colonists would come to communicate this geography of property lines, dispossession, and conquest. This material marker was the *fence*.

Colonization and Deforestation

For settler-pioneers, woodlands embodied clear imperatives related to colonial notions of land improvement.[12] To these newcomers, the forest was essentially unimproved land—wild, untamed, devoid of order, and in need of clearing and cultivating so that it could be rendered fit for civilized (sedentary and agricultural) habitation. In this sense, the forest loomed as the primary obstacle to the "Promised Land" that early colonists hoped to find in America, standing between them and survival. At the same time, the settler could find solace in overcoming this challenge to survival by felling the forest, thus following God's commandment to subdue the earth for human subsistence.

For the early colonist, the cleared patch of wilderness and the neatly fenced, "made" ground are what brought order and life itself to the landscape, and so pleased God. Writing in 1790, William Cooper, a land speculator and founder of Cooperstown whose interests focused on settling large tracts of land in New York (Cooper 1790, i), admitted that his "primary aim" in life was "to cause the wilderness to bloom and fructify" by felling the forest and turning unimproved land to land improved (quoted in Williams 1989, 13). His views followed those of Benjamin Franklin, who had earlier identified the frontier with "opportunity" and had equated the moral and spiritual improvement of society to the progress of "converting wilderness into a paradise of material plenty" (quoted in Williams 1989, 13). Thus, in addition to its material attributes, this process of felling the forest and rendering it into ordered and cultivated plots of land had a spiritual moniker: *redemption*.

While early colonists were inspired by this symbolic notion of land improvement leading to redemption, their activities in clearing woodlands also had a market-driven impulse. Insofar as settlers had to clear forests in the interior to establish farms and to secure building materials and fuel for survival, they were improving and transforming the landscape within horizons of subsistence. In so doing, they were able to perceive in trees a certain similarity with animal pelts. Both were potential commodities for profit, of course. But colonists discovered certain advantages in exploiting trees for profit rather than animals. Animal pelts required exchange networks with Amerindians. Timber, by contrast, provided colonists with a seemingly free resource that could be turned to profitable gain. In order to "improve" the forest, one had only to affix one's labor to the trees, cutting them down, splitting the wood, and shipping the lumber to market. In 1621, for example, when the Pilgrims sent their first shipment of goods back to England, William Bradford reported that the ship was "laden with good clapboard as full as she could stow" (quoted in Cronon 2003, 109). Thus in the early period of English colonization, the market was already prominent as a force on the landscape, with the forest becoming exploitable as lumber and part of a burgeoning profit-making industry.

Nevertheless, while the forest was being tapped economically by a new type of activity personified by the lumberman, the real agent of change in transforming the forest into a gridded landscape of property was the settler-farmer.[13] After initial settlement, colonists soon began expanding into the heavily forested interior, where they confronted the challenge of preparing land for cultivation. They discovered that certain types of trees, and the ecologies created from the interactions of trees, plants, and animals, were powerful agents in promoting well-nourished soils ideal for agriculture. After such areas were located, however, colonists invariably resorted to clear-cutting, harvesting some of the cut trees for profit but in the process destroying animal habitats and undermining the conditions that created rich soils suitable for farming.

In other forest areas where trees species did not offer good profit-making opportunities, colonists applied a method of clearing learned from Indians: they burned the trees. Yet in contrast to Indian practices of controlled burning to remove undergrowth and help regenerate animal habitats, colonists burned the entire forest environment in what was akin to clear-cutting, destroying both the forest and the animal life dependent on it. So extensive was this burning practice that colonists in New England were already regulating it by the 1630s in order to prevent fires from burning out of control across property boundaries. In policing the burning of forests, however, colonists did not only employ self-regulation; they also forced the regulations on nearby Indians, who were held liable in colonial courts for any damages their fires might cause to colonial homesteads. Such restrictions were one of the ways colonists impressed upon Indians the function of individual property lines in a bounded landscape.

As settlement expanded, with colonists clearing and burning forests, the landscape assumed a patchwork character as individual property owners demarcated their holdings with wooden fences. By fencing their farmsteads with wood, owing to its seemingly inexhaustible supply, colonists put further pressure on forest stocks. In this way, farms, fences, and deforestation worked in a mutually reinforcing way to create an environment of "fields and fences" (Cronon 2003, 127–56). More significantly, the fence-enclosed cultivated fields became symbols of an improved landscape signifying colonial ownership of rectilinearly bounded spaces (Cronon 2003, 130). In the long term, this regime of enclosed private spaces excluded Native Americans as it marched across the North American landscape (Greer 2012, 366).

Complementing this pattern of agrarian settlement was the emergence and proliferation of larger towns and cities, which posed even bigger problems for the sustainability of forests. With their expanding populations, towns required huge quantities of wood for fuel—the single biggest source of deforestation (Cronon 2003, 120). Colonial buildings also contributed to deforestation, full-timbered construction being the norm, unlike in England.

Thus, despite its seeming abundance, wood from forests was being depleted as fuel and as building material—with profound impacts on Indian subsistence systems. As early as 1642, the destruction of New England forests by colonists and its effects on the Native food economy were already a source of anxiety to the local Indians. In that year the Narragansett sachem Miantonomo remarked presciently about the time when "our fathers had plenty of deer and skins, our plains were full of deer, as also our woods, and of turkies, and our coves full of fish and fowl. But these English ... with scythes cut down the grass, and with axes fell the trees ... and we shall all be starved" (quoted in Cronon 2003, 162). Over a century later, in 1768, the Oneida chief Conoghquieson complained to Sir William Johnson, British superintendent for Indian Affairs, about English practices of destroying the forests and the wildlife in them, and barricading the forests with fences: "When our Young men wanted to go hunting the Wild Beasts in our Country they found it covered with fences," he observed, " so that they were weary crossing them. Neither can they get Venison to Eat, or Bark to make huts, for the Beasts are run away and the Trees cut down" (Graymont 2001, 527).[14]

Colonists, however, understood what they were doing to the forest not as something destructive but as something enlightened. They were improving the land. Essentially, colonists were adapting an English model of rural agrarian development to an American environment, clearing the forest being a necessary first step toward achieving the improved and enclosed landscapes of the English countryside.

Yet deforestation was only one of the manifestations of colonial land hunger that began to imprint grid lines onto the landscape. An even stronger set of impulses behind the inscription of property lines emerged from the way settlers used patterns of cultivation and animal husbandry as part of agriculture and land improvement.

From Deforestation to Cultivation and Animal Domestication

From the beginning of English settlement, colonists conceived of land improvement in the context not only of cultivating grain on enclosed plots of ground, but also of keeping livestock. The pasturing of cattle, goats, and sheep, the keeping of pigs, and the use of horses for plowing were well-established practices of English agriculture and reflected profound differences between English and Indian subsistence systems. Governor John Winthrop, in addition to disparaging Indians for "inclosing noe land," remarked upon how Indian people "had no tame cattle to improve the land," which meant they lacked an essential anchor to the soil. Yet when colonists first arrived at Plymouth in 1620–21, they also had no animals, while Massachusetts Bay Colony had but few. Only beginning in the last years of the decade and extending into the early 1630s and beyond did ships laden with livestock begin arriving regularly in the colonies, such that by 1634 William Wood of the Massachusetts Bay Colony could reflect upon the settlers' wealth in having an abundant supply of cattle, pigs, and goats (V. Anderson 1994, 603; V. Anderson 2004, 103–04; Cronon 2003, 128–29). Domesticated animals thus complemented cultivated and enclosed fields as material elements of rootedness to the landscape. In this way, land improvement, conferring upon the improver the right to property, became yoked—literally—to animals themselves.

What made colonial pastoralism an ongoing source of conflict between colonists and Indians, and what enabled domesticated animals to emerge as a potent force for changing the landscape, was the land hunger that attended the keeping of livestock and horses. Animals constantly compelled settlers to extend the boundaries of colonial property rights. Alongside the proliferation of cultivated fields, domesticated animals were on the frontlines of ongoing encroachment into Indian country and eventual removal of Indians from the landscape to accommodate this appetite for ever more land.

Land conflict between Indians and colonists where animals played a prominent role started ironically on the one area of the landscape where colonists at least initially had conceded some degree of Amerindian dominium: indigenous cultivated fields (V. Anderson 2004, 192). Encroachment arrived in the form of settlers' domesticated animals trespassing on and damaging Indian corn fields, a situation that Indians had never before encountered. A major reason for the problem stemmed from the way colonists cared for their livestock. Colonists let cattle and pigs forage far more freely than was customary in England, where livestock was typically shepherded by human labor. In North America, however, labor was scarce. What colonists did to overcome this scarcity and protect their own agriculture from damage by animal grazing and foraging was to enclose their own croplands with fencing, a remedy that marked the beginning of a proliferating mosaic of lines on the landscape (Cronon 2003, 134–35).

Although colonial courts at times recognized damages to Indian property, the law sought to remedy the problem by forcing Indians to accept fences around their own cultivated fields in much the same way that colonists were being forced to enclose their own fields. As early as 1633, a court in Plymouth Colony had ordered that no colonist should "set corne . . . without inclosure but at his perill." Similarly a Massachusetts court in 1642 affirmed that "every man must secure his corne," and if any damage should be done to fields by cattle, "it shall bee borne by him through whose insufficient fence the cattle did enter" (quoted in Cronon 2003, 134–35).

In some of the early cases involving trespass onto Indian corn fields, offending colonists were obliged to help protect Indian agriculture by contributing labor to build fences around Indian croplands. Such was the case in 1653 at the town of New Haven (Cronon 2003, 131). As part of the judgment, however, Indians had to agree to fence their fields in the future, a concession that proved a Faustian bargain. The fact that cultivated fields, both white and Indian, received legal protection only if they were properly fenced was part of a legal order promoting the redrawing of the map of the landscape as a system of enclosed spaces, one of lines and trespass (Cronon 2003, 135).

Even when Indians fenced their fields, they still faced the problem of encroachment from English pigs.[15] Let loose on coastal areas, pigs damaged Indian clam and oyster beds. Allowed to forage in forested areas, pigs competed with Indians for nuts, berries, and roots, consuming so much of the wild foodstuffs in woods that they drove away wild game (V. Anderson 1994, 618). When pigs walked into Indian hunting traps, colonists held Indians liable for damages to the ensnared animals (V. Anderson 2004, 198). Colonists, in effect, despite recognizing Indian property rights on cultivated fields, permitted animals—and by extension the animal owners—to have use rights to Indian subsistence areas in woods and on the coasts; meanwhile, Indians could not obtain compensation in colonial courts for damages because the English recognized such land to be empty. In these various ways, the animal economy of colonists encroached on the subsistence economy of Indians, drawing the two groups into conflict. At the same time, colonists in their encroachment were extending an ever-proliferating set of property lines across the landscape.

In addition to the incursions of livestock, a much broader set of encroachments onto Indian land derived from the pastoral economy itself (Cronon 2003, 137–50). "The country is yet raw," wrote one of the original Pilgrims, Robert Cushman, in 1621, promoting the improvement and civilization of the landscape, "the land untilled; the cities not builded; the cattle not settled" (quoted in V. Anderson 1994, 604). Even Roger Williams, the progressive founder of Rhode Island, who was more inclined to treat the Indians with civility, urged them to move from barbarism by "keeping some kind of Cattell" (V. Anderson 1994, 605). For the colonists, improving the wilderness was a cultural imperative to be accomplished not only through cultivation but also through the keeping of animals, leading to a constant redrawing of boundaries on the landscape (V. Anderson 1994, 604).

At the center of the livestock economy was the individual farmstead and the primary form of farmstead settlement, the agrarian town. In the case of both the individual farm and the agrarian town, animals played a pivotal role in shaping the landscape. Every individual farmstead had its house, its cultivated fields, and its outbuildings for the various subsistence activities of processing grains, making cloth, and making tools, but by far the largest portion of land was reserved as animal pastures. Indeed, livestock required more land than all other agricultural land uses put together. Farmers were also always seeking additional land with grass, not only for grazing but also for mowing to make hay to provision the animals during the winter. With an increasing colonial population, the animal population increased as well, and with more animals came more pressure to find additional land for pasture.

Animals also played a landscape-changing role on colonial croplands.[16] Plowing allowed small farmers to cultivate far larger tracts of land than their Indian counterparts. These large plowed fields, unlike Indian fields, were typically cultivated with a single soil-exhausting crop: corn. While the deep turning of English fields had some impact in destroying certain organisms necessary for soil replenishment, the practice of monoculture, especially of corn, exhausted soil nutrients most rapidly. By cultivating corn without the accompanying legumes, as Indians did in their fields, farmers were forced to abandon their cleared and plowed croplands within less than a decade because of soil exhaustion. As early as 1637, one colonial farmer remarked that the soil "after five or six years . . . grows barren beyond belief; and . . . puts on the face of winter in the time of summer" (quoted in Cronon 2003, 150). With fields so depleted, and with an ongoing need to provision animals, colonists would utilize the exhausted field as pasture and seek out new fields for cultivation. Thus the cycle of pasturing animals and planting crops would continue the incessant quest for new lands.

As individual farmsteads agglomerated into agrarian towns, the fundamental boundary on the farm between pastureland and land used for everything else became part of the territorial pattern. In a typical colonial town, the area allocated for pasturing was roughly two to ten times greater than that taken by cultivation (Cronon 2003, 139). At the same time, these boundaries were always temporary as an ever-expanding population of people and animals required ever new lands for grazing and haying. This need for land for animals was one of the primary reasons colonists sought Indian land for purchase on a constant basis. In those instances where Indians were reluctant to sell land, conflict ensued, with Indians finding themselves in increasingly untenable situations. Yet selling land was often preferable to the alternative of living in the shadow of ongoing encroachment (Cronon 2003, 138–39).

The settler economy, in addition to expanding ever outward, had the more visible effect of multiplying the bounding and fencing of the landscape. As the population increased, and as the amount of land needed for the expanding number of individual farmsteads grew, fencing emerged as a logical if almost irrepressible material force reshaping the colonial environment. Fencing came to demarcate not only the divisions between individual farmsteads, but also the distinctions between pasture and nonpasture activities on the land. Eventually these lines of fencing that bounded the landscape became cartographic representations on maps themselves (Cronon 2003, 137–38).

Finally, the role of livestock as commodities linking individual farmsteads to urban market centers wrought enormous changes on the Indian landscape owing to the ways in which the animal economy integrated town and countryside, primarily through road-building.[17] Pastured on farmsteads in rural areas, cattle or hogs could be driven and slaughtered for consumption in the urban markets, or alternatively animals were slaughtered, salted, and shipped long distances to foreign markets. Either way, roads emerged as pivotal elements of material infrastructure facilitating this circuit from pasture to slaughter and sale while profoundly transforming the land. In the late fall, farmers drove fatted animals to the coastal cities such as Boston, New Haven, and Providence, where they could be sold and slaughtered in local abattoirs. For these livestock drives, roads had to be constructed; these livestock roads, designed to move large herds from country to city, were typically between 99 and 165 feet wide (Cronon 2003, 140). This road-based system of communications bound the city and countryside into a single livestock economy and enabled farmers to orient their livestock production to commercial ends. By 1660, the livestock economy had vast connections to distant markets and was something of a marvel. Samuel Maverick, a merchant and one of the first Massachusetts Bay colony settlers, recollected that in 1626

> there was not a Neat Beast [cow], Horse or sheepe in the country and very few goats or hoggs. . . . Now [1660] it is a wonder to see the great herds of Catle belonging to every Towne. . . . The brave Flocks of sheepe, the great number of horses besides those many sent to Barbados and the other Carribe Island, and withall to consider how many thousand Neate Beasts and Hoggs are yearly killed, and so have been for many yeares past for Provision in the Countrey and sent abroad to supply Newfoundland, Barbados, Jamaica and other places. (quoted in Cronon 2003, 139)

In what would prefigure the American economy by the late nineteenth century, animal grazing and slaughter was thus already emerging as a major economic activity in the early colonial period. The meat economy, in turn, from pasturing animals to building roads for livestock drives, created an ever-growing hunger for land and ever more pressure on wilderness ecologies. An exploding population of animals dependent on grassland as well as an animal economy driven by accumulation translated into so many hectares of territory. As hectares of territory succumbed to the colonial agricultural economy of cultigens and animals, the landscape became increasingly a world of enclosed and fenced spaces. This pattern of expansion across the landscape took hold not just in New England but throughout the area of Anglo-American settlement.

The full range of colonial agriculture—cultivating the soil, grazing animals, and building roads to bring animals and grains into the rural-to-urban system of marketing and trade—was a paradox within the English property system, however, with its fixed property boundaries and anchors to specific pieces of ground. Colonial agriculture was anything but fixed. But the solution adopted by colonists for overcoming this contradiction was straightforward: settlers looked to expand those boundaries—and they would not let notions of Indian ownership stop them.

"Remove the Indians, Enclose the Landscape"

With settler encroachment complementing a legal and cultural environment that by the late eighteenth century had rendered Amerindians as tenants at-will, the status of indigenous peoples was increasingly tenuous. By 1790 in much of New England, Native Americans had lost all of their land, and so had virtually disappeared (Banner 2005, 194). Although the idea of removal had a legacy going back to the late 1600s, the idea of forcibly removing and relocating Natives did not become part of the public political discourse until after the American Revolution. From that moment, however, Amerindian removal became a goal of many Americans (Robertson 2005, 118). Even so-called reformers of the early nineteenth century regarded it as a way of protecting the Amerindian way of life.

Yet despite the public nature of the debate over relocation, removal was not something policymakers would force on Native Americans. Prior to the 1820s, public discourse regarding removal was essentially one of exchange and "fair" bargain. Amerindians would cede land in the East in exchange for lands in the West, which had become far more abundant as a result of the Louisiana Purchase in 1803. Consequently, policymakers would try to convince Native Americans of the mutual interest in their removal to western lands. This situation, however, changed dramatically in the 1820s, when the state of Georgia began an aggressive campaign to remove the Cherokees, Creeks, and Seminoles from the state (Robertson 2005, 119). It was thus in Georgia that the issue of removal and its impacts emerged most clearly. Consequently, Georgia became emblematic of the broader story about Amerindian dispossession and relocation in the rest of the country.

Arguably, the growth of the settler population in Georgia is what elevated the issue of removal into the public sphere (Banner 2005, 195). Of all the states at that time, Georgia had the largest Amerindian population, with bands of Creeks, Seminoles, and Cherokees constituting the dominant groups. In 1802 Georgia, like other states, ceded its claims on land in its western domains to the federal government. In return, the latter agreed to acquire western lands in Georgia held by Indians and then convey them to the state; Georgia would in turn make them available to settlers. Such were the terms of the Georgia Compact of 1802. From the time of the compact to 1819, the federal government, through treaties with southeastern Indians, secured 20 million acres, which were then ceded to settlers, enabling the settler population to more than double in size during that period (Hershberger 1999, 16; Banner 2005, 195).

Nonetheless, both settlers in Georgia and their political representatives were dissatisfied with the rate at which land was being transferred from Natives to whites. In the early 1820s, Georgia's congressional delegation declared that the federal government had failed to uphold the terms of the 1802 Compact, neither acquiring Indian land nor extinguishing Indian title fast enough. Meanwhile, settlers themselves were encroaching into Amerindian country, effectively changing the spatial demography of the state while setting the stage for land conflict pitting the rights of states against the federal government. In what had become common in the early 1820s, Thomas Cobb, a member of the Georgia congressional delegation, complained on the floor of the House of Representatives in 1820 that "Indian title to fully one-half, and probably the most valuable half, of the lands within the boundaries of the State is yet unextinguished" (quoted in Banner 2005, 195).

In 1824, President James Monroe admitted that he favored Indian removal in Georgia but cautioned state officials that the federal government could not force Native Americans to exchange their land for lands in the West (Banner

2005, 195). Nevertheless, under increasing settler encroachment and vigilant-ism, some Native groups believed that they had no choice but to negotiate terms of removal. As early as 1809, a group of more than a thousand Cherokees had agreed to trade land in Georgia for land in Arkansas. By 1820, roughly three thousand Cherokees—17 percent of the tribe—were living west of the Mississippi (Banner 2005, 194).

These "voluntary" exchanges differed little from the treaties and land pur-chases negotiated in the 1700s. Alexis de Tocqueville, who toured the United States at the height of the removal controversy in 1830, offered a sobering account of the process. For de Tocqueville, the "expulsion of the Indians often takes place at the present day in a regular and, as it were, a legal man-ner." When settlers approached the boundaries of Indian country, he noted,

> the government of the United States usually sends forward envoys who assem-ble the Indians in a large plain and, having first eaten and drunk with them, address them thus: . . . "sell us your lands." . . . After holding this language, they spread before the eyes of the Indians firearms, woolen garments, kegs of brandy, glass necklaces, bracelets of tinsel, ear-rings, and looking glasses. If, when they have beheld all these riches, the Indians still hesitate, it is insinu-ated that they cannot refuse the required consent. . . . Half convinced, half compelled, the Indians go off to dwell in new wildernesses, where the impor-tunate whites will not let them remain ten years in peace. . . . In this manner do the Americans obtain at a very low price whole provinces which the rich-est sovereigns in Europe could not purchase. (de Tocqueville 1835, 340–41)

This description of bribery and guile fits broadly with what transpired with the Creek Indians in Georgia. In 1821, the Creeks sold half of their land to the federal government for $50,000 plus annuities and other payments totaling roughly $400,000. Federal Indian commissioners then pressured the Creeks to sell their remaining land. When they refused, the government enlisted a dissident Creek leader, William McIntosh, to sell the remaining Creek land in exchange for land in Arkansas, bribing McIntosh with a $25,000 payment to consummate the deal known as the Treaty of Indian Springs. Although the Creeks managed to annul the treaty, the tribe, under intense pressure, ended up conveying the same land to the government. In effect, bribery, threats of force, and a willingness to deal with Indian splinter groups rather than official tribal leaderships were the hallmarks of U.S. policy regarding Indian removal. By 1827, Creeks were no longer living in Georgia.

The major controversy over Indian removal in Georgia, however, erupted with the Cherokees in 1824. In that year, in response to a solicitation from the federal government asking the tribe to move west, the Cherokee National Council informed President Monroe that it would not sell its land in exchange for land west of the Mississippi River (Robertson 2005, 119). When Monroe conceded that there was nothing the federal government could do to force the Cherokee sale, the state of Georgia charged the United States with being in violation of the Compact negotiated in 1802. In exchange for ceding claims to lands lying to the west of the state, the Georgia Compact gave the state the right to recoup Indian land within its boundaries, which the federal government was supposed to acquire through treaty and then convey back to the state. In 1827, the Cherokees reaffirmed their earlier decision not to sell their land, in a historic document modeled after the U.S. Constitution. In its first article, the Cherokee Constitution described the nation's territorial boundaries and included a statement that its lands "shall forever hereafter remain unalterably the same" (quoted in Robertson 2005, 122). Taking a different approach to removal than their Creek neighbors, the Cherokees were determined to remain in their lands.[18]

Confronted by the refusal of the federal government to force Cherokee land sales, as well as Cherokee resistance to sell, the state of Georgia—its congressional delegation and state lawmakers such as Governor George Troup—sought to force the issue and found in the 1823 *Johnson* case such an instrument of coercion. Using passages from Marshall's opinion in *Johnson* of Indians as tenants, Georgia lawmakers argued that "Indians were simply occupants—tenants at will," and that it was the federal government that was the landlord. If purchase of Cherokee land was not forthcoming, these lawmakers reasoned, "nothing remains to be done but to order their removal" (quoted in Banner 2005, 205).

Nevertheless, the Cherokees continued to resist the pressure to part with their land, and in response, Governor Troup and state lawmakers assumed a more active role in forcing a treaty on the Indians. Troup took the matter to the Georgia legislature, imploring state lawmakers to draft and pass eight resolutions in response to the Cherokee Constitution. In these resolutions, Georgia now claimed title to all Indian land within the state's territorial boundaries and resolved to overcome the Cherokees' refusal to sell. "The lands in question belong to Georgia," the drafting committee affirmed. "She must and she will have them" (quoted in Robertson 2005, 124).

A turning point in this campaign waged by Georgia lawmakers occurred with the election in 1828 of Andrew Jackson as the country's seventh president. In his first state of the union address in December 1829, Jackson made removal a major policy priority, emphasizing the need for Indians to be relocated west of the Mississippi (Hershberger 1999, 15). Although he still conceded that Indian emigration to the West should be voluntary, Jackson cautioned that if they refused, they would be dispossessed of the major portion of their land (Robertson 2005, 126). With an ally in the White House, the state of Georgia now increased its pressure on the federal government to remove Indians—if necessary, by force.

In the early months of 1830, Jackson played a key role in urging Congress to pass the Indian Removal Act, which they did on May 26, 1830; it was signed into law by the president two days later. The politics around the passage of the law, however, were polarized, with impassioned opposition as well as strong support, especially among slave states such as Georgia. While the Indian Removal Act did not explicitly authorize force to remove Indians from states such as Georgia, supporters within the state gave the law a new meaning. As law, the Indian Removal Act helped create a cultural climate that encouraged settler groups, many of them racist Indian-hating vigilantes, to take matters into their own hands and make it untenable for the Cherokees to remain (Cave 2003, 1337). The burning of Cherokee fields, slaughter of Cherokee livestock, and destruction of Cherokee homes were used by these groups to convince the Cherokees of the wisdom of removing themselves to the West (Perdue and Green 2008, 119). Jackson himself, disturbed by the delays in Cherokee removal, regarded harassment a legitimate strategy for encouraging their departure, allegedly remarking to a Georgia congressman: "Build a fire under them. When it gets hot enough, they'll move" (quoted in Cave 2003, 1339).[19]

Jackson was determined to force the Cherokees into a treaty but absent an agreement was prepared to let them languish at the hands of white settlers. Rather than enforcing the prohibitions against white settlement on Indian land, Jackson told Indian leaders that he lacked the power to protect them from both state governments and lawless whites. One Cherokee chief, Tiskinhah-haw, wrote to Jackson in 1831 saying that whites had invaded Cherokee land to "steal our property" and that soldiers, deployed ostensibly to protect Indians from this illegal encroachment, refused to help, but when Indians tried to resist the settlers, soldiers and settlers alike hunted them down "as if . . . they had been so many wild dogs" (quoted in Cave 2003, 1340). Four years later, Jackson responded to Cherokee petitioners trying to remain on their land, saying: "You cannot remain where you now are. Circumstances that cannot be controlled and which are beyond the reach of

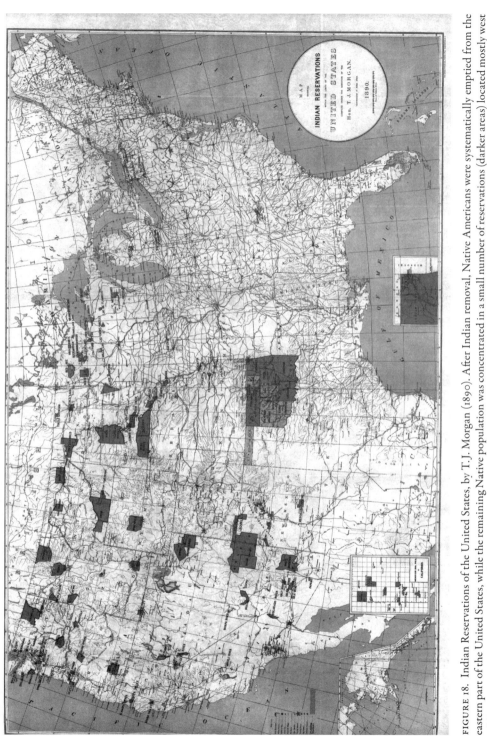

FIGURE 18. Indian Reservations of the United States, by T.J. Morgan (1890). After Indian removal, Native Americans were systematically emptied from the eastern part of the United States, while the remaining Native population was concentrated in a small number of reservations (darker areas) located mostly west of the Mississippi River. Reproduced by permission of the T.R. Smith Map Collection, University of Kansas Library.

human laws render it impossible that you can flourish in the midst of a civilized community.... Deceive yourselves no longer" (quoted in Cave 2003, 1340).

. . .

By 1840 virtually all of the southeastern Indian tribal groups—Cherokees, Creeks, Choctaws, and Seminoles—had been forcibly removed from their lands and relocated to what would become Oklahoma (Robertson 2005, 143). The state of Georgia constituted the main battleground of this campaign for dispossession and the making of property on the landscape. In the end, however, Georgia was but one chapter in a broader narrative that continued throughout the nineteenth century in which a geography of lines and boundaries consumed more and more of the landscape. By 1890, when the superintendent of the Census famously declared the "frontier" of unsettled lands was officially closed, very little Amerindian land remained. A discourse of land improvement and property rights—supplemented with notions of savagery and racism—had settled upon the landscape, fashioning a linear and gridded cartography of state, country, and municipal boundaries, while a ravaged and decimated population of Indians was enclosed in reservations (fig. 18).

PART THREE

"This Is Our *Land"*

REDEEMING THE PALESTINIAN LANDSCAPE

When we built Ariel, we never took one square inch of Palestinian land. This hilltop was empty.... Look at the hills around here. They [Palestinians] don't plant! They don't cultivate. We built something here.

RON NAHMAN, mayor of Ariel, August 14, 2005

In 1978 when the Israelis built Ariel, they took twenty dunums of land from me. My land was on that hillside, where I had one hundred olive trees. That was theft.

MOHAMMED A. I., farmer
from Marda, August 16, 2005/July 29, 2015

IF ONE TAKES LEAVE BY CAR on Route 60 from the biblical city of Bethlehem in the Palestinian West Bank toward Hebron, an unmarked road ten kilometers from the city limits, just past the Israeli settlement of Neve Daniel, leads to the home and farm of Daoud Nassar and his family. Mr. Nassar is the owner of 400 dunums (100 acres) of farmland purchased by his grandfather roughly one hundred years ago that today is planted with almost a thousand trees—olive, almond, fig, and citrus. The land, however, is surrounded by Israeli settlements built after 1967 whose residents are at best indifferent and at times openly hostile to their Palestinian neighbor, even going to the extreme of vandalizing some of the orchard trees on the farm. Under pressure from these settlers, Israeli authorities have initiated their own campaign against the Nassars. In 1991, Israeli law courts and surveyors were enlisted to reclassify Mr. Nassar's farm and home as Israeli state land, in an effort to repossess it for development of additional Israeli settlements, despite the Ottoman deeds possessed by the Nassars showing that the land belongs

FIGURE 19. Naḥḥālīn (left) and Beitar Illit as seen from the Tent of Nations (2016). Photo by author.

to the family as private property. While this contest bears the markings of innumerable other legal cases involving Palestinian farmers, Mr. Nassar has taken unusual steps outside the courts and beyond the reach of surveyors to resist such encroachments on his property. He has opened his land to visitors in seeking public support to preserve his farm as a model of environmentally sustainable agriculture, a campaign of peaceful resistance that he describes as building a "Tent of Nations." From the hilltop where Mr. Nassar's farm is located and where visitors have access to an expansive vista, even the casual observer cannot fail to notice, surrounding the Tent of Nations, a landscape that offers a metaphor of the difficulties facing Mr. Nassar and innumerable other Palestinian landowners.

Gazing north by northwest, the visitor encounters a landscape anchored by two townships, with vastly different architectural attributes and contrasting visual rhythms (fig. 19). In the foreground is the Palestinian agricultural town of Naḥḥālīn, its built-up area organized in a seemingly random but altogether organic pattern of building forms. Ottoman records reveal the town's existence at the time of the Ottoman conquest in 1516, but its origins are much older. To the north, perched on a hilltop above Naḥḥālīn, is the Israeli settlement of Beitar Illit, standing almost fortresslike, its highly planned built forms organized in linear and semicircular rows. Although the settlement boasts origins in "the era of the Second Temple 2,000 years ago," its regularized suburban geometry testifies to its modern pedigree dating to

1988. The differences in the visible attributes of these two communities also reflect very divergent fortunes. Beitar Illit is one of the two fastest-growing Israeli settlements, its current population of 45,000 projected to more than double to over 96,000 residents on an expanding footprint of land. Naḥḥālīn, by contrast, is experiencing a trajectory in the opposite direction. In 1967, Naḥḥālīn's farmers had access to roughly 15,000 dunums of land, but since that time the town has lost much of its farmland, including 1,500 dunums seized by the state of Israel for construction of the nearby Jewish settlements, primarily Beitar Illit (Applied Research Institute 2010, 17–18).

Such a landscape, marked by these two widely differentiated types of settlement, is commonly observable throughout the Palestinian West Bank and inside Israel itself, but observation alone limits what can be learned about the meaning of these built forms on the land. When we probe beyond direct observation, this landscape reveals a story of how a geometrically patterned order has come to dominate the land, constantly expanding its footprint on the land surface while forcing those from communities like Naḥḥālīn into ever smaller, more restricted and enclosed territorial spaces. How this landscape has emerged—how places such as Naḥḥālīn and Beitar Illit have become "neighbors"—and the meaning of this neighborly relationship is the subject of what follows.

SIX

Palestinian Landscapes

LANDHOLDING AND TENANCY IN
HISTORIC PALESTINE

IF WE ARE TO BELIEVE HERODOTUS, often called the "Father of History," Palestine had a definable geography, and the Palestinian people a recognizable identity, by the time the author of *The Histories* (ca. 440 B.C.E.) had written his enduring account of the Greco-Persian wars (Mohammed 2005, 87–88). Describing the Mediterranean coast south of Phoenicia down to Egypt, Herodotus writes that this area "is all known as Palestine" and "belongs to the Syrians known as Palestinians" (Herodotus 440 B.C.E., 472, 205). Later, during the tenth century C.E., one of the earliest Arab geographers, the Jerusalemite known as al-Muqaddasi, made similar observations. In a work considered one of the greatest early geographical treatises on the Middle East, *The Best Divisions for Knowledge of the Regions* (985), al-Muqaddasi emphasized the attributes of Palestine as a region with clear geographical boundaries, and "Palestinian" as a recognizable identity associated with its inhabitants (al-Muqaddasi 985, 85, 132, 139, 338; Mohammed 2005, 90).

While Palestine has an ancient pedigree, its modern contours were shaped most decisively by the Ottoman Empire, which seized control of the territory in 1516 and, with the exception of a brief period from 1831 to 1840, exercised sovereignty until the British takeover in 1917. Throughout the period of Ottoman rule, Palestine was a part of Greater Syria, and by the mid-sixteenth century Ottoman rulers had incorporated Palestine administratively into the empire by organizing it into subdistricts, or *sanjaqs*, affiliated with the primary district of Damascus. During the next three hundred years the Ottomans periodically altered these divisions, until in the nineteenth century the *Tanzimat* reforms resulted in an administrative reorganization of the empire, including the area of Greater Syria. In this reorganization, north coastal Palestine was incorporated into the vilayet of Beirut, the north mountain area was made part of the vilayet of Damascus, and the southern portion of Palestine was incorporated into a new administrative district known as the Mutasarrifate of Jerusalem, the latter forming the bulk of what is Palestine today (Abu-Manneh 1999; Pappe 2010, 9).

Ottoman records reveal that at the time of the conquest of 1516, most Palestinians resided in roughly five hundred villages, small to medium-sized settlements that anchored the primary economic activity of Ottoman Palestine, agriculture (Brawer 1990, 169; Inalcik 1994, 45). Although Palestine counted several urban centers—Jerusalem, Hebron, Gaza, Jaffa, Nablus, Ramle, and Safed—even these cities included large tracts of farmland near their built-up cores that engaged many urban residents in agricultural activities (Cohen and Lewis 1978, 19; Brawer 1990, 170). In this way, urban-based production and trade were tied to commodities deriving from the land such as grain and olive oil, which elevated agriculture to a position of primacy in local networks of commerce and industry (Pappe 2004, 18). Agriculture also dominated long-distance networks of industry and trade, bringing even small villages into communication with more distant Palestinian towns, with dominant regional trade centers such as Damascus and Cairo, and even with areas far beyond Egypt and Greater Syria (Doumani 1995). As the foundation of these rural-urban relationships, land assumed the dominant role in Palestinian economic life.

With land as the primary source of production in the Palestinian economy, Ottoman sovereignty and legal doctrine were the basic foundations of Palestinian land tenure (Mundy and Saumarez Smith 2007, 3). Crafted by imperial legal scholars and jurists, or muftis, Ottoman land law refined the inherited legacy of Islamic law by developing a system of landholding that elevated three primary actors: the Ottoman state, the peasant cultivator, and the tax-collecting intermediary (Issawi 1982, 135). From the interplay of these three groups emerged the so-called *miri* system of Ottoman landholding and tenure (the term *miri* coming from *amiryyah,* meaning princely or of the emirs) (Inalcik 1994, 120). Although the miri system continued to evolve over the four-hundred-year reign of the Ottomans, in its broad outlines, small cultivators, forming the vast bulk of the Palestinian population, possessed legal rights of usufruct on state-owned land. The surplus they produced was given over as a type of rent/tax to the state as overlord, but owing to the weak reach of Ottoman rule in Greater Syria, tax collection was the domain of local elites acting on behalf of the Ottoman sovereign. These intermediaries sent a portion of the revenue collected from cultivators to their state overlord and retained a portion for themselves. Cultivators, for their part, had a legal right to use miri land as long as they fulfilled their fiscal obligations (Mundy and Saumarez Smith 2007, 14). Moreover, through the institution of the village and local village control, cultivators forged a unique system of communal tenure known as *mushā*, which helped spread the risks of subsistence agriculture among members of the village collective while empowering cultivators with a system of control over cropping practices in the fields (Atran 1986, 277). Thus, while rights to land in the miri system derived from the law as a rule-making text, the law did not operate in a social vacuum. Rights to land emerged from the interplay of the law, administrators interpreting and enforcing legal codes, and especially cultivators seeking to create their own best practices on the land (Mundy and Saumarez Smith 2007, 7).

This chapter recounts the evolution of land tenure on the Palestinian landscape. Although this story begins with older Islamic notions of rights to land, the focus of this chapter is the Ottoman system of miri landholding. The broad themes that follow, then, include the coevolution of the miri system and the *mushā* adaptations to it in Palestine; early reforms in this system with respect to landholding and taxation and their effects on the Palestinian cultivator and the *mushā* system of tenure; and the Ottoman land reforms of 1858, which created a basis for Zionist newcomers to gain a legal foothold on the land from which they would eventually remake the Palestinian landscape.

ISLAMIC NOTIONS OF RIGHTS TO LAND

Landholding and tenancy in Ottoman Palestine derived many of its basic principles from Islamic law. According to the Qur'an, God alone was lord of the world and its material attributes: "to God belongs all that is in heaven and on the earth." Human beings were but temporary stewards of worldly goods needed for life; what they possessed for their material needs was essentially granted to them by God (Granott 1952, 85).

Within this framework of holy versus worldly, Islam by the late seventh century had crafted two criteria for entitlement to land. The first was "conquest" (Shehadeh 1982, 83). As stated by the Caliph Umar (r. 634–44), lands acquired by force became the property of the community of conquerors, while dominium *(raqaba)* over conquered lands was vested with the community, or *ummah Muhammadiyeh* (Joseph 1998–99, 114; Inalcik 1994, 103–4). The other principle that conferred rights to land focused on the idea of "reclamation"—in other words, reclaiming or improving land through cultivation (Shehadeh 1982, 83; Joseph 1998–99, 116). From the first principle emerged the idea of outright ownership; the second conferred rights of use.

Although these two principles appeared to derive from different foundations and confer different rights, they were related. Early Islamic law conceded that the lands of the Muslim conquest were inhabited by indigenous peasants who, prior to Islam, had cultivated land through customary rights of use. Therefore, early Islamic jurists insisted that the use rights of the cultivator had to be respected, but they qualified this notion by arguing that those rights ultimately derived from rights of ownership vested in the conqueror, who assumed the power of rent-gathering over the indigenous population (Inalcik 1994, 104). On the basis of this principle, indigenous cultivators required permission from the community of conquerors—the true owners— to undertake improvements and stake a claim to land. In other words, rights to land stemming from reclamation derived from the right to land through conquest (Joseph 1998–99, 116). These principles framed two distinct ideas about land ownership, one collective vested in the state, the other private and vested in the individual or the family.

During the early period of Muslim rule, Islamic legal theorists developed a third key principle that lay between conquest and reclamation, a special category of land designed specifically to finance "pious" activities. Although the early Islamic community sought to promote Islam in this way, most notably by building mosques, it accepted the need to provide certain public services as a prerequisite for a healthy society. Consequently, activities such as promoting education, caring for the infirm, building roads and bridges, and establishing places of rest for travelers and traders, though essentially public services, were conceived as pious activities (Gaudiosi 1988, 1233). As a consequence, piety and the provision of public goods and services became linked in Islamic jurisprudence. What emerged to finance these pious activities was a special instrument known as the *waqf,* or "Islamic trust," by which private persons would provide a service and receive some benefit in return (Kuran 2001, 842).

Within the waqf system, a person providing a public service placed the proceeds of a revenue-bearing asset into a trust as a source of funding for the service in question. Islamic law stipulated that such endowments be funded by an immovable asset: *land* (Kuran 2001, 846). Hence, village lands assumed a prominent economic role in the provision of public goods and services, with urban land and even entire towns such as Tulkarm becoming waqfs (al-Salim 2011, 65). Land placed in a waqf trust was held in perpetuity for the purpose of extracting revenue from it to fund these pious and public endeavors. As stipulated in Islamic law, the person converting land to a waqf for such a reason received compensation by being entitled to shelter some or all of his or her remaining property from taxes (Kuran 2001, 842). In this way, the waqf system, while encouraging the provision of public goods, enabled land to be changed in status to a tax-exempt asset, thereby shrinking the revenue base of the community, an issue that would continue to plague the heirs to the Islamic community in Palestine, the Ottoman Empire.

FROM ISLAM TO EMPIRE: NOTIONS OF OTTOMAN LANDHOLDING

When the Ottomans assumed sovereignty over vast areas of the Middle East, they inherited these Islamic traditions as the basis for rights to land. As the empire evolved, however, sultanic law reshaped Islamic law through legal codes compiled in the *Mecelle,* and in the process the Ottoman state crafted its own institutions of landholding and tenancy (Inalcik 1994, 104; Sluglett and Farouk-Sluglett, 1984: 410). In distinguishing between land possessed by right of conquest and entitlement to land by reclamation, Islamic legal theory established two broad categories of land, *ushr* and *kharaj* (Lewis 1979, 115; Ahmed 1980, 78–82). As the precursor to what in the Ottoman system became known as as *mülk,* ushr was roughly akin to freehold land belonging to those who had converted to and fought for Islam, or to land of Jews and Christians who had kept their faith but submitted to the Muslim conquerors. Kharaj, in contrast, referred to all other lands not in freehold belonging to the Islamic community that had been secured by conquest and was by far the more extensive of the two categories. The Ottomans retained this distinction but modified the notion of land possessed by the community, developing what was effectively a new classification: land owned by the state (Lewis 1979, 115). This notion of state-owned land is best understood by reference to Crown land in English land law, where the monarch is the legal owner of all land in the realm, but the land is effectively at the disposal of tenants who hold their land either directly or indirectly from the Crown. In Palestine under the Ottomans, the Sultanate was equivalent to the Crown, as the ultimate owner of all conquered land (Shehadeh 1982, 90). This resulted in two primary categories of land within the Ottoman Empire: mülk (freehold) and miri (state-owned but functioning as common land).

In the Ottoman context, mülk landholders possessed an entitlement corresponding to two sets of rights. While on the one hand they possessed the right of use *(tasarruf)* typically associated with miri land, mülk landholders also had close to an absolute right of possession *(raqaba)*, akin to severalty in English land law. As in the pre-Ottoman period, land in mülk ownership during the time of sultans comprised a small fraction of land in Palestine. In cities, mülk was confined to land set aside for dwellings along with areas appurtenant to dwellings for private gardens. In rural villages, this land was supplemented by certain cultivated orchards and gardens in immediate proximity to the built-up village core (Sluglett and Farouk-Sluglett 1984, 410).

Miri land, in contrast, was owned by the Ottoman state and comprised between 87 and 90 percent of agricultural land in the Empire (Inalcik 1994, 105). Early Ottoman religious and legal theorists, most notably Sheikh ul-Islam Ebussuud, the most revered religious figure in the realm (d. 1574), recognized the eminent domain of the state on such land. As the author of a definitive commentary on Ottoman land law, Ebussuud sought to clarify two important issues of the miri land regime: the status and legal persona of the cultivator, and the legal basis on which miri land generated tax revenues for the Ottoman state (Inalcik 1994, 112–13).

Under Suleyman I (r. 1520–66), the Ottomans gave priority to agriculture as the primary economic activity in the empire, recognizing in the cultivator a critical foundation of fiscal solvency. As a result, Ottoman administrators promoted a landholding system that they believed would enhance agricultural output that was taxable while providing cultivators with a secure place on the land (Inalcik 1994, 45). In equating the state's fiscal interests with a vibrant agricultural economy, state authorities were willing to entrust cultivators on miri land with durable rights of use but insisted that such rights derived from the sultan, thus preserving the state's ultimate ownership of the land (Inalcik 1994, 106). At times, this use right created certain anomalies, in that olive and fruit trees planted by cultivators on miri land were considered property of the cultivator, while the land itself belonged to the state (Islamoglu 2000, 31). This anomaly between state ownership of the ground and private ownership of what was on the ground invariably enabled cultivators to extend their nominal use rights into de facto proprietorship on the land (Joseph 2012, 83–84; Doumani 1995, 157–58). Over time, such practices evolved as rights of *custom* (Inalcik 1994, 106; Seikaly 1984, 404; al-Salim 2011, 65). Thus, similar to tenant farmers in England, Palestinian cultivators, despite not owning their land as freehold, gained customary rights to their holdings by sufferance (Granott 1952, 294).

By the seventeenth century, customary rights of use had evolved into an intermediate type of tenure with elements of tenancy alongside elements of proprietorship (Seikaly 1984, 404). Although technically cultivators could not sell their holdings or bequeath the land they cultivated to heirs, in practice they developed ways of acquiring heritable use rights on land that they were able to pass on (Joseph 2007, 33; Islamoglu 2000, 17). In many cases they even devised ways of buying and selling rights of usufruct and were able to register such transactions with local judges (Inalcik 1994, 112). In this way, cultivators learned to shape the system of landholding and promote their interests by establishing practices on the ground that became part of a system of customary rights to land.

Despite this evolving notion of usufruct, rights of cultivators on miri land under the Ottomans were always conditional. As long as cultivators continued to plant and make improvements, they retained the right to use the land. If, however, they left land untended for three years, the land reverted to the state. More importantly, in an affirmation of their tenuous status, cultivators of miri land and their family members faced harsh sanctions for abandoning their holdings, a subject of intense debate among Ottoman religious and legal theorists beginning in the 1600s (Mundy and Saumarez Smith 2007, 31–37). In the end, however, cultivators could be returned to their lands by force or, if not returned, made liable for the taxes owed on the land (Mundy 2010, 400–403).

In addition to these stipulations on cultivators, the Ottomans reserved special rights for land that was "plowed," which in Ottoman legal parlance meant cultivated with grain (Inalcik 1994, 106). In contrast to olive and fruit orchards, grain fields on miri land had special status aimed at protecting land critical to provisioning the Ottoman military with food for their imperial campaigns (Islamoglu 2000, 31). Accordingly, by the early 1700s Ottoman jurists had strengthened the claims of cultivators on land planted with grain by affirming their rights to it on the basis of labor invested in plots of plowed land, and not simply from general possession and use (Mundy and Saumarez Smith 2007, 37). Consequently, the Palestinian cultivator of grain fields secured rights to land similar to what Locke had outlined in his labor-driven theory of landed property rights.

Outside the boundaries of freehold mülk land and state-owned miri land, one other important category of land existed in the Ottoman system: land considered "dead," or *mawat* land. Borrowing from the Roman law idea of *terra nullius,* Ottoman jurists defined mawat as empty land without owners or land unsuited to cultivation owing to topography (Inalcik 1994, 120). Land abandoned by cultivators and left empty for long periods was also considered land in waste. Such land, however, presented opportunities for taxation, which Ottoman administrators continuously sought to exploit. In some cases, the state created tenancies on such land for peasant cultivators who would improve it and be taxed. In other cases, the sultan made grants of mawat land to elites for reclamation; they in turn would rent the land to cultivators while turning over some of the rent to the state. In still other cases, the state granted the land to elites to create a waqf that would fund religious or other public activity, again with a portion of the revenue accruing to the Treasury. Mawat land thus figured prominently in Ottoman discourses about land improvement and ways of augmenting the state Treasury. Following the formation of the state of Israel, significantly, mawat land would become the flashpoint of a controversial issue regarding land ownership, when the new nation began to seek legal foundations for reclassifying land in Palestine as Israeli state land (Inalcik 1994, 120–22).

TENANCY AND TAXATION

Under the empire, the landholding system assumed its attributes not only from the categories of land but also from two defining institutions, tenancy and tax collection, and the interplay of cultivators, the state, and tax-collecting intermediaries (Issawi 1982, 135; Inalcik 1994, 120).

Existing on the vast holdings of miri land in Palestine were mostly small peasant farmers—*fellaheen*—linked to the land in tenancies constituting the primary institution on the Palestinian landscape (Granott 1952, 288–89). Making up 80 percent of the population in Ottoman Palestine (Doumani 1995, 27), these cultivators developed a relationship with the state that elevated the status of the tax-collecting intermediary who stood between the Ottoman Treasury and the fellaheen. Like other landholding systems, the Palestinian cultivator incurred an obligation to pay the landowner—the Ottoman state—a fee for the use right to Ottoman-owned land. In Palestine, the fee or tithe was levied predominantly on the output from the land, with some tithes also levied on certain inputs (Cosgel 2005, 573–74). Unlike in England, where land ownership had devolved from kings to feudal lords who assumed much of the responsibility for paying taxes to the Crown but had legal rights to collect fees or exact services from tenants to finance such obligations, the Ottomans relied on a system of third-party intermediaries for the collection of revenue on state land from peasant cultivators. This system of rural taxation was known as the *timar* system (Sluglett and Farouk-Sluglett 1984, 410–11; Doukhan 1938, 97).

During the early period of Ottoman rule, administrators divided the empire, including Palestine, into fiefs or timars—land grants awarded to military officers who had helped extend Ottoman sovereignty through conquest (Lewis 1979, 121). While in the first instance the timar corresponded to a level of revenue expected from the land grant, the timar had a territorial component usually consisting of the land associated with a village or part of a village, or in some cases more than one village. In return for the grant, the timar holder assumed responsibility for collecting taxes from the land under his control. Prevailing during the sixteenth century, this system enabled Ottoman rulers to collect taxes from the empire's more outlying domains. Surveyors sent by Ottoman authorities to the countryside recorded names of village households along with their farmland holdings and from this information assigned a tax assessment for the village, which the timar holder then collected, usually in partnership with a village *sheikh* or headman, who solicited local families to fulfill the village tax quota (Cosgel 2005, 570; Inalcik 1994, 135, 138; Singer 1994, 46–54; Hoblos 2010, 117).[1] In practice, the timar holder demanded from villagers revenues greater than what was required by the Treasury, sharing the overage with local partners in a system rife with corruption and exploitation of small cultivators (Firestone 1990, 112). At the same time, timar holders not only levied assessments on village cultivators at whatever level they could force upon them, but they also emerged as creditors to the fellaheen when the latter were unable to pay what was demanded. In Palestine by the mid-sixteenth century, as a consequence, the fellaheen had become the most indebted group in Greater Syria, their economic position constantly deteriorating in ongoing cycles of taxation, indebtedness, and outright extortion (Rafeq 2008, 125).

Despite certain advantages of the timar system for Ottoman administrators, in the early 1600s the corruption endemic to this institution forced the Ottomans to replace timar holders with local notables who would bid for the tax collecting contract (Hütteroth 1973, 9; Lewis 1979, 123–24). Such were the origins of the institution known as *tax farming*. At its core were individuals bidding on the right to "farm" the taxes of a given area for a fixed period, often relying on the help of a village sheikh (Inalcik 1994, 65). As in the timar system, the tax farmer would send the contractually specified portion of this revenue to the Ottoman Treasury, pay off the village headman, and keep the rest (Pamuk 2004, 16). As a result, tax farming was prone to the same types of corruption as the timar system, including merciless exploitation of fellaheen (Kark 1997, 50). Although by 1695 the Ottomans attempted to replace short-term bid contracts with longer commitments by tax collectors, a reform known as *malikane,* tax farming as an institutionalized means of exploiting Palestinian cultivators remained little changed (Cohen 1973, 180; Granott 1952, 57). From this crucible of tax farmers allied with local elites and a revenue-hungry Treasury emerged a new institution on the Palestinian landscape that transformed landholding and tenancy both: the large privately owned landed estate.

LANDED ESTATES

Although large-scale landed proprietorships in Palestine had pre-Ottoman origins, the widespread appearance of this institution dates from the mid- to late 1700s, becoming even more pronounced during the nineteenth century. In addition to the tax farmer, a second and arguably stronger stimulus for this rural phenomenon originated not in the countryside but in towns. Urban notables who accumulated fortunes from commerce and industry, finding the Ottoman state, owing to perpetual fiscal difficulty, a willing seller of its miri lands, emerged as a new class of buyers of large landed property. At the same time, these urban families, along with their wealthy rural counterparts—not a few of whom had served as creditors of impoverished fellaheen—managed to acquire the land of their destitute customers when the latter were unable to pay their debts. And so a gradual transfer began of land from small cultivators into the hands of more wealthy elites, both rural and urban.

What resulted from the tendency of the state and small cultivators to sell, and the wealthy to acquire, was the proliferation of large estates by some of Palestine's most illustrious families. These included the Sursuk in the Jezreel Valley, the Kouri from Haifa, the el-Husseini from Jerusalem, the Abd el-Hadi and Touqan from Nablus and Jenin, the Badran and later al-Jayyusi and Hanoun from Tulkarem, the al-Farouki from Ramle, and the Shawa from Gaza (Sluglett and Farouk-Sluglett 1984, 413–14; Granott 1952, 80–82). Some of these families, notably the Sursuk, lived in Beirut and were absentee landowners. During the nineteenth century, therefore, as these families acquired more land, a profound transformation occurred on the Palestinian landscape, in which land became concentrated among a small class of private owners. By the early twentieth century, 144 large estates possessed 38 percent—3.1 million dunums of the estimated 8.2 million dunums (four dunums equals one acre)—of arable land in Palestine (Granott 1952, 39). This land transfer from nominally miri to private owners was one of the most pivotal events in the agrarian history of Palestine, not only because the land maintained by the Palestinian *fellah* generally decreased (Granott 1952, 38), but also because the transfer established the basis on which subsequent land sales to the Zionist movement would occur.

Paradoxically, the transfer of land to large estates did not result in large-scale, capital-intensive farms (Granott 1952, 40). In contrast to England, farms on estates in Palestine remained largely unconsolidated and continued to be farmed by small cultivators, some of whom had been freeholders but who had sold their holdings, effectively becoming tenants. Even as a tenant, however, the Palestinian cultivator still believed himself to be a proprietor on his land, despite paying a rent to a representative of the landowner who, like the tax collector, appeared once a year or so to take either a portion of the crop or cash as the price for the tenant's right of occupancy and use (Granott 1952, 288). Thus, the change to private landlordism did little to alter the status of the cultivator.

Yet despite the expansion of privately owned landed estates, expulsions of cultivators from these lands were rare (Granott 1952, 288). The proliferation of estates, moreover, led to a more widespread system of private land ownership and a more vibrant land market than had prevailed during earlier periods of the miri system. Nevertheless, this dual condition of private ownership and a robust land market exposed cultivators to new uncertainties and pressures for change. At the same time, cultivators in Palestine had recourse to an institution that helped them negotiate the possibility of exploitation and contributed a collective character to the landscape. This institution was *mushā* tenure.

THE CULTIVATOR AND MUSHĀ TENURE

Despite a resemblance to earlier nomadic and Bedouin practices of common pasturage, mushā evolved as a system of landholding and tenure compatible with village-based, sedentary agriculture (Atran 1986, 275). In this system, village cultivators shared rights to village land in collective ownership rather than owning separate individual plots (Fischbach 2000, 38–39). Drawing on notions of co-ownership and partnership that were already deeply ingrained in the agrarian culture of Palestine and Greater Syria, fellaheen adopted mushā tenure in the belief that collective management and pooling of risk were effective offsets to an agrarian environment rife with uncertainty for the small cultivator (Firestone 1990, 125). While estimates vary of how much Palestinian land was mushā, in practice very little agrarian land in Ottoman Palestine fell outside this system (Granott 1952, 174; Firestone 1990, 91).

Although mushā tenure varied by region and village, the system possessed two basic attributes that gave it the status of an institution for allocating rights to land (Firestone 1990, 92).

First, in the mushā village, use rights to land were held in collective ownership by members of the village community (Fischbach 2000, 38). At the same time, villagers did not actually own the land, but instead owned *shares* in the use rights to land in the village (Schaebler 2000, 246; Firestone 1990, 105–6).[2] Through village self-government, these collectively owned use rights were apportioned in shares called *ahsahm* (sing. *sahm*) and distributed to villagers, usually by family groups (Schaebler 2000, 246; Nadan 2003, 321). In this way, the mushā village resembled the English common field village with its collective decision-making and allocations of use rights on village land (Firestone 1990, 95). Even British administrators during the Mandate often equated the mushā system to English common fields (Bunton 2007, 9).

Second, the mushā system allowed the redistribution and equalization of shares of village land at one-to-five-year intervals through decisions of village self-government (Schaebler 2000, 244; Firestone 1990, 95; Atran 1986, 271, 277). In practice, the cultivated village environs were divided into large sections, usually numbering four quadrants corresponding to north, south, east, and west, with each individual quadrant roughly uniform in terms of soil type, topography, drainage, and access to and from the village (Firestone 1990, 92; Patai 1949, 439). Villagers were allotted shares in the various sections by family lineage—in essence, according to the capacity of each family to cultivate a certain number of shares, as determined by the number of animal-drawn plows or male laborers the family could mobilize (Firestone 1990, 92). Within family groups, the right to cultivate a share of mushā land was heritable and handed down from father to son. In another similarity to English common fields, shares of land did not accrue to families and individuals in single consolidated holdings but were instead scattered throughout the larger sections of village land (Patai 1949, 439; Granott 1952, 202)—further affirmation of the equalizing impulses of the mushā village community and English common field villages (Firestone 1990, 104). Even the plots themselves bore a certain resemblance to the long, narrow selions of English common fields (Granott 1952, 208). Boundaries separating these strips were marked only informally owing to periodic redistribution, imbuing landscapes with a largely open character. Because of redistribution, too, the cultivator generally did not work the same land over time, but moved around as shares were reallocated (Nadan 2003, 321).

While scattered land holdings reflected the need to equalize cropping risks across the community, the bounty harvested on an individual holding was not common property but belonged to the cultivator (Atran 1986, 275). Mushā tenure in Palestine was thus a mixed form of property, broadly comparable to the English common fields, where the harvest on individual strips of land belonged to the cultivator but communal decision-making prevailed. In both systems, collective forms of management coexisted with individual proprietorship over land (Schölch 1984, 142).

Although fundamentally an economic system of landholding, mushā tenure was also a cultural system embedded in the communal impulses of agrarian village life (Schaebler 2000, 288; Granott 1952, 231). At the core of this village-based communal culture was the extended Palestinian family group or *hamula,* which provided economic and social support to family members when the need arose. Such needs included the collective building of homes, communal payment of the tax on village lands, and village assistance during the harvest (Doumani 1995, 27–29). Because each village was home to a small number of families and derived much of its identity from those families, such collective support was only logical. The mushā system of land tenure was one more aspect of that cooperation.

This cultural foundation of mushā tenure is what enabled Palestinian cultivators to develop their own idea of moral economics, that elevated the right to use land for subsistence (Khalidi 1997, 99). This moral right, in turn, gave the cultivator a sense of being anchored to the landscape. Although the legal status of the cultivator was constantly evolving under the Ottomans, by the seventeenth century the state tacitly accepted the right of the cultivator to a place on the land (Mundy and Saumarez Smith 2007, 28–37). This right in turn, in addition to being part of Ottoman jurisprudence, was embedded culturally in mushā tenure and the Palestinian village as the central unit of agricultural life. Consequently, in contrast to the so-called "rational peasant" with preferences for markets, personal accumulation, and individual rights of landholding, Palestinian villagers operated in a cultural setting of collective and communal preferences. It is not that the Palestinian villager was an economically irrational actor; rather, the village setting enabled cultural preferences to shape rational economic choices as mushā tenure offered villagers a seemingly more viable and culturally familiar way of dealing with the economic vagaries of agrarian life (Schaebler 2000, 288).

LORDSHIP AND MUSHĀ TENURE

Arguably, the burden of taxes and rents on village communities in Ottoman Palestine was even more important in shaping the economic fortunes of cultivators and influencing their preferences for mushā tenure than the uncertainties affecting crop yields and harvests. These exactions, imposed by the state and its tax-collecting intermediaries, impoverished the cultivator from an early date in the history of the empire and had driven the returns on his land to near zero (Firestone 1990, 96). The relationship of cultivators to these actors helps explain how the institution of lordship emerged in Palestine, and why cultivators adopted land redistribution as a strategy for dealing with overlords acting as representatives of the state and in their own interests (Firestone 1990, 95–96).

With the Ottoman state pressuring its tax collectors for revenues, and with tax collectors seeking to offset their obligations with ever-increasing demands on villages for owed taxes, brutal exploitation arose. At the historical moment when taxes exceeded the capacity of a village to pay, the responsible intermediary descended upon the impoverished village and offered to strike a deal, in the form of credit (Firestone 1990, 113). As part of this "bargain," notables assumed partial or even total ownership of village lands, extracting from villagers a fee for the credit advanced commensurate with a share of the village crop.

Such were the origins of what in Europe is called the institution of lordship, in which the cultivator owes a rent or services in kind to an overlord in exchange for certain protections and the right to cultivate land. In the Palestinian context, an excessive fiscal burden compelled the village community to turn to an overlord to protect them from the intrusive power of the state and ensure the continuity of agricultural use rights by cultivators on village land (Firestone 1990, 98). In this arrangement, the reassignment of landholdings to the overlord would, at least in theory, insulate the villagers from the fiscal scrutiny of the state. But the result was that the local overlord now acquired shares in the mushā village lands, thereby becoming both patron and exploiter. As patron, the notable now assumed responsibility for the tax levied on the village; as exploiter, however, he used every conceivable strong-arm tactic to extract rents and tithes from the villagers, for payment of the taxes to the state and for profit to himself (Firestone 1990, 113–14).

In practice, the reassignment of control over village land did little to alter patterns of cultivation, since local notables did not till the land (Firestone 1990, 115). Instead, lands redistributed to local notables or overlords were let to village cultivators, who maintained the same use practices as always. At no time did cultivators consider themselves other than proprietors of what they farmed, despite the land coming under the control of an overlord and despite the continued designation of the land as state property (Firestone 1990, 105, 115). Thus, while villagers were in practice little more than sharecroppers in the mushā system, they were still able to retain their customary rights as producers on the land (Sluglett and Farouk-Sluglett 1984, 410–11).

Yet in what appeared to be a system-wide problem with mushā tenure, the periodic redistribution of holdings provided little incentive for cultivators to improve their land (Stein 1984, 14). "I cannot plant a tree on my lands," explained a cultivator interviewed by British Mandate authorities in 1931, because "next year they [the trees] will have passed to another's cultivation." The farmer goes on: "I cannot fertilize my fields; another shareholder will get the benefit next year, and why should I spend a pound per bag on manure for another person's advantage? I cannot build a stable for my horse or my cattle; it will belong to another next year" (quoted in Stein 1987, 34–35).

This lack of incentive was of concern to the Ottoman Treasury as well, because it limited the expansion of crops that could be taxed. Equally problematic for the Ottoman state was the ongoing involvement of tax farmers in the collection of revenues owed to the Treasury. In response, the state launched a two-pronged effort in the 1830s to develop new incentives for cultivators and to gain direct control of agricultural tax revenue by consolidating its administrative authority and breaking the power of tax farmers (Sluglett and Farouk-Sluglett, 1984, 412–13). Part of a major reorganization known as Tanzimat, this effort culminated in the Ottoman Land Code of 1858.

As a legal text, the Ottoman Land Code can be read in two different ways. On the one hand, the Code reveals continuity with the desire on the part of the Ottoman state to regain control over the administration of land that had been usurped by intermediaries ever since the late sixteenth century. On the other, the Code represented a break with Ottoman efforts to assert control over its miri domains in that it codified rights to individual titles to land and framed new rules on inheritance. From this starting point, the Land Code is less a seamless whole and more a combination of these two divergent readings (Mundy 1994, 59–60).

Whether the Code represents continuity or disjuncture, there is little dispute that it was designed to help remedy the endemic fiscal crises of the Ottoman state by increasing tax revenues from land (Sluglett and Farouk-Sluglett 1984, 413; Warriner 1948, 17). Because the primary source of revenue in the Ottoman state was agriculture, reformers sought wholesale changes in both the system of tax collection and the patterns of land tenure in order to reassert their right to the fiscal exploitation of the agrarian economy (Zu'bi 1984, 93; Quataert 1994, 854). What emerged from the Land Code was thus twofold: fiscal reform and land reform.

The impulses for the Tanzimat reform of taxation actually began with a decree of 1838, the aim of which was the elimination of the arcane and corrupt system of tax farming and the establishment of direct collection of taxes by salaried agents of the state (Shaw 1975, 422). Although the state had difficulty implementing this objective during the next two decades, the principle nevertheless became institutionalized and was restated in the opening to chapter 3 of the Law on the Registration of Census and of Properties in the Land Code, which stipulates "that in all the provinces the apportioning, collection, and management of taxes . . . be put under such a system as to win the confidence of the people and prove advantageous to the Imperial Treasury" (*Ottoman Land Code* 1892, 120). By means of these stipulations, the Ottoman regime sought to elevate itself as the sole tax collector in order to regain prerogatives it had relinquished over the centuries to tax-farming elites (Islamoglu 2000, 28; Sluglett and Farouk-Sluglett 1984, 413).

At the same time, as the Ottomans understood, capturing tax revenue is not only dependent on efficient administration, but is a function of output levels on the land. Influenced by French physiocrats who elevated land as the primary source of wealth, early Tanzimat reformers reordered levies on its most important source of revenue, cultivated produce, consolidating them into a single levy that amounted to a 10 percent assessment on agricultural yields (Islamoglu 2000, 28; Shaw 1975, 428; Shafir 1996, 31). With this change, cultivators could expand yields and so earn more absolute income, while the state would secure more revenue from the higher aggregate output.

Yet reformers also realized that higher taxable yields fell outside the strict parameters of fiscal administration. They therefore proposed two far-reaching changes in the system of landholding meant to provide cultivators with further incentives to improve their land. First, they determined to create a landholding system of privatized spaces on the landscape—in effect, a system of individual landed property on former miri lands (Islamoglu 2000, 32–33). To this end, in its opening chapter on miri land (article 8) the Code targeted the system of mushā tenure, aiming to weaken if not undermine it completely. "The whole land of a town or village cannot be granted in its entirety to all of the inhabitants," the Code states in a rebuke to mushā tenure, "nor to one, two, or three of them. Different pieces of land are given to each inhabitant and a title deed *(tapu sened)* is given to each showing his right of possession" *(Ottoman Land Code* 1892, 8). The logic behind this eradication of mushā tenure was straightforward. With durable rights of ownership to a specific plot, the cultivator had incentive to improve the land and expand output, being now entitled to the gains deriving from his improvement, with only a portion of the additional output accruing to the state as tax. As part of this bargain, however, the cultivator-turned-owner had to register his land with Treasury officials. In theory, the cultivator would accept this bargain because it would enable him to capture the profits from land improvement, despite the tax burden. And with registration, the state would be able to monitor the land and tax it.

Second, this regime of individual landed property promised a more robust land market built on codified rights to buy, sell, mortgage, and inherit land in a system of free exchange. With such rights, cultivators had additional incentives to improve land in order to capture the enhanced value for themselves or hand it down to heirs. Together, a landscape of private holdings reinforced by a more fluid, rule-inflected land market would—in theory—remedy the problem of insufficient revenue for the Treasury and generate higher yields from agriculture.

In addition to these more general aims, the Land Code proposed two provisions for encouraging an extension in cultivated areas and thus enhancing the taxable base. The context for these provisions in the mid-nineteenth century was one of population growth and economic expansion, with the state conceding that taxation was a function of its ability to regulate and capture portions of economic activity while reinforcing and encouraging it (Islamoglu 2000, 21). In these circumstances, the desire of cultivators to open new land was inevitable. Through the reforms of the Land Code, the Treasury sought to regularize how new land was opened and so gain more control of the resulting revenue streams.

The first of these provisions was in article 78, which institutionalized one of the most critical rights of the cultivator, the right to possess land by "prescription." In the wording of the article, a person possessing and cultivating miri land for ten years without dispute "acquires a right by prescription and whether he has a valid title-deed or not the land cannot be regarded as vacant, and he shall be given a new title-deed gratis for that land" (*Ottoman Land Code* 1892, 41–42). Despite the fact that article 78 also penalized cultivators who opened miri land under conditions of dispute, its intent is clear: rights of possession are accorded to cultivators who, with appropriate permission, open new land for cultivation.

Second, and perhaps more significant, was article 103, on "dead land." Article 103 enabled anyone in need of empty or dead land for cultivation to "plough it up gratuitously," with permission from an Ottoman official, "on the condition that the legal ownership shall belong to the Treasury, and all the provisions of the law in force concerning other cultivated land are applicable to this category of land also" (*Ottoman Land Code* 1892, 54). Though promoting cultivation on land without an owner and insisting on being able to recoup the cultivation taxes in accordance with provisions in the law, article 103 emphasized that, in the end, the right of ownership on dead land remained vested in the state. This provision would have far-reaching consequences later, when the state of Israel, on becoming sovereign in Palestine, inherited the Ottoman Empire's legal legacy.

THE LAND CODE IN PRACTICE

If the primary aims of the Land Code were to break the power of local notables as tax collectors and encourage a system of private ownership on state land by eradicating mushā tenure, the law had mixed results (Quataert 1994, 854–55). Although efforts at recouping power from tax-farming local notables had begun as early as 1839 with passage of the Gulhane Decree, the

Ottomans were unable to rid themselves of their dependence on these inter-mediaries, especially in the Syrian and Palestinian provinces. Consequently, despite the stated intentions of Tanzimat to implement a more centralized and rational method for the collection of taxes, tax farming continued to prevail throughout the empire even into the early twentieth century. Moreover, the state's goal of encouraging individual land ownership was challenged by wary peasant cultivators anchored to long-standing village-based traditions of communal land tenure and the collective regulation of plowing, harvesting and grazing, not to mention the collective responsibility of paying the village's taxes (Mundy 1994, 62). Despite the seemingly explicit prohibition of the mushā system in article 8 of the Land Code, Ottoman authorities had limited success in dislodging the Palestinian cultivator from this institution. In this regard, one of the most formidable impediments to private land ownership on the rural landscape—and one of the obstacles confronting the Zionist movement in its efforts to acquire Palestinian land—was the persistence of mushā tenure and the land-equalizing mushā village throughout Palestine (Quataert 1994, 854–55).

Part of the explanation for the persistence of mushā was the heroic assump-tion of reformers that the Palestinian cultivator was a "rational peasant," an actor responding logically to the prospects of profitable gain. According to this way of thinking, peasant cultivators should be naturally inclined toward individual landed property and the supposed rewards that go with it. In prac-tice, however, the Palestinian cultivator proved far more amenable to custom and tradition than to the promise of rewards from individual title to land. Reformers, in short, miscalculated the willingness of cultivators to accept individual ownership of their land on condition that they register it with Treasury officials. As a consequence, efforts to compel peasant cultivators to register their holdings with officials of the Census and Properties throughout Greater Syria largely failed (Mundy 1994, 60). A long-standing mistrust among cultivators toward tendering any such information to Ottoman authorities did not recede because of abstract notions of rewards from indi-vidual rights to landed property. Bound by communal traditions, cultivators feared that registration with Ottoman authorities would bring them new tax burdens along with unsavory obligations such as conscription (Mundy 1994, 60–61). In the end, when confronted with change Palestinian cultivators reanchored themselves to what was culturally familiar (Schaebler 2000).

In what emerged as an unintended consequence of the reform, cultivators, instead of registering their land to gain title as was expected, sought the protection of local notables as an offset to what they feared was an unwanted intrusion by the state into their lives (Mundy 1994, 61; Khalidi 1997, 95). For their part, local notables, both rural and urban, exploited this fear, offering themselves to cultivators as proxies for registering cultivators' land while offering to pay the taxes on the land or extending loans for other forms of peasant indebtedness. In this way, local elites managed to broaden their leverage over both the cultivator and the state as newly reconstituted tax farmers, who in the logic of the reform were supposed to have been eradicated (Shafir 1996, 35).

Nevertheless, for all of the difficulties encountered by Ottoman officials in compelling cultivators to register their holdings, some accepted the bargain, most notably in the Jerusalem corridor, where no large landowner registered land in place of cultivators who actually farmed the holding (Quataert 1994, 860). First-hand accounts of witnesses such as Samuel Bergheim of the Palestine Exploration Fund, for example, testify to the phenomenon of registration in a Palestinian mushā village, including some of its contradictory attributes. "The lands are divided by an Imperial Commissioner into various portions and given to individual villagers," writes Bergheim. Cultivators "receive title-deeds for individual ownerships, and each one is at liberty to sell his portion to whoever he pleases." Bergheim added, however, that this process engendered resistance on the part of villagers when they realized that registration meant taxation (Bergheim 1894). Nevertheless, the fact that such a high percentage of land in Palestine remained in mushā tenure suggests that the Ottomans' success in registering land was partial at best (Kark 1997, 56). Where registration by peasant holders did occur, it tended to be in the hill and mountain regions, while in the coastal region large landowners assumed title to the land of small cultivators and consolidated this inventory into estates. The large consolidated properties that had registration documents attached to them would be particularly attractive to the Zionists aiming to purchase land.

Another complication was the fact that Ottoman officials had in place only a very limited cadastral system for measuring and mapping land in Palestine, despite the intent to implement such a system as outlined in the Law on the Registration of Census and Properties in the Land Code.[3] Absent such a system, the Imperial Treasury was unable to connect individuals to plots of land for purposes of registration. Administratively, without a cadastral map to make the landscape "legible," the Ottoman state was effectively "blind," explaining in part why the state became dependent again on intermediaries as tax collectors (Scott 1998; Craib 2004). Although the Ottomans did attempt a cadastral survey in the Acre district of northern Palestine, it was extremely limited, with coverage of only 10 percent of the area (Kark 1997, 56–58). For the most part, there was little cadastral mapping in Ottoman Palestine (Doukhan 1938, 99).

Although transformation of cultivators into freeholders and eradication of mushā tenure may have been limited, the Land Code was arguably more successful in its aim of institutionalizing an open market in land. The Ottomans employed two mechanisms in pursuit of this aim. First, they extended and liberalized one of the most important elements of any land market, the system of heritable rights to land. This change encouraged families to improve what they owned, since the land would remain in their hands (Shafir 1996, 33). Second, and perhaps more significantly, the Land Code, together with provisions added to it over the next ten years, institutionalized an earlier set of reforms passed in the 1856 Reform Decree (the *Islahat Fermani*) that allowed "foreigners" to buy land. Prior to this change, foreigners were able to purchase land in Palestine only in exceptional circumstances and with a special *firman* from the sultan (Kark 1984, 359). The Land Code and its supplements rendered land more freely exchangeable without discrimination and gave land a more durable status as an asset that could be freely alienated by the owner. These changes, in turn, would help the Zionist movement in its quest beginning in the 1880s to acquire private Palestinian land as well as lands of the sultan himself.

If the Land Code registered some degree of success in promoting a market in land, the market at the same time fostered certain impacts unforeseen (Shafir 1996, 34–35). In seeking to liberalize the land market, reformers exploited a change already under way by the late eighteen and early nineteenth centuries: the acquisition of what was nominally miri land in the countryside by urban and rural notables and the establishment of large landed estates (Doumani 1992, 12). What ensued from the more "fluid inventory of land," therefore, was a concentration of wealthy elite buyers anxious to acquire large tracts of land (Kark 1984, 373; Shafir 1996, 34). And in this push to gain a stronger foothold as large landowners, notables, both rural and urban, had help from an unlikely source: the Palestinian fellah. Wary of coming under the control of the Ottoman administrator and fearing the resulting tax burden, the cultivator, despite being a newly entitled individual holder of his land, became a seller to local notables who offered to free the cultivator of his burden. In the process, the system of landholding in the aftermath of the Land Code became more concentrated as notables expanded their holdings and joined the growing ranks of estate owners, a phenomenon also crucial for the purchasing aspirations of the Zionist movement (Shafir 1996, 33–36).

In the end, three important and in many ways unintended outcomes resulted from the Land Code and its aftermath (Shafir 1996, 33–36). First, tax farming did not meet its demise but was instead resurrected in conjunction with the expanded socioeconomic influence of a large landed elite. Second, land ownership became more, not less concentrated, alongside the consolidation of a more entrenched landed elite, many of whom were absentee landowners from the cities. Finally, and perhaps most significantly, the mushā system, far from being eliminated, survived, although the pressures pushing the landholding system toward freehold were undeniable and the mushā system began a slow but gradual process of transformation. This transformation accelerated after the defeat of the Ottoman Empire in 1916–17 and the assumption of power in Palestine by British authorities after the Balfour Declaration (1917).

By the time of the British Mandate, an estimated 70 percent of village lands in Palestine were still in mushā tenure (Patai 1949, 441). Influenced by enduring ideas about "improvement" and "progress" and convinced that the enclosure of common land in England provided for the common good, British colonial administrators in Palestine had only contempt for the mushā system (Bunton 2007, 8–11). Arguably the most important of these colonial figures was Sir Ernest Dowson, an engineer and surveyor whose ideas on land administration—and harsh criticism of the mushā system—provided the foundation for British land policy in Palestine (Forman 2002, 61, 63).

The focus of Dowson's reform was the small Palestinian cultivator and the mushā system of land tenure (Biger 1994, 196). Though conceding that certain traditional land rights had to be part of the reform process, Dowson was convinced of the superiority of Western concepts of land ownership and the notion of the landscape as a parcelized grid of individual blocks of property (Forman 2002, 62–63). In his "Preliminary Study of Land Tenure in Palestine" from 1925, Dowson remarked caustically that the mushā rotation of occupants on the land was incompatible with good husbandry. "A temporary occupant will aim at extracting all he can from the land and will put nothing into it," he wrote (Dowson 1925, 18). Influenced by England's past experience with land held in common, Dowson and other officials of the Mandate government believed that "enclosure and partition of the common fields" was what was needed to help the Palestinian fellah (Bunton 2007, 10). Consequently, Dowson was intent on rationalizing the system of landholding by creating blocks of property that could be surveyed and registered with the Mandate Land Authority. Indeed, this agency succeeded in surveying and assigning official title on 5.6 million dunums of land, or roughly 25 percent of the total land area of Palestine (Forman 2002, 65).

The British policy of weakening the mushā system represented a victory for the Zionist movement. Mushā tenure, with its collective authority over land and aversion to being registered in blocks of individual private ownership, insulated large areas of village land from the land market, making the Zionist aim of acquiring land in Palestine through purchase more difficult to achieve. The Mandate policy of surveying and establishing private titles for land, however, challenged the collective nature of land management, thereby "freeing" land of its constraints as a tradable commodity and enabling it to be transferred more easily from Palestinian to Jewish owners (Forman 2002, 65). Yet British policy could not force such transfers. Even by 1947, Zionists had secured through purchase only about 8–10 percent of the arable land in Palestine, where the rural geography was still dominated by the Palestinian agricultural village and aspects of mushā tenure. The Zionist movement continued to confront the seemingly intractable obstacle of an agricultural population firmly anchored to the land and embedded in an agrarian-based economic system of production and trade linking villages to towns and cities. Only after the Zionists assumed sovereignty in what emerged as the state of Israel did this situation change.

SEVEN

From Imagination to Redemption

CRAFTING A HEBREW LANDSCAPE
ON PALESTINIAN LAND

FOR MUCH OF TWO MILLENNIA, an imagined geography resonated within Jewish culture. Through religious rituals, stories and legends, and metaphors in everyday speech, Jews conceived of themselves as refugees living in exile while yearning for a landscape distant from the diaspora where they had once flourished (Lockman 1996, 22; Zerubavel 1995, 16). Over time, these oral traditions and written texts reinforced a longing among Jewish communities for rebirth in the land they called Zion or *Eretz Yisrael* (Taub 2010, 24). Yet this longing for Zion represented something of a paradox. By the time of the Arab conquest of Palestine (c. 638), Zion contained only a fraction of its former Jewish population, and by the early modern period this landscape was firmly anchored to an Ottoman pattern of agrarian landholding cultivated by Arab Palestinian *fellaheen*. The land of Zion thus became imbued in the Jewish imagination with two meanings (Zerubavel 2002, 115). On the one hand, Jews in exile imagined Zion as a land forsaken, populated by "foreigners" and neglected by its existing Arab inhabitants. On the other, this landscape beckoned to the Jewish people for redemption, for a time in the future when Jews would again settle, populate, and cultivate this land—supposedly as God had ordained.

Paradoxically, this collective yearning for Eretz Yisrael was far removed from the idea of taking possession of soil and ground (Ezrahi 2000, 10). Instead, the connection of people to place in the Jewish imagination was based on a messianic longing in which Jews were obligated to await the coming of the Messiah—the so-called "end time"—before returning to the Holy Land (Aberbach 2008, 3; Masalha 2007, 2). In the period prior to this time of messianic redemption, therefore, Zion for the Jewish people was a place of reverence—and for some, a place of pilgrimage—but it was not a place where

Jews actively sought to build a new homeland. This perspective would change dramatically with the nineteenth-century advent of Zionism.

IMAGINED GEOGRAPHY: ZIONISM AND REIMAGINING ZION

Zionism represented a revolutionary departure from the idea that Jews should wait for signals from God before returning and redeeming the land of Zion (Avineri 1981, 1–13). The movement exploited the long-standing "love of Zion" in Jewish culture but emphasized that Zionists themselves, not divine providence, had to deliver Jews from exile by settling the ancient homeland (Goldman 2009, 271–72). By the time of Herzl's *Jewish State* (1896), Zionists had broken even more radically from traditional Jewish messianism in elevating the importance of land and territory to end the misery of Jewish life in diaspora. As part of this break, Zionists actively imagined the society they were trying to establish on the Palestinian landscape, conceiving it as something to be remade with a Hebrew character and redeemable through Jewish settlement (Troen 2003, 142; Troen 2007, 874). Ultimately, the land of Zion evolved in the Zionist imagination as a *state* for the Jewish people (Shamir 2000, 29). In this way, Zionists crafted a vision of an end to exile and a path to redemption in the context of land and soil, eventually adding to this vision the territorial elements of sovereignty and dominium, maps and boundaries, nation and state.

Confronted by this territorial project, Palestinians were far from passive. They refused to accept as fate or God's will the taking of their land by a group of people supposedly chosen for such a task. Indeed, Palestinians resisted when the territorial aims of Zionists became aggressive—resistance that began during the early decades of Zionist settlement and continues to this day (Khalidi 1997, 89–117; Swedenburg 1995; Taraki 2006).

Haskalah: *Toward an Imagined Hebrew Landscape*

As a source of inspiration for an imagined Hebrew landscape in Palestine, Zionism derived from earlier paths in Jewish thought. One view of Zionism's origins focuses on medieval Andalusia and the iconic Hebrew philosopher and poet Yehuda Halevi, who for some is the first "proto-Zionist" (Halkin 2010a,b). Equally compelling is the view that Zionism's "true forerunners" derive from nineteenth-century figures such as Zvi Hirsch Kalischer, who reconciled religious faith with an activist orientation to Jewish emancipation (Katz 1978). Between these perspectives is a third position that situates the lineages of Zionism within the eighteenth-century Jewish Enlightenment known as the *Haskalah*. A central concern of Haskalah philosophers—the *maskilim*—was the "Jewish Question": How were the Jewish people to overcome the age-old scourge of European anti-Semitism? Two outlooks coexisted among the intellectual elites of the Jewish diaspora regarding this vexing problem.

One outlook embraced the notion of assimilation. Inspired by the French Enlightenment ideals of liberty, equality, and fraternity, this viewpoint found support among a cadre of maskilim who challenged the rabbinical elite and invited others from the Jewish intelligentsia to embrace their secularist vision (Feiner 2011, xiii–xiv). These figures, influenced especially by the notion of equality between different groups, envisioned emancipation in the context of integration with newly emergent liberal and secular states such as France and parts of Germany. Most notable among this group was Moses Mendelssohn, arguably the most accomplished eighteenth-century Haskalah intellectual, who was himself assimilated and a friend of the German philosophers Immanuel Kant and Gotthold Lessing (Hertz 2007, 39). The "Age of Reason," with its emphasis on secularism, progress, and equality, thus provided Jews of a certain outlook with a vision to emancipation through integration into the societies around them.

Yet the Haskalah was far from monolithic. Emerging just as the impact of the European Enlightenment was waning, it opened the Jewish revival to the influence of another dynamic, eclectic movement, one that was challenging aspects of the European Enlightenment itself (Litvak 2012). This new movement was Romanticism.

Though influenced by the Enlightenment, Romantics proffered a trenchant critique of progress and the perfectability of human society over time. Whereas Enlightenment intellectuals expressed optimism about the human condition based on the proliferation of reason in the present, Romantics insisted that human improvement must derive from an engagement with the distant, primordial past. For Romantics, engagement with time immemorial revealed the uniqueness of different groups of people and the beauty of language on which these differences were based. Consequently, where Enlightenment advocates celebrated notions of equality, Romantics elevated the virtues of difference. This outlook in turn provided the inspiration for perhaps the most formidable political force of the nineteenth century and beyond: nationalism.

The Romantics, with their impulse toward nationalism, provided an alternative vision of Jewish emancipation within the Haskalah during the first half of the nineteenth century (Litvak 2012). Jewish Romantics sought inspiration for solving the Jewish question not from an enlightened Europe, but from the society of the ancient Hebrews. Thus, alongside the assimilationists there emerged a competing perspective for transforming Jewish life in the diaspora that focused on an idealization of the ancient Jewish homeland and a revival of a Hebrew-based culture. It was but a logical step for Jews inspired by Romanticism and nationalism to connect this vision of Jewish emancipation to a territorial container. One of the most important early protagonists of this territorially inspired Jewish nationalism was the Polish rabbi Zvi Hirsch Kalischer.

Coveting Zion: From Kalischer to Ben-Yehuda

By the mid-nineteenth century when Kalischer was writing, nationalism had already taken firm root in Europe, where most of the Jewish population was located. Like the longings of Italians, Hungarians, Germans, and Poles for a homeland, Jews inspired by nationalism believed the Jewish people to constitute a distinct nation deserving of a state of their own. Kalischer was instrumental in forging an early vision of Jewish emancipation focused on nationalist redemption of the land of Zion.

In *Seeking Zion* (1862), Kalischer contributed three ideas that would transform this longing into a more territorial project. First, he argued that land redemption would not occur through divine intervention but must result from human agency. As a rabbi, Kalischer conceded that redeeming the land of Israel had religious imperatives; the process, however, would begin not because "the Messiah will suddenly sound a blast on the great trumpet" but rather by awakening support for "the gathering of some of the scattered of Israel into the Holy Land" (Kalischer 1862, 111).[1]

Second, Kalischer emphasized the role of Jewish settlement in redeeming land (Shapira 1992, 16). "There must first be Jewish settlement in the Land," he wrote, for "without such settlement, how can the ingathering begin?" Mindful of the practical challenges in settling the landscape, Kalischer suggested "that an organization be established to encourage settlement in the Holy Land." Although he conceded that Jewish settlement in Palestine would need support from world Jewry, he argued that such assistance would not be sufficient to sustain the new agrarian communities. Instead, settlers would have to work the land with their own hands.

Third, Kalischer elevated agricultural over urban settlement as the key to the redemption of Eretz Yisrael, noting that the organization for settlement would have a mission of "purchasing and cultivating farms and vineyards." In promoting his vision for the future, Kalischer not only charted a pioneering path that anticipated territorial themes from later Zionism, but also broke with rabbinical tradition about the meaning of coveting Zion (Myers 2003, 65). Kalischer was also inspired by the nationalism around him, referring to the campaigns occurring in Europe to offer legitimacy to the nationalist aspirations of the Jewish people in pursuit of a territory of their own. "Let us take to heart the examples of the Italians, Poles and Hungarians, who laid down their lives and possessions in the struggle for national independence," he wrote. Following the example of these other peoples would "raise our dignity among nations, for they would say that the children of Israel, too, have the will to redeem the land of their ancestors."

What helped push Kalischer toward nationalism as the key to Jewish emancipation were the pogroms in Russia following the 1881 assassination of Alexander II. In such conditions, with Europe again seeming unable to curb anti-Semitic excesses and various national groups seeking to liberate themselves by claiming rights of self-determination, nationalism had a logical appeal to the Jewish people. Unlike assimilation which relied on the tolerance of outsiders, nationalism drew its vitality from a sense of shared identity among members of the community and the idea that emancipation resided ultimately within the community itself.

Even more passionately than Kalischer, the figure who, prior to Herzl, most clearly articulated this idea of emancipation as a project of the Jewish people and who advocated a national homeland for Jews to solve the Jewish question was Leo Pinsker. His 1882 pamphlet "Auto-Emancipation: An Appeal to His People by a Russian Jew" is a cogent argument for Jews to overcome anti-Semitism by reestablishing themselves as a nation and forging their own state. While observing that the Holy Land might one day become the homeland of the Jewish people, Pinsker cautioned against the "dream of restoring ancient Judaea." The more urgent task, he noted, was to find "a land of our own . . . which shall remain our property." Such a land had to embody both sovereignty, in the form of a national territory, and dominium, in that it would be inalienable and not for sale (Pinsker 1882, 194, 197). As a practical matter, Pinsker advocated for acquisition of land through purchase and envisioned a commission of experts that would choose where "several million Jews could settle." At the same time, he insisted that land acquired be contiguous so that a national territory could take shape. Pinsker concluded by reemphasizing that the Jewish question could only be solved by the Jewish nation living on its own soil, an outcome possible only through the efforts of the Jewish people alone (Pinsker 1882, 197, 198).

Kalischer and Pinsker focused on the virtues of Jewish settlement and statehood, but neither pondered the role of Hebrew in nation-building and state formation. This task was pioneered within the Zionist movement by Eliezer Ben-Yehuda. His work opened a new era in the development of Zionism, in which the revival of Hebrew emerged as pivotal for the settlement of Palestine and redemption of the land (Saenz-Badillos 1993, 269). He was also one of the first to initiate the trend among Zionists in Palestine of changing one's European name—he was born Eliezer Issac Perlman—into a Hebrew one. Thanks in part to him, the role of language linked to names in general became decisive in Zionist cartography and projections of a thoroughly Hebrew landscape in Palestine.

Ben-Yehuda first penned his views on Hebrew in the context of an 1879 debate between Peretz Smolenskin, editor of the Vienna-based Hebrew monthly *Ha-Shahar,* and several German-speaking, Haskalah-influenced Jewish intellectuals on the role of Hebrew in Jewish life (Avineri 1981, 84). This latter group considered Hebrew an anachronism best discarded by Jews in favor of German. Smolenskin, in contrast, argued that Hebrew represented a spiritual as well as cultural bond unifying Jewish communities in diaspora and should be maintained. Ben-Yehuda intervened in this debate in an open letter to *Ha-Shahar* entitled "A Burning Question," which Smolenskin changed to "A Weighty Question" (Saulson 1979, 16). In his essay, Ben-Yehuda sided with Smolenskin but situated the issue of language within the context of nationalism and Jewish nationhood, defining nationalism as a common identity among a group of people forged from a shared history and a common language (Ben-Yehuda 1879, 1). For the Jewish people, Ben-Yehuda insisted that this common language had to be Hebrew. Only as a spoken vernacular could Hebrew emerge as a language of high culture and a path to Jewish national regeneration. At the same time, he emphasized that only in an environment with a Jewish majority could Hebrew be resurrected as a living language. In this way, he cast his vision toward Zion for the revival of Hebrew but argued that the Jewish people had to reestablish themselves there in order for the language to take root. "The land of Israel will become the center for the entire people," he wrote, "and even those who live in the diaspora will know that 'their people' dwell in its land, that its language and its literature are there. The language too will flourish. . . . Herein lies our people's salvation and our nation's happiness!" (Ben-Yehuda 1879, 10–11). In what proved prophetic, Ben-Yehuda wrote that in reviving Hebrew, the Jewish people would have an advantage: "We possess a language in which we can even now write anything we care to, and which it is also in our power to speak if only we wish" (Ben-Yehuda 1879, 5).

In a follow-up letter to *Ha-Shaḥar,* Ben-Yehuda was even more explicit in linking the Hebrew language to land redemption, nation-building, and state formation, imploring his readers to imagine Hebrew as a vernacular suitable for the Jewish people to use in their own homeland: "Let us therefore make the [Hebrew] language really live again! . . . But we will be able to revive the Hebrew tongue only in a country where the number of Hebrew inhabitants exceeds the number of gentiles. Therefore, let us increase the number of Jews in our desolate land; let the remnants of our people return to the land of their fathers; *let us revive the nation and its tongue will be revived, too!*" (Ben-Yehuda 1880, 164).

In these passages, Eliezer Ben-Yehuda anticipates some of the most salient themes of the Zionist movement—language, land, and soil. From these two letters emerged images of a Jewish community returning to Eretz Yisrael, speaking Hebrew there, and redeeming a desolate land—as Theodor Herzl envisioned in his *Jewish State.*

Herzl: Imagining The Jewish State

In *The Jewish State* and *Altneuland,* along with entries in his diaries, Theodor Herzl at all times fashioned an intensely visual image of the future state homeland for the Jewish people. In his visions of landscape, Herzl developed some of the signature themes of the Zionist imagination about a barren territory in the Holy Land with landscapes poorly cultivated by their current Palestinian stewards. To this desolate landscape, however, Herzl added what would become the defining theme of his work: how the Jewish people, through ingenuity and hard work, would redeem the Holy Land—or whatever area they chose as a homeland—into a modern nation-state. In this vision of the future, Herzl emphasized how the Jewish state would recast the landscape itself—and so signaled the possible fate awaiting Palestinians on this remade land.

That Herzl was aware of indigenous inhabitants as a problem for Jewish state-building is evidenced in an underappreciated passage in *The Jewish State* in which the author criticizes immigration as a strategy for statehood. In 1896, Zionists were still debating the location of the future state, and Herzl conceded that statehood might be viable in Uganda or Argentina, where Jewish immigrants had already settled. Herzl pointed out, however, that gradual immigration might founder in such places, because at a certain point "the native population itself feels threatened," and proposed instead that the Jewish people acquire sovereignty on a piece of territory as the prelude to settlement (Herzl 1896, 29). Although Herzl ignores the indigenous throughout most of *The Jewish State,* his admission of potential conflict arising from a steady influx of Jewish newcomers in places already populated is prescient.

Herzl also confronted other difficulties in promoting a Jewish state in Palestine based on an 1899 encounter with the chief rabbi of France, Zadok Kahn. The rabbi informed Herzl about a letter he had received from Yusuf al-Khalidi, a Jerusalem notable who had served as the city's mayor. In his letter, al-Khalidi sympathized with Jewish suffering but observed that Jewish sovereignty over Palestine could only be achieved by force and would be resisted. Undaunted, Herzl responded that Zionism and its preoccupation with improvement would benefit the local population and that Palestinians would embrace Zionists as modernizers (Lockman 1996, 33–34).

When Palestine eventually emerged as the choice location for the Jewish state, Herzl focused on the unique attributes of Jewish inventiveness as a way of redeeming the Holy Land's supposedly neglected landscape. In an interview given in 1898 to *The Young Israel,* a London-based Jewish youth journal, Herzl actually referred to the improvement metaphor in Daniel Defoe. Commenting on what the Zionist movement confronted in building the Jewish state in Palestine, Herzl remarked: "All the instruments that we require we must make for ourselves, like Robinson Crusoe on his island" (Robinson 2013, 225; Bar-Yosef 2007, 91).

Especially revealing of Herzl's imagined landscapes of Palestine are writings from his trip there in 1898, in which two themes prevail. First, Herzl continues his reprise of an "Arab-blighted countryside." On disembarking in Jaffa, Herzl describes an environment suffering from "poverty, misery and heat," with nary a word of Jaffa as a city (Herzl 1958, 279). His picture of Jerusalem, with its dominant Arab Palestinian population, is even more harsh. "When I remember thee in days to come, O Jerusalem," he writes in his diary entry of October 31, "it will not be with delight. . . . Two thousand years of inhumanity, intolerance, and foulness lie in your reeking alleys" (Herzl 1958, 283). Second, and in sharp contrast, Herzl makes glowing references to the Jewish settlements of Beth Ha'am, Mikveh Israel, Rishon LeZion, and Rehovot that he visited. In an article about his trip titled "The Zionist Deputation in Palestine: A Travel Report" (1898), written for the newspaper he founded, *Die Welt,* Herzl again mentions the desolate landscapes he observed, contrasting them to Jewish settlements, which "are nothing short of amazing" (Herzl 1973, 33; Eisenzweig 1981, 281). What Herzl emphasizes in these descriptions of landscape is how the artifice of Jewish labor improves a desolate Palestinian wilderness (Braverman 2009b, 335), a theme that would inspire his most imaginative literary enterprise, *Altneuland* (1902).

Herzl's utopian novel juxtaposes Palestine in two time periods: the beginning of the century in 1901, and the future in 1923, after Palestine has been transformed by the establishment of the Jewish state. Images of decrepit physical and human landscapes are dominant themes in the Palestine of 1901. Jaffa, much as described in Herzl's diary, is a city "in a state of extreme decay," while in the countryside were blighted Arab villages and the bare slopes of deforested hills that "showed few traces of present or former cultivation" (42).[2] Jerusalem also comes in for an unsparing critique by Lowenberg, one of the novel's main characters, who speaks of a city of "ragged people in narrow musty lanes, beggars, sick people, hungry children, screeching women, shouting tradesmen," a city that "could have sunk no lower" (44). Jerusalem must have once been beautiful, Lowenberg laments. "Perhaps that is why our ancestors could never forget it and always wanted to return" (46–47).

Lowenberg and the novel's other main character, Kingscourt, indeed return in 1923 and marvel at what they see. They find Haifa a bustling city due "to the dignified behavior of the many Orientals" along with the "absence of draught animals on the streets." Indeed, the reference to the absence of animals is a subtle metaphor of a modernized space in which the city's former Arab character has given way to an urban landscape that is "thoroughly European" (61). Jerusalem has had a similarly modern makeover, its ragged and musty lanes transformed into a beautifully ordered metropolis. Herzl also casts a vivid imagined geography upon the rural landscape. "Do not expect to see the filthy nests that used to be called villages in Palestine," Herzl exclaims through the voice of Steineck, acting as a guide to the book's two main characters (120).

Arguably the most compelling episode in the book occurs in the presence of the novel's only Palestinian character, Reshid Bey, whom Herzl uses to affirm the virtues of the new society. As Bey and the book's main protagonists pass a stand of citrus trees, Steineck observes that the "Jews introduced cultivation here" (121). At this point Herzl corrects the record, in the voice of Bey, who says that citrus groves of Palestinians pre-dated the newcomers. Herzl then uses Bey to make a more important point: that Palestinians were unable to reap full advantage from citrus cultivation. Bey concurs, stating that harvests and profits increased after Jewish immigrants arrived and applied their know-how to the growing of oranges. Thus Herzl makes the subtle argument, in the spirit of Locke, that Zionists are deserving of the land because their superior methods of cultivation and their prowess at profitmaking represent improvements that entitle them to dominion on the landscape.

Herzl then enlists Bey to provide a more broad-based defense of the Zionist project. "Nothing could have been more wretched than an Arab village at the end of the 19th century," Bey concedes, affirming what Steineck had stated. "Now everything is different" (123). Through a Palestinian voice, Herzl promotes the common trope that the makeover of territory through colonization benefits colonizer and colonized alike. "When the swamps were drained," insists Bey, "the natives were the first to be employed and were paid well for their work!" Herzl also uses Bey to dispel the more troubling issue of whether Jews were "intruders" and whether Palestinians suffered as a result of Jewish immigration. "Were not the older inhabitants of Palestine ruined by Jewish immigration?" Kingscourt ask Bey, who is surprised by the question. Jewish settlement, Bey maintains, "was a great blessing for us" (122).

Despite the tenor of these exchanges, Herzl is aware of, if not uneasy about, Palestinian suffering and has thought carefully about rebuttals to those objecting to Jewish settlement in Palestine. There was indeed good reason for Herzl to harbor some anxiety about the Jewish state in Palestine. He had only to look at the United States to verify what can happen to an indigenous population confronted by colonization and settlement. Nevertheless, Herzl remained undaunted by such problems, invoking in *The Jewish State* the metaphor of modernization and improvement that had become symbolic of American achievements and the hallmark of the Zionist project in Palestine. Wherever "we moderns appear," he writes, "we transform the desert into a garden. . . . America offers endless examples of this" (Herzl 1896, 74–75).

Just prior to publication of *Altneuland,* Herzl provided another signal of his uneasiness about the problem posed by the Palestinian population in a proposed charter that he coauthored for the Zionist movement, aimed at the Ottoman sultan, for creation of a land development company in Palestine (Khalidi 1993).[3] The genesis of this document dates from the third Zionist Congress (1899), but it was not until May 1901 that Herzl finally managed to secure a meeting with Sultan Abdul Hamid II to discuss the concept. Later that year Herzl produced the draft, and in February 1902 he returned to Istanbul to negotiate its provisions. Although these talks broke down, the proposed charter offers insights into the thinking of Herzl and the Zionist movement about colonization and the situation on the ground.

As envisioned by Herzl, the Jewish-Ottoman Land Company (JOLC) would have had special prerogatives for colonizing Palestine. In the charter's preamble, Herzl writes: "His Majesty the Sultan grants and guarantees the JOLC the following special rights and privileges for the purpose of settling Palestine and Syria with Jews," while article 1 begins by granting the JOLC "a special right to purchase large estates and small farms (Jifliks of whatever kind), and to use them for agriculture, horticulture, forestry, and mining. . . . The JOLC is entitled to establish small and large settlements and to settle Jews in them" (quoted in Khalidi 1993, 44). The most important provisions of the document, however, are contained in article 3, which pertains to existing Palestinian owners and users of land to be purchased by the JOLC. Herzl proposes to compensate these individuals, but the manner of this compensation is revealing. "The owners shall receive plots of equal size and quality procured by it [JOLC] in other provinces and territories of the Ottoman Empire." In effect, the charter outlines a vision for Zionists to acquire lands in Palestine for Jewish settlement and to resettle the owners and occupiers of those lands *outside* Palestine.

In contemplating the possibility of moving Palestinians outside of Palestine, Herzl in a sense anticipated Zionist debates in the 1930s about the problem of a large Palestinian population in an eventual Jewish state. In those debates, some proposed "transferring" Palestinians from Palestine (Masalha 1992; Morris 2002). While at this point Zionists were in no position to implement such an idea, demographic facts in Palestine posed an obvious dilemma for a movement committed to creating a Jewish homeland in a territory overwhelmingly non-Jewish. Such inconvenient truths had already circulated within the Zionist movement years before Herzl's *The Jewish State,* most notably in a candid assessment of Zionism's problems in Palestine written by one of the most revered of Zionist intellectuals, Ahad Ha'am.

An Inconvenient Truth

"Truth from the Land of Israel" by Ahad Ha'am provided an eloquent if sobering admission of the so-called Arab problem confronting Jewish colonists in Palestine and was one of the first serious engagements with the fact that Palestine was not an empty country (Ahad Ha'am 1891, 160; Dowty 2000, 156; Avneri 1985, 122). "From abroad, we are accustomed to believing that *Eretz* Israel is presently almost desolate," he wrote. The truth, he noted, was far different. "In the entire country, it is hard to find tillable land that is not already cultivated." In observations at once cautionary and prophetic, Ahad Ha'am went on to remark:

> From abroad we are accustomed to believing that the Arabs are all desert savages. . . . But this is a big mistake. . . . The Arabs, and especially those in the cities, understand our desires in *Eretz* Israel, but they keep quiet and pretend not to understand, since they do not see our present activities as a threat to their future. . . . However, if the time comes when the life of our people in *Eretz* Israel develops to the point of encroaching upon the native population, they will not easily yield their place. (Ahad Ha'am 1891, 161–62)

Despite this realistic assessment of the dilemma facing the Zionist movement, Ahad Ha'am did not dissent from mainstream Zionist views of Palestinians (Dowty 2000, 159). Indeed, he writes of "the indolence of Arabs" and Palestine's "miserable condition" (Ahad Ha'am 1891, 160). The article, however, is a caustic denunciation of Zionists, whom the author likens to being "put to sleep with pretty tunes" from lyrcs singing love songs of Zion without an awareness of what Palestine really was. Unlike Herzl, who had little to say about the Palestinian population beyond overt disparagement, Ahad Ha'am recognized this population and understood its implications for the Zionist project.

Despite Ahad Ha'am's cautionary warnings, Zionists still described the country as barren and neglected. In *The Jewish State* and *Altneuland,* Herzl hinted that the work of the Jewish society to ameliorate neglect conferred upon the Jewish community a moral right to those areas where they had improved the ground with their own effort. In this way, despite overwhelming evidence of Palestinian presence, visions of a Jewish landscape in Palestine were able to emerge from a largely improvement-driven notion of rights to land. While Herzl signaled this idea in an effort to overcome the *realpolitk* of figures such as Ahad Ha'am, notions of entitlement to land through labor were soon to be articulated systematically within Zionism, in the person of Aaron David Gordon (1856–1922).

Hebrew Land through Hebrew Labor

For Gordon, the basic task of Zionism was to reestablish a national Jewish culture in Palestine for a people who had been living in diaspora, and to reattach the people of this culture to the soil from which they had been exiled. It was in this context that Gordon developed his idea about labor as the key to taking possession of land. While Zionists had argued that Jews would have to assume ownership of land in order to take control of the country, Gordon insisted that acquisition of, and settlement on land in Palestine was insufficient for the establishment of a Jewish homeland. Absent changes in outlook and activity, a culture of *galut* (diaspora) would continue even in Palestine (Gordon 1911a, 375). For this reason, Gordon argued that Zionism had to establish a culturally regenerated Jewish people in Palestine, "not a mere colony of Diaspora Jewry" (Gordon 1920, 382). The only way to do this was to anchor Jews to the soil through work on the land with their own hands.

> Labor is not only the force which binds man to the soil and by which possession of the soil is acquired; it is also the basic energy for creation of a national culture.... In Palestine we must do with our own hands all of the things that make up the sum total of life.... From now on our chief ideal must be labor.... The ideal of labor must become the pivot of all our aspirations. It is the foundation upon which our national culture is to be erected.... We need a new spirit for our national renaissance. That new spirit must be created in Palestine and must be nourished by our life in Palestine. What we need are zealots of labor—zealots in the finest meaning of the term. (Gordon 1911b, 373–74)

Gordon's difficulty in promoting this agriculturalist perspective among Zionists was that the two-thousand-year life of exile had essentially imprisoned the Jewish people within city walls, giving Jewish life a heavily urban bias (Gordon 1911b, 372). Indeed, Jews had developed an aversion to manual labor and agricultural life. Of the Jews who had lived in Palestine under the Ottomans, few had engaged in agricultural work. Gordon was convinced that if the Jewish people were to emerge with a justifiable claim to the soil of Palestine, then the Jewish community in Palestine would have to break free of the prejudices they had developed in exile about agriculture and manual work. Gordon even questioned the idea of Zionists taking possession of land in Palestine through purchase. "Not even by thousands of title deeds can national assets be acquired," he wrote. "A people can acquire its own land only by its own effort" (Gordon 1911a, 376). Despite these convictions, however, Gordon was not oblivious to the actual situation on the landscape, where Zionists confronted two intractable problems with respect to labor and land ownership.

The first problem concerned the employment policies of the Jewish community in Palestine, the *Yishuv*. During early Zionist settlement, new Jewish landowners had little choice but to employ Palestinians, owing to shortages of Jewish labor in a plantation-style approach to colonization. Yet how was land worked by non-Jewish labor to become the basis of a Jewish state? It was only during the second, much larger wave of Jewish colonization in Palestine—the Second *Aliya* of 1904–14—that the Yishuv debated and answered this question in an effort to establish a truly Hebrew landscape. Gordon was a central figure in these debates (Shafir 1996, 190–91).

In articles for *Hapoel Hatzair* (The Young Worker), the Zionist publication connected to the organization of the same name that he founded, Gordon maintained that the relationship of labor to land was central to Zionism. "If we do not till the soil with our very own hands," he wrote, "the soil will not be ours" (Gordon 1911c, 60). Gordon did admit to a problem, however, in putting this view into practice. The work that could be done by the landowner and his family was limited, he conceded, and therefore the landowner was obliged to hire labor. Yet for Gordon, there was no question of who was to work the land; the labor, he insisted, must be Jewish (Gordon 1911c, 62, 70–71). In his view, land did not have a Jewish pedigree if it was not worked by Jews. In this way, Hebrew labor would become inseparable from the project of creating a Hebrew landscape.

If Gordon was persistent about the obligation of Jewish landowners to hire their own in order for land in Palestine to become Jewish, by 1919–20 he was also clear about the second, more troubling issue confronting the Yishuv—"the problem between ourselves and the Arabs" (Gordon 1938, 24). Surprisingly, given his unyielding position on Jewish labor, Gordon was forthright in acknowledging the rights of Arabs who lived on and cultivated the land. Nevertheless, he emphasized that there was no need for the Jewish community to be submissive in its relations with the Arabs, and in this spirit Gordon sought to dispel the idea that Jewish settlement in Palestine uprooted and dispossessed the Arabs (Gordon 1938, 23–24). He denied that Arabs had been dispossessed by insisting that they had never exercised rights as masters of the land in Palestine, other than their rights as cultivators. Arabs, he pointed out, long ago surrendered mastery on the land to the Ottomans and therefore had no claims to the land on the basis of sovereignty through conquest (Gordon

1938, 24–25). Absent rights of sovereignty, Arabs, according to Gordon, could not claim that Jews were taking their land.

An Arab claim to Palestine based on dominium, Gordon further insisted, was also problematic. Though he was willing to concede the individual rights of cultivators, as a people, he said, "the Arabs, like ourselves, have nothing more than a historic claim to the land" (Gordon 1938, 25).[4] While it might appear that Gordon was conceding the historical legitimacy of Arab presence on the land, he was actually turning the argument in the other direction. Gordon argued that in the absence of either Arab or Jewish sovereignty in Palestine, both groups lacked possession of the land. Hence, neither group could be dispossessed. "It cannot therefore be said that we are taking the land from the Arabs" (Gordon 1938, 25).

In affirming that both groups had historical claims to land in Palestine, Gordon framed the problem on the land as one of free and open competition. "Of the two groups of people," Gordon asked, "which has the greater right to acquire land and enlarge its holdings?" (Gordon 1938, 24). In posing this question, Gordon was seeking criteria that elevate certain claims to land and enable certain claimants to prevail in competing for land. Taking a cue from the spirit of Locke, Gordon responded unambiguously to his own question: "Whoever works harder," he wrote, "creates more, gives more of his spirit, will acquire a greater moral right and a deeper vital interest in the land" (Gordon 1938, 24).

With the terms of this "peaceful competition" firmly established, Gordon had little doubt which of the two parties would prevail by working harder. "What did the Arabs produce in all the years they lived in the country?" he asked rhetorically. "The people who came after us did not create anything at all" (quoted in Sternhell 1998, 72). Palestinian claims to the land thus had little merit.

At the same time, Gordon harbored supreme confidence in the Jewish people to elevate physical labor as part of a spiritual national identity (Sternhell 1998, 70–73). In a short essay titled "The Dream of the Aliyah," Gordon uses familiar terms in describing the imagined Palestinian land as "wasted," "abandoned," and "desolate." What opens the heart and soul of the settler-pioneer to the life of aliyah in Eretz Yisrael is "work," not for wages, but labor that create a spiritual anchor to the land (Gordon 1938, 1).

At the core of Gordon's vision was the connection of land to improvement through labor. Because for Gordon the Palestinians were seemingly content to leave areas of the landscape barren, he was confident that the Jewish community would prevail as improvers of the land with a higher claim on it. Just as Locke resolved the problem of the Amerindian cultivator by emphasizing the superiority of the English planter to work and improve the landscape, Gordon resolved a similar problem by suggesting that Jewish settler-pioneers would work harder than their Palestinian counterparts and would thus be more deserving of the land. In this way, long-held ideas about rights to land through labor and improvement found a modern-day Jewish apostle. Although Gordon was willing to concede individual Palestinian rights on the land, his approach to the landscape was ultimately aggressive (Taylor 1974, 94). Only Hebrew labor would create a Hebrew landscape.

MAPPING THE IMAGINED GEOGRAPHY OF ZION

Just prior to the period of the British Mandate, Zionists from the fields of cartography and geography were already seeking to project their vision of a Hebrew Palestine onto maps (Benvenisti 2000, 14). For the Zionist movement, however, mapping was part of a broader campaign designed to show how the reemergence of a Jewish culture in "the Land of Israel" was part of a long-standing and unbroken Hebrew lineage on the land (Azaryahu and Kellerman 1999, 112). Evidence for the time-honored Jewish character of the landscape was lodged in so-called facts, deriving from numerous sources but culled primarily from archeological antiquities (Abu El-Haj 2001, 2002, 2006). With a bold materiality, antiquities testified to a vibrant Hebrew presence in ancient Palestine, which in turn connected Zionists to the present day. By overlaying this history onto the landscape where Jews were settling, Zionists were imbuing modern Palestine with an enduring Hebrew identity, creating potent arguments for taking possession of what rightfully belonged to the Jewish people. In order to formalize this historically derived claim on territory, Zionists seized on the often-hidden power of mapping to render objective and neutral what was an argumentative proposition about the Hebrew character of the Palestinian landscape

From 1914 onward, Zionist historians, geographers, linguists, and archeologists transcribed notions about Jewish rights to Palestinian land into a cartographic idiom. Their goal was a Hebrew map of Palestine. The first step in this process focused on the naming of geographical places, establishing a Hebrew toponymy for a landscape dominated by Arabic-speaking Palestinians. By "discovering" ancient Hebrew place-names on the Palestinian landscape and transcribing such geographical facts onto maps, Zionists crafted counterarguments about the landscape's Palestinian attributes, emphasizing instead the land's enduring Hebrew character. At the same time, by naturalizing Hebrew names for geographical features of the landscape, Zionists framed a new way of thinking about the land. Imbued with a Hebrew toponymy, the map of Palestine was transformed into the land of Eretz Yisrael, informing Zionists and others that what was depicted on the map was Hebrew land. In this way, the Hebrew map of Palestine provided a path to power for Zionists to stake a claim on the Palestinian landscape.

The efforts to fashion a cartographic representation of a Hebrew landscape in Palestine evolved alongside two interdependent cultural campaigns that lay at the core of Zionism. One focused on elevating Hebrew as the *lingua franca* of the Yishuv. Once established, the Hebrew language influenced the second campaign, which aimed at reconstructing Palestine's Hebrew past and refashioning the Palestinian landscape as a Hebrew space. These two initiatives provided the foundations for mapping what Zionists imagined as Palestine's Hebrew geography.

Hebrew Revival: Foundation of a New Cartography

The ascendancy of Hebrew as the lingua franca of the Jewish community in Palestine was one of the signature accomplishments of Zionism (Dieckhoff 2003, 104). For Jews from cultures as diverse as Yemen and the Ukraine, Hebrew was the instrument that enabled the newcomers to imagine themselves as a people—a community—with a shared identity and purpose in redeeming Palestine as a Jewish homeland. As it diffused across the geographical contours where this population was settling, the Hebrew language reshaped the character of the territorial space, effectively "hebraicizing" the landscape. Yet the eventual dominance of Hebrew within the Yishuv was never preordained. Herzl, among others, believed that Hebrew would be one of several languages in a future Jewish state, with German the likely language of cultivated Jews in Palestine (Dieckhoff 2003, 103; Berkowitz 1993, 51). The transition of Hebrew from a largely liturgical language to a spoken vernacular generated intense debate during the early years of Zionism, but despite strident opponents, Hebrew had a core of fervent backers.

As early as 1899 at the third Zionist Congress in Basel, one delegate, Leopold Kahn, challenged the assembly to become a Hebrew-speaking institution within twenty years (Berkowitz 1993, 62). Ten years later, at the ninth congress, amid still-contentious debate about Zionism and language, several speeches and some congress business were conducted in Hebrew for the first time. By the time of the next congress in Basel, in 1911, entire debates, constituting the official proceedings, were conducted in Hebrew. Foreshadowing this momentous change, Herzl's successor as president of the World Zionist Congress, David Wolffsohn, in his opening remarks to the congress, proclaimed "one God, one people, one language, one country, one Zionism!" (Berkowitz 1993, 68).

Parallel to events at Zionist congresses was the more critical issue of how Hebrew would diffuse within the Yishuv itself. Arguably, the institution most decisive for the spread of Hebrew was education. Within the early Yishuv emerged a network of schools beginning in 1886 in Rishon LeZion with Hebrew as the language of instruction (Ornan 1984, 225–226). By the opening years of the twentieth century, this network had spawned two organizations that played an important role in promoting a Hebrew education: the Committee for a National Hebrew Education and the Hebrew Teachers Association (Saposnik 2008, 25, 214).

Although the revival of Hebrew faced constraints and even opposition, it had never actually been a "dead" language (Parfitt 1984, 255). Hebrew had always played a role in Jewish prayer, and it played a role in the literary revival of the Haskalah as well. Even in Palestine prior to Zionism, Hebrew could be heard in Jewish quarters of cities in Ottoman Palestine with sizable Jewish populations such as Jerusalem (Parfitt 1972, 237–38). Consequently, by the opening years of the twentieth century, Jews in Palestine were creating their own colloquial innovations for Hebrew used in daily life (Saposnik 2008, 66).

In some way, the progress of Hebrew in the Yishuv was constrained by differences within the Zionist movement, pitting Zionists in Europe who favored a European approach to Jewish settlement and thought of the Yishuv as multilingual, against those in Palestine who favored Hebrew as an expression of local autonomy (Saposnik 2008, 213–17). By 1913, however, the idea of Hebrew as an instrument for creating a unified Jewish culture in Palestine, embraced by those favoring local control of language, had become firmly entrenched within the educated elite of the Yishuv and among notables in the Zionist movement (Berkowitz 1993, 76).

The institutionalization of Hebrew within the Jewish community in Palestine passed through two decisive transitional events, one the result of forces internal to the Yishuv, the second resulting from decisions made by the British Mandate authorities. The first of these two milestones occurred in

1913–14 and focused on the Tekhnion Institute in Haifa, the first school of higher education in the Yishuv, where a "war of languages" broke out between the institute's German-speaking Zionist founders and supporters of Hebrew as the Institute's language of instruction (National Library of Israel n.d.). Igniting the crisis was a decision in October 1913 by the institute's Board of Trustees that the language of instruction would be German. Protests by Hebrew-speaking students and teachers erupted into a mass movement featuring strikes and demonstrations that spread to other areas of Jewish Palestine, including schools in Jaffa and Jerusalem (Saposnik 2008, 224; Khurshid 2008, 42). Prominent intellectuals also played a role in this struggle as defenders of Hebrew, including Ahad Ha'am and Eliezer Ben-Yehuda. In a sharp rebuke to Dr. Paul Nathan, the main protagonist on the German side of the debate, Ben-Yehuda defended Hebrew as a language fully adaptable to modern intellectual life. "As the author of *The Dictionary of the Hebrew Language,*" Ben-Yehuda wrote, "I have the right more than any other person to decide whether it is possible to study sciences in Hebrew and I say and proclaim: indeed scientific study is possible in Hebrew! And if the terminology for the known branches of science is not yet perfected as much as necessary--this is only a question of time" (quoted in Fellman 1973, 138).

Owing to these pressures, the Board of Trustees reversed its decision about German in January 1914, agreeing on Hebrew as the language of instruction at the Tekhnion Institute. This decision affirmed that Hebrew was more than a liturgical language; it was also a language adaptable to science and education, and to the culture of modern life (Dieckhoff 2003, 103).

Waged as a campaign against "foreign languages," the conflict and its outcome provided momentum for the expansion of Hebrew not only in Palestinian Jewish schools but also within the Yishuv more broadly as the central element of a new Jewish culture in Palestine (Saposnik 2008, 232). One of the most telling metaphors of the ascendancy of Hebrew was the creation in 1925 of Hebrew University in Jerusalem, the first university of the Yishuv dedicated to promoting an educational culture anchored in the Hebrew language. In this newly ascendant role as a vernacular language, Hebrew emerged as the foundation of a locally based Zionist and Jewish nationalism. "On three things is our world founded," declared A. D. Gordon's organization, Hapoel Hatzair (The Young Worker): "on Hebrew soil, on Hebrew labor, and on the Hebrew Language!" (quoted in Saposnik 2008, 227).

In the early 1920s, Hebrew promoters within the Zionist movement brought their campaign to a new level by convincing British authorities to recognize Hebrew as an official language of the Mandate Government. This campaign exploited Britain's own policy goals for Palestine as outlined in the Balfour Declaration, with its explicit aim of promoting a Jewish homeland in Palestine. After the declaration was inserted into the final document of the San Remo Peace Conference (1920), leaders of the Yishuv had an opening to seek British support for the declaration's stated objective. Consequently in 1922, educators at the Hebrew Language College in Jerusalem, in a memo to Sir Herbert Samuel, British High Commissioner in Palestine, argued for the need to institutionalize Hebrew within Britain's Mandate for Palestine as part of the mutual interest shared by the British and the Yishuv. In a calculated admission of the challenges still facing the Yishuv in promoting Hebrew among Jewish newcomers, and with an appeal to the British for help in overcoming this difficulty, authors of the memo wrote:

> A National Home for the People of Israel in the Land of Israel is not possible unless the People of Israel are completely and definitely unified. However, such unity is not possible as long as in the Land of Israel there are Jews speaking the scores of languages of the Diaspora. . . . In his response to the salutatory letter from the Language College, His Lordship agreed to announce that "he would be concerned for the rights of the Hebrew Language." In his talk with our president, he declared that he would soon issue a formal order in accordance with which the Hebrew language will become *one of the three governing languages* in Palestine. . . . We hope that the day is near. (quoted in Saulson 1979, 63–64)

In the end, British authorities acceded to this demand. In 1922, Hebrew took its place alongside English and Arabic as one of three official languages in British-ruled Palestine. At that time, the total population of Mandate Palestine was 757,182, of whom 590,390 were Muslims, 73,024 were Christians, and 83,794 (roughly 11 percent) were Jews (Government of Palestine 1922, 5, table 1).

Arguably, the most far-reaching impact of Hebrew as an official language in Mandate Palestine occurred within the Yishuv itself. As Hebrew extended its reach within the Jewish community, it emerged as an attractive means for the diverse Jewish immigrants in Palestine to integrate into the new society and gain a sense of themselves as members of a unified nation anchored to a common language and territory (Shamir 2000, 7, 33; Dieckhoff 2003, 100–102). By 1931, the dominance of Hebrew as the language of the Yishuv in Palestine had become indisputable (Azaryahu and Golan 2001, 182). As part of this linguistic revival, many of the Zionist immigrants adopted Hebrew names. Among the latter was David Grun, who as David Ben-Gurion would become Israel's first prime minister.

For the Zionist movement, restoring the Hebrew language was part of a broader effort to connect an ancient Hebrew society to a modern population of Jewish settlers. Mediating this connection between past and present was the concept of *return* (Dieckhoff 2003, 104). Zionists insisted that Jews were returning to their homeland to take their place in the pantheon of modern nations and build a modern nation-state. In order for this idea of return to be viable, however, the Zionist movement had to imbue the territorial space of Palestine with an enduring Jewish character. While restoring the ancient lingua franca in Palestine and recreating a Hebrew-speaking population was fundamental in aligning present to past and legitimizing the notion of return, the Zionist movement was involved from 1914 onward in an ambitious effort to cast the historical geography of Palestine with an almost timeless Jewish character. This effort focused on excavating the landscape.

Excavating a Hebrew Presence in Palestine

In 1914, a group of Zionist intellectuals in Palestine, many active in the Hebrew language campaign, launched a new initiative, the "Society for the Reclamation of Antiquities," aimed at advancing knowledge of what the group claimed were the historical and geographical roots of the Land of Israel. Although its initial efforts were short-lived owing to the outbreak of the Great War, the group was reconstituted in 1920 as the "Jewish Palestine Exploration Society" (JPES). In the following year, the JPES launched its first archeological excavation in Tiberias under the direction of Nahum Slouschz, chair of modern Hebrew language and literature at the Sorbonne and one of the period's most accomplished Zionist intellectuals (Fine 2005, 23). Slouschz and the JPES, led by David Yellin, the group's first president, and Eliezer Ben-Yehuda, its first vice president, would find inspiration for restoring a Jewish society in Palestine in the rediscovery of a Hebrew-speaking Jewish society in Palestine's distant past. For the JPES, archeology was the instrument for realizing what Herzl had earlier imagined as *Altneuland:* an ancient Hebrew society providing the historical foundations for renewal of the Jewish nation in the modern world (Abu El-Haj 2002, 46).

The revival of Hebrew and the rediscovery of Palestine's Hebrew historical geography reflected a logical convergence. Since the time of Herzl, Zionists had debated, and then actively sought to establish, a Jewish homeland in the territory of the ancient Hebrews. Such a project emphasized the idea of a "return to Zion" as the basis of redemption for the Jewish people (Azaryahu and Kellerman 1999, 112). The legitimacy of returning to Zion, however, hinged on the historical presence of a Hebrew-speaking Jewish population and culture in Palestine. In this sense, Zionists sought to align the geographical space of Palestine with a historically long-standing Hebrew nation located there. For the JPES, this reconstruction of past landscapes elevated a specific type of historical inquiry above all others—archeology—and a distinct material object at the core of this research practice—*antiquities* (Abu El-Haj 2002, 38).

As material artifacts, antiquities had particular salience for Zionists seeking affirmation of Palestine's Hebrew past. With their tangible links to ancient Israel, Hebrew antiquities were akin to a type of "deed" marking Jewish land. In this sense, the JPES enlisted antiquities as a blunt instrument to lay claim to the Palestinian landscape based on its attribution as the ancestral homeland of the Jewish people. Where antiquities were unearthed and catalogued as evidence of an ancient Hebrew society, they provided a verifiable, material foundation for the landscape's long-term Jewish character and status in the past as Eretz Yisrael. Antiquities also had compelling ideological resonance. Unearthing ancient Jewish artifacts on the Palestinian landscape worked to naturalize a Jewish identity with the land, validating the idea of returning to Zion in the present. By integrating the history of Jewish presence in Palestine into the texture of the landscape itself, the Zionist movement had formidable arguments, crafted from antiquities, to justify the idea of taking possession of Judaism's ancestral homeland (Fine 2005, 23; Abu El-Haj 2002, 38; Azaryahu and Kellerman 1999, 112).

This appropriation of antiquities to verify continuity between the Jewish past and the Zionist present was already part of the archeological work of the JPES as described in its *Proceedings* (1925) by some of the best-known luminaries of cultural Zionism. In addition to Slouschz, Yellin, and Ben-Yehuda, contributors to the early work of the JPES included Yizhak Ben-Zvi, Avraham-Ya'akov Brawer, Judah Magnes, and the other great Zionist archeologist, Eleazar Sukenik, all of whom considered archeology indispensable for Zionist nation-building (Fine 2005, 23). In an affirmation of this aim, Iyal Press wrote that "excavations ought to be carried out here by the Jewish [Palestine] Exploration Society in order to reveal the traces of former Jewish occupation" (Press 1925, 65).

Prior to the articles in the *Proceedings,* Slouschz penned what was perhaps the clearest description of the political agenda in Zionist archeology in a 1921 article for the journal *Hashiloach* (Fine 2005, 24).[5] Noting that excavations in Palestine undertaken by non-Jews brought to light much about what was "distinctive to Israel in its land," Slouschz stated that, as Jews, "our ideology and purpose differ from that of most Gentile scholars." For Slouschz, the task for Zionist archeology was clear: "to learn and to know what the people of Israel accomplished and created during the period when their political lives were normal [and] to trace the development of our language, crafts, and industries." Such topics, he wrote, though of little importance to Christians, "are an entire Torah for us" and complimented the work of the JPES, who he said understood these issues and spearheaded the Tiberias excavations. For Slouschz, what was unique about the excavation of Tiberias was the fact that it was a postbiblical site where the Hebrew language became standardized and went through revitalization; where Jews were a nation speaking their own language; and where the Jewish people were anchored to their own land not simply from their religion but through their own material, political, and cultural life. In this way, Slouschz revealed extraordinary insight about archeology as a means of promoting the mission of Zionism. Archeology also embodied the spirit of Herzl's utopian novel *Altneuland,* connecting the ancestral Jewish homeland to the new land of Jewish return (Abu El-Haj 2002, 46; Fine 2005, 24). By sharpening the resonance of the Hebrew past on the Palestinian landscape, archeology for Slouschz and the Zionist movement helped fire the imagination of Palestine as a Jewish land (Abu El-Haj 2002, 45).

Following the excavations at Tiberias, an ever-increasing inventory of archeological discoveries, mostly ancient tombs and synagogues, continued to provide robust evidence of a unique Hebrew cultural past in Eretz Yisrael, a theme repeatedly emphasized in the JPES *Bulletin* (Abu El-Haj 2002, 50; Abu El-Haj 2001, 74–76). Based on these artifacts, Zionists could claim to be returning to the distinct ancestral homeland of the Jewish people. In one example of excavations, at the Tomb of Jehoshaphat near Jerusalem, Dr. Aaron Mazie remarks that the pediment carvings of grapes, figs, pomegranates, olives, dates, and citrons "show definitely a) that they pertain to a Jewish tomb and b) that they were executed according to the conventions of early Jewish art form." At the end of his article, Mazie writes: "We are bound to conclude that the Jews had a native art, born out of love of their country and of its fruits, and of veneration towards their religion and liturgy" (Mazie 1925, 68, 71). From the Galilee to Hebron, tombs and synagogues not only testified to a Hebrew history in these localities, but once they appeared as locales on maps, excavations of Jewish antiquities formed a widening cartographic arc of ancient Jewish presence on the Palestinian landscape, broadening claims on land in contemporary Palestine (Abu El-Haj 2002, 50). So compelling was this territorially defined historical Jewish presence that by 1934 Shmu'el Yeivin, one of two co-editors of the JPES *Bulletin,* was able to remark to the Tel Aviv branch of the JPES that the group's "most important achievement of the decade" was "the discovery of Hebrew Palestine" (from Abu El-Haj 2001, 73). This discovery, in turn, provided inspiration for the next step in the making of a Hebrew map of the landscape, which began with naming places.

Renaming Places

If Zionists relied on the historical reconstruction of Palestine as a Jewish place to justify their return to the area, they engaged in an equally aggressive effort to assign Jewish attributes to the landscape by immersing it in a Hebrew toponymy (Azaryahu and Kellerman 1999, 112; Cohen and Kliot 1981). This campaign to graft Hebrew place-names onto the landscape was intimately connected to the territorially focused revival of the Hebrew language. By reordering the landscape with Hebrew place-names, and by transcribing this Hebrew-named landscape onto maps, Zionists were crafting the cartographic elements of Palestine as an imagined Hebrew land.

As an instrument of this imagined geography, toponymy is actually a system of arguments about the landscape with two basic attributes (Azaryahu and Golan 2001, 181). First, place-names, once established, seemingly become part of physical landscapes, such that "place" and "name" become virtually inseparable. Second, place-names, once fused with material features of the landscape, assume a rarefied status when transferred to maps, becoming objective facts about land while shedding any hint of the arguments embedded in the creation and selection of the place-name itself. Although place-names on maps appear as benign representations of a reality on the landscape, names are replete with cultural signals that shape how people imagine the territorial world in terms of who is sovereign on the land, who belongs on the land, and who is an outsider (Peteet 2005, 153, 157; Azaryahu and Golan 2001, 180–81).

Among Zionist geographers, historians, and cartographers, Hebrew place-names were critical to redeeming the ancestral homeland. For this group, the Hebrew homeland had succumbed for too long to outsiders who had neglected the land and had inscribed it with a foreign, Arabic toponymy. During the period of the Mandate, this Arabic toponymy continued to dominate the geography of Palestine, with roughly 3,700 Arabic names describing cities, villages, and various features on the land (Ben-Ze'ev 2007, 115; Azaryahu and Golan 2001, 183). For those Zionists seeking to rediscover a Hebrew history and culture in Palestine, reinscribing this landscape with Hebrew place-names was a logical extension of the earlier campaign to revive Hebrew and rid the country of "foreign" languages. What many Zionists also understood is how the placement of Hebrew names on maps created a powerful cartographic counternarrative affirming the Hebrew character of a landscape dominated by Palestinians.

Zionist involvement in naming places in Palestine actually began in the 1880s with the first Zionist settlements. The convention adopted by the newcomers for naming new communities was to take inspiration from the Hebrew Bible. The founders of Petah Tikva chose a prophecy of hope from the prophet Hosea, and for Rishon LeZion, the biblical verse from Isaiah, "First to Zion." More or less spontaneously, early Zionists were forging continuity between ancient Israel and the territory now being settled by ancient Israel's modern-day Zionist descendants.

As Jewish immigration to Palestine expanded between 1903 and 1928, the Zionist movement sought institutional control over the process of naming newly created Jewish settlements. In 1925 it empowered a committee under the auspices of the Jewish National Fund (JNF) to manage this mission. The focus was on selecting names for new Jewish settlements from biblical texts, Mishnaic-Talmudic references, and recent Zionist luminaries (Cohen and Kliot 1981, 229; Benvenisti 2000, 14). During the pre-state period from 1925 to 1948, this committee managed to give 215 Jewish communities in Palestine Hebrew names (Azaryahu and Golan 2001, 183).

Even prior to 1925, Zionist cartographers, geographers, and historians sought not only to name new Jewish communities but also to affix these Hebrew places-names to maps in an effort to transform Palestine into a territory of the Zionist imagination—Eretz Yisrael. With this project, these specialists sought an expanded role for place-naming, one that went beyond the new Jewish settlements to the rest of Palestine under British control. Spearheaded by JPES notables such as David Yellin, this campaign targeted the Royal Geographical Society's Committee for Names, which had jurisdiction over the designation of geographical places in Palestine. Zionists pressured the British for representation on the committee, and as a result three JPES members were added as advisers: Yellin himself; Izhak Ben-Zvi, an archeologist who would become Israel's second president; and Avraham-

Ya'akov Brawer, arguably the most eminent Hebrew geographer and cartographer of the time (Benvenisti 2000, 12). The drafting of a map of the Land of Israel with Hebrew place-names was an integral part of the overall project of hebraicizing Palestine—restoring a people, reviving a language, and redeeming a land.

This advisory group from the JPES focused first on the 1922 Census of Palestine undertaken by the British (Press 1925, 89–90; Abu El-Haj 2001, 85). British officials had prepared a list of names of Palestinian villages and asked the JPES advisory group to determine the historical Hebrew names of these villages, resulting in the first inventory of Hebrew place-names for a number of settlements and villages in Palestine. Zionists expected the British to publish this inventory in its first *Transliterated Personal and Geographical Names for Use in Palestine* of 1931, but this did not happen (Benvenisti 2000, 24; Abu El-Haj 2001, 86). Two reasons account for the omission.

First, British authorities were wary of the growing antagonism between Jewish settlers and Palestinians following riots between the two groups in 1929. Because Mandate Palestine was dominated by Arabic-speaking Palestinians with their own names of places, and because the British were reluctant to exacerbate conflict by overturning this reality, British authorities decided to render the dominant colloquial Arabic toponymy into written Arabic as well as English and Hebrew. While acknowledging Hebrew as an official language, the British reserved Hebrew names for places where the Jewish population had attained a 20 percent threshold. Consequently, of the place-names transliterated in Palestine, only 5 percent were Hebrew names. In the end, place-names published by the British were for the most part English renderings of Arabic names that reflected the dominant Arab character of the landscape (Benvenisti 2000, 24–25; Abu El-Haj 2001, 86–91).

Second and perhaps more important, the British were not about to cede their authority to designate place-names in Palestine. While they granted the Zionist movement the right to name Jewish places, the British regarded the assignment of place-names on the larger Palestinian landscape as their sovereign prerogative (Benvenisti 2000, 24). This policy—restricting Hebrew place-names to areas sufficiently Jewish—generated intense animosity among Zionists toward the British.

Interpreting this policy as a provocation, the Zionist community launched an aggressive campaign against the Mandate Government through the JPES and the Va'ad Leumi (Jewish National Council), the supreme institutional authority of the Yishuv in the pre-state period. In a document titled "Memorandum on Method of Transliteration of Geographical and Personal Names" (1932), Ben-Zvi implored British authorities to use translations of the Hebrew place-names from lists generated in 1922–24 by the JPES; in addition, he submitted an amended list of names "corrected in accordance with the principles laid down by our experts." The future president of Israel also emphasized that ancient Hebrew place names "belong to the country," while the "tendency to Arabicise Hebrew names is prejudicial to scientific and historical accuracy." Hebrew place-names, he argued, were objective facts that the Mandate Government was obliged to respect because of the official status of the Hebrew language in Palestine (quoted in Abu El-Haj 2001, 86–91).

Alongside this debate was an equally bitter disagreement over the Hebrew name for Palestine itself. What the Mandate Government's Names Committee proposed as the Hebrew equivalent for Palestine was the Hebrew word for Palestine—*Palestina*—followed by the Hebrew letters *aleph* and *yod* (or EY), standing for Eretz Yisrael (Abu El-Haj 2001, 82). (The committee also decided to designate the territory of the British Mandate as Palestine—English—and Filistin—Arabic.) Opposing this designation on behalf of the Yishuv, Yellin argued that Eretz Yisrael had always been the Hebrew name for Palestine. Citing biblical, Talmudic, and even non-Jewish sources, Yellin wrote that changing the name to Palestina EY not only subverted Hebrew convention but was contrary to a neutral, scientifically derived designation dating from time immemorial. Accordingly, Yellin insisted that "the proper name used for centuries be restored" (Abu El-Haj 2001, 84–85).

What was objectively revealed to Zionists as the landscape of a Hebrew-speaking people with their own way of designating places contradicted what was self-evident to Palestinians: a dominant 1,200-year-old Arabic-speaking socioeconomic life on the land with its own descriptive Arabic toponymy. In seeking to designate Palestine as Eretz Yisrael and spread Hebrew place-names across the landscape, the Zionist movement was attempting to enclose the area linguistically and cartographically as a possession of the Jewish people (Abu El-Haj 2001, 85). Although the movement was severely limited in designating place-names during the pre-state Mandate period, their efforts during the 1930s were but a prelude. A far more ambitious campaign of place-naming would occur after the State of Israel emerged in 1948 and the Zionists gained control over the institutions of power and authority.

From Names of Places to Place-Names on Maps

While archeology and contemporary Jewish settlement carried material affir-
mations of a Jewish landscape in Palestine, and while Hebrew names for
Jewish places reinforced such facts, maps designating these places in Hebrew
were potent instruments in "hebraicizing" the Palestinian landscape for both
Zionists and constituencies external to Zionism (Bar-Gal 2004, 38). At the
same time, maps of Hebrew space in Palestine in this period were part of a
fractious debate internal to Zionism focusing on the borders of Eretz Yisrael.
Two basic positions on this issue had emerged within the Zionist movement,
one represented by Chaim Weizmann, who accepted as a *fait accompli* the
British offer of Transjordan to the emir Abdallah and the Hussein family,
the other personified by Menachem Ussishkin, who demanded that Eretz
Yisrael include Transjordan and opposed any partition of the area under the
British Mandate into separate spheres. Ussishkin, who became president of
the Jewish National Fund in 1923, used that organization to promote his
vision of "Greater Israel." Many Zionist maps of the period were created
under the auspices of the JNF and thus conveyed Ussishkin's maximalist idea
of Israel extending to both sides of the Jordan River.

Hebrew maps during the 1920s and 1930s thus had a dual purpose. On the
one hand, they conveyed to the outside world a vision of Palestine as a
Hebrew space. On the other, they contained barely concealed JNF propaganda that projected the organization's maximalist idea of this Hebrew space
to other Zionists (Bar-Gal 2003, 140). Despite these different aims, both
arguments could be integrated as part of the same map in which Jewish presence extended over a wide expanse while Palestinian presence was diminished or even absent.

Two types of maps produced by the Jewish National Fund communicated
these dual claims of a Hebrew landscape within a greater Eretz Yisrael (Bar-
Gal 2003, 140). One type corresponded to maps created by professional cartographers. A second type corresponded to symbolic maps created not by
mapmakers but by graphic artists. In 1923, the JNF began to commission
both types of maps as part of a deliberate effort to convey certain claims
about land and territory in the area of the Mandate.

In terms of scientific maps, the most important early example was a map
created in 1925 by Avraham-Ya'akov Brawer at the behest of the JNF (fig. 20).
Titled "Eretz Yisrael," Brawer's map embodied two fundamental attributes
of early Zionist cartography. The first had to do with the borders of Eretz

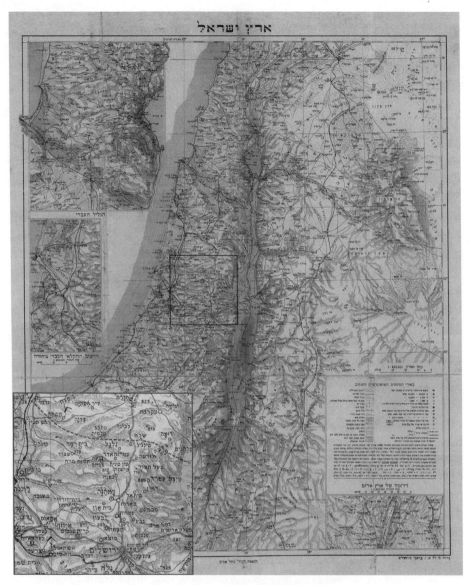

אֶרֶץ יִשְׂרָאֵל

FIGURE 20. Map of Eretz Yisrael, by Avraham-Ya'akov Brawer (1925). The inset features Jerusalem (bottom center) and, in addition to Palestinian towns, shows Jewish communities such as Motza and Kiryat Anavim just north of Jerusalem. Source: National Library of Israel Pal 1295, System Number 2367244. Reproduced by permission of Moshe Brawer and the National Library of Israel.

Yisrael, the second with the representation of Jewish settlement, and hence of a Hebrew territorial space. With respect to the borders of Eretz Yisrael, Brawer's map contains what is arguably the most prominent feature of pre-state JNF cartography: the alignment of the Jordan River and the three inland bodies of water down the center of the map's north-south axis (Bar-Gal 2003, 7). Although the map does demarcate the border established by the Mandate Government separating Palestine and Transjordan, the border is only faintly delineated, while the territory depicted outside the border works to undermine this notion of boundary. The map's prominent title, too, challenges the suggestion of a boundary, emphasizing that Eretz Yisrael does not stop at the Jordan River. What is thus projected by Brawer in the map is a territory that does not distinguish between land east and west of the Jordan River, a territory called the Land of Israel.

In certain respects, Brawer's map of Eretz Yisrael corresponded to geographical ideas about the borders of the country expressed in his 1927 book *Ha'aretz* (The Land [of Israel]). There, Brawer distinguished three border systems to describe the Land of Israel: (1) "biblical borders of the land of Israel"; (2) "natural" borders within the biblical boundary, consisting of four distinct geographical areas—the coastal plain, the mountain area, the Jordan Valley, and land east of the Jordan River; and (3) "political borders" implemented by the British Mandate, which drew a line along the Jordan River separating "Palestine" from Transjordan (Bar-Gal 2004, 37). In his map, Brawer elevated the first two categories while muting the political borders, creating a subtle set of arguments about the territory of Eretz Yisrael. For Brawer, Eretz Yisrael encompassed the four natural zones that traverse Palestine and Transjordan and extend north to the Litani River and the southern part of Lebanon. At the same time, by affixing the central north-south axis of the map along the Jordan River and muting the border created by the British, Brawer subtly hinted at the absence of British occupation of the territory. What was ultimately represented was a Hebrew territorial space, designated by the toponym Eretz Yisrael, which extended from the Mediterranean to the east beyond the Jordan River, and from Sidon in the north to the Negev in the south.

Brawer's map was also pioneering in that it was the first Hebrew map to depict virtually all the Jewish settlements in Palestine in 1925 (Moshe Brawer, author interview, July 26, 2015). Although a small number of Palestinian cities are represented, such as Nablus (designated by the Hebrew, Shechm) and Hebron (Hevron), Brawer used toponymy to develop an argument about the

Hebrew character of a geographical space that was still fundamentally Palestinian. While this projection of a Hebrew territorial space in the Land of Israel typified pre-state Zionist cartography and paralleled other Zionist efforts at hebraicizing the Palestinian landscape, Brawer's map was connected to a critical educational mission within the Yishuv focusing on geography and homeland in which Brawer himself was influential (Bar-Gal 1996; Bar-Gal 2004, 226; Bar-Gal 2000, 115). In his *Teaching "Homeland" in Elementary School* from 1930, Brawer insisted on the use of maps for the study of *molodet* (homeland), the aim of which was "to tie the cords between the Jewish people and its land that had been broken by oppressors and to connect the distant [Hebrew] past with the present and future" (quoted in Bar-Gal 1991, 7). By delineating Jewish settlements in a Hebrew idiom, and by anchoring these settlements cartographically to the idea of Eretz Yisrael, Brawer crafted lessons that projected a Hebrew geography onto land still overwhelmingly non-Jewish.

At the same time that the JNF solicited the map from Brawer, the organization was actively involved in designing maps of the second type, primarily for propaganda purposes (Bar-Gal 2003, 141). Intended for a much larger distribution, such maps projected a more didactic set of arguments about the Hebrew character of Palestine. One such map, from 1925 (fig. 21, *left*), provides a stark contrast to Brawer's scientifically rendered map but crafts a similar point of view about Palestine's Hebrew character.

The map's arguments are represented by a highly stylized set of graphic images. Land acquired and settled by Jews is shown in bold hues of blue and green, but the most striking feature of the map is the area where Jews have not settled. Comprising most of the map, this area is rendered in stark white, suggestive of an empty landscape. Although the towns of Tulkarem and Jenin are designated, the map as a graphic instrument essentially erases Palestinian presence, beckoning to donors and settlers with the idea that most of Eretz Yisrael is not yet redeemed. Subsequent JNF renditions of this map contained a textual cartouche that complemented the visually rendered arguments about the land and its redemption. The text in the cartouche asked map viewers to ponder the small area of Jewish settlement relative to the territory as a whole and implored them to do their utmost for the task of redemption ahead. In this way, an imagined geography about land was linked explicitly to a plea for action to realize the imagined vision.

The symbolic map of 1925 marks the beginning of a trend in which graphic artists, working as mapmakers, crafted one of the signature design elements

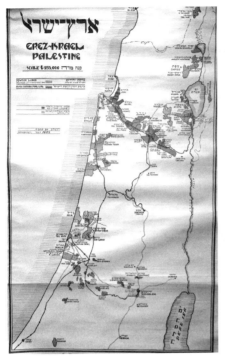

FIGURE 21. *Left:* Map of Eretz Israel (1925). From the private collection of Moshe Brawer. Photo taken by author with permission of Moshe Brawer. *Right:* The Blue Box (c. 1934). Reproduced by permission from an anonymous private museum collection.

of JNF cartography in terms of a sparse, even invisible Palestinian presence on the land (Bar-Gal, 2003: 149). This theme would emerge more forcefully by 1934, in what was perhaps the most widely disseminated symbol of JNF fundraising for land purchases in Palestine: the celebrated JNF Blue Box (fig. 21, *right*).

The JNF first developed the boxes in 1902–4 as an instrument for collecting funds from Jews worldwide in order to buy land in Palestine. Equally critical, however, was the ideological role of the boxes as advertisements to world Jewry for Zionism and the JNF. This dual aim was acknowledged in a JNF booklet of 1921 explaining "the value of the JNF Box," in which the box is an "eternal fundraiser in the house, the synagogue, the clubhouse" and "performs constant and perpetual propaganda work for the JNF wordlessly" (Bar-Gal 2003, 34). What enabled the box to perform this ideological mission was the symbolic content printed on it and the mass diffusion of this content with the placement of millions of boxes in Jewish homes and institutions worldwide (Bar-Gal 2003, 38; Bar-Gal 2003, 1). It was the design on the box, however, that carried this ideological function, a design deriving from the lineage of JNF symbolic mapping and appearing on the cover of the organization's magazine, *Karnenu* (Our Fund).

In November 1928, the JNF decorated the cover of *Karnenu* with a map of Eretz Yisrael that shared the basic design of the symbolic map of 1925 and carried the same arguments about the landscape as *terra nullius*. One significant change in the map on the *Karnenu* cover, however, was the absence of a border along the Jordan River. So popular was this cover of *Karnenu* in conveying the Hebrew character of land in Palestine that the JNF decided to use its basic design for its blue collection boxes (Bar-Gal 2003, 146–47).

By 1934, when the *Karnenu*-like map first appeared on its Blue Boxes, the JNF had appropriated the box as a powerful instrument of meaning-making. Like the *Karnenu* representation, the Blue Box map had no borders. Instead *Eretz Yisrael* extended into southern Lebanon, while the seemingly empty territory represented in white stretched across the Jordan River and actually wrapped around the right side of the box, suggesting a vast *terra nullius* to the east (fig. 21). Undoubtedly, however, the most revealing feature of the map was the elimination of any Palestinian presence. Apart from the limited areas of Jewish settlement, the Land of Israel beckoned to future Jewish settlers as an open and blank slate.

From Projecting to Taking

Even as Zionists were using history, toponymy, and cartography to project a Hebrew vision of the Palestinian landscape, the movement was also engaged in taking actual control of land. One source for this activity is the "Report on Immigration, Land Settlement, and Development" (1930) of John Hope Simpson, a British official charged with investigating the causes of rioting between Jews and Palestinians in 1929. Although the Yishuv was critical of the report (Granott 1952, 99), one of the assertions in the document about the source of tension between Jews and Arabs—the land acquisition and labor policies of the Yishuv—had been affirmed earlier by a Zionist writer, Yitzhak Epstein, in a 1907 essay titled "A Hidden Question."

According to Hope Simpson (1930, 52–54), the fraught relationship between the Yishuv and Palestinians derived from the conditions by which

Zionist entities bought, held, sold, and leased land. These conditions, he argued, were exclusionary and caused dispossession. To support this argument, Hope Simpson quoted from the 1929 constitution of the Jewish Agency, which specified that lands acquired by the Jewish National Fund "be held as the inalienable property of the Jewish people" and that all work on this land be undertaken by "Jewish labour." The constitution also makes reference to JNF lease agreements, stipulating that "the holding shall never be held by any but a Jew" and that the lessee will execute all work connected with cultivating the holding "only with Jewish labour." For Hope Simpson, these policies of labor and land purchase resulted in land being "extra-territorialized." "It ceases to be land from which the Arab can gain any advantage either now or at any time in the future. Not only can he ever hope to lease or cultivate it, but, by the stringent provisions of the leases of the Jewish National Fund, he is deprived forever from employment on that land. Nor can anyone help him by purchasing the land and restoring it to common use" (Hope Simpson 1930, 54).

The observations made earlier by Epstein were in some ways even more forceful. Epstein noted that in Palestine, when land changed hands, the custom among Palestinians was for the tillers of land to remain and cultivate. By contrast,

> When we [Jews] buy such a property, we evict the former tillers.... If we do not want to deceive ourselves, we must admit that we have driven impoverished people from their humble abode and taken bread out of their mouths.... Can we really rely on this way of acquiring land? Will it succeed, and does it suit our purpose? One hundred times no.... If there are farmers who water their fields with their own sweat and their own mother's milk, it is the Arabs. (Epstein 1907, 41–42)

Both Epstein and Hope Simpson offer a cautionary assessment of Zionist land and labor policies. For Hope Simpson, the Zionist boycott of Arab labor is "a constant and increasing source of danger to the country.... As long as these provisions exist in the Constitution of the Zionist Organization, in the lease of the Keren-Kayemeth and in the agreement of the Keren-Hayesod, it cannot be regarded as desirable that large areas of land should be transferred to the Jewish National Fund" (Hope Simpson 1930, 55–56). In the environment of the Mandate, members of the pre-state Yishuv had imagined a Hebrew landscape—and were telegraphing, with facts on the ground, how they intended to shape that space.

LAWFARE: THE LEGAL REMAKING OF THE
PALESTINIAN LANDSCAPE

During the British Mandate, the Jewish community benefited from British patronage in settling land but lacked sovereignty over the territory it coveted for statehood (Shamir 2000, 9, 29). This situation changed in 1947–49 after the Yishuv emerged victorious in a campaign of war and assumed sovereignty over 78 percent of Mandatory Palestine, reconstituted as the State of Israel. Within this territorial container, the state's new rulers took control of the institutions for creating systems of rights, notably the institution of the law. Most dramatic in this regard was the overhaul of landed property rights. After 1948, the State of Israel rewrote laws on rights to land that disqualified Palestinians as owners of their landed property and transferred this resource to the state for reallocation to the country's Jewish citizens, an unmistakably overt use of the law as an instrument of force (Forman and Kedar 2004).

At the same time, sovereignty enabled Israel's rulers to reinforce this institutionalized process of dispossession and land transfer with state-sponsored cultural measures designed to replace the Arab Palestinian landscape with a landscape Jewish in character. Foremost in this category was the creation in 1949 of an official place-names committee within the prime minister's office. Focusing initially on the Negev, this committee was expanded in 1951 to alter place-names throughout the country. Its ultimate goal was the creation of a Hebrew map of the newly constituted state that would function as a cultural instrument to educate the Jewish population about its connection to what was being redefined as a Hebrew landscape. This committee of place-names continues to operate to this day.

From transformations engineered by this campaign of lawfare emerged a different landscape, remade on the ground and renamed on maps in the image and likeness of the landscape's new rulers.

Law and Geographical Place-Names

When the State of Israel emerged in 1948, the Jewish Palestine Exploration Society was renamed the Israel Exploration Society (IES). Yet the IES continued to emphasize research to enhance "the connection between the People of Israel and the Land of Israel" (Benvenisti 2000, 11–12). In this role, the IES would be linked to one of the most politically charged cultural projects undertaken by the new state: the creation of a Hebrew toponymy for the landscape and its incorporation into a new map of the Land of Israel.

In July 1949, Prime Minister Ben-Gurion, feeling a sense of urgency, summoned eight associates from the IES and Josef (Yosef) Weitz from the JNF as the core members of a cabinet-level Committee for Designation of Place Names in the Negev (Negev Names Committee, or NNC). In March of that year, the Israeli army had quelled the remaining Arab resistance in the Negev and begun the process of expelling 90 percent of the region's Bedouin population to neighboring Egypt and Jordan. Although the 1947 UN partition plan had allotted a large portion of the Negev to the Jewish state, military conquest over the entire Negev changed the territorial configuration of what was now Israel. Thus the Jewish state gained sovereignty over an area overwhelmingly Arab and Bedouin in character that now comprised 60 percent of the new state's territorial footprint (Benvenisti 2000, 11–12).

For Ben-Gurion and the Jewish state, the extension of Israeli sovereignty into this territory presented a paradox. In 1948, the Negev's Jewish population amounted to 475 persons, or less than one half of 1 percent of the total (Amara and Miller 2012, 73). Owing to its overwhelmingly Arab Bedouin character, the Negev—*Naqab* in Arabic—was known almost exclusively through Arabic place-names. Ben-Gurion's committee sought to change this state of affairs.

According to Naftali Kadmon, who served on the Names Committee for almost fifty years, the Negev was Ben-Gurion's obsession. "Ben-Gurion moved to the Negev as an example to the rest of the country to affirm its importance for the future Jewish state," he explained. "Like many Israelis, Ben-Gurion wanted to establish a Hebrew environment for cultural matters including the geography of the country, so it was natural to create a Hebrew environment in mapping the Negev." The task of the NNC, Kadmon emphasized, "was to remake the Arab landscape of the Negev with Hebrew place-names as a starting point for creating a Hebrew map of the new country" (author interview, September 29, 2014).

The NNC was an instrument of cultural reengineering designed to promote a new vision among the Jewish Israeli public about the Negev as the patrimony of the Jewish people (Benvenisti 2000, 14). The time-honored practice of place-naming—creating a vocabulary of cultural signs influencing how people perceive, understand, and imagine the territorial world around them—enabled the NNC to achieve this educational and cultural aim. With 90 percent of the Bedouin population evicted from the Negev between 1949 and 1954, the NNC conducted its work on what committee chair Zalman Lifshitz characterized as a cartographic blank slate. "There is no point in keeping [Arabic place-names]," said Lifshitz, "since there are almost no Bedouin there." In addition to the expulsions, however, there was another reason Lifshitz referred to the area as empty of Bedouins. Alongside the evictions, the State of Israel forcibly removed the remaining ten thousand Bedouins from different areas of the Negev and transferred them to a small area near Beersheva known as the "Enclosure Zone" (*Siyag* in Hebrew; see below). There the Bedouin were confined, forbidden to exit or reenter the Siyag without permits from the government, and were without basic public services. Moreover, Lifshitz claimed—dubiously—that the Bedouin were nomads who did not put down roots. He thus concluded that, just as the Bedouin are without anchors to the land, "so also are the Bedouin place-names not rooted there" (quoted in Benvenisti 2000, 18).

Although some in the NNC resisted erasing the Arab Bedouin cartography of the Negev, a letter to committee chair Lifshitz from Ben-Gurion himself reminded committee members what the state expected from them. "We are obliged to remove the Arabic names for reasons of state," the prime minister wrote unflinchingly. "Just as we do not recognize the Arabs' political proprietorship of the land, so do we not recognize their spiritual proprietorship and their names" (quoted in Benvenisti 2000, 14).

At the completion of its work in March 1950, the NNC had established 533 Hebrew names for geographical features in the Negev along with names for 27 new Jewish communities (Benvenisti 2000, 23). In the official gazette of place-names published the next year, it was noted that under the British Mandate extending the Hebrew toponymy beyond Jewish settlements had foundered owing to British opposition. By contrast, the NNC had carried out a large-scale reclassification of a singularly Arab landscape owing to an official legal mandate. In this way, sovereignty enabled the state's new leaders to exploit the power of law and institutionalize place-naming as a change agent on the landscape (Benvenisti 2000, 24–25).

If the new state waged a successful campaign against an existing Arab toponymy in the Negev, it also sought to reverse much of the toponymic work of the British Mandate and even the pre-Mandate surveys of the (British) Palestine Exploration Fund (PEF). In the surveys of Claude Conder and Herbert Kitchener, the PEF had recorded roughly nine thousand Arabic place-names in the late 1870s (Benvenisti 2000, 29). In 1881, Edward Henry Palmer, a professor of Arabic at Cambridge University and the PEF's Arabic language expert, transliterated these place-names into English, with descriptions in English of the Arabic toponyms. From Palmer's list, names such as Ain el Muthniyat (Spring of the Lands Twice Turned over for Sowing) and Ain Umm el 'Aml (Spring of the Mother of Work), and even the unsavory Khallet ez Zibil (Dell of Manure), testify to a colorful toponymic heritage (Palmer 1881, 2–3, 6). During the British Mandate, Zionists had argued to the British that Arabic place-names were primarily arabicized versions of Hebrew names and that therefore the Hebrew names should be restored. This argument, however, met with limited success; the British guarded their sovereign prerogative on the assignment of place-names in Palestine and were not about to cede this task to the Yishuv. As a result, maps of Palestine made by the British prior to and during the Mandate were infused with an Arabic toponymy deriving from the work of Kitchener, Conder, and Palmer that emphasized the Arab character of the land, inflaming the Zionist community (Benvenisti 2000, 30).

It was precisely this Arab character of the Negev landscape that emerged as the target for the NNC. Now backed by state power and the "blank slate" created by the mass expulsions of Bedouins, the committee was able to recreate a biblical and Hebrew landscape where for centuries Bedouins had predominated. "The names we found," states the NNC summary regarding its ten-month task, "not only sound strange to our ears. . . . Many of the names are offensive in their gloomy and morose meanings, which reflect the powerlessness of the nomads." Indeed, numerous place-names that derived from Bedouin descriptions of the land were considered by the Zionists as epithets. Consequently, the Bedouin place of Bir Khandis (Well of the Shadow of Death") became the Hebrew Be'er Orah (Well of Light), while Ain Weiba (Spring of the Plague) emerged with the biblical name of Ein Yahav (Spring of Yahav). By means of these revisions, Hebrew was projected onto the vast topographical spaces of the Negev landscape (Benvenisti 2000, 17, 19–20).

By the time the NNC had concluded its work, not only had it established Hebrew names for the 560 places in Negev, but it had also produced a map of the area, described by the committee as "a Hebrew map of the Negev, cleansed of foreign names in which every placed is called by a Hebrew name" (Kadman 2015, 93–94). For Ben-Gurion, this campaign to create Hebrew names for places in the Negev was complementary to the military conquest of the Negev Bedouin. "By granting Hebrew names to all areas of the Negev," he proclaimed in an address to the NNC, "you have removed the infamy of alien and foreign tongues from half the state of Israel, and completed the action begun by the Israel Defense Forces" (quoted in Kadman 2015, 93).

In March 1951, the government of Israel created a new committee—the Government Names Committee (GNC)—with an official mandate for the designation of place-names throughout the entire state. Immediately confronting the committee was new Jewish settlements in or near the hundreds of abandoned and destroyed Palestinian villages. For this reason, names for Jewish settlements emerged as the first priority of the GNC. Committee chair Avraham Biran announced in August of that year that the names assigned to places by the committee would be published in the official government gazette *(Reshumot)* and that their utilization by state and local authorities and public institutions "shall be obligatory" (quoted in Benvenisti 2000, 25). Moreover, only the place-names assigned by the committee would be recorded on maps of the new state, a fact that showed how the power of the state and the power of maps had essentially merged.

In most cases, crafting names for these new Jewish settlements involved substituting a Hebrew name for the Arabic one, on the assumption that the Arabic name derived from an earlier, more "authentic" Hebrew name. Thus the abandoned Palestinian village of Faradiyya became Parod, Dallata reemerged as Dalton, and Bayt Dajan became Beit Dagon. In other instances of Jewish settlements established on or near emptied Palestinian villages, if the Arabic name had no Hebrew equivalent, the GNC used the names of biblical characters, such as Aviel, or phrases from the Hebrew Bible, such as Te'ashur (from Isaiah, referring to "trees that will blossom on the way of the redeemed in the wilderness"). Of the roughly 770 Jewish settlements created within the pre-1967 borders of Israel, names for 350 corresponded to this broad definition of biblical Hebrew (Benvenisti 2000, 34–35).

As Jewish settlements multiplied, the GNC developed new methods for naming them. In the case of 170 communities where the Arabic name had no ancient Hebrew equivalent, the committee assigned names from agriculture and nature, such as Avivim (from *aviv,* springtime). For another 70 settlements, the GNC chose symbolic names from Hebrew, such as Hosen, meaning strength. Finally, for 20 percent of the settlements on Hebrew maps of Israel, the GNC chose famous modern Zionist figures for place-names. The GNC was careful not to allow foreign influences in these names; thus the kibbutz named for the American Supreme Court justice Louis Brandeis, for example, was not transliterated from English but was instead hebraicized into the name Ein ha-Shofet (Spring of the Judge).

In addition to settlements, the GNC assigned Hebrew names to features of the landscape—water courses, springs, tells, mountains, hills, and ruins. While the starting point for assigning names to such landscape features was biblical, most names were taken from flora, fauna, or birds or were translations of Arabic names into Hebrew. In its first nine years of work, the GNC established 3,000 new place-names for settlements and feature of landscape, including 780 streams and 520 springs. Reports of the GNC show that "little by little, a closed circle evolved: . . . first a mountain, stream, or ruin was assigned a name, and then everything else in the vicinity—gullies, plains, caves, hills, and crossroads—was given a name derived from the first. . . . And so it went on and on: thousands of names changing meaning, erasing an entire universe" (Benvenisti 2000, 37–39).

Ultimately, for Biran and the GNC, the point of renaming places was to situate them on maps as a way of forging a national consciousness about the landscape and connecting Jewish Israelis to what was now being conveyed as Jewish and Hebrew land (Benvenisti 2000, 39). In transcribing this toponymy into cartographic language, Israeli mapmakers created an entirely new set of arguments about the Hebrew character of the land. While these cartographers retained Arabic names for Palestinian communities that remained after 1948, the Arabic toponymy for geographical features of the landscape was erased. In addition, the GNC made the critical decision to eradicate the memory of Palestinian villages whose residents were evicted or fled. "We have ascertained that no traces are left of the abandoned villages," stated Biran at a committee meeting in 1959, "their names are hereby abolished." There are few similar examples anywhere of such deliberate radical changes in the making of a map (Benvenisti, 2000, 42, 53).

On the landscape was a social and physical reality vastly different from what existed before 1948. All but a tiny fraction of the Palestinian and Bedouin population had been driven forcibly from the land. To the victors went spoils of war, including the power to create a cartography that celebrated this story of conquest in muted tones of scientific objectivity.

Law and Landed Property Rights

Alongside Israeli cartographers renaming places and affixing these place-names to maps, Israeli legal experts were enlisting the law as an instrument for transferring land from Palestinians to Jewish Israelis in order to remake the imagined geography of a Jewish space into an actual Hebrew space. In this manner, the State of Israel was following the practice of other settler societies (Forman and Kedar 2003, 494). In the Israeli case, rewriting the law allowed land possessed by Palestinians to be transformed into a new ownership category: "Israel Lands" (Forman and Kedar 2004). Israeli lawmakers discovered, however, that the state needed a second mechanism to formalize the state's title to the Palestinian land it coveted. It thus implemented a second process termed "settlement of title," focusing initially on the Galilee where a large Palestinian population remained after 1948, with the aim of forcing them to verify ownership of their holdings. In those instances— almost always—where Palestinians did not possess documentation for their holdings, settlement of title resulted in the transfer of Palestinian land into the pool of state-owned land. By the early 1960s, through legislation and settlement of title, the state had secured roughly 93 percent of the land surface inside Israel as state property. To Israeli jurists and lawmakers, this process of turning Palestinian land into state property was entirely lawful. To Palestinians, the process was one of organized plunder under cover of meticulously conceived legal procedures (Tamari 2005, 90). However the process is characterized, what emerged from the creation of Israel Lands was a vastly unequal system of rights to landed property and an ethnically divided territorial space (Kedar 2001, 999).

From Palestinian Land to "Israel Lands." When Israel emerged from the conflict of 1947–49, only about 13.5 percent of the roughly 20.6 million dunums of land in the new state was under formal Jewish ownership, either by private individuals or by the state (Forman and Kedar 2004, 812). Much of this discrepancy between Jewish sovereignty over the territory of Israel and the pattern of land ownership within it derived from the enormous inventory of landed property left behind by Palestinian refugees. In 1947, roughly 900,000 Palestinians were living in what became Israel. Of this number, roughly 750,000 were uprooted from their homes during the conflict and became refugees, effectively evicted and exiled when the new state forcibly barred them from returning to their land and property (Ben-Ami 2007, 42–45). Meanwhile, 300 new Jewish settlements were established by 1950, the same number as were created between 1882 and 1948, and Jewish immigrants more than doubled the state's Jewish population to 1.4 million by 1951 (Benvenisti 2000, 178).

Nevertheless, a legal dilemma confronted the new state. Palestinian refugees were still the legal owners of their landed property, which extended over a vast area of the new state (Kedar 2001, 946). The State of Israel aimed to remedy this discrepancy by creating a legal route to gain control of refugee land (Forman and Kedar 2004, 812). This legal campaign of turning Palestinian landed property into state-owned land occurred in four overlapping phases.

The first phase of this process began prior to the formation of the state in March 1948, when armed units of the Yishuv, known at that time as the Haganah, routed Palestinian forces and took control of landed property in ninety abandoned Palestinian villages (Golan 1995, 406; Fischbach 2003, 14–15). Concurrently, some Jewish settlements seized Palestinian land illegally, and in response, Ben-Gurion empowered a Ministerial Committee on Abandoned Property to frame procedures for taking control of Palestinian land. This effort resulted in the first instrument to legalize the seizure of Palestinian landed property, the Fallow Lands Regulations (Forman and Kedar 2004, 813).

Drafted in June 1948, Fallow Lands granted temporary possession of abandoned land to what was now the state; this measure in turn compelled Israeli lawmakers to work on legislation to vest land abandoned by Palestinian owners *permanently* in a new state institution. The result was the Absentee Property Regulations, passed in December 1948. Although these regulations were also temporary, they outlined the two core elements that would become part of the most important piece of legislation passed by Israel on the issue of refugee landed property, the Absentee Property Law. First, the regulations established a new status for certain persons—"absentees"—and used this status to identify abandoned land that could be repossessed. Three attributes identified the absentee, but the most important focused on those individuals who had been citizens of Mandate Palestine and who at any time after November 1947, and for any reason, had left their place of residence. Even if such persons had returned, they were still designated absentees. These regulations thus eliminated rights to land for a whole class of people. Second, the regulations created an official position, "Custodian of Absentee Property" (CAP), with the power to seize property from those designated as absentees. These regulations signaled in broad outline the provisions of the Absentee Property Law and the Development Authority Law, which lay at the center of phase two (Forman and Kedar 2004, 813–14).

In this second phase, Zalman Lifshitz played a decisive role as Ben-Gurion's Special Advisor on Land and Border Demarcation in seeking to make permanent the Absentee Property Regulations established in phase one. In a "Report on the Need for Legal Settlement of the Issue of Absentee Property" (March 1949), submitted to Ben-Gurion and key ministries, Lifshitz cautioned that the transitory nature of the Absentee Property and Fallow Land Regulations precluded the government from permanently fixing the status of these properties (Forman and Kedar 2004, 816).[6] Citing Pakistan, where in 1948 the government legalized the expropriation of property belonging to departed Hindu and Sikh individuals, Lifshitz recommended that Israel craft similar legislation in order to make permanent the regulations for Absentee Property and Fallow Land.

By the end of 1949, lawmakers had drafted two bills that appeared before the Israeli Knesset, the Absentee Property Bill and the Development Authority Bill. For the Absentee Property Bill, lawmakers extended the definition of "absentee" to include not only those who were outside the country as refugees but also those who had temporarily left their homes during the hostilities, but remained inside the country and returned home when hostilities had ceased. In the new bill, this group, who were actually citizens of Israel, assumed a different classification: "present absentees." Roughly 25–50 percent of the Palestinians remaining in the State of Israel were classified as present absentees (COHRE/BADIL 2005, 41). Accordingly, the Custodian had the prerogative of confiscating not only the property of Palestinian refugees designated as "absentees" but also land belonging to Palestinians still in the country but classified as "present absentees."

Central to the second piece of legislation was the establishment of a new entity, the Development Authority (DA), as an intermediary for the transfer of absentee property to the state and the Jewish National Fund. In the language of the bill, however, the term *absentee* was deliberately omitted. Instead, the bill emphasized the role of the DA as a catalyst for the country's development. Lawmakers, though, clearly intended the DA to process land expropriated under the provisions of the Absentee Property Bill for reallocation to Jewish Israelis. Indeed, the singular purpose of the Absentee Property and Development Authority bills was not lost on lawmakers and heads of ministries. "We are in a very delicate situation," warned Finance Minister Eliezer Kaplan to members of the Knesset Economics Committee in January 1950, shortly after the two bills were proposed. "We are totally mistaken if we think we are holding spoils with which we can do as we please" (quoted in Forman and Kedar 2004, 818).

Despite Kaplan's foreboding message, the Knesset passed both laws, the provisions of which were fully understood by Palestinians still in the country.

Speaking of the Absentee Property Law, Tawfiq Tubi, a Palestinian member of the Knesset, articulated the Palestinian opposition succinctly. "This law is a symbol," he said in the Knesset. "It is an expression of the discrimination practiced against Arab inhabitants of this country. . . . In accordance with the provisions of this law thousands of Arab inhabitants of the country are regarded as 'absentees' although they are citizens of the state—and they are being plundered of their right to their property. The Custodian, assisted by the law, is plundering them of their rights as citizens. . . . The real function of this honorable Custodian is to plunder more and more" (quoted in Jiryis 1973, 91–92).

Indeed, the vast amount of absentee land available under the law for reallocation to Jewish Israelis, alongside the land taken illegally from Palestinians inside Israel who were not absentees, was creating conditions that some Israeli lawmakers found indefensible (Jiryis 1973, 83; Foreman and Kedar 2004, 819). During debates on the Absentee Property Bill, certain Knesset members insisted that the inclusion of present absentees was untenable and so voted against it. Even the Custodian of Absentee Property, Moshe Porat, recommended that the legal definition of *absentee* match the normal meaning of the word and that the state return property taken from so-called present absentees (Segev 1986, 82). This recommendation, however, was not implemented. For the state, the problem was not preventing illegal seizures of Palestinian land, nor ending the expropriation of land of Palestinian citizens of Israel who were classified as present absentees. Instead, Israeli jurists began to work on ways of legalizing both these means of acquiring land. These efforts came to fruition during the third phase in the development of the Israeli land regime, which culminated in the Land Acquisition Law of 1953.

The purpose of the Land Acquisition Law was to legalize land seizures carried out against both nonabsentees and present absentees by retroactively classifying their land as indispensable for "security" or "development." In this way, the government avoided the issue of the seizures' legality by shifting the focus away from the status of the landowner. As explained in the law's preamble, although security and development may not have been the reasons for expropriation of land at the time of the taking, such imperatives were ongoing and could thus be retroactively applied as justification for the seizure. In a sober critique, Finance Minister Kaplan admitted to this ruse of turning expropriations done without a legal basis into something lawful when he stated that the law aimed "to legalize certain actions taken during and after the war." Once reclassified as necessary for security or development, Kaplan concluded, these lands could never be returned to their owners (quoted in Jiryis 1973, 99).

By 1953, as the third phase in the evolution of the Israeli land regime came to a close with passage of the Land Acquisition Law, the impacts on the landscape were palpable. The State of Israel had built 370 new Jewish settlements from 1948 to 1953. Of these, 350 had been constructed on land confiscated by the state in accordance with the various land laws passed since 1950 (COHRE/BADIL 2005, 41).

The fourth and final phase in the evolution of the Israeli land regime focused on creating a system of governance for the state and quasi-state entities such as the Jewish National Fund that had played major roles in the pre-state land policy of the Zionist movement. By 1950, the JNF still owned 2.1 million dunums of land in Israel, second only to the 16.7 million dunums claimed by the state, and the Fund was intent on retaining a position of primacy in the new land regime. What eventually emerged was a system centralized in a new state institution, the Israel Lands Administration (ILA); within this framework the JNF and one other institutional actor, the Development Authority, retained decisive roles by virtue of their status as major landholders (Forman and Kedar 2004, 822–23).

The ILA institutionalized a system whereby the state, the Development Authority, and the Jewish National Fund, which by 1951 collectively owned or controlled 92 percent of the land in Israel, held this inventory in a "closed reservoir." This closed reservoir of the ILA consisted of a series of institutional and administrative barriers that prevented land from entering a free market and thus becoming accessible to non-Jews. Owing to these barriers, land in the reservoir could only be transferred to the JNF or the DA; the DA, in turn, could only transfer land to the state or the JNF. Finally, the JNF, by its own bylaws, was forbidden to sell land at all and could only lease land to Jews. In this way, land appropriated through various land laws was consolidated into an inventory of nationalized property that was centralized within the ILA with no outlet except to organizations of Jewish Israelis (Forman and Kedar 2004, 823–25).

Estimates vary as to the amount of absentee land that became state property. A report issued in November 1948 by a committee chaired by Yosef Weitz estimated that abandoned Palestinian land amounted to 2 million dunums. Omitted from this estimate, however, was land outside village boundaries defined as dead land and thus state property, and village land considered common (Fischbach 2003, 43–44). "Every village and town had land for common uses which was open with no fences," explains Ali Z., a resident of Sahknin, one of the larger towns in the Galilee. "When the Israelis came in 1948–49, they confiscated this common land" (author interview, September 8, 2014). Meanwhile, the United Nations Conciliation Commission for Palestine (UNCCP) arrived at a very different number. In its 1951 report, the UNCCP estimated refugee land appropriated by the state at 16.3 million dunums; this included privately owned Palestinian agricultural land as well as land in the Negev appropriated by the state as "dead land" (Fischbach 2003, 120–21). More recent estimates place the figure at 4.2–5.8 million dunums (Golan 1995, 403, 431; Fischbach 2003, 41). Whatever the amount, there is little dispute that an enormous inventory of land not owned by members of the Yishuv or by the State of Israel in May 1948 had changed hands by 1960 under the auspices of the Absentee Property Law, the Development Authority Law, and the Land Acquisition Law. In addition to abandoned refugee land seized by the state, roughly 40–60 percent of the land belonging to Palestinian citizens of Israel classified as present absentees was also expropriated (Kedar 2001, 948). Consequently, a campaign waged through the law effectively transferred land from one group of owners to another.

Lawfare and Settling Title on the Frontier. Although the laws of the 1950s transformed millions of dunums of Palestinian land into state property, there remained land in Israel still possessed by Palestinian Israelis but no less coveted by the new state for redemption (Kedar 2001, 949). Two regions revealed heavy concentrations of land in this category, the Galilee in the north and the Negev (Naqab) in the south, which together constituted 80 percent of the territorial footprint of the Israeli state. In these areas, Palestinians in 1948–50 far outnumbered Jewish Israelis, which meant that the Jewish state confronted the anomaly of a Palestinian majority on 80 percent of its land. Accordingly, the Galilee and Negev were designated as "frontier areas" which the government aimed to settle with Israeli Jews. This project of "Judaizing" the landscape, however, depended on state land to anchor Jewish settlement (Forman 2005, 116).[7] In order for the state to make strides in its project of land redemption, especially in the Galilee, Palestinian landholders somehow had to be dispossessed. In the end, much of this Palestinian property would come into the state's inventory through a legal mechanism that supplemented the legislation of the 1950s: settling title on land (Kedar 2001, 993).

Settlement of title opened a second legal front in the transfer of land from Palestinians to the State of Israel (Kedar 2001, 948). Following the conflict of 1947–49, when large areas of the fledgling state were emptied of Palestinians and Israeli lawmakers passed legislation that reclassified this population as "absentee," their land became state property. Yet this wholesale reclassification lacked precise demarcations, and even Israeli officials were forced to concede that land remade into state property by virtue of the laws of the 1950s had to be given precise legal descriptions before it could pass into the state's landed inventory (Forman 2005, 16). Such land had to be surveyed, its boundaries configured on maps, and title for the bounded and mapped land assigned and recorded. Through the process of survey, settlement of title enabled the government to identify specific plots of absentee land, verify the ownership status of those plots, and, once verified as absentee, claim those plots as property of the state.

In the Galilee, settlement of title sought to enlarge the inventory of state land by compelling Palestinians to *prove,* through documents, that they were the land's legal owners. Palestinians who held rights to their land through the Ottoman notion of continuous occupancy and cultivation were invariably unable to meet this requirement. As result, their land passed into the category of state property. This newly designated state property became the foundation of Jewish settlement, enabling the Judaization of frontier areas to commence (Kedar 2001, 993; Forman 2005, xiii).

In addition to delineating absentee property and identifying undocumented Palestinian land, the process of settling title admitted to an equally ambitious aim: imposing a modern cadastral system of property on the landscape. Prior to the formation of Israel, the Ottomans, even after the reforms of 1858, recorded patterns of landholding in Palestine only through text descriptions (Kark 1997, 49, 56). Even the British, despite ambitious intentions to survey the area of the Mandate, managed to map landholding on only 20 percent of the Palestinian landscape (Gavish 2005, 201). Unlike its predecessors, the State of Israel was determined to survey and map its domains, not only to identify the patterns of dominium on its territory but also to extend the standards of modern landed property rights over informal customary practices of possession. Israeli insistence on this project stemmed from the way that modern landed property lends itself to greater levels of control by the sovereign power.

Modern landed property reshapes landscapes into *grids* of subdivided plots of land (Shamir 1996, 237; Blomley 2003). Each bounded space of the grid corresponds to an owner and is an area where the owner's rights begin and end. Such a system renders the landscape "legible" in terms of who owns each plot and the boundaries inside which owners exercise the primary right of land ownership: the right to exclude (Scott 1998, 33–36). For this legible grid of landed property to become operational, however, a certain type of information is needed, which is acquired through survey (Blomley 2003). If indeed knowledge is power, then the knowledge of the landscape obtained through survey is what the State of Israel was seeking in extending modern landed property across its domains and imposing settlement of title on its land.

In undertaking surveys for the settlement of title operation, Israeli policymakers claimed that the state was fulfilling objectives inherited from the British Mandate's Land Settlement Ordinance of 1928. Following passage of that ordinance, the British Land and Survey Department carried out extensive surveys during the next twenty years in an effort to settle land titles for Mandatory Palestine. Despite the best efforts of the actors involved in this massive undertaking, however, by the end of the Mandate in 1947 only 20 percent of the country had been surveyed (Gavish 2005, 260, 201). Thus the Israeli government was able to claim that the Land Settlement Ordinance of 1928 and the British settlement of title operations that emerged from it furnished the new state with a legal basis for settling title on Palestinian land, a position at the center of the Israeli land regime to this day (Kedar 2001, 938).

When, by the mid-1950s, the Israeli government carried out the initial reallocation of land to Jewish Israelis in those areas of the country emptied of Palestinians, they did so on the basis of rough and preliminary surveys (Kedar 2001, 949). Although this process did not meet the standards of land measurement desired by the new state, the government was content to survey and settle title on abandoned land reallocated to Israeli Jews at a later date. What interested the government for immediate survey were those areas of the country—frontier areas—where Palestinians still predominated, especially the Galilee, which had never been subjected to settlement of title even under the British (Kedar 2001, 949). Despite a relatively large Palestinian population, the Galilee experienced its own flight of refugees in 1948–49 and therefore had a sizable footprint of land emptied of people and classified as absentee (Falah 1991, 70). Because this land had not been surveyed, Israel had yet to formalize title to this land as state property. Surveys in the Galilee were thus aimed at affirming and verifying the state's claims for what it considered its own land.

For the State of Israel, a sense of urgency attended the task of settling title on land in the Galilee, stemming from government fears that Palestinians would find a legal route from Ottoman law to preserve their land. Historically, under the Ottoman Land Code, Palestinians had acquired rights to land that was legally owned by the state—rights of "adverse possession"—by continuously using it. Article 78 of the code stipulated that a person in possession of miri land (see chapter 6) who planted the holding continuously "for ten years without disturbance" gained a prescriptive right along with the equivalent of a title grant to that land; article 103 enabled improvers of dead land, also legally state property, to gain a similar right if they kept the land continuously planted (*Ottoman Land Code* 1892, 41–42, 54–55; Forman 2006, 801; Abu Hussein and McKay 2003, 118). Although cultivators were obligated to register land thus obtained with the Ottoman authorities so that the land could be taxed, registration was rare. Instead, possession of land, whether miri or mawat, occurred informally, while tax collection remained the province of village sheikhs and local Ottoman-employed tax collectors (Fischbach 2013, 303). Although the British introduced critical changes to the Ottoman land system, Mandate authorities accepted the basic framework of Ottoman land law and its notions of entitlement to land (Bunton 2007, 5–6). As successor to these empires, Israel was also beholden to the land system it had inherited, and short of overturning the Ottoman Land Code (which it did eventually do in 1969), the state could not simply eradicate Ottoman notions of rights to land.

Israeli officials justified the need for the survey with a narrative that accused Palestinians in the Galilee of illegally seizing state-owned absentee land during the conflict of 1948–49. According to this narrative, Palestinians who managed to remain in the Galilee had exploited the disorders of wartime and expanded onto land abandoned by their neighbors with the aim of keeping it, or had tended it to preserve its cultivated status for its banished owners (Forman 2006, 801). From the state's perspective, such land was absentee land belonging to the state. In many cases, land so possessed by Palestinians belonged to family members who had fled the conflict. Nevertheless, the government insisted that Palestinians who had gained control of any absentee land, regardless of whether it belonged to family members, were squatters on state property deserving of eviction. Israeli officials also emphasized that Palestinians in the Galilee had seized land belonging to the state by virtue of its status as public land. Such "unassigned state land" included *matruka* land, normally proximate to villages and used for common purposes, from roads to grazing, which Israelis officials now claimed as state property. Thus, in the narrative circulated by Israeli officials, Palestinians had illegally seized state land, both absentee and unassigned, and were trespassers.

In 1956, in an admission that these "trespassers" had a legal route to the land they occupied by virtue of the Ottoman Land Code, Moshe Levin, director of the Development Authority, cautioned that in two years, unless the government could settle title for absentee and unassigned lands as state property and enforce laws of trespass on them, it confronted the possibility of losing those lands in accordance with Ottoman-based laws of adverse possession (Forman 2005, 126). "The state needs to prove ownership of the seized state land within two years," Levin warned, "or lose it" (quoted in Forman 2005, 132). A year later, a report of Israel's State Comptroller reached a similar conclusion, conceding the "danger that illegal occupants of . . . [state land] are likely to acquire for themselves rights to this land through its cultivation under the Ottoman Land Code" (quoted in Kedar 2001, 950). This vulnerability to the ten-year prescription period compelled Israel to launch settlement of title operations in the Galilee in August 1956, with the aim of identifying state-owned land used by Palestinians, who in the Israeli narrative had gained control of it illegally (Forman 2006, 801).

Directing the settlement of title operation was a Supreme Land Settlement Committee (SLSC) represented by the ministries of Justice, Labor, and Finance, the prime minister's Arab affairs advisor, the JNF, and the military, all of whom collectively framed the policy goals of the process (Forman 2006, 802). In order to implement the actual survey work, the SLSC created an Operations Committee specifically for the Galilee, where the settlement of title operation targeted forty-two Palestinian villages comprising 702,000 dunums of land (Kedar 2001, 950–51). Of this total, preliminary assessments suggested that 400,000–450,000 dunums, or roughly 57–65 percent of the land in the Galilee, was recoverable as state land for Jewish settlement (Forman 2005, 120). That the survey process aimed explicitly at demographic reengineering was affirmed by Yosef Weitz, head of the JNF Land Department and a member of the Galilee Operations Committee, who in 1957 stated that the goal of settling title was "the Judaization of the Galilee" (quoted in Kedar 2001, 951). Two years later, Yosef Pinhasovitch, director of Israel's Department of Land Registration and Settlement, was even more explicit. "Present work is not being carried out for settlement of title purposes only," he explained. "Rather, it is being undertaken for the specific purpose of clarifying the possibility of settlement in areas populated predominantly by Arabs" (quoted in Forman 2006, 801).

Despite the time pressure on the state to conduct the survey, work proceeded more slowly than expected. In response to the delay and the looming expiration of the ten-year prescription period, the government resorted to a far-reaching legal remedy: the Prescription Law. Passed by the Knesset in March 1958, the law evolved from senior government officials' belief that legislation was needed to prevent Palestinians in the Galilee from gaining control of state lands (Forman 2005, 134). In its final form, the law challenged the prescriptive rights of Palestinians on virtually all miri land, becoming one of most profound changes to the land regime handed down from the Ottomans and British (COHRE/BADIL 2005, 45). Two key provisions in the law enabled the state to overturn long-standing practices of landholding on state-owned land.

First, the law increased the period of time needed to acquire prescriptive rights to land from the ten years specified in articles 20 and 78 of the Ottoman Land Code to fifteen years. In this way, if Palestinians had seized state land in 1948–49, as government officials claimed, the law preempted them from gaining rights to that land in 1958 by virtue of the extension in the prescription period. At the time that the law was being debated, the meaning of this proposed change in the prescription period was clear to Palestinians. For Palestinian lawyer Elias Koussa, the bill was unjust "because it will strip Arab landowners, farmers and villagers of a considerable amount of land, possibly in the neighborhood of a quarter-million dunums" (quoted in Forman 2006, 140). If there was any ambiguity about the state's intent in revising the rule on prescription, a report of the Israel Lands Administration in 1965 clearly conceded the rationale of the law. "In reference to the Galilee, the report notes that "there was a danger of the acquisition of rights by prescription according to the Statute of Limitation (1958) regarding all State land, and those of the Custodian of Absentee Property and the Development Authority. Particularly in the area of the minorities [Palestinians] where various elements began to take over State land, ... there was worry that these lands would be taken away from the hand of the ILA and transferred to the ownership of the trespassers" (quoted in COHRE/BADIL 2005, 45).

Second, the law stated that for "any land" acquired after March 1, 1943, the period from 1958–63 would not count toward prescription, effectively increasing the prescription period for land acquired in 1943–48 to twenty years. This provision not only provided the state with more time to complete settlement of title before prescription resumed (Forman 2005, 143). By foreclosing maturation of the time period needed for obtaining prescriptive rights to miri land, the law effectively abrogated one of the most common pathways used historically by Palestinians to gain rights to the soil (Kedar

2001, 972). In what can only be described as lawfare in its most undisguised form, Israeli officials regarded the five years, 1958–63, when prescription was halted as a window of opportunity to eliminate prescription entirely and repossess Palestinian land on the pretext that Palestinians had failed to meet the prescription standard and were thus holding state property illegally (Forman 2002, 72).

The extension of the prescription period to fifteen years and the five-year freeze on prescription from 1958 to 1963 were not arbitrary but reflected decisions by high-level Israeli policymakers on how best to prevent Palestinians from defending claims to their land (Forman 2002, 70–71). In February 1958, as debate on the Prescription Law continued, leading officials in the Justice Ministry asked Reuven Aharoni, the Land Settlement Officer for the Northern Districts, to recommend a length of time needed to preclude Palestinians from using prescriptive rights of continuous cultivation to claim state land. Aharoni said at least fourteen years and also affirmed that Palestinians should be prevented from counting the first five years after passage of the law. These recommendations, incorporated into the final version of the 1958 law, resulted from long-running discussions within the government on how to use a new source of evidence in the campaign to enlarge the footprint of state land: aerial photography inherited from the British Mandate (Forman 2002, 70–72; Forman 2005, 97, 232).

In 1944–45, the British completed extensive aerial photography of Palestine—known as the PS series—in preparation for cadastral surveying of the country (Gavish 2005, 262). Although the surveys were only partially completed, photographs of Palestinian landscapes including the Galilee taken by the British provided important information to the State of Israel, above all on the cultivated or uncultivated status of land. In the context of the Prescription Law, the Israeli government now had a formidable instrument—the seemingly irrefutable evidence of photography—to challenge Palestinians on claims to land based on continuous cultivation (Kedar 2001, 982).

In order to exploit these photographs as evidence, the state had first to adjust the time period for prescription to account for the dates when the photos were taken. For this reason, the final language of the Prescription Law pushed the date for affected land back to 1943. Second, while the state began using aerial photography by 1959 to determine whether parcels of Palestinian land had been cultivated in 1944–45, the admissibility of the photos as evidence became a matter of controversy in Israeli courts. Only in the 1961 Supreme Court case of *Ahmed Nimr Badran v. State of Israel* was the issue formally decided in favor of aerial photos as evidence in cases of Palestinian claimants on unassigned land (Forman 2011, 32–34; Forman 2005, 98–99). Finally, the state needed a way of assessing the photographs for evidence of land left unplanted. Israeli courts devised a novel legal doctrine known as the "Fifty Percent Rule," which stipulated that the land surface of a particular plot had to be at least 50 percent planted in order for it to be considered cultivated.

Prior to Israeli rule, Mandate courts had determined whether a parcel of land was cultivated based on the notion of "reasonable cultivation." In *Habiby v. Government of Palestine* (1940), the Mandate court decided that cultivated land required a level of planting that was "reasonably possible" for the type of land and the particular crops planted (Forman 2009, 674). Moreover, Mandate law, following the spirit of Locke and English improvement doctrine, accepted "plowing and fencing" as proxies for the cultivation requirement (Kedar 2001, 977). By 1960, however, this doctrine was being tested in Israeli courts, with aerial photography providing the primary form of evidence and Israeli analysts assessing these photos in terms of what constituted cultivated land.

In one of the early court decisions leading up to the 50 percent standard, *State of Israel v. Khatib and Da'ash* (1960), aerial photography "expert" Moshe Saban testified that land in the Palestinian village of Deir Hanna planted by Palestinian defendants did not qualify as cultivated based on his reading of the British aerial photos of the land in question (Forman 2009, 672–73). Only subsequently, in three Israeli Supreme Court decisions, did the notion of cultivated land assume a new legal threshold different in spirit from article 78 and the Mandate court decision in *Habiby*. The turning point in this legal history was the ruling in *al-Khatib v. State of Israel* (1962), in which Supreme Court justice Haim Cohen reinterpreted article 78 to mean that for a parcel of land to be cultivated, "most" of the surface area of the parcel had to be planted (Forman 2009, 683; Forman 2011, 34). Despite the seeming objectivity of the standard, it was still open to interpretation by so-called experts such as Saban whether particular plots of land were "mostly" cultivated.

These changes—extending the prescription period and reinterpreting the meaning of cultivated land—enabled the supposedly neutral artifact of aerial photography to evolve into a formidable tool used by the State of Israel to contest and ultimately strip Palestinians of their claims to land (Kedar 2001, 976).

In addition to elevating aerial photos as evidence for contesting Palestinian claims to land, settlement of title and the Prescription Law established a new set of documentary standards for verifying possession of land (Kedar 2001,

973). By the mid-1950s, Israeli courts affirmed these new standards by insisting that title to unregistered land be verifiable not only on the basis of possession and cultivation but also through documented registration. In order to authenticate their claims for prescriptive rights to land, Palestinians had to submit documentary evidence—essentially registration documents—proving uninterrupted cultivation of their holdings, documents that most Palestinians could not produce (Kedar 2001: 973–84).

Blocked from accessing rights of prescription, subjected to a new set of criteria on the meaning of cultivation, and forced to verify ownership of their land through new standards of documentation, Palestinian landholders had little chance of demonstrating that their land legally belonged to them. Consequently, the State of Israel not only engineered a solution to the time-sensitive issue it faced settling title on absentee and unassigned land in the Galilee. Settlement of title also enabled Israel to conduct a comprehensive review of Palestinian landholding according to the criteria of a cadastral-based landed property system. Essentially, it grafted a grid onto the landscape in the Galilee. Where Israeli survey teams did not find documentation of ownership for the spaces in the grid, the state remade those spaces into state property. In the end, manipulation of the prescription period, new rules on registration documents, and changes in the meaning of cultivation resulted in the expropriation of more than 200,000 dunums of land from Palestinian possessors (Kedar 2001, 973).

If the process of settling title in the Galilee made it more difficult for Palestinians to qualify as landholders and brought miri land more firmly under state control, Israeli policymakers also sought to bring still another major source of Palestinian land into state ownership: dead (mawat) land improved by Palestinians. Representing a large portion of the land held by Palestinians in the Galilee and thus occupying a sizable footprint on the landscape, dead land emerged in the settlement of title operation as a strategic source of land for Jewish settlement. At the same time, dead land required a different legal strategy in order to be recast into state property, but it turned out to be an easier process than was the case with miri land (Forman 2005, 104).

Like miri land, mawat land, defined in articles 6 and 103 of the Ottoman Land Code, was technically state property, to which Palestinians historically had proprietary rights of use (Tute 1927, 15, 97). During the British Mandate, however, the British modified language in the Ottoman Land Code regarding rules for taking possession of dead land and attempted to restrict its use as a source of proprietary land rights for Palestinians, emphasizing instead the role of mawat land as property of the state. This revision by the British created an ideal precedent for the State of Israel. For Israeli legal experts, the British reinterpretation of the Ottoman Land Code strengthened the legal status of mawat land as state property to which Israel, as the successor to the British, was legally entitled. Consequently, one of the primary strategies of Israel during the settlement of title operation in the Galilee was to find as much wasteland as possible, whether or not it was cultivated by Palestinians, so as to bring it into the inventory of state land.

In order to repossess this land, the State of Israel needed to transform two key provisions in the mawat law inherited from the previous regimes. First, it reinterpreted the definition of dead land in article 6 of the Ottoman Land Code. Second, it exploited the Mawat Land Ordinance (1921) passed by the British that modified article 103 of the Ottoman Land Code regarding rules for opening up and registering dead land. In reworking these two frameworks, Israel, through its Supreme Court, crafted new legal doctrine for entitlement to improved dead land that left Palestinians who had cultivated such land without rights to it.

Article 6 of the Ottoman Land Code defined dead land as unoccupied "waste" not possessed by anyone, lying outside a village or town. In addition, three locational criteria attached to the definition, such that dead land (1) began where a human voice at the outermost location of an inhabited place could not be heard; (2) was 1.5 miles from that outermost location; or (3) was thirty minutes distant from said location. On the basis of this rather open-ended definition, article 103 of the Ottoman Land Code attempted to encourage cultivation of dead land as part of a land improvement strategy to enhance the tax base of the empire. At the same time, article 103 enabled villagers in an era of rural population growth to extend cultivation beyond village limits while allowing improvers of dead land to obtain a title grant "gratis" if the improvement was undertaken with permission. Finally, article 103 enabled improvers who opened up land *without* permission to obtain the rough equivalent of a title grant by payment of a fine (*Ottoman Land Code* 1892, 54–55). Article 103, in any event, left no doubt that dead land that was opened up and made arable, much like cultivated miri land, still belonged to the state as ultimate title holder in perpetuity (*Ottoman Land Code* 1892, 54; Tute 1927, 97; Forman and Kedar 2003, 514).

The Mawat Land Ordinance of 1921 passed by the British reversed the spirit of article 103 of the Ottoman Land Code that had rendered dead land available to the enterprising cultivator (Bunton 2007, 45). The ordinance also contained a provision regarding the unauthorized revival of dead land, which characterized the cultivator of waste without permission not as a contributor to the general interest but as a trespasser. "Any person who without obtaining the consent of the Administration breaks up or cultivates waste land shall obtain no right to a title-deed for such land," the ordinance stated, and such a person "will be liable to be prosecuted for trespass" (quoted in Kedar 2001, 936). The ordinance additionally required those who had revived dead land prior to 1921 to register their improvement with the British Land Registrar within two months following passage of the law. As a consequence, dead land transitioned under British rule from being a source of new land for an expanding village population to a resource for the state that was off-limits to village cultivators (Forman 2011, 36).

Despite this change, however, British administrators and Mandate courts rarely contested cultivators who failed to register their improvement. Even more importantly, British authorities did not practice eviction in the event of a failure to obtain registration documents (Kedar 2001, 952). In the revised version of the ordinance from 1934, moreover, the two-month registration requirement was omitted, thereby restoring the rights of cultivators to obtain a title grant on improved but unregistered waste by paying a fee (Abu Hussein and McKay 2003, 140). Nevertheless, the language in the ordinance that defined unauthorized cultivation of waste as trespass, and the designation of mawat land as state property, presented Israel, as successor to the Mandate, with the legal basis to recast the doctrine for dead land in accordance with its aim of gaining control of such land. In this campaign, the Israeli legal system reinterpreted article 6 and exploited British revisions of article 103 to its own advantage, rendering it virtually impossible for Palestinians to claim rights of possession on mawat land.

The turning point in the Israeli transformation of mawat jurisprudence was a Supreme Court case, *State of Israel v. Saleh Badran* (1962), which redefined the doctrine for acquisition of dead land on the basis of three new principles (Forman 2011, 36–40).

The first change institutionalized in *Saleh Badran* concerned the method of defining land as mawat. While article 6 of the Ottoman Land Code had outlined three ways of measuring distance to establish a plot's status as dead land, the Israeli judges in *Saleh Badran* determined that the 1.5-mile criterion was the only objective metric for determining if land was dead. As a result of this "clarification," virtually all land outside the 1.5-mile perimeter of villages became dead land able to be claimed as state property available for the development of

Jewish settlements (Kedar 2001, 955–56). With this ruling, a large portion of the landscape was immediately transformed into state property.

The second change established a new standard for defining a village or inhabited place of settlement where measurement of the 1.5-mile perimeter could begin. The *Saleh Badran* decision stipulated that the distance had to be measured from the outermost spot of a locality that was in existence in 1858 when the Ottoman Land Code was established. This provision of specifying a time frame for what constituted a village had profound ramifications as a means of reclassifying land as dead and thus state property. An expanding population in Palestine after the mid-nineteenth century created larger numbers of people in existing villages and led to the establishment of new settlements. This pattern, in turn, compelled villagers from both the expanding villages and the new settlements to open otherwise mawat land for cultivation while reducing the territorial footprint of land considered empty. For existing villages, this meant land beyond the 1.5-mile boundary. New settlements, by contrast, were invariably located beyond the 1.5-mile boundary of existing villages and were thus situated entirely on dead land. In effect, the map of Palestine in terms of dead land was being redrawn by demographic change. Indeed, in his detailed 1927 commentary on the Ottoman Land Code, R. C. Tute, president of the Mandate's Land Court in Jerusalem, observed that existing villages and towns in Palestine had expanded owing to population growth and the number of villages had increased. His conclusion was inescapable: "The limits of the mewat have retreated with the advance of habitation . . . [and] the mewat lands of the State are being steadily reduced" (Tute 1927, 98).

It was precisely the reduction of mawat land stemming from Palestinian economic development after the mid-nineteenth century that the *Saleh Badran* decision was intended to reverse. According to *Badran,* in villages established after 1858, land *inside* the 1.5-mile perimeter, which would normally qualify as village land where villagers would cultivate and establish prescriptive rights after ten years of continuous planting, was now reclassified as mawat and so became technically state property. In using a historical date to define what constituted a village, Supreme Court justices in *Badran* understood that if any settlement could qualify as a legitimate point from which to establish a 1.5-mile perimeter for miri land, then the surface of the landscape for dead land would be greatly reduced in size (Kedar 2001, 959). In this way, large areas of the Palestinian countryside, despite new settlements, were classified by judicial fiat as dead land and thus state property.

The third and perhaps most far-reaching transformation codified in the *Saleh Badran* decision occurred in the registration requirements for improving dead land. While Ottoman law allowed improvers who had failed to register to obtain a title grant by paying a fee, the British Mawat Ordinance was less amenable to leaving portions of the landscape available for improvement by the individual cultivator (Bunton 2007, 45). British authorities demanded landholders who possessed dead land by virtue of improvement to register their holdings within a two-month period in 1921 (February–April) or lose their land. In practice, the registration clause of the British Mawat Land Ordinance received flexible enforcement—until the State of Israel proposed to enforce it rigidly in the early 1960s. In *Saleh Badran,* the Israeli Supreme Court exploited Mandate precedent and held that the registration requirement codified in the British Mawat Land Ordinance was indeed enforceable, the objective being to verify whether Palestinians had revived dead land in accordance with the ordinance (Forman 2011, 39). Palestinians unable to document registration of their revival of land within the two-month period specified in the 1921 Mawat Land Ordinance were thus vulnerable to claims by the state that the land they were cultivating—and perhaps had been cultivating for generations—was state property on which they were trespassers.

In 1962, in the wake of *Badran,* Israeli courts made certain that Palestinians claiming rights to mawat land had documentary evidence attesting to the registration of their land improvement between February and April 1921. Moreover, Palestinian cultivators not only carried the burden of producing registration documents for their revival of dead land; they also had to prove continuous cultivation from the date they took possession of the land as a result of reviving it. Such evidentiary requirements made it virtually impossible for Palestinians to claim rights to land through the doctrine of improvement (Forman 2005, 196).

In the end, settlement of title operations, alongside the legislation of the 1950s, left Palestinians dispossessed of both miri and mawat land, with little recourse apart from the Israel courts. Roughly eight thousand court cases initiated by Palestinians followed the settlement of title operation in the early to mid-1960s (Jiryis 1976a, 16). Not surprisingly, the state prevailed in roughly 85 percent of these cases. In the process, the State of Israel acquired hundreds of thousands of dunums of land from Palestinians in the Galilee—all through legal means (Kedar 2001, 952). What emerged in the Galilee as a result of this legal campaign was a new order on the landscape anchored by Jewish settlements that have surrounded and effectively enclosed Palestinian

FIGURE 22. Judaization on the ground: Yuvalim (background), located on land formerly belonging to residents of Sakhnin (foreground) (2014). Photo by author.

villages and towns, constraining their growth and development and creating an ethnically segregated geography (Falah 1991, 82, 72).

One of the best vantage points for viewing this new territorial order in the Galilee is the town of Sakhnin, the second largest city in the area to undergo settlement of title, after Um al-Fahm (Forman 2005, 112). "In the 1950s," explains Ali Z., a lifetime resident of Sakhnin, "the town had access to 70,000 dunums of land." Today, with 25,000 people, Sakhnin controls less than 10,000 dunums. "Basically, we have been stripped of our land except in the built area of the town" (author interview, September 7, 2014). On the hillsides where some of Sakhnin's farmland and common grazing land were once located stand newly built Jewish settlements known as *mitzpim,* meaning "lookout communities." Across Sakhnin's northern side lie the Jewish settlements of Ash'har, Eshbal, Maale Z'vi, and Lotem, while to the southeast sits Hararit. Most prominent among these hilltop settlements, however, is Yuvalim, located on the northwest side of Sakhnin (fig. 22).

Totaling roughly 20,000 residents, these communities have been allocated 180,000 dunums of land by the local Misgav Regional Planning Council, which assumed jurisdictional control over the land taken by the state from Sakhnin and two other nearby Palestinian towns, Arraba and Deir Hanna. Collectively, these hilltop settlements enclose Sakhnin in an envelope of

Jewish territorial space, immobilizing the town and preventing it from expanding. With their land expropriated, villagers from Sakhnin have lost their agricultural roots, becoming wage laborers dependent on work in the very settlements that have taken their lands (Falah 1991, 75; Shafir and Peled 2002, 112–25). In the process, Palestinians from the Galilee have lost anchors to the land itself.

If lawfare provided the legal infrastructure for a Judaized landscape in the frontier area of the Galilee, the other frontier area, the Naqab (Negev) of the Bedouin, was poised to undergo an equally dramatic territorial transformation. In the case of the Bedouin, however, the law was even more draconian, and in the Naqab, Israeli authorities combined the law with another instrument to remake the landscape. That instrument was trees.

"ENCLOSURE ZONE": PLANTING A HEBREW LANDSCAPE IN THE NAQAB (NEGEV)

In 1953, the State of Israel hosted forty-nine countries at an exhibition called "The Conquest of the Desert," showcasing the fledgling nation's reclamation accomplishments in the Negev Desert (Zerubavel 2009, 33). In remarks celebrating the exhibit's opening, Israeli president Yitzhak Ben-Zvi insisted that conquering the desert was necessary because of the damage inflicted on the land by desert-dwelling Bedouin tribes. "Settlement shrank and the desert expanded," he explained, because the Bedouin made their living from herding and gathering wild plants, not from cultivating the land. The president went on to observe caustically that "Israel is not a country of nomads and desert tribes" (*Conquest of the Desert* 1953, 6). For Ben-Zvi, conquest of the desert was embedded in a historically traditional Jewish practice of planting the land with trees, cultivating it with crops, and settling it with people who had languished during the long exile from their homeland.

Although the early Zionist movement had largely overlooked the Negev, by the late 1930s Zionist leaders, among them David Ben-Gurion, began to target the desert region as critical to a future Jewish state (Ben-Gurion 1937). In 1948, Yosef Weitz, chairman of the Jewish National Fund, spoke about the role of the Negev in the country's future: "The Hebrew State will have to embark on a wide settlement strategy in its first three years," he said, "[a] big part of it in the Negev. . . . In the Negev we'll be able to implement immediately our development laws, according to which we shall expropriate land according to a well-designed plan" (quoted in Yiftachel 2006, 193). By 1953 when the "Conquest of the Desert" exhibit was taking place, Weitz's words on expropriation seemed prophetic.

From 1948 to 1954 the State of Israel was engaged in forcibly removing the Bedouin from the Negev and placing them in an area near Beersheva known as the Siyag, or "enclosure zone." There they were confined until 1966 without basic services, forbidden to build durable housing structures, required to obtain permits to enter and exit the Siyag, and dispossessed of their land. As the Bedouin languished in the Siyag, the state opened a second phase in its campaign of conquest by launching a wave of Jewish settlements on lands from which they had been removed (Yiftachel 2006, 198). According to Khalil A., a resident of al-Sira, a Bedouin village located in the Siyag but unrecognized by the State of Israel and thus not visible on Israeli maps, "What the State of Israel did in removing the Bedouin from their land and transferring them to the enclosure zone was exactly what the United States did in removing the Indians from their lands and placing them in reservations" (author interview, September 20, 2014).

Conquering the desert thus has two different meanings. For promoters of the Jewish state, it is akin to planting the landscape with trees, cultivating it with crops, and settling it with a population of Jewish Israelis. For the Bedouin of the Naqab, conquering the desert refers to a still-ongoing process of uprooting the people of the desert and dispossessing them of their land.

In this process of making the desert bloom, afforestation has played a pivotal role. According to Weitz, also known as the "Father of Israel's Forests," tree-planting has served as both "prelude" and "partner" to redeeming the Palestinian landscape and settling it with Jews. For Weitz, a landscape planted with trees marks territory both materially and symbolically as a space for Jewish settlement (Weitz 1974, 135, 55). The Zionist movement revered tree-planting as a practical way of physically anchoring the Jewish people to the soil (Kadman 2015, 41). Thus tree-planting and settlement-building emerged as complementary strategies in the creation of a Jewish landscape where a non-Jewish Arab and Bedouin landscape once prevailed.

What has enabled tree-planting to become so central to the transformation of the system of land ownership in the Naqab is an imagined geography of the desert that has designated the land where the Bedouin reside as dead land (Yiftachel, Amara, and Kedar 2013). This doctrine of the "Dead Negev" classifies the living space of the Bedouin as empty, without settlements, without greenery, in need of planting by those committed to redeeming the land.

In a legal sense, the doctrine has recast the land of the Bedouin as land without owners and thus the property of the state. Materially, in creating state land from the supposedly empty land of the Bedouin, the Dead Negev doctrine has allowed vast portions of the landscape where Bedouin once lived to be remade into Jewish space. How this imagined geography of the Negev as dead land emerged, and how it has inspired the campaign of conquering the desert and making it bloom, is the story that follows.

The Desert and Trees: Contested Imaginations

Even prior to Zionism, the desert played a pivotal role in the Jewish imagination of Palestine. Alongside its revered status, Palestine for Jews had succumbed to a desertlike condition at the hands of Arabic-speaking "foreigners." The latter had rendered the country's once-vibrant landscape desolate, in need of redemption by those Jews courageous enough to return from the diaspora and remake it anew.

Once Zionists established settlements in Palestine in the late nineteenth century, the idea of the desert shifted to those areas outside of Jewish habitation where emptiness and disorder prevailed (Zerubavel 2009, 35). Seeking to differentiate themselves from such barren areas, early Zionist settlers emphasized the importance not only of cultivation but of plowing their fields in orderly straight lines, in contrast to what they perceived as the vast areas of disorderly uncultivated waste nearby (Zerubavel 2008, 210). As part of their negative impression of the landscapes around them, Zionists harbored deeply ambivalent attitudes toward the agricultural practices of Palestinians. "They [Palestinians] never cleared their fields of stones and never improved them," wrote Melech Zagorodsky in 1919, chief agronomist for the Zionist Federation in Palestine, echoing Locke about Amerindian agriculture and the virtues of land improvement. "In truth, [the Palestinian] does not plow; instead he scratches the surface of his soil with his plowshare" (quoted in Neumann 2011, 84).

From the earliest period of Zionist colonization, Jewish settlers conceived of tree-planting as the antithesis of the desertlike landscape around them and a way of restoring the land to what it had been in the time of the ancient Hebrews. According to the JNF's Weitz, Hebrew scripture presented evidence of four regional forest landscapes of "mixed woods of fruit and forest trees" in ancient Israel. He refers to the tenth-century Arab geographer al-Muqaddasi, who, in listing a specific pine nut among thirty-six items found only in Palestine, affirmed the conifer as indigenous to the area (al-Muqaddasi 985, 297). According to Weitz, by reforesting the country, Jewish settlers were liberating the land from the desolation imposed on it by its Arab usurpers and carrying out a sacred imperative to return the landscape to what it once was and what it was destined to be when redeemed by people chosen for the task (Weitz 1974, 3–20).

European and American travelers during the nineteenth century also described the Holy Land in terms of a profound fall from grace. One of the most authoritative, if disparaging, accounts of Palestine's desert landscape was written by the celebrated secretary of the Palestine Exploration Fund, Edward Henry Palmer, a fluent speaker of Arabic who had only disdain for the Bedouin Arabs. "Wherever he goes," Palmer wrote of the Bedouin, "he brings with him ruin, violence and neglect. . . . Many fertile plains from which he has driven its useful and industrious inhabitants become, in his hand, a parched and barren wilderness" (Palmer 1871, 297). The most famous of these travel requiems was penned by Mark Twain. "Of all the lands there are for dismal scenery," he wrote in *The Innocents Abroad* (1869), "I think Palestine must be the prince. The hills are barren, . . . the valleys are unsightly deserts. . . . It is a hopeless, dreary, heart-broken land." Interestingly, Twain added that Palestine was a land with "no timber" (quoted in Tal 2013, 23).

There is indeed striking symmetry between these travel narratives and the political narrative of the Zionist movement. Both emphasized the disjuncture between the ancient, once-verdant landscape and the neglected landscape of the present wrought by the supposed misdeeds of Arabs (Tal 2013, 23). For Weitz, tree-planting aimed to remedy such misdeeds; as such, it derived from the same impulses that inspired Zionists to revive Hebrew, restore Hebrew place-names, and settle the landscape with Jews. Ultimately, however, at the core of this narrative was an interpretive and subjective historical geography—a set of invented traditions—that elevated and idealized the society of the ancient Hebrews and castigated the society of the Palestinians.

If Zionists and Westerners imagined Palestine as once forested, Palestinians also harbored images of an enduring, arboreal landscape (Bardenstein 1999, 149). For Palestinians, however, the landscape embodied a very different history, with very different meanings for trees and land. Instead of a Golden Age of afforestation punctured by a decline into desert, the environmental history of Palestine for this group has been dominated by trees of a specific type: fruit-bearing trees, of which the olive, with an eight-thousand-year history in Palestine, is the primary cultigen (Tal 2013, 11). "Planting trees is indigenous to Palestinian culture," explains Abdul-Latif K., an agricultural hydrologist from the West Bank village of Jayyous, in an emphatic rebuke of Palestine as "desert." "We have been planting olives, citrus, figs, almonds, and carob in this land for hundreds of years and probably longer. All of these trees—but above all, olive trees—are what sustain us. They are our heritage and what we pass to our children. The Israelis believe that they came here and made the desert bloom. *We* made it green here" (author interview, September 10, 2014).

In addition to conceiving of their own tree-planted landscapes as verdant, Palestinians have long considered trees as "field," in contrast to Zionist ideas of "forest." Although this split has an ancient genealogy, it also denotes a more modern distinction between fruit-bearing trees, akin to cultivated fields, and non-fruit-bearing "futile" trees (Braverman 2009a, 31–37). Whereas the forests so esteemed by Zionists are stands of trees "bearing no edible fruit" (Weitz 1974, 11), Palestinians appreciate fruit-bearing trees as providers of sustenance. Even the Hebrew Book of Deuteronomy speaks of protecting fruit trees from cutting while excluding forest trees from this injunction (Weitz 1974, 426). Palestinians thus accord fruit trees, above all the olive, a privileged role on the landscape, embodying the labor of cultivation, whereas futile trees are considered inferior as wild growth.

The split between trees as forests and trees as fields also highlights differences in the way Zionists and Palestinians conceived of trees establishing rights to land. For Palestinians, use rights on land for tree-planting derived from the need for sustenance endorsed in Ottoman law. Despite certain nuances in the Ottoman Land Code that separated the property right in trees from the use rights in the land, the code distinguished land planted with fruit trees as cultivated, in contrast to land where futile trees grow wild. By conferring rights of use to cultivators of land, and by affirming the status of fruit orchards as cultivated fields, Ottoman Land Law provided rights to land to cultivators of orchards in contrast to non-fruit-bearing trees (Braverman 2009a, 37).

Zionist Tree-Planting

When the first Zionist settlers arrived in Palestine in the late nineteenth century, the arboreal landscape they encountered was dominated by the olive tree. Although olives were one of seven holy species in the Hebrew Bible,

Zionists had an uneasy relationship with the olive-dominated landscape, associating it with "foreigners" who had allowed the land to degenerate into waste and interpreting it as something to be overcome and redeemed (Braverman 2009b, 337). Most early Zionist settlers were from Eastern Europe, where conifer forests prevailed. Pine trees thus provided Zionists with a familiar material symbol for confronting the olive-dominated landscape of Palestinians while easing the transition of Zionists to their newly adopted homeland (Braverman 2009b, 343; Baer-Mor 2009).

While tree-planting was part of early Zionist settlement, systematic efforts at afforestation were launched under the auspices of the Jewish National Fund (Cohen 1993, 47). Although early afforestation included the planting of fruit trees, by 1913 the JNF had shifted to conifers, which soon became the signature element of Zionist tree-planting. In addition to their symbolic meaning of imbuing territory with a distinctly Hebrew identity, conifers had practical advantages for Zionists. Cultivated in dense stands, conifers clearly differentiated Hebrew space from landscapes planted with fruit trees by Palestinians; they were also fast-growing and the cheapest way of planting the land. More strategically, tree-planting was an instrument to secure land for settlement following purchase. One of the constraints of early Zionist settlement was a shortage of settlers to take possession of land immediately after it was acquired. Tree-planting prevented the land from lying fallow and risking claims of adverse possession by Palestinians. In the end, however, pre-state afforestation activity of the JNF was quite modest. In 1927, the planting of trees by the JNF covered only about 5,000 dunums. Thereafter, the area forested by the JNF expanded annually, reaching a peak in 1936 when close to 44,000 dunums were planted. The numbers then declined during and after the Revolt of 1936–39, until 1948. During the Mandate, too, the British were actively engaged in tree-planting, which helped the Zionist cause (Cohen 1993, 47–49, 58).

One of the first decrees of the Mandate Government was an Ordinance for Regulation of Forest Lands and the Protection of Trees (1920), intended to promote forest reserves as a remedy for soil erosion (Tal 2013, 31–35; Survey of Palestine 1946, 423–24). The process for designating these reserves proved unworkable, however, and an amended ordinance (1926) appeared, with two key provisions not present in the original (Braverman 2009a, 38–39; Tal 2013, 33, 43). The first involved legal protections for forest trees planted in reserves, which eventually included conifers, eucalyptus, oak, and poplar (Braverman 2009a, 39). The second removed obstacles for establishing forest reserves by targeting uncultivated land for afforestation (Cohen 1993, 54). Both modifications proved enormously valuable to the Zionist movement. While the legal protections afforded to futile trees in forest reserves enhanced the status of the trees planted by the JNF on Jewish-owned land, more critical was the designation of uncultivated "dead" land for official tree-planting. This provision placed new constraints on Palestinian villagers seeking to open up empty land for cultivation. In a report titled "Forest Reservations in Palestine" (1946), Amihud Goor, a member of the Yishuv whom the British appointed as conservator of forests, conceded this aim, noting that the 1926 ordinance enabled Mandate authorities to designate any wasteland as a forest reserve where "no new claims to ownership based on cultivation are allowed to arise" (Survey of Palestine 1946, 426; Cohen 1993, 53).

Not surprisingly, Palestinians bitterly resented afforestation (Tal 2013, 46). With the Palestinian population having doubled between 1922 and 1944, rural families were seeking to open new land for cultivation and perceived in forest reserves a threat to their rights as cultivators. To counter this threat, Palestinians planted fruit trees and cultivated crops on land set aside for tree-planting, hoping to claim land in accordance with the Ottoman Land Code (Tal 2013, 44). In extreme cases, Palestinians destroyed trees planted by the Mandate Government or launched arson attacks on the trees planted by the JNF (Segev 2001, 361; Cohen 1993, 58). This resistance to tree-planting expanded during the Palestinian Revolt of 1936–39 against the Zionist movement and British rule. For Palestinians, tree-planting had assumed a familiar pattern in which land sales to the JNF were invariably followed by the appearance of conifer trees and then Jewish settlers. During the 1930s, such sales resulted more frequently in evictions of Palestinian cultivators, and while the number of Palestinian households dispossessed may have been arguably low— roughly eight thousand—examples of fellaheen evicted spread deep resentment (Metzer 1998, 93; Morris 2001, 123). Even Ben-Gurion conceded what Palestinians at the time feared: "There is a fundamental conflict," he wrote at the beginning of the revolt. "We and they . . . both want Palestine. . . . They see the best lands passing into our hands. . . . Their fear is . . . losing the homeland of the Arab people which we want to turn into the homeland of the Jewish people" (quoted in Morris 2001, 122, 136).

The cycle of land acquisition, tree-planting, settlement-building, and resistance reached a temporary hiatus in 1939 with the defeat of the Arab Revolt. From that moment, the fortunes of the Zionist Yishuv and the Palestinians diverged. While a catastrophe awaited Palestinians in 1947–49, an arguably even greater tragedy befell the Naqab Bedouin at the hands of conquerors determined to plant forests in the desert and make it bloom (Jiryis 1976b, 122).

Siyag: Enclosing and Confining the Bedouin

In 1951, as the State of Israel was engaged in removing Bedouin from the Naqab and transferring them to the Siyag, Prime Minister David Ben-Gurion delivered an impassioned speech in the Knesset outlining a vision to redeem the country by covering its landscapes with trees. "We will not be faithful to one of the two central goals of the state—conquering the desert—if we confine our efforts solely to the need of the hour," he stated. "We must eventually plant half a million dunums per year" (quoted in Cohen 1993, 61). Although Israel did not meet Ben-Gurion's lofty goal, the state, under the auspices of the Jewish National Fund, expanded forest cover inside the territory of Israel from 20,000 dunums in 1948 to 230,000 dunums by 2013, reshaping the landscape physically and culturally (Kadman 2015, 42). For Weitz, Ben-Gurion's vision was most urgent in the Negev, where by 1949 the JNF had initiated an intensive forestation effort, the primary aim of "covering the desolate countryside with green trees" (Weitz 1974, 195). In this way, Bedouin removal from the Negev, and tree-planting where Bedouin had been removed, emerged as complementary elements of a single campaign: to erase the Bedouin landscape and create a Hebrew landscape in its place.

The wartime campaign that brought the Naqab under Israeli control shattered its Bedouin society. In 1948, the Bedouin population was roughly 75,000–100,000 organized into ninety-five tribes and eight confederations (Abu-Saad and Creamer 2012, 24). From 1948 to 1954, fully 90 percent of this population—seventy-six of the ninety-five Bedouin tribes—left the area, most forcibly expelled by the Israeli military, the rest fleeing to Jordan, Egypt, and the Gaza Strip (Pappe 2015, 62). During this same six-year period, Israeli forces were engaged in a second offensive of removing the remaining Bedouin from their land and transferring them to the enclosure zone (Falah 1989, 78). The Siyag thus counted nineteen of the original ninety-five Bedouin tribes. Seven of these, however, already lived within the Siyag and were not moved; the twelve tribes moved to the enclosure zone were mostly from the northwest Naqab, the land most heavily cultivated by the Bedouin (fig. 23) (Abu-Saad 2008, 4). Almost overnight, the Naqab, except for the Siyag, was erased of Bedouin, most of whom became a landless people (Falah 1985c, 363).[8] It

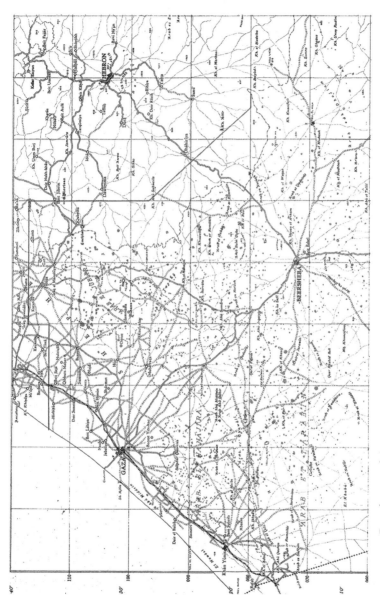

FIGURE 23. Distribution of the Nomad Population of the Beersheba District (detail, 1947). Each dot on this map of the Northwest Naqab, derived by the British from aerial photos and the 1946 national census, represents a Bedouin dwelling or tent. Source: Israel State Archives, Map 298. Photo by author; reproduced by permission of Israel State Archives.

was this removal and transfer of the Bedouin to the Siyag that enabled Zalman Lifshitz, head of the Negev Names Committee, to remark in 1949 that the once-fractious issue of retaining Arabic place-names in the Negev was irrelevant since there were no longer any Bedouin there.

Owing to this population transfer, the Naqab emerged as a type of *tabula rasa* where the new state was determined to create a Jewish landscape (Falah 1996). Indeed, the northwestern part of the Naqab, with its relatively good soil accounting for the large concentration of Bedouin prior to 1948, had been a target even for the limited Jewish settlement during the pre-state period (Abu-Saad 2008, 5). Already in 1937, Ben-Gurion had pondered an aggressive vision for Jewish settlement in the south, writing that the Negev had been made barren under Bedouin stewardship and that the Yishuv could not tolerate an area capable of absorbing tens of thousands of Jews to remain vacant. "We must expel the Arabs and take their place," Ben-Gurion wrote prophetically; "if we are compelled to use force in order to guarantee our right to settle there, our force will enable us to do so" (Ben-Gurion 1937).

Despite relying on force to subdue and confine the Bedouin, the state also sought a more legally durable justification for replanting the desert with Jewish Israelis. The government now reclassified Bedouin land using the same legislative instruments deployed in the Galilee, notably the Absentee Property Law and the Land Acquisition Law (Amara 2013, 28). Both laws exploited Bedouin removal to classify this group as absentees and their land as abandoned in order to provide a legal basis for the transformation of Bedouin land into state land. By March 1954, as a result, the Development Authority had transferred an estimated 1.2–1.9 million dunums of Bedouin land, mostly from the northwest Naqab, into the inventory of Israel Lands (Falah 1989a, 79; Fischbach 2003, 260–61; Amara 2013, 36).

Moreover, as in the Galilee, the state subjected the Naqab to the process of settling title to verify documented ownership rights to land. By 1966, as a consequence, most of the Naqab had been declared dead land and thus state property (Amara 2103, 36, 46).[9] Of the total land area in the Naqab—roughly 12 million dunums—settlement of title had occurred on 9 million dunums, of which 7.5 million dunums was reclassified as state land. What had not been subjected to settlement of title was the northwest Naqab, where the state anticipated that it would encounter resistance to its efforts to classify these former areas of Bedouin habitation as dead land. In 1970, however, the government did open this area to the settlement of title operation, along with the Siyag itself. Bedouins indeed resisted this effort, filing 3,220 formal claims for rights to land covering 1.5 million dunums in the northwestern portion of the district.

In response to these claims, in 1975 the government assigned Plia Albeck of the State Attorney's Office to chair a special committee empowered to make recommendations on the status of land in the northern Negev. Albeck had already earned a reputation, based on legal work she had done in the aftermath of the 1967 Six-Day War (see below), affirming the legality of Israel's settlement enterprise in territories conquered in that conflict. In its "Summary Report of the Experts Team on Land Settlement on the Siyag and the Northern Negev" (1975), Albeck's committee upheld the state's position that the lands claimed by the Bedouin constituted dead land in accordance with the Ottoman Land Code and the British Mawat Land Ordinance. In making this recommendation, the committee crafted the outlines of subsequent government policy on Bedouin land issues in the Negev, at the center of which stood nonrecognition of Bedouin land rights (Swirski 2008, 31). To promote its arguments, the committee used a highly selective reading of historical source material on Bedouin society, which emerged as the core of the doctrine known as the "Dead Negev" (Yiftachel, Amara, and Kedar 2013).

The "Dead Negev"

According to the findings of the Albeck Committee, the Bedouin were a nomadic people who had never established rights in the land through either settlement or cultivation. In reaching this conclusion, the committee affirmed the Negev as dead land, allowing for nonrecognition of Bedouin land rights. Subsequently, in 1984, the Israeli Supreme Court, in its landmark decision of *al-Hawashlah v. State of Israel,* affirmed the committee's position, both with regard to the Bedouin as a people without landed property and the Negev as empty land.

The legal issue central to the *al-Hawashlah* case was how to define mawat land (Kram 2012, 130). The thirteen Bedouin appellants, who earlier had lost a case in the Beersheva District Court regarding rights to several plots of land, argued that their rights to these lands derived from practices of custom conducted since time immemorial (Shamir 1996, 238). The Israeli Supreme Court, however, defended the district court decision and the findings of the Albeck Committee, affirming that the land in question was dead land on the basis of two criteria. First, the Court determined that the land was dead according to the Ottoman Land Code. Second, the Court determined that the land was not owned because the appellants could offer no documentary proof of their ownership rights in accordance with the British Mawat Land Ordinance of 1921. In reality, these two legal judgments were superseded by cultural judgments about Bedouin society and by cultural differences over the meaning of terms such as *cultivation* and *settlement*. These legal issues also turned on different visions of land ownership, one based on practices of customary rights, the other derived from a cadastral-based grid codified and archived in registration documents and parcel maps.

In contesting the arguments of the Bedouin appellants, Eliyahu Halima, Chief Justice of the Supreme Court, revisited claims of the lower court and the Albeck Committee about Bedouin society and concluded that the plots of land in dispute were barren both presently and historically (Shamir 1996, 238). Land in the Negev, the Court insisted, had never been owned by anyone. Referencing the studies of the Negev made in 1870 by Edward Henry Palmer, Halima stated that Palmer had found only desolation and nomadic Bedouins who did not cultivate the land and did not occupy it. According to Halima, the state had therefore managed to establish the two conditions that typify dead land (Yiftachel, Kedar, and Amara 2012, 8–9). Halima and the Supreme Court also had at their disposal the judgment of the lower court as to what constitutes "cultivation," which echoed key themes in the improvement and enclosure discourse of Locke. "It is important to know how the law perceives the concept of working and reviving the land," the Court announced. "This concept means: seeding, planting, ploughing, constructing, fencing and all types of adaptations and improvements such as clearing of stones and other improvements performed on a dead land," all of which should result in "a total, permanent, and persisting change in the quality of the worked land" (quoted in Shamir 1996, 241). Oblivious to the idea of the law as culturally constructed, the Court imposed on the appellants a set of standards for land ownership not specific to the Bedouin but deriving from cadastral surveys of gridlike spaces, registration documents, and parcel maps (Shamir 1996, 234).

In a fundamental way, the Court was making law by imposing cultural judgments on two of the most fundamental aspects of Bedouin society: their system of settlement and their pattern of cultivation. According to the Court, Bedouin settlement and the cultivation that supported it did not constitute permanent occupation or agricultural improvement sufficient to alter the character of the land as dead. From the vantage point of the Court, the Bedouin tent that anchored Bedouin settlement was mobile rather than a dwelling, thus rendering the idea of Bedouin settlement—along with the Bedouin themselves—as something fleeting. Similarly, the agriculture of the Bedouin was either ignored or rendered as somehow an insufficient improvement on dead land. As a consequence, Bedouin society, according to the Court, maintained only "abstract possession" of the land, not having any claim to it based on being anchored to the ground through practices of settlement and cultivation (Shamir 1996, 241).

Despite the historical and anthropological evidence used by the state and courts to insist on the Negev as dead land, these institutions ignored a body of source material suggesting an alternative interpretation of Bedouin claims to land. Such sources range from the sixteenth-century Ottoman census, to nineteenth-century travelers. Zionists themselves also contributed evidence of Bedouin ownership of land, describing cultivated fields and the purchase of land from Bedouin, similarly contradicting the idea of the Negev as dead (Yiftachel, Kedar, and Amara 2012, 5).

One feature of the Ottoman census of 1596 consists of detailed lists of tax payments from Bedouin tribes for crops of wheat and barley, suggesting sedentary activity related to cultivation (Yiftachel, Kedar, and Amara 2012, 25; Hütteroth and Abdulfattah 1977, 28, 68–69). During the nineteenth century, some Western travelers to the Negev provided images of the area quite different from the one-sided impressions of Palmer, referenced by Judge Halima in the *al-Hawashlah* case. Henry Tristam, whose 1858 journey through the Negev admits to much of the area as barren, nevertheless recorded impressions of Beersheva at variance with Palmer's. "One feature in particular marks Beersheba," Tristam wrote. "This is the cultivation of large portions of unfenced land for corn [wheat] by the Arabs. Here for the first time since leaving Jericho, we came upon arable land. The rich low-lying flats for the Wady Seba are ploughed, . . . for wheat and barley" (Tristam 1865, 372). Some twenty-five years later, Edward Hull, a surveyor with the Palestine Exploration Society, recorded his travels in the Negev. Despite comments about the desolation east of Beersheva, Hull's impressions of the area northwest of the town were strikingly different. "The country we traversed," he reported, "was spread with a deep covering of loam of a very fertile nature. . . . The District is extensively cultivated by the Terabin Arabs. . . . The extent of the ground here cultivated is immense, and the crops of wheat, barley, and maize must vastly exceed the requirements of the population" (Hull 1885, 138–39).

When the Ottomans established Bir es Saba (Beersheva) in 1901 as an administrative center, they negotiated a purchase of 2,000 dunums of land from the confederation of al-Azameh tribes in a seemingly open admission of Bedouin rights to land (Falah 1989a, 76). But it was a survey of the Negev undertaken by the Palestine Land Development Company in 1920 that provided some of the most compelling evidence of the Bedouin as cultivators and landowners. Supervised by the director, Dr. Yaacov Tahon, the Summary Report of the survey observes that in the Beersheva region, 2.66 million dunums of land were "owned" by the Bedouin, of which 35 percent were cultivated, while in the northern Negev roughly 50 percent of the land was under crop (Yiftachel, Amara, and Kedar 2013, 32). The report also gives a breakdown of land ownership among the Bedouin confederations, of which the Tiyaha, Azameh, and Terabin were the largest.

Whatever historical and anthropological evidence existed to affirm Bedouin claims to land in the Negev, the Court and the State of Israel had a powerful rejoinder. The Bedouin had few documents attesting to official registration of their lands. Moreover, Israeli demands for such documents provided an objective rationale for denying such claims—and, further, denying that dispossession had taken place (Shamir 1996, 241; Weizman and Sheikh 2015, 51).

In the end, the doctrine of the dead Negev, together with the court cases affirming it, provided a seemingly inevitable ideological and legal arsenal for a state intent on remaking the Negev landscape. On this landscape, an Arabic-speaking population formerly residing on and using lands estimated at 3 million dunums presented a formidable obstacle to a state seeking to Judaize territory under its control (Yiftachel 2013, 294). Turning the land of the Bedouin into state property provided Israel with the wherewithal to accomplish this aim. On the ruins of Bedouin removal, this new landscape emerged and took shape, embodied most visibly in Jewish settlements and conifer trees.

Planting the Desert

With a barely visible Jewish population in the Negev, tree-planting emerged as a pivotal element in the state's early planning for redemption of the frontier (Weitz 1974, 143). In order to attract Jewish residents to an otherwise austere environment, Israel undertook a dramatic expansion in afforestation in the early 1950s as part of a newly framed planning process (Kaplan 2011, 27). For Weitz, these early efforts at tree-planting aimed at "brightening the otherwise dreary grayness of the bare Negev expanse" while "providing relief for the eye of the settler" (Weitz 1974, 143).

Alongside this tree-planting activity emerged new Jewish towns and settlements on the Negev landscape. Beersheva was remade as a Jewish city, while Yeruham and Dimona were built as new Jewish towns in the 1950s, followed in the 1960s by Arad, east of Beersheva, and Okafim and Netivot, in the north and west, where most of the Bedouin lived prior to their removal. In addition to these towns, rural settlements also appeared. From 1948 to 1954 the number of kibbutzim (communities with shared ownership of farms) doubled from twelve to twenty-four, while the number of moshavim (cooperatives with individually owned farms) increased from two to twenty-eight, with most of these settlements in the northwestern Negev. By 1961, roughly sixty new Jewish towns and settlements occupied the Negev landscape. In Israel's Physical Master Plan for the Negev of 1976, one hundred Jewish agricultural settlements were projected for the northwestern Negev and along the border with the West Bank (Falah 1989a, 83). By the late 1980s, ninety-five new Jewish communities, including the towns of Lehavim and Meitar, had been established in the Negev as part of the state's overall policy of settlement-building and dispersal of the Jewish population in areas of the frontier (Kellerman 1993, 250–51; Shachar 1998, 213).

With the appearance of new settlers and settlements, the cartography of the Negev and the landscape itself changed dramatically. Where Bedouin dwellings once prevailed as the dominant form of settlement, a new settlement landscape emerged anchored by the towns of Netivot and Okafim and peopled by Jewish Israelis. Even more striking is the spatial configuration of this settlement activity on the perimeter of the Siyag, where the remaining Bedouin population was still concentrated. Encircling the various Bedouin communities within the enclosure zone is a ring of Jewish towns anchored by Beersheva, Lehavim, Meitar, Arad, Dimona, and Yeruham (fig. 24). This spatial strategy of enclosing the Bedouin within a Hebrew landscape reflected what the government had envisioned for the Bedouin as part of its Master Development Plan for the Negev Region of 1966.

Master Plan: From Bedouin Townships to "Unrecognized" Villages. Once the State of Israel ended military rule over the country's Palestinian and Bedouin populations in 1966, the government confronted a dilemma: what to do with a group of people it had confined in the Siyag for almost twenty years. Eight years earlier the Israeli military, in a document titled "Permanent Arrangement of the Bedouins of the Siyag in the Negev," had signaled what would become the basic outlines of Israeli policy toward the Negev Bedouins

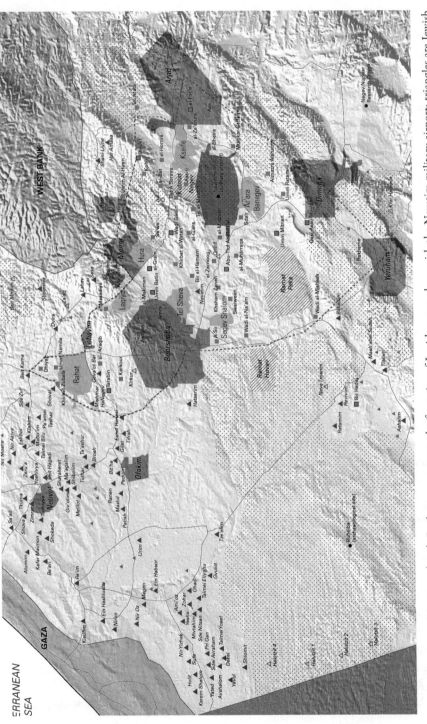

FIGURE 24. Map of the Siyag (2015). Dark areas represent the footprint of Jewish towns along with the Nevatim military airport; triangles are Jewish agricultural settlements; medium dark areas are Bedouin townships; small squares are Bedouin villages, both recognized and unrecognized. Dotted line demarcates the Siyag, where Bedouins are still concentrated. Map designed by Francesco Sebregondi/Forensic Architecture. Reproduced by permission.

(Negev Coexistence Forum for Civil Equality 2016, 6). Conceding that the aim in concentrating the Bedouins in the Siyag was to clear land for Jewish settlement, the report recommended that the Bedouin community be more intensively concentrated in a small number of towns. Both of these aims—settling territory with Jewish Israelis and concentrating the Bedouin in ever-smaller territorial spaces—emerged as central themes in the 1966 Master Plan for the Negev (Falah 1989a, 83).

In fundamental ways, the 1966 plan reflected the two most basic practices of Israeli planning: demographic engineering and the reorganization of territorial space. Maintaining the numerical hegemony of Jews inside Israel and distributing this dominance spatially across state territory have always been the central axes of Israeli planning and development (Yiftachel 2006, 36, 105; Shachar 1998, 210). By 1961, this demographic and spatial orientation had remade the Negev with new Jewish towns and agricultural settlements, as well as a Jewish population in the Beersheva district that soared to 81 percent of the total 97,200 residents (Central Bureau of Statistics 2015, table 16.2).

Despite the hardships of confinement, the Bedouin population had more than doubled during the period 1948–66 to roughly 25,000. Although numerically still much smaller than the Jewish population in the region, but with a birth rate reputed to be the highest in the world, the Bedouin posed two urgent development imperatives for the Israeli planning establishment, as reflected in the 1966 plan. First was the need to increase Jewish migration to the Negev and expand settlement-building in order to offset the anticipated increases in the Bedouin population. Accordingly, by 1972 the Jewish population stood at 85 percent of a total population of 201,200 (Central Bureau of Statistics 2015, table 16.2). Second, and perhaps more important, the 1966 plan aimed to shrink even more completely the presence of Bedouin on the landscape of the Jewish state. To achieve this, the 1966 plan proposed the development of nine urban townships within the Siyag, later reduced to seven, where Bedouin would be "encouraged" to relocate (Falah 1989a, 83–84; Adalah 2011, 9).

By 1968, the state had framed specific development plans for the first of these Bedouin towns, Tel Sheva, which was established the following year. Following Tel Sheva came Rahat (1971), Segev Shalom (1979), Kseife (1982), Ar'ara Ba Negev (1982), Lakiya (1985), and Hura (1989). Once relocated to these townships, the Bedouin would be occupying 2.5 percent of the roughly 3 million dunum area they had inhabited prior to 1948, and less than 1 percent of the Negev's total 12.6 million dunums (Goldberg Commission 2011, 28–29).

Much of the land for these townships was taken from Bedouin tribes that had not been transferred but had maintained a hold on their land within the Siyag. In order to gain title to this land, the government used special legislation, the Negev Land Acquisition Law (1980). The largest land transfer stemming from this law occurred with the Bedouin of Tal al-Malah, when the state seized 65,000 dunums from the village to build the townships of Kseife and Ar'ara Ba Negev along with the Nevatim military base and airport. The seven thousand people dispossessed from these land seizures were moved to one of the two new townships in a process of forced relocation (Falah 1989a, 80; Amara and Miller 2012, 77–78). In other cases, a small sum was given as compensation to induce the Bedouin families to relocate to the townships. No matter how the moves were accomplished, the government required residents to give up all claims to land, including any ancestral lands outside the enclosure zone. In exchange, families moving to the townships received a lease to a plot of state-owned land to build a house. Since the townships are zoned urban, herding of livestock and cultivation were prohibited. Although some Bedouin secretly kept livestock, they were essentially forced into agreements with the government to relinquish their cultural way of life as a condition for living in these segregated environments.

While the townships offered Bedouins access to basic services otherwise denied them for decades, compelling some to relocate and accept the government's terms, an equal number of Bedouin opposed relocation (Falah 1983, 314). Generally speaking, the idea of living without the possibility of cultivating crops or herding livestock was anathema to the historical culture of the Bedouin. More specifically, they objected to the fact that they would not be owners of their land but rather lessees, a concept foreign to Bedouin culture. Then too, many of the Bedouin who had claimed land during settlement of title operations in the Negev were naturally reluctant to relinquish their claims by moving to the townships. Finally, Bedouin were loath to reside on land claimed by other Bedouin. As a result, the land confiscated from Bedouin communities such as Tal al-Malah to create townships was severely compromised because few if any Bedouin will move to land that rightfully belongs to other Bedouin. All of the townships, with the exception of Segev Shalom, have sizable percentages of land claimed by Bedouin, ranging from Hura, with 20 percent of its land the object of claims, to Kseife, with fully 87 percent of its land claimed by nearby Bedouin (Goldberg Commission 2011, 28–29).

These objections meant that roughly half the Bedouin population resisted the government plan to relocate them to the townships. What emerged from this resistance to relocation was the phenomenon of "unofficial" settlement on the landscape, meaning that the government did not recognize such settlements and did not provide them with basic services. Without schools, medical clinics, and infrastructure such as water, electricity, and roads, these communities remain unmarked on Israeli maps of the Negev, known only as "unrecognized villages." They represent an effort to preserve Bedouin culture. "We call the townships *hotels*," explains Fadi M., director of the Regional Council for the Unrecognized Villages in the Negev (RCUV). "There are no jobs [there], and there is no life. All you can do in the townships is sleep" (author interview, September 19, 2014).

By 1999 there were forty-six unrecognized villages, of two basic types: those located on ancestral land that predate 1948, such as al-Sira and Tal al-Malah, whose residents were not moved; and those composed of internally displaced residents transferred to the Siyag. The former make up 70–75 percent of these villages, the latter up 25–30 percent (RCUV/BIMKOM 2012, 11). Dispersed primarily across the northern portion of the Siyag, unrecognized villages were designated by the government as "illegal," while the villagers themselves were classified as trespassers on state-owned land liable for prosecution in criminal courts in accordance with the state's Law of Planning and Building (Nevo 2003, 186). From the perspective of a government intent on Judaizing the Negev, the existence and territorial spread of these Bedouin villages was an impediment to state aspirations to develop Jewish towns and settlements inside the area of the Siyag. Although the government eventually recognized eleven of these villages in 1999, explains Fadi M., and provided them with a minimal level of service, their status is little different from that of unrecognized villages (author interview, September 19, 2014).

Currently, the forty-six unrecognized villages have a total population of 108,000, roughly 50 percent of the total Negev Bedouin population (RCUV/ BIMKOM 2012, 5; Central Bureau of Statistics 2015, table 16.2). Despite the efforts of the Regional Council of Unrecognized Villages to develop a master plan showing that recognition of the unrecognized villages and the provision of services to them would be no different than what occurs in nearby Jewish rural localities and would be less costly than the government's Township Plan, there is no indication that Israeli authorities are prepared to extend such recognition to the Bedouin community (RCUV/BIMKOM 2012, 6–7). Indeed, the opposite seems true.

By the early 2000s, the government of Israel embarked on an aggressive campaign of policing to eradicate Bedouin presence in unrecognized villages, spearheaded by a special paramilitary unit operating across different ministries known as the Green Patrol (Abu-Saad and Creamer 2012, 42–43). The most notorious of these policing operations has involved the demolition of thousands of Bedouin homes, and in some cases entire villages, which the state contends is a matter of enforcing the law against trespassing and illegal construction on state-owned land. This policy was promoted by the Ministry of the Interior in a document known as the Markovitch Commission Report (1986, updated 1989), in accordance with the country's Planning and Building Law of 1965. Demolitions followed from this report during the 1990s, then decreased during the latter part of the decade, only to be reinstated in 2001 when eight Bedouin homes in the Negev were demolished. As the decade progressed, the number of demolitions increased dramatically, from 63 in 2003 to 96 in 2006 and 227 in 2007 (Human Rights Watch 2008, 117).

By 2010, the annual figure on Bedouin house demolitions had reached 456, while in 2011 the figure jumped dramatically to 1,000. From that time the number has remained in the range of roughly 500–1,000 demolitions per year. Even housing in recognized villages has been targeted, with demolitions occurring at roughly the same rate as in the unrecognized villages (Negev Coexistence Forum for Civic Equality 2011, 16; 2014, 12; 2017, 14). Because the state considers virtually all houses in unrecognized villages to be illegally built, they automatically have demolition orders attached to them. "They [the Green Patrol] came to my house and stuck a notice on my door stating that my house is on state land and faces demolition," explained Khalil A. of al-Sira. "They don't put your name on the notice, only a number. My number is 67. If they put your name on the notice, that would mean that you are somebody and that you exist. They don't want you to exist" (author interview, September 20, 2014).

In 2011, the government reorganized its enforcement policies connected to illegal construction in the Negev and placed responsibility for this activity within the Ministry of Public Security and a new unit known as the Coordination Directorate of Land Law Enforcement in the Negev. A special police detachment—Unit Yoav—was assigned as the enforcement arm of the Coordination Directorate, with the stated duty of keeping "state lands free of infiltrations and illegal construction, and available for use according to government discretion."[10] Although the ministry and the Coordination Directorate make no specific reference to house demolitions, this activity has intensified with the creation of Unit Yoav, and nowadays demolitions of Bedouin houses in the Negev occur on a daily basis (Noach 2014, 1–2).

National Outline Plan 22: Tree-Planting in the Negev. If creating a landscape of demolished houses represents an instrument of brute force to compel the Bedouin to relinquish their land and move to the townships, it functions alongside a more subtle type of landscape reorganization: the planting of trees. Codified in the National Plan for Forests and Afforestation—National Outline Plan 22 or NOP 22—tree-planting is a signature practice for spreading Hebrew space on the landscape and is the most visible element in "greening" the desert (Kaplan 2011). For the Bedouin, however, tree-planting has a different set of meanings, being connected to the spread of Jewish settlement and concurrent shrinkage of Bedouin space. Where trees are planted and where forest areas expand, areas for Bedouin settlement and circulation contract and disappear. Thus tree-planting, too, becomes a control technology. By recasting the landscape symbolically as Jewish space, Zionist tree-planting drives the Bedouin to seek the few remaining spaces on the land—mostly townships—where conifers have not intruded to mark the areas as Jewish. Zionist tree-planting also reorders the landscape physically, becoming an imposing and intimidating material technology for restricting the routes of circulation of Bedouins in territorial space, with impacts similar to the hedge and fence in the English enclosures (Blomley 2007).

Until 1976, afforestation had been part of the state's master planning process, inaugurated in 1951 with Israel's first nationwide plan (Yiftachel 2006, 193). Framed under the direction of Ariel Sharon, this plan targeted three areas for Judaization: the Galilee, the Jerusalem corridor, and above all the Negev, where the state aimed to settle a burgeoning immigrant population in new Jewish settlements. "Only by settling and developing the Negev," Ben-Gurion emphasized, "can Israel, as a modern, independent and freedom-seeking nation, rise to the challenge that history put before us" (quoted in Yiftachel 2006, 193). Thus, alongside his clarion call for afforestation in the same year, Ben-Gurion outlined a vision for the country's future that was anchored in the Negev and built on a foundation of Jewish settlements and forest trees.

As Ben-Gurion's point person for afforestation, the JNF's Weitz aggressively organized tree-planting in the Negev during early statehood. By 1967–68, afforestation was being pursued in ninety-eight locations spread throughout four Negev subregions in a calculated program to remake the desert and appeal to a population of new settler-pioneers (Weitz 1974, 144; Tal 2013, 114). Perhaps the most ambitious project of early JNF afforestation in Israel was the Yatir Forest, conceived by Weitz in 1964 on the northern edge of the

FIGURE 25. "Making the Desert Bloom": Yatir Forest (2014). Photo by author.

Siyag. With four million mostly coniferous trees on 30,000 dunums, it remains the largest forest in Israel (fig. 25) (Rotem, Bouskila, and Rothschild 2014, 15). Soon to follow was the Lahav Forest covering 27,000 dunums, first planted in 1952 but expanded in 1971. Later JNF forests in the Negev include Meitar, Kramim, and Beersheva, along with expansions in the western portion of the Negev where some of the earliest Negev settlements took shape (Kaplan 2011, 30).

In 1976, the state drafted a plan specifically for afforestation and delegated the JNF, the state Planning Authority, and the Israel Lands Administration as the primary institutions responsible for the plan's implementation (Kaplan 2011, 11). Redrafted numerous times, National Outline Plan 22 was eventually ratified in 1995, but in the interim, afforestation in the Negev had become one of the state's most prominent planning priorities. By 1994, the Beersheva district had the second largest area of planted forests in Israel, with 115,000 dunums, and by the time NOP 22 was ratified, the Beersheva district constituted the largest area planned for future forests, estimated at 55,000 dunums (Kaplan 2011, 67). More recently, still in accordance with NOP 22, the vast bulk of forest planting and land preparation for forests in all of Israel has occurred in the Beersheva region (Kaplan 2011, 30). In 2010, 69 percent of the planting and land preparation by the JNF for afforestation in Israel occurred in the Beersheva region, while the figure for 2011 was 73 percent (Rotem, Bouskila, and

Rothschild 2014, 17). These efforts have transformed the forest lands in the Negev as tree-planting has swept aggressively throughout the Siyag.

Tree-planting in the Negev is, together with the effort to concentrate the Bedouin in townships, part of a strategy to take control of land and mark it as Jewish space. Where trees are planted, Bedouin crops and livestock—and ultimately Bedouin communities—are unable to thrive on the landscape. Tree-planting, then, is a way of reorganizing landscape to create pressure on Bedouin presence and coerce them to relinquish their place and move where the government wants them. Nowhere is this combination of demolition and afforestation more formidable than in the Bedouin village of al-Araqib.

Al-Araqib

Al-Araqib is located on the extreme northwestern corner of the Siyag. Most of its lands belonged to the al-Uqbi tribe, which in 1905 sold some of its land in the eastern part of al-Araqib to the nearby al-Turi tribe. In 1951, the Israeli military governor for the area ordered the al-Uqbi to evacuate the village for six months to allow for military training exercises, after which they could return. Three years later, after being repeatedly denied the right to return to their land, the al-Uqbi returned anyway, but they were soon forcibly evicted; since that time the tribe has been served continuously with restraining orders prohibiting them from going to their land. The al-Turi tribe was also evicted in the 1950s, but unlike the al-Uqbi, they returned several times each year with livestock herds, and during parts of the year they cultivated wheat on the land, believing that because it was purchased the land still belonged to them. The al-Turi were also joined during that time by three other tribal groups, the Abu-Medeghem, Abu-Freih and Abu-Zayed (Weizman and Sheikh 2015, 46–50; Adalah 2013, 2).

In 1998, the situation in al-Araqib changed dramatically when the Jewish National Fund began to plant the first of what would be several forests in the surrounding lands. The two largest were the Mishmar HaNegev Forest and the Givot Goral Forest. Some of the planting was placed directly on croplands of the village, which were uprooted to make way for the forest trees. Upon seeing the tree-planting, the al-Uqbi again attempted to return to the village but were denied; meanwhile, however, the al-Turi and the three other tribes decided to establish a permanent presence on the site. By 2002, when a first demolition of the village occurred, four hundred people from the four tribes were living there. From the perspective of the state, urgency warranted this harsh tactic: plans had already been formulated for a new Jewish settlement in the vicinity of al-Araqib, Giv'ot Bar.

On January 19, 2004, trailers representing temporary housing for Giv'ot Bar were moved onto the ancestral lands of the al-Uqbi, just on the edge of al-Araqib village, as a first step toward the permanent Jewish settlement. In the Negev, however, Jewish settlement compels the state to satisfy two preconditions on the landscape: afforestation is one, and a landscape cleared of Bedouin is the other. Al-Araqib had become the site of a battle over land. In this battle, the landscape itself was enlisted as a weapon of war.

From 2004 to 2010, as villages in the Negev were being demolished with ever greater frequency, demolition of al-Araqib occurred piecemeal. The situation changed, however, in July 2010, when the state embarked on a full-fledged battle for the lands of the village. This moment marked the beginning of monthly—and sometimes more frequent—razings of the village. Between July 2010 and February 2016, Israeli police and military units demolished the village roughly eighty-five times. Despite this formidable power, the village, though largely emptied of residents, continued to resist.

Meanwhile, tree-planting in the vicinity of al-Araqib intensified, expanding ever more invasively onto village croplands. Surrounding the village in addition to the Mishmar HaNegev Forest and the Givot Goral Forest are the Ambassadors Forest and the Forests of the German States (fig. 26). Planted in accordance with the National Forest Master Plan, along with local and regional forest plans and the afforestation efforts of the Jewish National Fund, these forests lie to a large extent on land claimed by the villagers. All of these forests are currently undergoing expansion, becoming more concentrated and increasing their footprint on the landscape.

Villagers from al-Araqib describe the ways in which tree-planting is shaping the fate of the village. "A great historical injustice has been done here," said Awad of the Abu Freih tribe, referring to the Forests of the German States,

> because this land belongs to my father and grandfather and now it has been planted with trees with the help of funding from various German state governments. You can see a new landscape here, but it is a landscape that has created a whole new layer of history over our presence in this place. My family has been erased from here. . . . This is no longer a place for me. I am not comfortable even coming here, which is why we [author and interviewee] did not use the main entrance. This forest has been made for the people who live there in Lehavim. (author interview, February 28, 16)

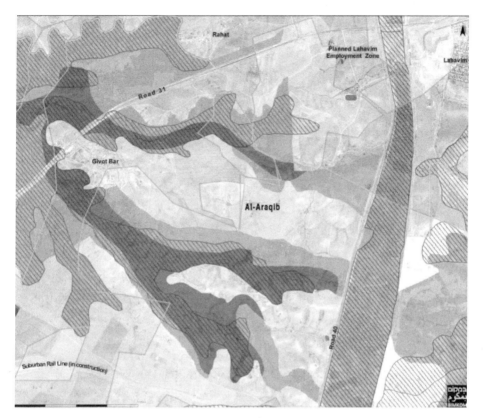

FIGURE 26. Map of Forests surrounding al-Araqib (2011). Cross-hatching represents areas in the National Master Plan for Forests. Shaded areas without cross-hatching represent local, regional, and JNF forest plans. The area east of Road 40 is the Givot Goral Forest; the areas immediately surrounding al-Araqib belong to the Mishmar HaNegev Forest. Source: Bimkom Planners for Planning Rights. Reproduced by permission.

A similar theme is sounded by the Sheikh of al-Araqib, Sayah al-Turi, who is also the leader of a resistance campaign against demolition of the village and the seizure of its land. "Those trees around our village are planted on our lands," he said. "They are enemy soldiers." His son Aziz provided an even more dramatic accounting of JNF tree-planting, including an emphatic rebuttal to the doctrine of the Dead Negev. "Where you [author] came into our village, all of it was green. Now it has changed. Our area is yellow; and the JNF planting is green. . . . We made the desert green. We planted everything green here. We planted wheat and olives. But the JNF destroyed *our* green—destroyed the Arabs' green and planted a new history on our land. They want to delete the Arabs' history, and so with their trees they plant a new history and try to make us disappear" (author interview, September 21, 2014).

• • •

On June 29, 2016, during the holiday month of Ramadan, Israeli army bulldozers, accompanied by soldiers and police, demolished the village of al-Araqib for the hundredth time. In the immediate aftermath of the destruction, representatives of the JNF—which has been waiting to plant the village lands with a "forest" of conifer trees, insisting that the land belongs to the JNF—were again perusing the area. Nonetheless, the villagers' campaign to remain steadfast continues, against all odds. "Even if they destroy Al-Araqib two hundred times, I am not moving," vowed Hameq Abu Madigem, a resident of the village (quoted in Wilson 2016).

In a matter of decades, a profound historical transformation has occurred on the landscape of the Naqab. Where Bedouin communities once prevailed in an area of roughly three million dunums, cultivating crops of wheat and barley and herding livestock, an entirely new landscape has emerged marked by Jewish settlements and conifer trees. In this process of change, as larger areas of the Naqab are enclosed as Jewish space, Bedouins have been moved into ever-diminishing territorial spaces, their footprint on the landscape continuously shrinking. As this process continues, the Bedouin, much like Native Americans, are pushed into townships by a state promoting the expansion of communities populated by a new generation of Jewish settler-pioneers spreading across the land.

"A STONE IN THE FIELD": ISRAELI SETTLEMENTS AND THE ENCLOSED LANDSCAPE OF NAḤḤĀLĪN

"Naḥḥālīn is a very special village in Palestine," says Ibrahim Bader, Naḥḥālīn's mayor since 2013 (author interview, February 24, 2016). He has spent all of his fifty-seven years in the town, located seven kilometers from Bethlehem and ten kilometers from Jerusalem. According to Mayor Bader, Naḥḥālīn, now with roughly eight thousand residents, is one of the three oldest settlements in Palestine. "We have archeological evidence, verified by UNESCO, of glass-making here that is three thousand years old," he says proudly. The name of the town, he continues, derives from the Arabic word *nahl,* meaning bee, and Naḥḥālīn means the "town of beekeepers." It has always been a fertile area," he explains, with many different types of flowers, so that historically beekeeping has flourished here. But not so much today." Naḥḥālīn is also famous for its springs, of which the most important is Ain Faris. "We also have many problems here that make our situation very difficult," he admits. Since 1948, he says, Naḥḥālīn has been close to the border with Israel, and the conflict between the two groups of people is intense. "The Israeli army has come across the border numerous times, and we have martyrs from these incursions," says Bader, referring to March 1954, when Israeli soldiers came into the village and killed four people, and to April 1989 during the First Intifada, when the Israeli border police and army invaded Naḥḥālīn and killed five people. "Now our biggest problem comes from the Israeli settlements all around us," Bader says (fig. 27). "They take our land, and they have ruined the water from our springs."

"Two weeks ago," he continues,

> I was at the Israeli DCO [District Command Office] to discuss with the commander the hazards from the high voltage transmission wires that they placed in the Valley [of the Cow] between us and the settlement of Beitar Illit. When I was there, I noticed a drawing on a piece of paper hung on the wall. On this drawing was a football field and on the field representing the players were Israeli settlements from the area—Beitar Illit, Geva'ot, Rosh Tzurim (Zurim), Neve Daniyyel, and the others from Gush Etzion. In the middle of field was a big stone labeled, "Naḥḥālīn." The meaning of this drawing was obvious. You can't play the football game with a big stone in the middle of the field. Somehow you have to remove it.

In a historical sense, the Israeli settlements surrounding Naḥḥālīn, along with the other settlements in the West Bank, are recent additions to the Palestinian landscape, having emerged following the Six-Day War of June 1967. Since that time, Israeli settlements have proliferated, with the settler population continuing to grow much faster than the general Israeli population. In the wake of this ever-expanding settlement cartography, an old landscape of hilltops reserved for grazing, cultivation, or open space has given way to tracts of intensive construction and development. As this old landscape vanishes, the right of Palestinians to circulate across the land has become compromised by the creation of ever-widening zones of impassable space (Shehadeh 2008, xiii). Indeed, a 1996 military order declared all settlements and their surroundings to be closed to Palestinians except by special permit, thereby formalizing large areas of trespass on the landscape

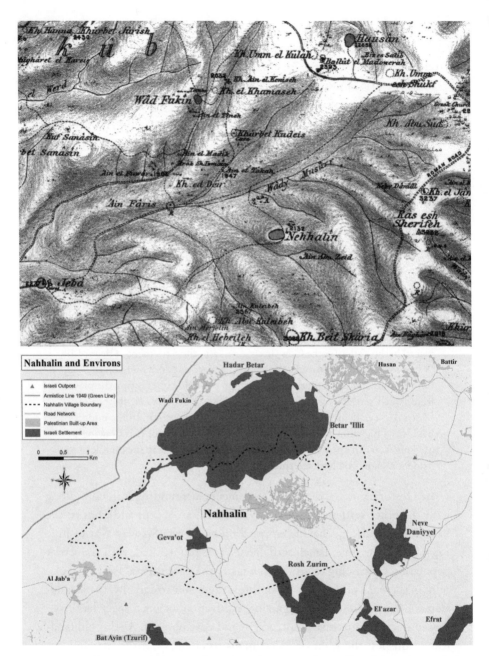

FIGURE 27. Naḥḥālīn, 1880 and 2016. *Above:* Map of Western Palestine (detail) by C.R. Conder and H.H. Kitchener for the Palestine Exploration Fund (1880). *Below:* Naḥḥālīn and Environs (2016). Map of Western Palestine reproduced by permission of The David Rumsey Map Collection, www .davidrumsey.com. Naḥḥālīn and Environs designed by Issa Zboun, Applied Research Institute of Jerusalem (ARIJ), and reproduced by permission of ARIJ.

(BIMKOM 2008, 17). Most fundamentally, what have disappeared in this settlement-dominated landscape are rights to land itself—the right to build a home, the right to cultivate crops, and the right to roam freely on the land.

Encircled by Neve Daniyyel, Rosh Zurim, Geva'ot, and Beitar Illit, Naḥḥālīn bears witness to this process of disappearance stemming from the proliferation of West Bank settlements. At the same time, located just over the Green Line in the Palestinian West Bank but a mere ten kilometers southwest of Jerusalem, Naḥḥālīn is situated in the midst of the other major land conflict stemming from the 1967 war: the expansion of Jerusalem's territorial footprint into the West Bank to create a city under Israeli sovereignty three times its former size, where the State of Israel is also settling its Jewish citizens. These two processes of creating a Jewish landscape from what was Palestinian territorial space in the West Bank and Jerusalem represent enclosure: the redrawing of boundaries on land, and the reassignment of rights to land within the redrawn areas. In the West Bank and the environs of Jerusalem, large tracts of land have been redrawn and reassigned as Jewish space. Meanwhile, Palestinian spaces are disappearing—as in Naḥḥālīn.

War, Occupation, and Settlement-Building

When the State of Israel emerged victorious in the war of June 1967, it found itself in control of the entire territory designated as "Palestine" during the British Mandate. For the victors, the primary territorial acquisitions from the war consisted of the Gaza Strip, taken from Egypt, and, taken from Jordan, the West Bank, which also included the eastern portion of Jerusalem. (Israel also gained control of the Golan Heights from Syria, though that was outside Mandate Palestine.) Central to the government's approach to its conquered territories was a doctrine proposed in July 1967 by the former Israeli general turned labor minister Yigal Allon. His doctrine came to be known as the Allon Plan.

In basic outline, the plan consisted of three interrelated aims: (1) creating a secure territorial space for the State of Israel, (2) acquiring territory, and (3) settling acquired areas with Jewish Israelis. In order to establish "a strong defense alignment," Allon insisted on relocating sections of the Green Line, the de facto border established between Israel and its Arab neighbors following the armistice of 1949. Israel's eastern border would be moved to the Jordan River, and Allon proposed that Israel absorb areas of the West Bank with "a minimum of Arab population," thus enlarging the state's territorial footprint (Allon 1967, 186; Allon 1976). These areas of supposedly light Palestinian presence, however, comprised roughly 40 percent of the West Bank, primarily along the Jordan Valley in the area known as the "Rift," roughly 12–15 kilometers west of the Jordan River; the Judean Desert west of the Dead Sea as far as Hebron; and a strip of land linking the Jordan Valley to Jerusalem (Harris 1980, 38). In this way, Allon elevated territorial enlargement as the route to building a more secure Israeli state.

At the same time, Allon argued that defensible space had to align with a social and political space containing Jewish presence and proposed to establish Jewish settlements in the areas of Israeli control, including Palestinian East Jerusalem. Once established, settlements would enable the political border to move wherever Jewish settlement occurred (Shehadeh 1997, 3). In this way, Jewish sovereignty over territory would follow the settlement of Jewish Israelis, and a viable political space would emerge more or less aligned with the security space (Allon 1976, 49–50). Despite never being formally ratified, the Allon Plan, with its emphasis on security, territory, and settlement, guides Israeli policy in the West Bank to this day (Harris 1980, 36).

In seeking to settle its newly conquered territories, the Israeli government confronted a dilemma similar to that of 1948: how to establish state sovereignty on lands not owned by the state in order to settle and Judaize them? While the situation in the West Bank (and Gaza) differed from that in Israel proper, there was an important similarity between the frontier areas of the Galilee and the Negev in 1948, and territories conquered by Israel in 1967 (Forman 2009, 688). In both instances, Israeli officials concluded that the state required a legal foundation that it lacked at the outset in order to claim land for its settlement goals. Despite lacking sovereignty in the newly conquered territories, Israeli legal theorists argued that international law *does* allow an occupying power to confiscate land for military purposes related to security. Military administrators therefore emphasized the nexus between security and settlement-building, and used this nexus to requisition land for what was characterized as a security function.

Notwithstanding the effort to link Jewish settlement to security, the plan to annex territory and settle Jewish Israelis in the annexed areas presented Israeli authorities with serious legal problems. Article 47 of the Fourth Geneva Convention (1949) clearly forbids the annexation of occupied territory secured by military conquest, and article 49 prohibits the settling of civilians in territory under military occupation. Moreover, in September 1967 the Israeli Foreign Ministry solicited an opinion from one of its own

The third category of land seized by military order for inclusion as state property was dead land, primarily in the Judean Desert, regarded as having no owners; this category was similar to the dead lands in the Naqab seized under the doctrine of the "Dead Negev." Roughly 350,000 dunums of land w fell into this classification (Harris 1980, 118).

The fourth category consisted of land registered to Jewish owners prior to 1948 and added another 30,000 dunums to the inventory of state land in the West Bank (Abu-Lughod 1982, 49). Finally, the Occupation regime used a Jordanian law to expropriate land for "public needs," not to build settlements but as infrastructure for settlements; the law was revised, however, to eliminate all avenues of appeal by landowners. These expropriations were upheld by the Israeli High Court based on the rationale that the infrastructure, mostly roads to connect the settlements, enhanced the transportation network of the Palestinian population—a dubious claim, since many of these roads were off limits to Palestinians (B'tselem 2002, 60–61).

Despite differences in these various categories, several might be enlisted simultaneously for settlement-building. A prime example is the settlement of Shilo, established in 1978, which occupies 740 dunums of privately owned Palestinian land seized for security reasons, 850 dunums of so-called state land, and 41 dunums expropriated for public purposes (B'tselem 2002, 47).

In addition to these categories of appropriatable land, the military regime established a top-down planning process for settlement-building by means of Military Order No. 418, issued in 1971. Entitled "Order Concerning Planning Law for Towns, Villages, and Buildings," this decree created a separate planning framework for settlements, with authority concentrated in a single planning body, the Higher Planning Council (HPC), which includes no Palestinian representation. While the order disenfranchises Palestinian communities from the planning process, it empowers settler groups through a Settlement Subcommittee that works in conjunction with local military commanders in selecting settlement sites. Specific language in Order No. 418 allows settlement provided the site selected does not include an existing city or village (BIMKOM 2008, 39–45). This seemingly benign phrasing opened the way for widespread settlement of the West Bank by Jewish Israelis.

By 1979 Israel had gained control of roughly 30 percent of the land in the West Bank for settlement-building. Israeli military surveyors had completed preliminary surveys of this inventory as early as 1976, but much of the land proved unsuitable for settlement-building. Holdings were often scattered, with additional land—invariably private Palestinian land—needed for assembly into feasible settlement sites (Halabi, Turner, and Benvenisti 1985, 44). Owing to the piecemeal character of this approach, pressure mounted on land experts to devise more comprehensive methods for land seizure in order to continue and even expand the settlement project. By the late 1970s, Israeli land experts were framing plans for turning land into state property in the conquered territories. What was emerging from the surveys of West Bank lands was an extremely ambitious idea: conceiving of, and categorizing, the entire West Bank as the national patrimony of Israel, and on this foundation reclassifying unplanted or underutilized land in the West Bank as uncultivated and thus eligible for expropriation. This grandiose vision would eventually take shape following a landmark Israeli Supreme Court case known as *Elon Moreh* (1979).

From Elon Moreh *to the "50 Percent Rule"*

The catalyst for implementing this ambitious plan to expropriate vast amounts of West Bank land was a 1979 military survey that estimated land in the West Bank without registered title to be 1.53 million dunums (Abu-Lughod 1982, 49). Representing almost 30 percent of all West Bank land, this inventory of land without title was in theory "unassigned," that is, land without an owner and therefore claimable by the state as (again in theory) land without ownership. Equally compelling was the Ministry of Defense estimate that only 200,000 dunums of land in the entire West Bank (roughly 3.6 percent) could be considered privately owned (*Israel & Palestine Monthly Review* 1980, app. p. 6). The State of Israel, of course, already had vast experience in seizing control of land without registered title—in the Galilee during its settlement of title operation and in the Negev from Palestinian and Bedouin landholders. With only a small fraction of the land base under clear legal title, the landscape was akin to a clean slate of virgin territory open to acquisition by a state well acquainted with the necessary legal instruments.

As was the case in pre-state Israel, West Bank landholders who tended their holdings continuously gained prescriptive rights to their otherwise miri land in accord with Article 78 of the Ottoman Land Code. During the British Mandate, cultivators with prescriptive rights gained a more durable right of ownership over their land, but at the same time the British strengthened state claims on otherwise unassigned land as "state domain" (Forman 2009, 680). To identify private landholdings and state domain, the British initiated a survey in the territory of the Mandate in the 1920s, but by 1948 only 20 percent of Mandate Palestine had been covered, meaning that most of Mandate Palestine consisted of landholdings without officially surveyed and registered title.

When the State of Israel assumed control of the West Bank in 1967 from Jordan, it inherited a land system similar to what it inherited from the British in 1948. In the West Bank, although the Jordanian regime had resumed the land survey initiated by the British, by 1967 only 33 percent of the land had been covered, leaving most West Bank land without registered title (Forman 2009, 689). After assuming control of the West Bank, Israeli authorities suspended this survey, leaving the bulk of West Bank land unassigned. It was this inventory of unregistered West Bank lands, estimated at 1.5 million dunums, that the state coveted for settlement. The task of transforming this inventory into state land went to the same Plia Albeck who would later preside over the Commission on Bedouin Lands (see above). To transform this inventory into state land, Albeck had a body of law, developed in Israel, that had successfully dispossessed Palestinians of their holdings. Although the legal environments on the two sides of the Green Line were different, the basic issue of turning unassigned land into state property was sufficiently similar inside Israel and in the West Bank that the legal strategy used in Israel was, in theory, exportable to the conquered territories (Forman 2009, 693).

It was the legal environment surrounding the so-called *Elon Moreh* case that motivated the State of Israel to test the adaptability of Israeli land law for the West Bank. In *Dweikat et al. v. Government of Israel* (1979)—the case known as *Elon Moreh*— the Israeli Supreme Court established a new legal basis for the requisition of land to be used for settlement in the territories conquered by Israel. In this case, sixteen Palestinian landowners, led by Mustafa Dweikat from the village of Rujeib near Nablus, whose property was confiscated by military order to build the settlement of Elon Moreh, contested the expropriation and brought a petition to the High Court of Justice. In what was by most accounts a shocking decision, the court declared as void the issue of security as a basis for the seizure of private Palestinian land to build Israeli settlements across the Green Line. In reaching this decision, the court ruled that the confiscation of land for the building of settlements was not a temporary seizure but rather a permanent confiscation, since the settlement was intended as a permanent home for settlers. Two unusual anomalies in this case enabled the court to reach this decision. First, the petitioners invited several former Israeli generals, including opposition Labor Party leader Chaim Bar Lev, to testify as to whether Elon Moreh fulfilled the criteria for being essential for security. Surprisingly, Bar Lev challenged the arguments of the military, stating that the settlement would not enhance Israel's defenses (Weizman 2007, 106). Second, and arguably even more damaging to the IDF, was the testimony of Gush Emunim, the radical settler group seeking to establish Elon Moreh. In the person of Menachem Felix, Gush maintained that the right to settle the land was based not on reasons of security but instead on a biblical commandment. Felix also argued that the settlement was anything but temporary. "Basing requisition orders on security grounds," he noted, "can be construed only one way: the settlement is temporary and replaceable. We reject this conclusion" (quoted in Weizman 2007, 108).

With such testimony from the petitioners, Israeli generals, and the settlers themselves, the Supreme Court ended the practice of using military orders for the seizure of private Palestinian land to build civilian settlements. Although the decision returned land to the Palestinian plaintiffs, the victory for the petitioners was a pyrrhic one. It was the judgment in *Elon Moreh* that compelled the state to design a different set of legal practices for the acquisition of land to build settlements (Shamir 1990, 788–89). At the core of the new strategy for establishing state land across the Green Line was the instrument of state land "declarations," tied to a reinterpretation of article 78 of the Ottoman Land Code and the meaning of "cultivated" land (Forman 2009, 692–93).

Following the *Elon Moreh* decision, Albeck and the State of Israel embarked on a thoroughgoing effort to identify land in the Occupied Territories without registered title. Under the Ottomans, cultivated land was basically miri land that technically belonged to the Ottoman Treasury but was possessed by cultivators through rights of usufruct. The land targeted by Albeck's team—1.5 million dunums—was in the strict sense miri land (Forman 2009; B'tselem 2012, 23). If the state could demonstrate that the land in question lacked registration documents or was "uncultivated," the land, according to Israeli interpretation of Ottoman law, was without ownership and so could revert to the state.

In seeking out uncultivated land, Albeck had a newly minted precedent from inside Israel known as the "50 Percent Rule." A series of court rulings from the early 1960s had succeeded in redefining the metric for land considered "cultivated." To fit this definition, land had to be over 50 percent covered with planting; less than 50 percent coverage meant the parcel in question was "uncultivated" (Forman 2009, 683). Albeck's team sought out as a first step all land that appeared to be less than 50 percent cultivated. Cultivators in possession of land judged to be under this threshold without registration documents immediately lost rights to their land. Even for land planted at 50 percent or over, if cultivators were unable to prove continuous planting of their plots for the ten-year prescription period, they too lost rights to their holdings. In effect, by terminating the process of land registration in 1968, when only about 33 percent of the land in the West Bank had been surveyed, the State of Israel created an inventory of land readymade to be state property. By invoking the 50 percent rule alongside strict standards of documentation to verify ownership, the state mobilized a formidable legal instrument for redeeming the West Bank landscape (Kedar 2001, 988; Forman 2009, 685). The instrument in question consisted of the state designating land as state property by "declaration."

The use of the declaration to create state land became widespread during the 1980s as the Israeli settlement project expanded into the more densely populated hilltop areas of the West Bank and the need for land in areas of Palestinian presence became paramount. Alongside the proliferation of state land declarations to requisition land for settlement-building was a trend to constrict the physical space of the Palestinian population. This approach was reflected in a dramatic reduction in the approval rate of Palestinian building permits and more vigilant enforcement of existing building code and house demolitions for dwellings built "illegally" without permits. During the 1980s, the figure for approved building permits for Palestinians was already decreasing dramatically, and by 2000–2007 the military regime in the West Bank known as the Civil Administration rejected 95 percent of the 1,624 Palestinian applications for building permits. Currently, the approval rate is 1 percent. This phenomenon of shrinking the Palestinian space in the West Bank has been exacerbated by the Oslo peace process, which divided the West Bank into Areas A, B, and C, the latter accounting for all land outside tightly drawn boundaries of Palestinian villages and towns and representing the 60 percent of West Bank land where Palestinian farmland is located. In Area C, the IDF's Civil Administration has complete control and discretion on what can be done with the land. Area C is essentially a blank check for the reclassification of Palestinian land into Israeli state property (BIMKOM 2008, 10).

Palestinians whose land is declared state property can do little to prove that the land they cultivate, often in the family for generations, belongs to them. By declaring land to be state property, and by requiring the Palestinian cultivator to prove ownership, the state has been able to move enormous amounts of Palestinian land into the state inventory. It was in this way that the victory for the Palestinian plaintiffs in the case of *Elon Moreh* was a pyrrhic one (BIMKOM 2008, 27).

Settling Jerusalem

If settlement-building in the West Bank (along with Gaza and the Golan Heights) was a decisive outcome of the Six-Day War, Jerusalem was arguably even more central in the broader project of resettling Palestinian territorial space with Jewish Israelis (Klein 2008, 56). The city has long assumed a mythical status in the Jewish imagination as the eternal capital of the Jewish people, even though during the Ottoman period and the British Mandate it had a mixed population, indeed with a decidedly Arab-Palestinian majority (Abowd 2014, 22). From 1948 to 1967, Jerusalem was divided between Israel, which conquered the western portion during the 1948–49 war and transformed it into a Jewish city, and Jordan, which controlled the eastern portion. Heavy fortifications marked the boundary between the two sectors, and there was little contact between the Jewish side and Palestinian East Jerusalem. Upon sweeping through the Jordanian side of the city in June 1967, however, the Israeli army dismantled the barriers, expelled several hundred Palestinians from the Old City's celebrated Mughrabi quarter, and declared Jerusalem a unified city under Israeli sovereignty. Once unified under Israeli control, the long-standing vision of Jerusalem as a Jewish place was projected into plans that reordered patterns of development and demography and reshaped the urban landscape to fit this imagined geography (Said 1995, 6). Anchoring this vision was the settlement of Jewish Israelis in the city's eastern Palestinian sector, implementing one of the most critical policy goals of the Israeli government: to engineer the demography of Jerusalem such that an overwhelming majority of the city was Jewish.

Legally, Jerusalem and its environs differed from the West Bank and Gaza in terms of settlement policy. Palestinian East Jerusalem and roughly thirty of its suburbs, all of which were located across the Green Line, were annexed by the state as sovereign domain and attached to the western part of the city to form the expanded "Jerusalem Municipality."[11] This annexation totaling 70,500 dunums extended the boundaries of Jerusalem to the north, south, and east, increasing the city's area by roughly three times relative to its pre-1967 size (Efrat 1988, 13). Inside these enlarged boundaries, 68,600 Palestinians from East Jerusalem and its mostly agricultural suburbs were absorbed into the unified city as "residents," with the contours of the annexed area configured to take the maximum amount of land with a minimum Palestinian population (BIMKOM 2014, 17; Khamaisi 2006, 121).

From the outset, planning and development for the Israeli capital have been driven by the policy goal of maintaining a Jewish majority representing at least 70 percent of the total population (BIMKOM 2014, 15). More recently, this policy was articulated in the first official plan for both the western and eastern portions of the city, the Jerusalem 2000 Outline Plan, parts of which were released in 2004 (BIMKOM 2014, 49; Shragai 2010, 10; Chiodelli 2012, 7–8). The primary element of the Outline Plan is contained in a document titled "Report Number 4: The Proposed Plan and the Main Planning Policies," which summarizes the Jerusalem 2000's most important objectives in seventeen separate chapters. On the one hand, Report Number 4 notes how the settlement of Jewish Israelis in Palestinian East Jerusalem has diversified the city. At the same time, the report admits to the spatial segregation of Palestinians and Jewish Israelis, insisting that such separation is the preference of the two groups. Accordingly, Jerusalem 2000 divides the city into planning zones based on religious identity, with different objectives for Israeli Jews and Palestinians (Nasrallah 2014, 167). Arguably the most important part of the report is chapter 7, "Population and Society," in which the demographically driven policy objectives of the plan are clearly stated. "Demographic balance" in Jerusalem, chapter 7, section 1, notes, "demands the safeguarding of a ratio of 70% Jews compared to 30% Arabs [sic]."[12]

This emphasis on "demographic balance" has resulted in two complementary planning strategies for Jerusalem (Yiftachel and Yacobi 2006, 173). First, the Israeli leadership used settlement-building as the foundation for expanding the Jewish population and promoting the city, culturally as well as demographically, as a Jewish place. The government was able to move Jewish Israelis into Jerusalem settlements far more quickly than in the Occupied Territories of the West Bank, exploiting the proximity of these settlements to Jewish Jerusalem. By 1978, the Jewish population in the annexed Palestinian area of East Jerusalem had reached 47,000, or 32 percent of residents, compared to a total West Bank settlement population of 7,800 (Harris 1980, 145). Prior to 1967, this area was exclusively Palestinian. Second, the city's leadership strictly enforced planning and zoning codes severely restricting Palestinian building, thus impeding development of the city's Palestinian areas while keeping the Palestinian population from increasing (Cheshin, Hutman, and Melamed 1999, 10, 32). By the mid-1990s, the state complemented these planning restrictions with a draconian campaign of demolishing Palestinian buildings constructed without permits, a practice that continues to this day (Klein 2008, 64; Yiftachel and Yacobi 2006, 173).

Settlement-building has occurred cartographically across two wide arcs. Along the edge of West Jerusalem, the State of Israel developed an inner ring of Jewish settlements designed to push the boundaries of Jewish Jerusalem eastward by connecting the Jewish part of the city to the settlements (Harris 1980, 53). These settlements included Ramot, Ramat Shlomo (originally Reches Shuafat), Ramat Eshkol, French Hill, East Talpiot, and Gilo. This inner ring, however, was soon complemented by an outer ring consisting of the settlements of Neve Ya'akov, Pisgat Ze'ev, and Har Homa (fig. 28).

The cartography of settlement-building, in turn, has resulted in the spatial fragmentation of Palestinian communities in the annexed East Jerusalem area, where transport links have played a key role. In forging transport corridors between Jewish settlements and Jewish West Jerusalem, and between the settlements themselves, planners have bisected the annexed area with routes that bypass Palestinian East Jerusalem and its hinterland. This locational bias in transport planning has led to the isolation and spatial partitioning of East Jerusalem communities (Groag 2006, 176–77). As a result, as settlements expand and intensify their transport links to West Jerusalem, East Jerusalem and its hinterland communities have evolved into enclosed enclaves, disconnected physically from nearby West Bank Palestinian suburbs such as Abu Dis just over the municipal boundary and cut off physically as well as culturally from West Jerusalem. The outcome is an urban system of shattered connections isolating East Jerusalem from its hinterlands (Klein 2008, 56, 65).

While the formation of Municipal Jerusalem enlarged the city's physical boundaries, it simultaneously eroded the boundary between sovereign Israel and its conquered territories. The removal of the Green Line around Jewish West Jerusalem in turn created momentum for a compelling imagined geography. If the Green Line could be breached to create an enlarged Municipal Jerusalem replete with Jewish settlements, why not remove the Green Line in other locations to make Jerusalem even larger, inclusive of more West Bank territory and more Jewish residents? This question became part of an ongoing public discourse among Israeli politicians, planning experts, and the public that rendered the boundaries of Jerusalem—and the Green Line itself—increasingly unstable (Shlay and Rosen 2010, 359). As this discourse intensified, Jerusalem became the subject of even more far-reaching visions of grandeur. By the mid-1990s, a potent concept had emerged, without official

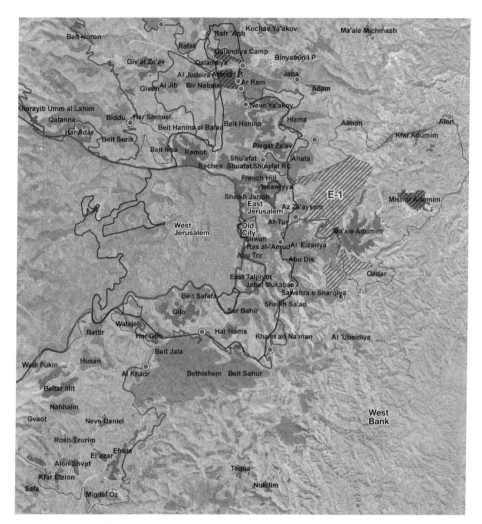

FIGURE 28. Map of "Greater Jerusalem" (2016), showing the area annexed to create the enlarged municipal boundary of Jerusalem. The line of annexation runs from Ramot north to Kafr 'Aqb and winds its way south and east to Beit Sahur, then west to incorporate Har Homa and Gilo. Along this line, but deviating slightly in certain places, is the Wall. At the settlement of Har Gilo, the Wall extends southward toward al-Khadr until Midgal Oz (part of the Gush Etzion Bloc), at which point the planned route of the Wall angles to the west, incorporating Naḥḥālīn on the Israeli side when completed. Map reproduced by permission of Terrestrial Jerusalem.

authorization in any planning documents or legislation but debated nonetheless: the concept of "Greater Jerusalem" (Halper 2002, 11).

In the most recent public discussions about Greater Jerusalem, one area frequently mentioned for annexation to the Israeli capital is the bloc of settlements making up Gush Etzion, including Beitar Illit. "Polls show that even now Gush [Etzion] is part of the territory over which there is a national consensus that Israel must retain it permanently," writes Israeli journalist Israel Harel in *Haaretz*. "It's a good reason to choose it as a turning point in Israel's absorption policy. The connection between Gush and the 1967 lines is geographically simple, natural and desired historically by most Jews" (Harel 2015). Indeed, Yitzhak Pindruss, the former mayor of Beitar Illit, insists that Beitar "is part of Jerusalem" but admits that it is "over the Green Line," thus suggesting that annexation remains a contentious political issue (author interview, February 29, 2016).

As debates continue on the merits of annexation, the State of Israel is pursuing a type of de facto annexation by means of a highly visible form of landscape architecture: a wall. The Israeli government has been building just such a barrier since 2002–3, ostensibly as a remedy to terrorism, but the route of the barrier suggests far different motivations. In the area of Gush Etzion, where roughly half of the barrier is complete, the planned route of the Wall will place the area of Gush Etzion—including Naḥḥālīn—on the Israeli side, effectively rendering the area Israeli territory (see fig. 28). Increasingly isolated due to encirclement by Israeli settlements, its land continually shrinking because of confiscations, Naḥḥālīn is being severed from the villages and towns to which it has historically been connected, ever more enclosed as the Wall is more fully built out.

A Vanishing Landscape

On Conder and Kitchener's map of 1880 (see fig. 27), Naḥḥālīn appears as one of several similarly sized agricultural villages in the Bethlehem Governorate, located in proximity to Bethlehem and the dominant central place in the region, if not the entire territory of Palestine, Jerusalem. By the end of the British Mandate, Naḥḥālīn had a population of 620 and a land area comprising 17,269 dunums, its fields and orchards yielding crops of wheat, barley, grapes, and olives (Hadawi 1970, 57, table 1). With roads providing access to the two larger cities, Naḥḥālīn was a moderate-sized node in a network of agricultural villages, marketing its produce in nearby Bethlehem as well as Jerusalem, where the market was larger and the prices higher for producers of agricultural goods (de Jong 2007, 24).

It was in the environs of Naḥḥālīn that Israel launched the first of its settlements in the West Bank, Kfar Etzion.[13] Although Kfar Etzion was located on land outside Naḥḥālīn's village boundary, it spawned development of other settlements that would eventually comprise the bloc of settlements known as Gush Etzion. Following in the wake of Kfar Etzion and situated directly on the perimeter of Naḥḥālīn were the settlements of Rosh Tzurim (1969), Neve Daniyyel (1982), Beitar Illit (1984), and Geva'ot, which though established in 1984 only recently received permits for a residential community. In addition to these five settlements, the bloc counted an additional seven—Har Gilo, Keidar, El'azar, Migdal Oz, Alon Shvut, Bat Ayin, and Efrata—creating an outer ring of settlement activity surrounding not only Naḥḥālīn but also nearby Palestinian villages such as Husan, Battir, and Wadi Fukin. In addition to being the first West Bank settlement, Kfar Etzion set a precedent for what would become one of the most prevalent tactics for establishing settlements: establishing the rudiments of dwellings and settlement infrastructure on the land—creating so-called "facts on the ground"—which allowed them to demand, and receive, government approval (Friedman 2005). Since 1967 the settlements of Gush Etzion have been among the most aggressive in gaining control of nearby lands. "We used to have 17,000 dunums of land," says Mayor Bader of Naḥḥālīn, "but now our area is only 5,000 dunums. Lands taken from Naḥḥālīn, Husan, and Wadi Fuqin have been used to construct the settlements all around us" (author interview, February 24, 2016).

Undoubtedly, the settlement that has affected Naḥḥālīn most is Beitar Illit, currently the second-largest West Bank settlement, with close to 50,000 residents, and one of the two fastest-growing Israeli settlements (United Nations 2007, 28; Central Bureau of Statistics 2016). Beitar Illit is also one of only four West Bank settlements classified by Israel as a "city." Due to its size, its rate of growth, and projections in its master plan of a final built-out population of close to 100,000, Beitar has been and continues to be one of the largest ongoing construction sites in the entire West Bank (Friedman 2005).

As with other settlements of Gush Etzion, the origins of Beitar Illit lie in the process of declaring areas of the West Bank Israeli state land (Bardin and Etkes 2015). "Beitar Illit sits on state land," insists Yitzhak Pindruss, who is from one of the forty original families that moved into the settlement when the first houses were completed in 1990 and is also a former mayor and deputy mayor of the city. "When we started construction, the hilltop for Beitar was empty land. There was nothing there. We did not take any land that belonged to anyone" (author interview, February 29, 2016).

Pindruss echoes what Israeli leaders have maintained over the past two decades: the State of Israel does not confiscate land from Palestinians to build settlements but instead builds settlements on land belonging to the state (Ofran 2009). A celebrated report, however, authored in 2005 by Talia Sasson of the State Attorney's Office, counters such claims. Sasson documented systematic confiscations of private Palestinian land by settlers who, assisted by complicit government officials, established numerous unauthorized *outposts* on the landscape, that is, clandestinely placed trailers or similar temporary housing on Palestinian land, which were later granted legal status as official settlements.[14] While the proliferation of outposts and their designation as settlements has resulted in the transfer of land from Palestinians to Jewish Israelis, what Pindruss as well as Israeli leaders in general do not explain is how land in occupied Palestine designated as state property and thus part of the "reservoir" of Israel lands (see above) becomes the property of the State of Israel in the first place.

In practice, Israel has exploited the fact that most of the land in the conquered territories was never surveyed, and ownership never registered, so when Israel took over the West Bank in 1967, what they found was an inventory of land theoretically without owners, ready to be designated as state property. At the same time, Israel has exploited the division of territory in the West Bank stemming from the Oslo Accords, which deemed 60 percent of land in the West Bank to be under complete Israeli control. By virtue of these two mechanisms, the State of Israel has acquired virtually unlimited discretion to declare land outside Palestinian built-up areas as state patrimony, challenging Palestinians to prove in Israeli courts that their holdings belong to them.

Challenging the benign characterization "state land" and the culturally relative notion of land as "empty," Mayor Bader of Naḥḥalīn recounts how Palestinians lost land when Beitar Illit was being built. "Members of the two main families in Naḥḥalīn, the Najajarahs and the Shakarnehs, had land on that hill with wheat and olives," he says. "In the summer and autumn, the hill was used by shepherds. Just before they started construction of Beitar Illit in 1989, they put notices on the ground saying that the area was state land and had to be evacuated. Soon after, they came and cut the olive trees and began to move heavy equipment onto the hill. Before the first houses were built, the land was lost" (author interview, February 24, 2016).

FIGURE 29. Beitar Illit (background), seen from the northern part of Naḥḥālīn (foreground) (2016). Photo by author.

Another villager, Adnan, tells a more personal story of what he witnessed on the hill where Beitar Illit sits. "When I was a young kid, I could look from an area near our house and see the hill because we live on the northern edge of Naḥḥālīn," he says.

> There were olive trees there, and some people from the village cultivated land on the hill but most of the land was for grazing. My father kept a herd of animals and was able to graze his flocks because there was space on the mountain and water from the springs. Sometimes I would go with him, and I have memories of olive trees and animals on that hill. Almost overnight everything changed. When I was eight, they began to build Beitar Illit. I remember it because they used explosives to level the mountain. When I saw them destroying the land with dynamite, I was sad. . . . When you look at a Palestinian village such as Naḥḥālīn, you see something old that has grown up organically. When you look at Beitar Illit, you see something *imposed* on the land (fig. 29).

Adnan then describes how the pressure on the land caused by settlements surrounding the town is affecting life within Naḥḥālīn itself:

> In Naḥḥālīn we have no space to expand for construction of new buildings. All of the land around us is Area C [a reference to the Oslo Accords]. There is intense competition between residents for space inside Naḥḥālīn, and the

result is that the price of land within the town is exploding. Even my family members cannot find places inside Naḥḥālīn that are affordable. In this way, the settlements nearby are not only taking the lands around us; they are affecting life inside our own village. This situation is forcing the young to move from Naḥḥālīn—which is exactly what the State of Israel wants! Israeli leaders want to concentrate us in bigger towns such as Bethlehem; they consider places such as Naḥḥālīn to be hurdles that they want to remove. (author interview, February 26, 2016)

In referencing the Oslo peace process, Adnan hints at yet another mechanism for enlarging the land base of settlements and shrinking the lands of Palestinian villages and towns: the reconfiguration of municipal boundaries. Beginning in the mid-1990s, the Civil Administration in occupied Palestine redrew the municipal boundaries for virtually all Palestinian communities in the West Bank, essentially shrinking them to fit the built-up areas. In addition, as part of the Oslo II Peace Agreement signed in 1995, Israel divided the West Bank into three administrative categories: Area A, where Palestinians had autonomy; Area B, where Israel and the Palestinians shared autonomy; and Area C, under full Israeli control with restricted access for Palestinians. In the wake of the agreement, fully 61 percent of the West Bank was designated by Israel as Area C, where the Civil Administration effectively prohibits any Palestinian construction. Any construction discovered by Israeli authorities in Area C faces demolition. In the area of Naḥḥālīn, this administrative system effectively squeezed the village and villagers into the town's built-up core, as virtually all of the land outside the redrawn municipal boundary was designated as Area C, with most of the land in this category either closed or off-limits to Palestinians (United Nations Office for the Coordination of Humanitarian Affairs 2011). In this way, Naḥḥālīn's historical boundary of 17,269 dunums was reduced to 1,132 dunums, with no possibility for the town to expand and only highly restricted access to surrounding lands.

In stark contrast, the boundaries for Israeli settlements, especially settlements such as Beitar Illit that are expanding rapidly, are undergoing constant enlargement. On March 24, 2013, for example, the Israeli Civil Administration Settlement Committee issued an order, published in the *Al-Quds* daily newspaper, informing the villagers of Naḥḥālīn of a modification to Master Plan 426/1/3/13 for Beitar Illit by which Beitar's boundaries would be expanded southward toward Naḥḥālīn (POICA 2013). The modification included rezoning thirty dunums of land on Beitar's southern edge, formerly classified by the Israeli Civil Administration as "nature reserves," into a residential area in order to add seventy housing units to the settlement. As the settlement boundaries of Beitar Illit encroach ever closer to Naḥḥālīn, the town has little capacity for growth or development.

This ongoing reconfiguration of municipal boundaries has led to the destruction of the open landscape and the abrogation of the right to circulate freely across land. The territorial footprint of settlements alone creates vast areas of space that is impassable for Palestinians. Even the land immediately outside settlement boundaries constitutes territory that Palestinians dare not breach, so when the boundaries of Jewish settlements are expanded, the area newly proximate to the boundary becomes the equivalent of expropriated land off-limits to Palestinians (BIMKOM 2008).

Related to this formal enlargement of settlement boundaries and the shrinking space allotted to Palestinians is a less formal, but no less formidable, boundary marker on the landscape: the violence perpetrated on a daily basis by settlers against Palestinians (Fields 2012; Munayyer 2012). Palestinian croplands in the vicinity of settlements are routinely subjected to vandalism or even destruction by settlers signaling to cultivators that the areas of cultivation are dangerous. Such areas thus become impassable spaces owing to fears on the part of cultivators that their presence there will incite further settler violence. In this way, settler violence becomes a way of marking the landscape, conveying to Palestinians that entry into the area is fraught with risk.

Arguably, the most formidable instrument changing the landscape in the West Bank remains the declaration of state land. Since 1979, and especially during the past two decades, state land declarations in the West Bank have occurred so frequently as to become more or less standard routine.[15] In the case of Naḥḥālīn, since the 1980s until 2012 roughly 3,000 dunums of land within the town's historical boundary have been confiscated as Israeli state land and reallocated for the establishment of the nearby settlements of Beitar Illit, Geva'ot, and Rosh Tzurim (Applied Research Institute–Jerusalem 2012).

In August 2014, the Israeli Ministry of Defense/Civil Administration Land Authority of Judea and Samaria issued an order for the expropriation of 3,799 dunums of land from five Palestinian towns, including Naḥḥālīn, in the largest seizure of land in the last thirty years (Levinson and Koury 2014). While most of the affected land was outside Naḥḥālīn's historical municipal boundary, three parcels lie within it. Two of the parcels lie to the south and

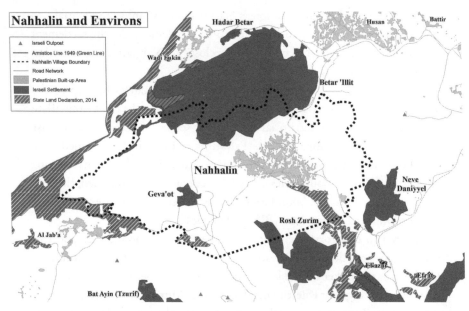

FIGURE 30. Map of Naḥḥālīn and Environs (2016), showing state land declarations as of 2014 (cross-hatching). Map designed by Issa Zboun, Applied Research Institute of Jerusalem (ARIJ), and reproduced by permission of ARIJ.

west of Geva'ot. The third, lying between the settlements of Rosh Zurim, El'azar, and Neve Daniyyel, projects forcefully toward the built-up area of Naḥḥālīn (fig. 30).

Despite the relatively small size of the two 10-dunum parcels to the south and west of Geva'ot, the configuration of the settlement and the two expropriated parcels provides a cartographic picture of how Jewish settlements expand and encroach their way into Palestinian land. Initially a military outpost, Geva'ot in 1998 was designated a planned civilian settlement—officially a "neighborhood" of the nearby settlement of Alon Shvut—with 60 residential units. In 2000, a plan was approved for a much larger settlement of 6,000 units, even though only about sixty residents were actually living in Geva'ot at that time. It was not until 2012 that the Ministry of Defense actually approved the first significant expansion plan of 523 housing units for Geva'ot. It is in this context of planned expansion that the two 10-dunum parcels confiscated in August 2014 begin to form a coherent settlement cartography. What the map reveals are the outlines of a triangulated settlement footprint anchored by Geva'ot's existing land, the 10-dunum parcel of expropriated land directly to the south, and the third to the southwest. It is within this triangulated area that a future and much larger Geva'ot is likely to sit.

The third piece of land confiscated by the 2014 declaration is much larger, 160 dunums. In addition to encroaching directly onto land abutting the built-up area of Naḥḥālīn, the expropriated parcel will provide contiguity between the settlements of Rosh Zurim, El'azar, and Neve Daniyyel. Such contiguity, in turn, is but a prelude to future infill development enabling the settlements surrounding Naḥḥālīn to grow and occupy even more land.

The location of the 160-dunum parcel also starts to create closure on the western flank of a plot of Palestinian land just inside the southeastern perimeter of the historical municipal boundary of Naḥḥālīn, land belonging to the Nassar family, promoters of the Tent of Nations (see opening to Part 3 above). Long accustomed to resisting their land being declared state property, and forced to endure the acts of nearby settlers who on several occasions have vandalized and uprooted their olive and fruit orchards, the Nassars confront an additional obstacle in remaining on the landscape with the placement of this expropriated parcel of land. To these settlers—and to the State of Israel—the Nassars' land is an obstacle, a stone to be removed. In many ways, what is occurring in Naḥḥālīn and what is occurring on the Nassar farm are parallel stories of power and territorial space; of boundaries being reconfigured, land confiscated or under threat of confiscation, and ultimately portions of the landscape passing from one group of people to another. In the face of continuing encroachments, Naḥḥālīn and the Nassar family are determined to resist and remain steadfast. It remains to be seen what the map will convey ten years from now.

• • •

In the late 1870s, just prior to the first Zionist settlements in the Palestine, the Jewish population of what came to be Palestine under the British Mandate was somewhere between 2–4 percent of the total population (Schölch 1985, 488; McCarthy 1990). By the end of the British Mandate in 1947, the Jewish population had increased to roughly 32 percent of the total, although Jewish settlements, forged from purchases of land, occupied only an estimated 8–10 percent of the land surface. Today, both of these figures are vastly different, reflecting a profound spatial transformation (al-Rimmawi 2009). The Jewish population in the area of Mandate Palestine is approximately 50 percent of the total, but Jewish settlements dominate the landscape both inside Israel and in the territories occupied by the state. Land under the control of the Jewish state and Jewish settlements accounts for roughly 90 percent of the land surface in what was Palestine under the British Mandate. In the historical space between these sets of facts is a story of power imprinted into the landscape. Zionists came to imagine the Palestinian landscape as Hebrew space and with the instruments of maps, property law, and landscape itself set out to recast that space in the image of their imaginings. As part of this process, they inscribed areas once the domain of Palestinians with new legal rules of property ownership, dispossessing the established occupants while imposing an entirely new pattern of stewardship and building. What emerged was a landscape transformed materially and culturally into Hebrew space, a process that continues to this day.

EIGHT

Enclosure in a Historical Mirror

ON AUGUST 5, 1765, the *Northampton Mercury,* a local newspaper for the English county of Northamptonshire and the oldest newspaper in England, carried an unusual story about a "Tumultuous Mob" that had assembled in a common field in the town of West Haddon, ostensibly for a football match but instead it "pulled up and burnt Fences designed for the Inclosure of the field" (quoted in Neeson 1993, 193). The destruction of fencing, which resulted in monetary damages of 1,500 pounds, had come in the throes of a failed counter-petition filed by villagers to halt the enclosure of the 800-acre common field. Fencing, along with stone walls and quickthorn hedges, was the most visible and accessible symbol of enclosure in early modern England and had emerged as a prime target of those resisting the transformation of common land into private property (Charlesworth 1983, 1; Neeson 1984, 128–30, 136). Even prior to the eighteenth-century Parliamentary Enclosure Act, "fence-breaking" had become sufficiently widespread as to be deemed a criminal act, with a minimum fine of six shillings for the offender (Oliver 2012, 196).

Two decades after the breaking of fences in West Haddon, the *Georgia Gazette* of October 25, 1787, reported on a similar series of violent incidents in Greene County, Georgia, initiated by Creek Indians against the property of white settlers. Such activity was becoming common along an extremely confrontational borderland in that soon-to-be new state. Along with the killing of colonists' livestock and torching of corn crops, the *Gazette* reported on the burning of fences protecting the property of these settlers (Haynes 2013, 213). As in England, the fence-burning reported by the *Gazette* was neither isolated nor unique. Much like the enclosure fence in England, the colonial fence in the United States was well understood by Native Americans as a symbolic marker of settler encroachment onto Native lands and had been the object of direct actions by Amerindians to reclaim land they imagined to be their own (Ethridge 2003, 147). Indeed, at the signing of the Treaty of Fort Stanwix in 1784, the Oneida chief, Conoghquieson, had addressed colonial negotiator William Johnson on the declining size of Oneida lands, stating his antipathy to colonial fencing in stark terms: "When our Young men wanted to go a hunting the Wild Beasts in our Country they found it covered with fences," said Conoghquieson, "neither can they get Venison to Eat, or Bark to make huts for the Beasts are run away and the Trees cut down" (quoted in Graymont 2001, 527).

Finally, in an article dated February 19, 2010, the Israeli daily newspaper *Haaretz* reported on the five-year anniversary of weekly protests taking place in the Palestinian village of Bil'in, thirty kilometers west of Ramallah. The target of these protests was the fence and wall erected by the State of Israel on land belonging to the villagers. Constructed ostensibly as protection for the Israeli settlement of Mod'in Illit, which was in the process of being built behind the fence and wall on lands of the village, the barrier effectively confiscated a portion of Bil'in's land by creating an impassible line of metal, concertina wire, and concrete separating villagers from their farmland. "Bil'in Protesters Dismantle Section of West Bank Separation Barrier," proclaimed *Haaretz* in the headline to its story, which described how protesters managed to tear down a section of the fence, causing at least $100,000 in damage before they were subdued by the Israeli military and police (Pfeffer 2010).

"Where there is power, there is resistance," Michel Foucault famously observed in his *History of Sexuality,* but what is striking in these three examples of protest is how, despite such different circumstances, those resisting dispossession directed their antipathy at the same material object in opposing the loss of their land. The parallels in these protests give rise to a vexing question. If, as Foucault suggests, power and resistance are inextricably linked, and if protesters in different contexts target the same symbol in resisting loss of land, does the fence as a recurrent target of resistance against dispossession suggest an enduring pattern of power in the seizure and remaking of land?

DISTINCT STORIES OF DISPOSSESSION

It is hardly surprising that the English enclosures, the seizure of Native American land, and Palestinian dispossession exhibit significant differences.

Each of these cases reveals different actor groups spearheading the enclosure of landscapes, alternative spatial environments where groups resisting but eventually removed from the landscape were placed, and different physical outcomes on the land itself. Most fundamentally, these three cases differ by the degree to which they reflect the influence of three complementary routes to modernization—capitalism, colonialism, and nationalism. In all three cases, the groups with territorial ambitions were motivated by the impulses of capitalist development, colonial settlement, and nationalist state-building, but the enclosed landscapes created by these actor groups reflected these influences in unique configurations.

English enclosure was most fundamentally an economic phenomenon, part of the agrarian prelude to the making of a modern capitalist industrial order (Aston and Philpin 1985). Yet enclosure also reflected decidedly nationalist impulses, as agrarian improvement tied to the privatization of land became part of an influential discourse and set of policies by the mid-seventeenth century defining the common good and the national interest (Tarlow 2007; Appleby 1978, 101, 183). As part of this nationalist discourse, enclosure assumed a decisive role in the project of land improvement, not only to provide sustenance for a burgeoning population but also to provision military conscripts for pursuit of the national interest through the making of war. At the same time, enclosure of the English commons and land lying in waste became part of the justification for English colonial ventures in North America (Horn 1994, 129)—a fusion best personified by John Locke, himself an advocate of enclosure as well as a colonial official. In this way, conflict on the land based on differences in economic class between improvers of land and those anchored to the land by custom assumed nationalist as well as colonialist overtones.

Similarly, while the dispossession of Native Americans clearly resonates as a manifestation of colonization, colonial settlement was intimately connected to both economic modernization and an incipient American nationalism. Driven by land hunger, settlers transformed the Native landscape into measurable plots of ground in an economic process whereby a continent-wide land surface became commodified into bounded parcels to be possessed, bought, and sold. This bounding of the landscape into a grid of modern landed property, and the spread of this property grid across territory that was so fundamental to colonization, helped shatter the Native landscape of use rights on the land (Cronon, Miles, and Gitlin 1992, 15). To be sure, the modern ideology of nationalism also played a role in this process of settling, parcelizing, and commodifying the landscape. Nationalism in the guise of a supposedly unique American destiny to populate a vast area of North America inspired and ultimately justified colonial settlement and the spread of the landed property grid that followed in its wake. The conceit that white settlement represented the fulfillment of this destiny helped carve out an ever-widening arc of territorial spaces that were emptied of their former Amerindian occupants and turned into enclosed and bounded parcels of land belonging to whites. Motivated by impulses of racial superiority and inspired by their designation as agents of destiny, colonial settlers pursued an economic and modernizing mission in enclosing the landscape, but one steeped in an unmistakably nationalist ideology.

In Palestine, the primary driver for the seizure of Palestinian land was, and continues to be, the nationalist impulses of state-building articulated in Zionist ideology, in which Palestine emerged as the territorial container for the nationalist aim of forging a state for the Jewish people. Nevertheless, this project relied from the start on practices of colonization, with state-building and colonial settlement in Palestine becoming not just interdependent but virtually indistinguishable. Zionist nationalism, state-building, and colonization were simultaneously suffused in a thoroughly modernizing development discourse based on the idea of ameliorating an empty and neglected landscape (LeVine 2005, 15–27). This outlook justified Zionist settlement of Palestine, as Herzl himself emphasized, and the taking of Palestinian land on the basis of the Zionist capacity for developing a supposedly barren and unmodern territorial space. Thus, what was fundamentally a nationalist project of state-building was integrated with colonial settlement and economic modernization as a set of practices for dispossessing Palestinians of their land. Although the conflict over the land is decidedly *not* based on religion, religious differences do separate the conflict's major protagonists, Zionist Jews on the one side and Palestinian Muslims and Christians on the other. Such differences animate the efforts of Zionists to enclose and remake the Palestinian landscape into Jewish spaces while identifying those dispossessed of their land by this practice of enclosure.

The individual cases are also differentiated by specific variations in outcomes on the land. Two are especially noteworthy. One pivots around the baseline systems of landholding, in which the group spearheading enclosure enlisted a particular type of landscape architecture to challenge the existing system of landed property rights. The second focuses on the spatial redistribution of the disinherited after they were dispossessed of their land.

Atop the openly configured areas of English common fields, including areas of common waste, emerged a system of individual landed property rights that abrogated the common uses once attached to these areas and rendered them off-limits to the small cultivators who formerly exploited them as a collective resource. Motivating this change was the idea of creating a more economically productive and efficient system of agriculture in spaces where common uses had once prevailed. Driving this change, in turn, was the profit-driven, rent-maximizing estate farm. Proliferating across the English countryside, the rent-maximizing estate transformed common-held, open landscapes into privately owned, geometrically regularized spaces, demarcated materially as well as symbolically by fences, walls, and hedges. What resulted was a landscape remade into bounded exclusionary spaces that restricted the right to roam freely across what had once been open land.

Differentiated from the common fields of England were the highly mobile, use-oriented agricultural fields, hunting and fishing grounds, and foraging areas of Native Americans who shifted locations seasonally as they sought out new territory for sustenance. On the landscapes where this use-based landholding system once prevailed emerged an exclusionary system of rights to plots of ground, in which whites had privileged access to rights of ownership. This transformation was effected by the settler-homestead, which encroached upon and proliferated across a Native landscape of use rights, remaking that landscape into a fenced and bounded grid of property lines demarcating exclusionary territorial spaces reserved for whites. Though similar to the eradication of the common fields, the replacement of Native landscapes with spaces of landed property owned and controlled by settlers was driven by notions of white racial superiority while the takeover of Native land was justified by ideas about the superiority capacity of white Europeans to improve the landscape.

Finally, on the lands of Palestinian agrarian communities, where the cooperative system of rights to land known as mushā tenure once prevailed, there emerged a land regime that reserved rights to land as the private preserve of the Jewish state and Jewish Israelis. What drove, and continues to drive, the process of eradicating a landscape of Palestinian spaces and replacing it with a landscape of Jewish space is the Jewish settlement, which is ever expanding its territorial footprint on the land surface. With its more geometrically regularized patterns of housing, agricultural cultivation, and overall development, the Jewish settlement creates a landscape symbolizing cultural trespass, and in the West Bank, spaces that are legally off limits to

Palestinians and made impassable by physical barriers of fences, gates, and walls. In this case, the eradication of Palestinian space and the proliferation of Jewish space on the landscape is supported by a system of entitlement privileging the rights of Jewish Israelis.

In this way, systems of landholding associated with groups of people anchored to the landscape through tradition and custom evolved along distinct historical pathways, only to be replaced by landed property regimes that led to exclusionary spaces on the land. In England, rights to land became vested in the category of economic privilege and class interest. In the American colonies and United States, rights to land became vested in the category of race and the color of one's skin. In Palestine/Israel, despite a conflict that is not fundamentally religious but over rights to land, such rights emerged on the basis of religious affiliation and a system that privileged those classified as Jews.

From the vantage point of the disinherited, enclosed landscapes redistributed the bodies of the dispossessed in different places and in different ways, resulting in vastly divergent fates. Commoners in England were uprooted from their land, remade into wage earners, and redistributed spatially, at times remaining on the land as agricultural laborers, at other times forced to migrate to cities as part of a broad demographic process of urbanization and industrial modernization. Some commoners seeking to resist enclosure were put in prison and in extreme cases subjected to capital punishment as a way of convincing those inclined to disrespect private landed property to take heed of the new lines inscribed on the land. Amerindians, in contrast, were uprooted from their land far more brutally and brought to the precipice of near-genocidal extinction by overt power and force. Ultimately, Native Americans were moved and pushed into ever smaller areas on the landscape, represented by the institution of the Indian reservation. Palestinians from what emerged as present-day Israel were uprooted from their land and driven into exile in massive numbers in 1947–49. Those remaining on either side of the Green Line inside Israel and in the territories occupied by Israel continue to lose land and have been relegated to ever-shrinking areas by a system of settlements always seeking new land for Jewish Israelis.

All told, there are good reasons for arguing that these three case studies of dispossession offer distinct pathways to modernity and unique worlds of domination and subordination on the land. At the same time, the question persists: Does the recurrence of the fence as a target of those protesting against the enclosure of their land suggest a different way of looking at these three cases of landscape change?

If on one level each case study of dispossession in *Enclosure* is unique, a far more striking conclusion from the comparison is the broadly aligned parallelism of the three landscapes. Most fundamentally, the three landscapes reveal a unified story about the reconfiguration of territorial space in transitions to the modern world, in which new systems of exclusion are inscribed onto land. Regardless of whether the primary influence in creating enclosed, exclusionary spaces on these landscapes was capitalism, colonialism, or nationalism, all these routes to modernity embodied wholesale spatial reorganization. Thus, one of the most compelling results emerging from the comparison of these landscapes is the recurrent territorial imperative of groups with power enclosing land as a route to a modern order.

In broad outline, the narrative central to *Enclosure* focuses on the interplay of power and geographical space. "Space is fundamental in any exercise of power," Foucault once remarked (Foucault 1984, 252). At the same time, power is an enactment involving human agency and choice. The way human actors enlist space in the exercise of power is through the practice of "territoriality," the conscious and active effort of individuals or groups to shape development in a place by asserting control over a geographical area (Sack 1986, 9). *Enclosure* documents the recurrent practice of territoriality across three case studies in which powerful actor groups target territorial landscapes as a platform for building what they insist is a modern order on the land.

Within this frame of territoriality, the storyline across the three case studies focuses on a common outcome from landscapes enclosed: *dispossession*. In all three cases, dominant groups with modernizing aspirations engaged in systematic efforts at "clearing" the landscape of people in order to implement their visions of a modern order. Yet these groups found the route to their vision of modernity blocked by groups of people already anchored to the landscape through systems of rights to land deriving from custom and tradition. What followed were struggles between groups already present on the landscape and modernizers aiming to reorganize systems of landed property rights. In the course of these confrontations, the groups with power successfully uprooted and removed the people tied to the land, then proceeded to substitute themselves as the landscape's new owners, stewards, and sovereigns.

This pattern of dispossession, whereby one group of people is supplanted on the landscape by another, and where land assumes a different legal, cultural, and material status as a result, is the common outcome in all three cases of *Enclosure*. What emerges from this recurrent act of removal and supplanting is the enclosed landscape. At the same time, animating the effort to enclose landscapes and dispossess people of their land is the notion of "difference." The three case studies reveal how categories of difference—whether in terms of class, race, or religion—become the basis for conflict on the land, and how the resolution of such conflict results in the establishment of reconfigured systems of exclusionary space on landscapes. In this sense, all three enclosure landscapes embody parallel stories of how dispossession becomes materialized on the land.

Within these broad outlines, the routes to enclosed landscapes and dispossession reveal recurring elements and themes. All three case studies bear witness to the influence of imagination—imaginative geography—on groups with land hunger, in what is an empirical affirmation of Edward Said's theoretical account of how groups with territorial ambitions come to act on their territorial aims. In all three cases, groups with modernizing aspirations and territorial ambitions essentially reimagine the landscapes they covet. In this process of reimagining geography, English landed classes, settler colonists, and Zionists justify to themselves and others why they deserve to take control of the land they covet. In the course of reimagining landscapes, these groups change the meaning of who belongs on the land, elevating themselves as the land's rightful owners and stewards while relegating groups already anchored to the land as undeserving of a place on the land, and in some cases as trespassers. This recurrent influence of landscapes reimagined is a compelling finding of the three case studies.

The most striking—and perhaps most surprising—finding in *Enclosure,* however, is the enduring influence of "land improvement" as the ideological inspiration for the reimagination of landscape and a driver of the process to enclose and take possession of land. With a focus on improving land as the basis for rights to ownership, this discourse inspired an entire class of landed elites in England beginning in the sixteenth century to seek profit from land, and to lay claim to portions of the landscape given to common uses that turned no profit. As part of an initially English outlook, this discourse found resonance among English colonists in North America, from the men of the Virginia Company and later John Winthrop along with John Locke, to early Anglo-Americans such as William Robertson, James Sullivan, and Hugh Henry Brackenridge. Also surprising with respect to this discourse, given its venerable origins and lineage, is how it resurfaced in the ideology of Zionism

(Braverman 2009a, 76). "We found a neglected and empty land and planted it to make it bloom" is the oft-heard refrain that emanated from the time of Herzl through Ben-Gurion. Today, this discourse about improving land—"making the desert bloom"—plays a decisive role in justifying Jewish sovereignty and dominium over land in Israel/Palestine. It is the central ideological element in the doctrine of the "Dead Negev" that continues to claim Bedouin land for Jewish settlement inside Israel, even as it justifies Jewish settlement on supposedly empty and uncultivated hilltop land in the occupied West Bank. *Enclosure,* then, is a story not only about power materialized into land, but also about "discourse materialized," as ideas about improving land continue to shape the physical landscape (Schein 1997, 664).

Undoubtedly, the most robust finding in *Enclosure* relates how the protagonists with land hunger all enlisted the same instruments of force to seize control of the land they coveted. Inspired by a shared ideology of land improvement and a similar imagination of themselves as sovereigns of the landscape, English estate owners, Anglo-American settlers, and Zionists turned to maps, the law, and landscape architecture to gain possession of the land they desired. Indeed, while there are differences in the way these actors deployed these instruments—Zionists, for example, used cartography more actively as propaganda than either estate owners or Anglo-American colonists to promote their vision of the Palestinian landscape as Hebrewland—all three groups used these technologies of power to assert their entitlement to land. Although *Enclosure* is reticent to suggest a generalizable model for dispossession and the enclosure of land, the recurrent use of the same instruments to enclose and take possession of landscapes is the strongest evidence in this study of a model of the enclosure process across time and territory.

Another of *Enclosure's* significant findings focuses on the similarities in the baseline systems of landholding across the three cases and the parallel trajectories in how these systems evolved as power became inscribed onto the landscape. In each case, systems of landholding deriving from custom and imbued with collective rights of use and cooperative forms of management came under attack by modernizers. The latter sought to eradicate those systems and impose a land regime given to the creation of more measurably "legible" spaces on the landscape. English common fields; Amerindian agricultural fields, foraging areas, and hunting and fishing grounds; and Palestinian village lands in mushā tenure all embodied systems of landholding with long-standing customary practices and strong collective and cooperative traditions of use rights and governance. In all three cases, modernizers, confronted by these collectively driven systems of landholding, overturned and replaced them with patterns of landholding deriving from cadastral surveys that established landscapes of ownership on geometrically regularized, measurable plots of ground. In these more rectilinear plots of ground, land emerged with new conditions of exclusion. Under the hegemony of estate owners, white settlers, and Zionists, the cadastral-based system of landholding enabled the creation of exclusionary landscapes in which spaces reserved for private ownership, white ownership, and Jewish ownership were fundamentally similar in their exclusionary character.

In all three cases, too, a particular element of landscape architecture functioned as the material carrier of this exclusionary regime on the land. In England, it was the rent-maximizing farm associated with the great estates that embodied parliamentary enclosure and expanded the footprint of privatized spaces on the landscape, a revolutionary change on the land represented by untold miles of fences, walls, and hedges (Allen 1992; Bermingham 1986). In colonial America it was the settler homestead expanding across territory, creating a landscape of enclosed spaces demarcated by fences that reserved an ever-expanding footprint of land as white space while diminishing the land and territorial space once the domain of Amerindians (Cronon 2003, 127–56). In Palestine, the Jewish settlement swept—and continues to sweep—across the landscape, enclosing territorial spaces in geometrically ordered patterns of development demarcating Jewish space, while promoting the proliferation of a vastly different pattern of cultivation and planting on the landscape, represented by the conifer tree. As they expand across the landscape, these built forms not only reinforce the exclusionary character of the spaces they occupy; they also function as powerful cultural markers imbuing the spaces where they are situated and the surrounding landscapes with symbolic messages regarding who belongs within and who lies outside these boundaries of belonging. In this way, rent-maximizing estate farms, settler homesteads, and Jewish settlements project the same cultural meaning about belonging and trespass.

Marked by these built forms of landscape architecture and distinguished by a new pattern of exclusion on the land, these rectilinear landscapes push the dispossessed into different and invariably smaller territorial spaces. The enclosed and privatized landscape in England casts commoners outside the areas of enclosure, sending them to workhouses, urban and rural, or, for those unable to find work, to the poorhouse. The settler landscape in the United States encroaches into vast territorial spaces, enclosing those spaces in white-settler proprietorship while driving Amerindians into reservations. The Zionist landscape, in creating an exclusively Jewish territorial space, sends Palestinians into exile as refugees, while those remaining are driven into an ever-smaller territorial footprint on the landscape in the face of ongoing Jewish settlement. In each case, people once anchored to the land through rights of custom are forced into new territorial spaces in a recurrent process of removal. While these spaces of removal differ, what is recurrent is the process of removal itself.

In the end, the disinherited had good reason to target fencing in their effort to resist the loss of their land. A broad historical arc stretching from early modern England to colonial America to contemporary Palestine reveals a long-standing pattern of territoriality—reshaping development in a place by seizing control of land—with resistance as a response. Along this arc groups with territorial ambitions enclose landscapes in new systems of exclusion. In the cases explored in *Enclosure,* this process witnessed the transformation of land in terms of identity and meaning as landscapes became private, white, or Jewish.

As part of the process of taking land, and as a symbol of their own territorial power, the makers of exclusionary spaces inscribe the landscape with a similar piece of landscape architecture: fences, hedges, and walls. These elements not only imbue landscapes with more geometrically regularized spaces that more easily define who belongs in such spaces and who is trespassing; they also function as material barriers, helping to create and reinforce impassable and exclusionary space, and in this sense are instruments of dispossession (Blomley 2007). Their presence on the land conveys potent cultural and symbolic meaning about the dispossessed and disinherited as trespassers. It is therefore not at all surprising that across the ages and in different places this element of landscape architecture, so instrumental in the process of enclosure and dispossession, should emerge as a prime target of those seeking to protect their land.

There are many who argue passionately that the conflict in Israel/Palestine is different from all others, that the historical trajectory of enclosing landscapes in systems of exclusion does not apply to the making of modern Israel and the dispossession of Palestinians. Such skeptics might do well to heed the words of Ze'ev Jabotinsky, considered the ideological inspiration of the modern-day Likud Party in Israel. In his prescient essay "The Iron Wall" (1923), Jabotinsky conceded the parallels between what the Zionists were doing and what English colonists did in North America. No indigenous people will ever accept the expropriation of their land without resisting, he insisted. Jabotinsky would no doubt understand the similarity between English commoners' efforts to defend their rights to common land, Native Americans' fight to protect the lands of their ancestors, and the struggle of farmers from Bil'in to regain land taken from them for Jewish settlement. All speak with the same voice in trying to destroy fencing on what they call their own land.

Enclosure is ultimately a story, told in three acts, about lines drawn on the ground and the use of power—including violence—to convey that the enclosed areas belong to "us" and are off limits to those different from us. In all three acts of *Enclosure,* power begets resistance, but there is one difference worth noting among the three groups: For English commoners and Native Americans, the account of enclosure has already been inscribed into the landscape. Those stories have reached their conclusion. In Palestine/Israel, in contrast, power met by resistance remains an unfinished story, very much part of a landscape still open to change.

NOTES

CHAPTER ONE. THE CONTOURS OF ENCLOSURE

1. Thompson (1963, 1971) argued that it was the mental universe of historical actors—how they understood their world—not simply their material conditions, that motivated their activity.

2. Hanafi (2009, 2013) uses the term "spacio-cide" to describe the territorial focus of the Zionist project, but control of land and territory are also central to the English Enclosures and Anglo-American colonization.

CHAPTER TWO. EARLY MODERN ENGLISH LANDSCAPES

1. Field systems derive from four basic elements: *topography,* including soil, relief, and drainage; *climate,* focusing on temperature and precipitation; *biology,* such as the crops cultivated and the livestock reared; and *culture,* such as systems of land tenure, the density and habits of populations, and technology (Baker and Harley 1973, 68).

2. By contrast, Kerridge (1992, viii) counts forty-two farming regions in early modern England.

3. The Hundred Rolls was a national survey of land tenure undertaken by Edward I, similar to the Domesday survey of 1086; it was not used as extensively as Domesday (Lachmann 1987, 42; Raban 2006).

4. Thirsk (1964) cites four attributes, but the fourth focuses on the manor court discussed above.

5. Merton also recognized the right of lords to enclose waste land to prevent common uses provided that sufficient land was left to tenants for grazing.

CHAPTER THREE. FROM LAND REIMAGINED
TO LANDSCAPES REMADE

1. Two further editions (1610 and 1618) appeared in Norden's lifetime, and a fourth appeared in 1738.

2. Quotations from Locke are from chapter 5 of *Two Treatises of Government* (1690, 285–302).

3. From a vast literature, see, e.g., Wordie 1983; Chapman 1987; Turner 1980; Yelling 1977, 11–16.

4. Prior to parliamentary enclosure, "referees" had the limited role of advising parties in disputes. By the late seventeenth century, these referees began overseeing the division of lands, but it was only with parliamentary enclosure that their role as commissioners became more formalized. See Kain, Chapman, and Oliver 2004, 31.

5. Information on Whytham in this paragraph and the next comes from Allen 1992, 99–100.

6. Information on West Haddon is from Neeson 1993, 188–207.

7. Admittedly, the number of smallholders displaced from the land by enclosure throughout England remains contested. Nevertheless, diverse sources (Turner 1980, 63–93; Allen 1992; Neeson 1993; Mingay 1968, 15; Beckett 1983, 1984; Thompson 1966, 515) reveal a rough consensus on the fate of smallholders during Parliamentary enclosure.

8. Information on de Grey and Tottington in this paragraph and the next is from J. Gregory 2005.

CHAPTER FOUR. AMERINDIAN LANDSCAPES

1. The population numbers of these communities have long generated debate. Early-twentieth-century estimates of the North American population at contact hovered around one million, but in the 1970s larger estimates appeared. Thornton (1987, 15–41) puts the population at seven million, while Denevan (1992a, 291) puts it at roughly four million. For an overview of the debate, see Thornton 1987 and Daniels 1992. For a strident critique of the methods and data used by scholars to calculate these populations, see Henige 1998.

2. Although agriculture involved two transitional innovations—the *protection* and *encouragement* of wild-growing plants—it has features distinct from protecting and encouraging plant growth. First, agriculture involves the cultivation of plants that would not otherwise survive without human intervention. Second, agriculture is marked by increases in human labor and technology, together with transformations on the landscape from these inputs. Finally, agriculture involves greater levels of stewardship for the cultivation of crops, and therefore increasing levels of attachment to the landscape to provide such stewardship (Doolittle 2000, 23–27).

3. Cahokia declined by the late fourteenth century, however, resulting in the out-migration of the Mississippians by the time of contact, mostly to areas of the Southeast eventually populated by Choctaws, Creeks, and Chickasaws.

4. Although a single indigenous cosmology is a heuristic conceit, a set of core beliefs common to diverse Amerindian groups with respect to land, people, and the spirit world can be delineated (Lewis 1998a, 53).

5. David S. Jones (2003) contests the argument that the collapse of Indian populations resulted from the spread of pathogens among people who lacked immunity to them. For Jones, the collapse of Indian populations resulted from colonization itself, which undermined the material foundations of Indian societies and weakened their ability to resist diseases. This alternative to the "virgin soils epidemics" does not, however, change the fact that diseases devastated Indian populations.

CHAPTER FIVE. REIMAGINING AND
REMAKING NATIVE LANDSCAPES

1. Much of this paragraph is based on Buckle 1993.

2. For this paragraph, see Armitage 2000, 97.

3. From 1669 to 1675, the proprietors of the Carolina colony employed Locke as their secretary. From October 1673 to December 1674, Locke held positions with the English Council for Trade and Foreign Plantations, and from 1696 to 1700 he was secretary to its successor, the Board of Trade. No major political thinker prior to the nineteenth century so actively applied theory to colonial practice as Locke did, by virtue of his involvement with the drafting of the *Fundamental Constitutions* of the Carolina colony. See Armitage 2004 and Edwards 2011.

4. Aspects of the map described in this paragraph are covered by the detail of place-names.

5. Information on the Holme map in this paragraph and the next comes from Klinefelter 1970, 41–45.

6. John Winthrop in "The City on the Hill" was arguably the first to signal this idea. The term was first coined in 1845 by John L. O'Sullivan, editor of the *Democratic Review,* who referred to America's "manifest destiny to overspread the continent allotted by Providence for the free development of yearly multiplying millions."

7. This paragraph and the next rely on Short 2004, 132–36.

8. This paragraph relies on Banner 2005.

9. The law was renewed at three-year intervals with minor modifications until 1802, when a more finalized version was put in place pending the final version of the law enacted in 1834, which is the law today.

10. Information on preemption rights comes from Banner 2005, 160–68.

11. The most detailed account of the case is in Robertson 2005. See also Banner 2005, 178–90.

12. Information in this paragraph is from Williams 1989, 10–14.

13. This paragraph and the next are based on Cronon 2003, 114–19.

14. I am grateful to Max Edelson for bringing this reference to my attention. See also Taylor 2006, 37.

15. For what follows in this paragraph, see Anderson 1994, 606–9.

16. For what follows, see Cronon 2003, 146–48.

17. For what follows, see Cronon 2003, 139–41.

18. Cherokees had good economic reasons for resisting removal. They had adopted Anglo-American farming more thoroughly than other tribes and by the 1820s were producing cash crops, notably cotton, at times on plantations with black slaves. Because they had increased the value of their land, they had good reason not to sell and move west (Banner 2005, 199).

19. Removal of Indians in Georgia and the opening of Indian land for settlement had economic ramifications. With removal, millions of acres of Indian land opened up for cotton plantations, allowing expansion of the cotton economy and the system of slave labor (Hershberger 1999, 17). Thus, Indian removal was part of sectional conflict.

CHAPTER SIX. PALESTINIAN LANDSCAPES

1. Such surveys did not map land, a practice introduced only in the late period of Ottoman rule and only in northern Palestine (Kark 1997, 53, 56–58).

2. Co-ownership differed from communal property. While no provision existed in Islamic or Ottoman law for communal property, co-ownership was consistent with the idea of partnership in Islamic civil law and Ottoman land law and was therefore suitable for the land-equalizing activity of the mushā village (Firestone 1990, 105–6).

3. The cadaster is an official register of the ownership, boundaries, and value of landed property in which the data are typically both textual and cartographic.

CHAPTER SEVEN. FROM IMAGINATION TO REDEMPTION

1. Quotations in this paragraph and the next rely on Kalischer 1862, 112–14.

2. In what follows, page references are to Herzl 1902.

3. Information in this and following paragraphs on the JOLC comes from Khalidi 1993.

4. Gordon points out, however, "that our claim beyond question is the stronger" (Gordon 1938, 25). Gordon does not specify the reason for his claim, but presumably he believes that the Jewish people have a longer presence in Palestine dating from antiquity and therefore their historical claim is more legitimate.

5. This paragraph, including quotations from *Hashiloach,* is based on Fine 2005, 24–25.

6. The following discussion relies on Forman and Kedar 2004, 816–25.

7. *Judaization* was actually the term used by Israeli state entities including the Israeli Defense Forces which employed it interchangeably with *settlement* and *development* (Forman 2005, 116).

8. Originally, military authorities told the Bedouin that they would be allowed to return to their land. To date, however, none of the Bedouin have been allowed to return (Goldberg Commission 2011, 9). As a result, the *Siyag* witnessed the development of squatter-like settlements built by Bedouin families who were moved but not allowed to construct durable housing (Abu-Saad and Creamer 2012, 26). Israeli authorities also prohibited Bedouin from cultivating land or grazing animals which basically ended their agrarian, pastoral life (Falah 1985b, 41–42).

9. The remainder of this paragraph and the next rely on Amara 2013, 36–37, 46.

10. http://mops.gov.il/English/PolicingENG/Negev_Land_Law_Enforcement/Pages/default.aspx.

11. Three legal changes formalized this territorial annexation and municipal expansion. On June 21, 1967, the government amended its Law and Administration Ordinance by empowering itself to designate areas of the Land of Israel where "the State's laws, jurisdiction, and administration apply," while attaching to the amended ordinance a description of territory in East Jerusalem that was now part of Israel (Benvenisti 1976, 109). On June 28 the government issued a "Proclamation on the Enlargement of the Municipality of Jerusalem" in which the boundaries of the enlarged city were defined in an annex to the decree, and on the following day the offices of the mayor of East Jerusalem and the Municipal Council were summarily terminated by an Order Dissolving the Jerusalem Municipality (Abdul Hadi 2007, 183–84). The unification and annexation were later codified by the state in 1980 in the Jerusalem Capital of Israel Basic Law (Jabareen 2010, 31).

12. Chapter 7 goes on to admit that the target ratio will not be met. Since the mid-1990s, the demographic balance inside Jerusalem has revealed a trend incompatible with the aim of maintaining the 70 percent Jewish majority. Estimates for 2020 place the Palestinian population at 40 percent, a number that for many in the Israeli political establishment is untenable. For this reason, Jerusalem 2000 has never been officially ratified, although in broad outline it is still being followed as Israeli policymakers try to find a solution to this "demographic threat." See English translation of Local Outline Plan Jerusalem 2000, Report No. 4, by the Coalition for Jerusalem (document in author's possession); also Chiodelli 2012, 17.

13. Kfar Etzion was a kibbutz during the later years of the British Mandate and was the site of a losing battle, with large losses of life on the Zionist side, in 1948, passing to Jordanian control from 1948 to 1967 (Friedman 2005).

14. See especially the lengthy interview with Sasson by David Horovitz (2012).

15. For an excellent chronicle of these declarations, see http://poica.org, especially material under the subheadings Military Orders, Israeli Plans, and Settlements.

REFERENCES

Aaronsohn, Ran. 1990. "Cultural Landscape of Pre-Zionist Settlements." In *The Land That Became Israel: Studies in Historical Geography*, edited by Ruth Kark, 147–63. New Haven, CT: Yale University Press.

———. 1995. "The Beginnings of Modern Jewish Agriculture in Palestine: 'Indigenous' versus 'Imported.'" *Agricultural History* 69 (3): 438–53.

Abdul Hadi, Mahdi, ed. 2007. *Documents on Jerusalem*. Vol. 2. Jerusalem: Passia.

Aberbach, David. 2008. *Jewish Cultural Nationalism: Origins and Influences*. London: Routledge.

Abowd, Thomas Philip. 2014. *Colonial Jerusalem: The Spatial Construction of Identity and Difference in a City of Myth, 1948–2012*. Syracuse, NY: Syracuse University Press.

Abu El-Haj, Nadia. 2001. *Facts on the Ground: Archeological Practice and Territorial Self-Fashioning in Israeli Society*. Chicago: University of Chicago Press.

———. 2002. "Producing (Arti) Facts: Archaeology and Power during the British Mandate of Palestine." *Israel Studies* 7 (2): 33–61.

———. 2006. "Archaeology, Nationhood, and Settlement." In *Memory and Violence in the Middle East and North Africa*, edited by Ussama Makdisi and Paul A. Silverstein, 215–33. Bloomington: Indiana University Press.

———. 2008 . "The Big Dig: Nadia Abu El-Haj Interviewed by Jeffrey Inaba." *C-Lab*, vol. 17: Content Management. http://c-lab.columbia.edu/0098.html.

Abu Hussein, Hussein and McKay, Fiona 2003. *Access Denied: Palestinian Land Rights in Israel*. London: Zed Books.

Abu-Lughod, Janet. 1982. "Israeli Settlements in Occupied Arab Lands: Conquest to Colony." *Journal of Palestine Studies* 11 (2): 16–54.

Abu-Manneh, Butrus. 1999. "The Rise of the Sanjak of Jerusalem in the Late Nineteenth Century." In *The Israel/Palestine Question*, edited by Ilan Pappé, 36–46. London: Routledge.

Abu-Rabia, Safa. 2008. "Between Memory and Resistance, an Identity Shaped by Space: The Case of the Naqab Arab Bedouins." *HAGAR: Studies in Culture, Polity, and Identities* 8 (2): 93–119.

Abu Ras, Thabet. 2012. "The Arab-Bedouin Population in the Negev: Transformations in an Era of Urbanization." www.europarl.europa.eu/meetdocs/2009_2014
/documents/droi/dv/138_abrahamfundstudy_/138_abrahamfundstudy_en.pdf,
67–124.

Abu-Saad, Ismael. 2008. "State Rule and Indigenous Resistance among Al Naqab
Bedouin Arabs." *HAGAR: Studies in Culture, Polity, and Identities* 8 (2): 3–24.

———. 2011. "The Indigenous Palestinian Bedouin of the Naqab: Forced Urbanization and Denied Recognition." In *The Palestinians in Israel: Readings in History,
Politics, and Society,* edited by Nadim N. Rouhana and Areej Sabbagh-Khoury,
121–27. Mada al-Carmel: Arab Center for Applied Social Research. http://
mada-research.org/en/files/2011/09/ebook-english-book.pdf.

Abu-Saad, Ismael, and Cosette Creamer. 2012. "Socio-Political Upheaval and Current
Conditions of the Naqab Bedouin Arabs." In *Indigenous (In)Justice: Human Rights
Law and Bedouin Arabs in the Naqab/Negev,* edited by Ahmad Amara, Ismael
Abu-Saad, and Oren Yiftachel, 18–66. Cambridge, MA: Harvard University Press.

Abu Sitta, Salman. 2012. "Living Land: Population Transfer and the Mewat Pretext
in the Naqab." *al-Majdal,* no. 49: 18–27. www.badil.org/phocadownload/Badil_
docs/publications/al-majdal49.pdf.

Adalah: The Legal Center for Arab Minority Rights in Israel. 2011. "Nomads
against Their Will: The Attempted Expulsion of the Arab Bedouin in the
Naqab—The Example of Atir–Umm al-Hieran." www.adalah.org/uploads
/oldfiles/eng/publications/Nomads Against their Will English pdf final.pdf.

———. 2013. "From Al-Araqib to Susiya: The Forced Displacement of Palestinians
on Both Sides of the Green Line." www.adalah.org/uploads/oldfiles/Public/files
/English/Publications/Position_Papers/Forced-Displacement-Position-Paper-
05–13.pdf.

Addington, Stephen. 1772. *An Inquiry into the Reasons for and against Inclosing
Open-Fields.* 2nd ed. Coventry: J. W. Piercy.

Ahad Ha'am. 1891. "Truth from Eretz Israel." Translated by Alan Dowty. *Israel
Studies* 5 (2): 160–79.

Ahmed, Ziauddin. 1980. "Ushr and Ushr Land." *Studia Islamica* 19 (2): 76–94.

Akerman, James K. 1995. "The Structuring of Political Territory in Early Printed
Atlases." *Imago Mundi* 47: 138–54.

Albers, Patricia, and Jeanne Kay. 1987. "Sharing the Land: A Study in American
Indian Territoriality." In *A Cultural Geography of North American Indians,* edited
by Thomas E. Ross and Tyrel G. Moore, 47–91. Boulder, CO: Westview Press.

Allegra, Marco. 2013. "The Politics of Suburbia: Israel's Settlement Policy and the
Production of Space in the Metropolitan Area of Jerusalem." *Environment and
Planning A* 45 (3): 497–516.

Allen, Robert C. 1992. *Enclosure and the Yeoman: The Agricultural Development of
the South Midlands.* Oxford: Clarendon Press.

———. 2001. "Community and Market in England: Open Fields and Enclosures
Revisited." In *Communities and Markets in Economic Development,* edited by
Masahiko Aoki and Yujiro Hayami, 42–69. Oxford: Oxford University Press.

Allon, Yigal. 1967. "Alon Plan 23 July, 1967 [Excerpts]." In *Documents on Jerusalem*, vol. 2, edited by Mahdi Abdul Hadi, 186. Jerusalem: Passia.

———. 1976. "The Case for Defensible Borders." *Foreign Affairs* 55 (1): 38–53.

al-Muqaddasi, Aḥsan al-Taqāsīm fī Maʾrifat al-Aqālīm. 985. *The Best Divisions for Knowledge of the Regions*. Translated by Basil Collins. Reading, UK: Garnet, 2001.

al-Rimmawi, Hussein. 2009. "Spatial Changes in Palestine: From Colonial Project to an Apartheid System." *African and Asian Studies* 8 (4): 375–412.

al-Salim, Farid. 2011. "Landed Property and Elite Conflict in Ottoman Tulkarm." *Jerusalem Quarterly* 47: 65–80. www.palestine-studies.org/sites/default/files /jq-articles/47-_Landed_Proerty_2.pdf.

Amara, Ahmad. 2013. "The Negev Land Question: Between Denial and Recognition." *Journal of Palestine Studies* 42 (4): 27–47.

Amara, Ahmad, and Zinaida Miller. 2012. "Unsettling Settlements: Law, Land, and Planning in the Naqab." In *Indigenous (In) Justice: Human Rights Law and Bedouin Arabs in the Naqab/Negev*, edited by Ahmad Amara, Ismael Abu-Saad, and Oren Yiftachel, 68–125. Cambridge, MA: Harvard University Press.

Amara, Ahmad, and Oren Yiftachel. 2014. "Confrontation in the Negev: Israeli Land Policies and the Indigenous Bedouin-Arabs." The Rosa Luxemburg Foundation. www.rosalux.co.il/confrontation_in_the_negev_eng.

Anderson, Charles. 2015. "Will the Real Palestinian Peasantry Please Sit Down? Towards a New History of British Rule in Palestine, 1917–1936." LSE Middle East Center. http://eprints.lse.ac.uk/64741/1/Anderson_Will the real Palestinian Peasantry _author_2015.pdf.

Anderson, Jerry L. 2007. "Britain's Right to Roam: Redefining the Landowner's Bundle of Sticks." *Georgetown International Environment Law Review* 19 (3): 375–435.

Anderson, Virginia DeJohn. 1994. "King Philip's Herds: Indians, Colonists, and the Problem of Livestock in Early New England." *William and Mary Quarterly* 51 (3): 601–24.

———. 2004. *Creatures of Empire: How Domestic Animals Transformed Early America*. Oxford: Oxford University Press.

Andrews, Thomas. 1738. *An Enquiry into the Causes of the Encrease and Miseries of the Poor of England*. London: A. Bettesworth and C. Hitch.

Anonymous. 1785. *A Political Enquiry into the Consequences of Enclosing Waste Lands, and the Causes of the Present High Price of Butchers Meat. Being the Sentiments of a Society of Farmers in ———shire*. London: Printed for L. Davis.

Applebaum, Robert, and John Wood Sweet, eds. 2005. *Envisioning an Empire: Jamestown and the Making of the North Atlantic World*. Philadelphia: University of Pennsylvania Press.

Appleby, Joyce Oldham. 1978. *Economic Thought and Ideology in Seventeenth-Century England*. Princeton, NJ: Princeton University Press.

Applied Research Institute–Jerusalem. 2010. *Nahhalin Village Profile*. http:// vprofile.arij.org/bethlehem/pdfs/VP/Nahhalin_vp_en.pdf.

———. 2012. "'Significant Paradoxes': The Israeli Settlements Spread as Mold in the Occupied Palestinian Territory." http://poica.org/poica/2012/06/significant-paradoxes-the-israeli-settlements-spread-as-mold-in-the-occupied-palestinian-territory.

———. 2013. *Marda Village Profile.* http://vprofile.arij.org/salfit/pdfs/vprofile/Marda_vp_en.pdf.

Aronson, Geoffrey. 2006. "Disengagement's Uncertain Fate." *Report on Israeli Settlement in the Occupied Territories* 16 (4). http://fmep.org/wp/wp-content/uploads/2015/01/16.4.pdf.

Armitage, David. 2000. *The Ideological Origins of the British Empire.* Cambridge: Cambridge University Press.

———. 2004. "John Locke, Carolina, and the Two Treatises of Government." *Political Theory* 32 (5): 602–27.

Armstrong, W. A. 1990. "The Countryside." In *The Cambridge Social History of Britain,* vol. 1: *Regions and Communities,* edited by F. M. L. Thompson, 87–153. Cambridge: Cambridge University Press.

Aston, T. H., and C. H. E. Philpin. 1985. *The Brenner Debate: Agrarian Class Structure and Economic Development in Pre-industrial Europe.* Cambridge: Cambridge University Press.

Atran, Scott. 1986. "Hamula Organisation and Masha'a Tenure in Palestine." *Man,* n.s., 21 (2): 271–95.

Aumann, Moshe. 1975. "Land Ownership in Palestine, 1880–1948." In *The Palestinians,* edited by Michael Curtis et al., 21–29. New Brunswick, NJ: Transaction Books.

Avineri, Shlomo. 1981. *The Making of Modern Zionism: Intellectual Origins of the Jewish State.* New York: Basic Books.

Avneri, Arieh L. 1984. *The Claim of Dispossession: Jewish Land-Settlement and the Arabs, 1878–1948.* New Brunswick, NJ: Transaction Books.

Axtell, James. 1975. "The White Indians of Colonial America." *William and Mary Quarterly* 32 (1): 55–88.

———. 1985. *The Invasion Within: The Conquest of Cultures in Colonial North America.* Oxford: Oxford University Press.

Aylmer, G. E. 1980. "The Meaning and Definition of 'Property' in Seventeenth-Century England." *Past & Present,* no. 86: 87–97.

Aytekin, E. Attila. 2009. "Agrarian Relations, Property, and Law: An Analysis of the Land Code of 1858 in the Ottoman Empire." *Middle Eastern Studies* 45 (6): 935–51.

Azaryahu, Maoz, and Arnon Golan. 2001. "(Re)naming the Landscape: The Formation of the Hebrew Map of Israel, 1949–1960." *Journal of Historical Geography* 27 (2): 178–95.

———. 2004. "Zionist Homelandscapes (and Their Constitution) in Israeli Geography." *Social and Cultural Geography* 5 (3): 497–513.

Azaryahu, Maoz, and Ahron Kellerman. 1999. "Symbolic Places: A Study in the Geography of Zionist Mythology." *Transactions of the Institute of British Geographers* 24 (1): 109–23.

Azaryahu, M., and R. Kook. 2002. "Mapping the Nation: Street Names and Arab-Palestinian Identity: Three Case Studies." *Nations and Nationalism* 8: 195–213.

Baer-Mor, Yael. 2009. "The Israeli-Palestinian Conflict: The Botanical Version." Paper presented at the European Council of Landscape Architecture Schools "Landscape and Ruins" Conference, University of Genoa. www.ybm.co.il/pdf/pub_01.pdf.

Bailey, Mark. 2002. *The English Manor, c. 1200–c. 1500.* Manchester: Manchester University Press.

Baker, Alan R. H. 1973. "Changes in the Later Middle Ages." In *A New Historical Geography of England,* edited by H. C. Darby, 186–247. Cambridge: Cambridge University Press.

———. 2003. *Geography and History: Bridging the Divide.* Cambridge: Cambridge University Press.

Baker, Alan R. H., and Gideon Biger, eds. 2006. *Ideology and Landscape in Historical Perspective: Essays on the Meaning of Some Places in the Past.* Cambridge: Cambridge University Press.

Baker, Alan R. H., and Robin A. Butlin, eds. 1973. *Studies of Field Systems in the British Isles.* Cambridge: Cambridge University Press.

Baker, Alan R. H., and J. B. Harley. 1973. *Man Made the Land: Essays in English Historical Geography.* Totowa, NJ: Rowman and Littlefield.

Banner, Stuart. 2002. "Transitions between Property Regimes." *Journal of Legal Studies* 31 (S2): S359–S371.

———. 2005. *How the Indians Lost Their Land: Law and Power on the Frontier.* Cambridge, MA: Harvard University Press.

Barber, Peter. 1992. "England II: Monarchs, Ministers, and Maps, 1550–1625." In *Monarchs, Ministers, and Maps: The Emergence of Cartography as a Tool of Government in Early Modern Europe,* edited by David Buisseret, 57–98. Chicago: University of Chicago Press.

———. 2005. "John Darby's Map of the Parish of Smallburgh in Norfolk, 1582." *Imago Mundi* 57 (1): 55–58.

Bardenstein, Carol B. 1999. "Trees, Forests, and the Shaping of Palestinian and Israeli Collective Memory." In *Acts of Memory: Cultural Recall in the Present,* edited by Mieke Bal, Jonathan Crewe, and Leo Spitzer, 148–68. Hanover, NH: University Press of New England.

Bardin, Hillel, and Dror Etkes. 2015. "The Fraud of Gush Etzion, Israel's Mythological Settlement Bloc." http://972mag.com/the-fraud-of-gush-etzion-israels-mythological-settlement-bloc/102133.

Bar-Gal, Yoram. 1991. "The Good and the Bad: A Hundred Years of Zionist Images in Geography Textbooks." Queen Mary and Westfield College Research Paper No. 4, London.

———. 1994. "The Image of the 'Palestinian' in Geography Textbooks in Israel." *Journal of Geography* 93 (5): 224–32.

———. 1996. "Ideological Propaganda in Maps and Geographical Education." In *Innovation in Geographical Education,* edited by J. van der Schee and H. Trimp,

67–79. The Hague: Netherlands Geographical Studies, IGU, Commission on Geographical Education.

———. 2000. "German Antecedents of the Department of Geography at the Hebrew University of Jerusalem: Historical Perspective." *Geographische Zeitschrift* 88 (2): 112–23.

———. 2003. *Propaganda and Zionist Education: The Jewish National Fund, 1924–1947*. Rochester, NY: University of Rochester Press.

———. 2004. "From Berlin to Jerusalem—Professor David Amiran and the Atlas of Israel." *Erdkunde* 58 (1): 31–41.

Bar-Gal, Yoram, and Bruria Bar-Gal. 2008. "'To Tie the Cords between the People and Its Land:' Geography Education in Israel." *Israel Studies* 13 (1): 44–67.

Barnai, Yacob. 1992. *The Jews in Palestine in the Eighteenth Century: Under the Patronage of the Istanbul Committee of Officials for Palestine*. Tuscaloosa: University of Alabama Press.

Barnwell, P. S., and Marilyn Palmer, eds. 2007. *Post-Medieval Landscapes: Essays in Honor of W. G. Hoskins*. Macclesfield, UK: Windgather Press.

Barr, Julianna, and Edward Countryman. 2014. "Maps and Spaces, Paths to Connect, Lines to Divide." In *Contested Spaces of Early America*, edited by Julianna Barr and Edward Countryman, 1–28. Philadelphia: University of Pennsylvania Press.

Barrell, John. 1972. *The Idea of Landscape and the Sense of Place, 1730–1840: An Approach to the Poetry of John Clare*. Cambridge: Cambridge University Press.

Bar-Yosef, Eitan. 2007. "A Villa in the Jungle: Herzl, Zionist Culture, and the Great African Adventure." In *Theodor Herzl: From Europe to Zion*, edited by Mark H. Gelber and Vivian Liska, 85–102. Tübingen: Max Niemeyer.

Bederman, David J. 2010. *Custom as a Source of Law*. Cambridge: Cambridge University Press.

Beckett, J. V. 1982. "Decline of Small Landowners in Eighteenth- and Nineteenth-Century England: Some Regional Considerations." *Agricultural History Review* 30 (2): 97–111.

———. 1983. "The Debate over Farm Sizes in Eighteenth- and Nineteenth-Century England." *Agricultural History* 57 (3): 308–25.

———. 1984. "Patterns of Land Ownership in England and Wales, 1660–1880." *Economic History Review* 37 (1): 1–22.

Beitar Illit. N.d. http://betar-illit.muni.il/eng/?CategoryID=166.

Ben-Ami, Shlomo, 2007. *Scars of War, Wounds of Peace: The Arab-Israeli Tragedy*. Oxford: Oxford University Press.

Ben-Arieh, Yehoshua. 1990. "Perceptions and Images of the Holy Land." In *The Land That Became Israel: Studies in Historical Geography*, edited by Ruth Kark, 37–53. New Haven, CT: Yale University Press.

Ben-Artzi, Yossi. 1996. "Imitation or Original? Shaping the Cultural Landscape of Pioneer Jewish Settlement in *Eretz* Israel (1882–1914)." *Journal of Historical Geography* 22: 308–26.

Bendall, Sarah A. 1992. *Maps, Land, and Society: A History with a Cartobibliography of Cambridgeshire Estate Maps, 1600–1836.* Cambridge: Cambridge University Press.

———. 1993. "Interpreting Maps of the Rural Landscape: An Example from Late Sixteenth-Century Buckinghamshire." *Rural History* 4 (2): 107–21.

———. 1997. "Estate Maps of an English County: Cambridgeshire, 1600–1836." In *Rural Images: Estate Maps in the Old and New Worlds,* edited by David Buisseret, 63–90. Chicago: University of Chicago Press.

Bending, Stephen, and Andrew McCrae, eds. 2003. *The Writing of Rural England, 1500–1800.* New York: Palgrave Macmillan.

Ben-Gurion, David. 1937. Letter to his son, Amos, October 5, 1937. Obtained from the Ben-Gurion Archives, translated into English by the Institute of Palestine Studies, Beirut. www.palestineremembered.com/download/B-G LetterTranslation.pdf.

Ben-Naeh, Yaron. 2008. *Jews in the Realm of the Sultans: Ottoman Jewish Society in the Seventeenth Century.* Tübingen: Mohr Siebeck.

Bennett, J. A. 1991. "Geometry and Surveying in Early-Seventeenth-Century England." *Annals of Science* 48 (4): 345–54.

Benvenisti, Meron. 1976. *Jerusalem: The Torn City.* Minneapolis: University of Minnesota Press.

———. 2000. *Sacred Landscape: The Buried History of the Holy Land since 1948.* Berkeley: University of California Press.

Ben-Yehuda, Eliezer. 1879. "A Weighty Question." In *Eliezer Ben-Yehuda: A Symposium in Oxford,* edited by Eisig Silberschlag, 1–12. Oxford: Oxford Centre for Postgraduate Hebrew Studies, 1981.

———. 1880. "A Letter of Ben-Yehuda." In *The Zionist Idea: An Historical Analysis and Reader,* edited by Arthur Hertzberg, 160–65. Philadelphia: Jewish Publication Society, 1997.

Ben-Ze'ev, Efrat. 2007. "The Cartographic Imagination: British Mandate Palestine." In *The Partition Motif in Contemporary Conflicts,* edited by Smita Tewari Jassal and Eyal Ben-Ari, 98–121. London: Sage.

———. 2011. *Remembering Palestine in 1948: Beyond National Narratives.* Cambridge: Cambridge University Press.

Beresford, Maurice. 1961. "Habitation versus Improvement: The Debate on Enclosure by Agreement." In *Essays in the Economic History of Tudor and Stuart England,* edited by F. J. Fisher, 40–69. Cambridge: Cambridge University Press.

Bergheim, Samuel. 1894. "Land Tenure in Palestine." In *Palestine Exploration Fund, Quarterly Statement for 1894,* 191–99 London: Palestine Exploration Fund and A. P. Watt and Son.

Bergman, Samuel Hugo. 1963. *Faith and Reason : An Introduction to Modern Jewish Thought.* New York: Schocken Books.

Berkowitz, Michael. 1993. *Zionist Culture and West European Jewry before the First World War.* Cambridge: Cambridge University Press.

Bermingham, Ann. 1986. *Landscape and Ideology: The English Rustic Tradition.* Berkeley: University of California Press.

Biddick, Kathleeen. 1990. "People and Things: Power in Early English Development." *Comparative Studies in Society and History* 32 (1): 3–23.

Biger, Gideon 1992. "Ideology and the Landscape of British Palestine, 1918–1929." In *Ideology and Landscape in Historical Perspective,* edited by A. R. H. Baker and Gideon Biger, 173–96. Cambridge: Cambridge University Press.

———. 1994. *An Empire in the Holy Land: Historical Geography of the British Administration in Palestine, 1917–1929.* New York: St. Martin's Press.

BIMKOM: Planners for Planning Rights. 2008. *The Prohibited Zone: Israeli Planning Policy in Palestinian Villages in Area C.* http://bimkom.org/eng/wp-content/uploads/ProhibitedZone.pdf.

———. 2014. *Trapped by Planning: Israeli Policy, Planning, and Development in the Palestinian Neighborhoods of East Jerusalem.* http://bimkom.org/eng/wp-content/uploads/TrappedbyPlanning.pdf.

BIMKOM and B'tselem. 2009. *The Hidden Agenda: The Establishment and Expansion Plans of Ma'ale Adummim and Their Human Rights Ramifications.* www.btselem.org/download/200912_maale_adummim_eng.pdf.

Birtles, Sara. 1999. "Common Land, Poor Relief, and Enclosure: The Use of Manorial Resources in Fulfilling Parish Obligations, 1601–1834." *Past & Present, no.* 165: 74–106.

Bisharat, George E. 1994. "Land, Law, and Legitimacy in Israel and the Occupied Territories." *American University Law Review* 43 (2): 467–561.

Black Hawk (Ma-Ka-Tai-Me-She-Kia-Kiak). 1834. *An Autobiography.* Edited by Donald Jackson. Champaign: University of Illinois Press, 1955.

Blackhawk, Ned. 2006. *Violence over the Land: Indians and Empires in the Early American West.* Cambridge, MA: Harvard University Press.

Blansett, Lisa. 2003. "John Smith Maps Virginia." In *Envisioning an Empire: Jamestown and the Making of the North Atlantic World,* edited by Robert Appelbaum and John Wood Sweet, 68–91. Philadelphia: University of Pennsylvania Press.

Blith, Walter. 1652. *The English Improver Improved; or, The Survey of Husbandry Surveyed, Discovering the Improveableness of All Lands.* London: Printed for John Wright.

Bloch, Marc. 1966. *French Rural History.* Berkeley: University of California Press.

Blomley, Nicholas. 2003. "Law, Property, and the Geography of Violence: The Frontier, the Survey, and the Grid." *Annals of the Association of American Geographers* 93 (1): 121–41.

———. 2007. "Making Private Property: Enclosure, Common Right, and the Work of Hedges." *Rural History* 18 (1): 1–21.

Blum, Jerome. 1981. "English Parliamentary Enclosure." *Journal of Modern History* 53 (3): 477–504.

Bodin, Jean. 1566. *Method for the Easy Comprehension of History.* Translated by Beatrice Reynolds. New York: Octagon Books, 1966.

Boelhower, William. 1988. "Inventing America: A Model of Cartographic Semiosis." *Word and Image* 4 (2): 475–97.

Bogart, Dan, and Gary Richardson. 2010. "Estate Acts, 1600–1830: A New Source for British History." *Research in Economic History* 27: 1–50. www.socsci.uci .edu/~dbogart/research_econ_history_paper.pdf

———. 2011. "Property Rights and Parliament in Industrializing Britain." *Journal of Law and Economics* 54 (2): 241–74.

Bonfield, Lloyd. 1989. "The Nature of Customary Law in the Manor Courts of Medieval England." *Comparative Studies in Society and History* 31 (3): 514–34.

———. 1996. "What Did English Villagers Mean by 'Customary Law'?" In *Medieval Society and the Manor Court,* edited by Zvi Razi and Richard Smith, 103–16. Oxford: Clarendon Press.

———. 2010. "Seeking Connections between Kinship and the Law in Early Modern England." *Continuity and Change* 25 (1): 49–82.

Bonfield, Lloyd, and L. R. Poos. 1996. "The Development of the Deathbed Transfers in Medieval English Manor Courts." In *Medieval Society and the Manor Court,* edited by Zvi Razi and Richard Smith, 117–43. Oxford: Clarendon Press.

Brace, Laura. 1998. *The Idea of Property in Seventeenth-Century England: Tithes and the Individual.* Manchester: Manchester University Press.

Brackenridge, Hugh Henry. 1814. *Law Miscellanies.* Union, NJ: Lawbook Exchange, 2001.

Braddock, Michael J., and John Walter, eds. 2001. *Negotiating Power in Early Modern Society: Order Hierarchy and Subordination in Britain and Ireland.* Cambridge: Cambridge University Press.

Braund, Kathryn E. 1993. *Deerskins and Duffels: The Creek Indian Trade with Anglo America, 1685–1815.* Lincoln: University of Nebraska Press.

Braverman, Irus. 2009a. *Planted Flags: Trees, Land, and Law in Israel/Palestine.* Cambridge: Cambridge University Press.

———. 2009b. "Planting the Promised Landscape: Zionism, Nature, and Resistance in Israel/Palestine." *Natural Resources Journal* 49 (2): 317–61.

Brawer, Moshe. 1990. "Transformation in Arab Rural Settlement." In *The Land That Became Israel: Studies in Historical Geography,* edited by Ruth Kark, 167–80. New Haven, CT: Yale University Press.

Broad, John. 1999. "The Fate of the Midland Yeoman: Tenants, Copyholders, and Freeholders as Farmers in North Buckinghamshire, 1620–1800." *Continuity and Change* 14 (3): 325–47.

Brooks, Christopher W., and Michael Lobban. 1997. *Communities and Courts in Britain, 1150–1900.* London: Hambledon Press.

Brückner, Martin. 2006. *The Geographic Revolution in Early America: Maps, Literacy, and National Identity.* Chapel Hill: University of North Carolina Press.

Brückner, Martin, and Kristine Poole. 2002. "The Plot Thickens: Surveying Manuals, Drama, and the Materiality of Narrative Form in Early Modern England." *English Literary History* 69 (3): 617–48.

Brundage, James A. 2008. *The Medieval Origins of the Legal Profession: Canonists, Civilians, and Courts.* Chicago: University of Chicago Press.

B'tselem. 2002. *Land Grab: Israel's Settlement Policy in the West Bank.* www
.btselem.org/download/200205_land_grab_eng.pdf.
————. 2008. *Access Denied: Israeli Measures to Deny Palestinians Access to Land
around Settlements.* www.btselem.org/download/200809_access_denied_eng.pdf.
————. 2012. *Under the Guise of Security: Israel's Declarations of State Land in the
West Bank.* www.btselem.org/download/201203_under_the_guise_of_legal-
ity_eng.pdf.
Buck, A. R. 1992. "Rhetoric and Real Property in Tudor England: Thomas Starkey's
'Dialogue between Pole and Lupset.'" *Cardozo Studies in Law and Literature* 4
(1): 27–43.
Buckle, Stephen. 1993. *Natural Law and the Theory of Property: Grotius to Hume.*
Oxford: Oxford University Press.
Buisseret, David, ed. 1992. *Monarchs, Ministers, and Maps: The Emergence of Car-
tography as a Tool of Government in Early Modern Europe.* Chicago: University
of Chicago Press.
————, ed. 1996. *Rural Images: Estate Maps in the Old and New Worlds.* Chicago:
University of Chicago Press.
Bunton, Martin. 1999. "Inventing the Status Quo: Ottoman Land-Law during the
Palestine Mandate, 1917–1936." *International History Review* 21 (1): 28–56.
————. 2007. *Colonial Land Policies in Palestine, 1917–1936.* Oxford: Oxford Uni-
versity Press.
Burckhardt, John Lewis. 1822. *Travels in Syria and the Holy Land.* New York: AMS
Press.
Burden, Robert, and Stephen Kohl, eds. 2006. *Landscapes and Englishness.* Amster-
dam: Rodopi.
Butzer, Karl W. 1990. "The Indian Legacy in the American Landscape." In *The Mak-
ing of the American Landscape,* edited by Michael P. Conzen, 27–50. Boston:
Unwin Hyman.
Calloway, Collin G., ed. 1994. *The World Turned Upside Down: Indian Voices from
Early America.* London: Palgrave Macmillan.
————. 1998. *New Worlds for All: Indians, Europeans, and the Remaking of Early
America.* Baltimore: Johns Hopkins University Press.
————. 2003. *One Vast Winter Count: The Native American West before Lewis and
Clark.* Lincoln: University of Nebraska Press.
————. 2007. *The Shawnees and the War for America.* New York: Penguin Books.
Campbell, B. M. S. 1990. "People and Land in the Middle Ages." In *An Historical
Geography of England and Wales,* 2nd ed., edited by R. A. Dodgshon and R. A.
Butlin, 69–121. London: Academic Press.
Carr, E. H. 1966. *What Is History?* Basingstoke, UK: Palgrave, 2001.
Carstensen, Vernon. 1988. "Patterns on the American Land." *Publius* 18 (4): 31–39.
Cave, Alfred A. 1988. "Canaanites in a Promised Land: The American Indian and
the Providential Theory of Empire." *American Indian Quarterly* 12 (4): 277–97.
————. 2003. "Abuse of Power: Andrew Jackson and the Indian Removal Act of
1830." *The Historian* 65 (6): 1330–53.

Central Bureau of Statistics. 2015. *Statistical Abstract of Israel, 2015.* www.cbs.gov.il /reader/shnaton/templ_shnaton_e.html?num_tab=st02_16x&CYear=2015.

———. 2016. *Localities, Their Population and Additional Information.* www.cbs.gov.il/reader/?MIval=%2Fpop_in_locs%2Fpop_in_locs_e.html&Locality Code=3780.

Chaplin, Joyce. 1997. "Natural Philosophy and an Early Racial Idiom in North America: Comparing English and Indian Bodies." *William and Mary Quarterly* 54 (1): 229–52.

Chapman, John. 1987. "The Extent and Nature of Parliamentary Enclosure." *Agricultural History Review* 35 (1): 25–35.

Chapman, John, and Sylvia Seeliger. 2001. *Enclosure, Environment, and Landscape in Southern England.* Gloucestershire, UK; Charleston, SC: Tempus.

Charlesworth, Andrew, ed. 1983. *An Atlas of Rural Protest in Britain, 1548–1900.* Philadelphia: University of Pennsylvania Press.

Charlesworth, Andrew. 1991. "An Agenda for Historical Studies of Rural Protest in Britain, 1750–1850." *Rural History* 2 (2): 231–40.

Cheshin, Amir S., Bill Hutman, and Avi Melamed. 1999. *Separate and Unequal: The Inside Story of Israeli Rule in East Jerusalem.* Cambridge, MA: Harvard University Press.

Chiodelli, Francesco. 2012. "The Jerusalem Master Plan: Planning into the Conflict." *Jerusalem Quarterly*, no. 51: 5–20.

Chowers, Eyal. 2012. *The Political Philosophy of Zionism: Trading Jewish Words for a Hebraic Land.* Cambridge: Cambridge University Press.

Clark, Gregory. 1998. "Commons Sense: Common Property Rights, Efficiency, and Institutional Change." *Journal of Economic History* 58 (1): 73–102.

Clark, Gregory, and Anthony Clark. 2001. "Common Right in Land in England, 1475–1839." *Journal of Economic History* 61 (4): 1009–36.

Clark, John. 1794a. *General View of the Agriculture of the County of Hereford.* London: Colin McRae.

Clark, John. 1794b. "On Commons in Brecknock." In *Annals of Agriculture and Other Useful Arts,* compiled by Arthur Young, 22:632–38. London. goo.gl/ aAyWIM.

Clarke, G. N. G. 1988. "Taking Possession: The Cartouche as Cultural Text in Eighteenth-Century American Maps." *Word and Image.* 4 (2): 455–74.

Cohen, Amnon. 1973. *Palestine in the Eighteenth Century: Patterns of Government and Administration.* Jerusalem: Magnes Press, Hebrew University.

———. 1984. *Jewish Life under Islam: Jerusalem in the Sixteenth Century.* Cambridge, MA: Harvard University Press.

Cohen, Amnon, and Bernard Lewis. 1978. *Population and Revenue in the Towns of Palestine in the Sixteenth Century.* Princeton, NJ: Princeton University Press.

Cohen, Saul B., and Nurit Kliot. 1981. "Israel's Place Names as Reflection of Continuity and Change in Nation Building." *Names* 29 (3): 227–46.

———. 1992. "Place-Names in Israel's Ideological Struggle over the Administered Territories." *Annals of the Association of American Geographers* 82 (4): 653–80.

Cohen, Shaul Ephraim. 1993. *The Politics of Planting: Israeli-Palestinian Competition for Control of Land in the Jerusalem Periphery*. Chicago: University of Chicago Press.

COHRE (Centre on Housing Rights and Evictions)/BADIL: Resource Center for Palestinian Residency and Refugee Rights. 2005. *Ruling Palestine: A History of the Legally Sanctioned Seizure of Land and Housing in Palestine*. Geneva and Bethlehem. www.miftah.org/Doc/Reports/2005/RulingPalestine_full.pdf.

Coke, Edward. 1642. *The Second Part of the Institutes of the Laws of England*. London: M. Flesher and R. Young.

Cole, Daniel H. 2001. "An Unqualified Human Good: E. P. Thompson and the Rule of Law." *Journal of Law and Society* 28 (2): 177–203.

Collins-Kreiner, N., Y. Mansfield, and N. Kliot. 2006. "The Reflection of a Political Conflict in Mapping: The Case of Israel's Borders and Frontiers." *Middle Eastern Studies* 42 (3): 381–408.

Comaroff, John L. 2001. "Colonialism, Culture, and the Law: A Foreword." *Law and Social Inquiry* 26 (2): 305–14.

Comaroff, John L., and Jean Comaroff. 2006. "Law and Disorder in the Postcolony: An Introduction." In *Law and Disorder in the Postcolony*, edited by Jean Comaroff and John L. Comaroff, 1–56. Chicago: University of Chicago Press.

Conder, C. R., and H. H. Kitchener. 1883. *The Survey of Western Palestine: Memoirs of the Topography, Orography, Hydrography, and Archeology*. Vol. 3: *Judea*. London: Committee of the Palestine Exploration Fund. www.archive.org/stream/surveyofwesternp03conduoft#page/n6/mode/1up.

Conquest of the Desert Exhibition and Fair. 1953. Catalogue. Jerusalem: Jerusalem Post Press.

Cook, Jonathan. 2011. "The Negev's Hot Wind Blowing." Middle East Research and Information Project. www.merip.org/mero/mero102511?ip_login_no_cache=09c84b916eeecaeb616427485f3f78f2.

Coones, I. P. 1985. "One Landscape or Many?" *Landscape History* 7: 5–12.

Cooper, William. 1790. *A Guide in the Wilderness*. 3rd ed. Cooperstown, NY: Freeman's Journal Co. 1936.

Cordell, Linda S., and Bruce D. Smith. 1996. "Indigenous Farmers." In *The Cambridge History of the Native Peoples of the Americas*, vol. 1, pt. 1, edited by Bruce G. Trigger and Wilcomb K. Washburn, 201–66. Cambridge: Cambridge University Press.

Cormack, Leslie. 1991. "'Good Fences Make Good Neighbors': Geography as Self-Definition in Early Modern England." *Isis* 82 (4): 639–61.

———. 1997. *Charting an Empire: Geography at the English Universities, 1580–1620*. Chicago: University of Chicago Press.

Cosgel, Metin M. 2005. "Efficiency and Continuity in Public Finance: The Ottoman System of Taxation." *International Journal of Middle East Studies* 37 (4): 567–86.

Cosgrove, Denis E. 1998. *Social Formation and Symbolic Landscape*. Madison: University of Wisconsin Press.

————. 1999. "Mapping Meaning." In *Mappings,* edited by Denis Cosgrove, 1–10. London: Reaktion Books.

————. 2006. "Modernity, Community, and the Landscape Idea." *Journal of Material Culture* 11 (1–2): 49–66.

Cover, Robert M. 1986. "Violence and the Word." *Yale Law Journal* 95 (8): 1601–29.

Cowper, John. 1732. "An Essay Proving That Inclosing Commons and Common-field Lands Is Contrary to the Interests of the Nation." London: Printed and sold by E. Nutt at the Royal-Exchange; J. Roberts in Warwick-Lane; A. Dodd without Temple-Bar; and at the Bible in George-Yard, Lombard-Street.

Crane, Jeff. 2015. *The Environment in American History: Nature and the Formation of the United States.* London: Routledge.

Crashaw, William. 1610. "A Sermon Preached in London Before the Right and Honorable Lord Lawarre, Lord Gouvernor and Captaine General of Virginia." Originally presented February 21, 1609. http://eebo.chadwyck.com/search/full_rec? SOURCE=pgimages.cfg&ACTION=ByID&ID=V9559.

Crawford, Rachel. 2002. *Poetry, Enclosure, and the Vernacular Landscape, 1700–1830.* Cambridge: Cambridge University Press.

Cronon, William. 2003. *Changes in the Land: Indians, Colonists, and the Ecology of New England.* New York: Hill and Wang.

Cronon, William, George Miles, and Jay Gitlin. 1992. "Becoming West: Toward a New Meaning of Western History." In *Under an Open Sky: Rethinking America's Western Past,* edited by William Cronon, George Miles, and Jay Gitlin, 3–27. New York: W. W. Norton.

Cumming, William P. 1982. "Early Maps of the Chesapeake Bay Area: Their Relation to Settlement and Society." In *Early Maryland in a Wider World,* edited by D. B. Quinn, 267–310. Detroit: Wayne State University Press.

Dahlman, Carl. 1980. *The Open Field System and Beyond: A Property Rights Analysis of an Economic Institution.* Cambridge: Cambridge University Press.

Daniels, John D. 1992. "The Indian Population of North America in 1492." *William and Mary Quarterly* 49 (2): 298–320.

Daniels, S., and S. Seymour. 1990. "Landscape Design and the Idea of Improvement, 1730–1900." In *An Historical Geography of England and Wales,* edited by R. A. Dodgshon and R. A. Butlin, 487–520. London: Academic Press.

Darby, H. C. 1973. "The Age of the Improver: 1600–1800." In *A New Historical Geography of England,* edited by H. C. Darby, 302–88. Cambridge: Cambridge University Press.

————. 2011. *The Draining of the Fens.* Cambridge: Cambridge University Press.

Darvill, Timothy. 1997. "Landscapes and the Archeologist." In *Making English Landscapes: Changing Perspectives,* edited by Katherine Barker and Timothy Darvill, 70–91. Oxford: Oxbow Books.

David, Abraham. 1999. *To Come to the Land: Immigration and Settlement in Sixteenth-Century Eretz-Israel.* Tuscaloosa: University of Alabama Press.

David, P. A. 1991. "Computer and Dynamo: The Modern Productivity Paradox in a Not-Too-Distant Mirror." In *Technology and Productivity: The Challenge for Economic Policy*, 315–47. Paris: OECD.

Davies, David. 1795. *The Case of Labourers in Husbandry, Stated and Considered, in Three Parts*. Bath: Printed by R. Cruttwell. https://books.google.com/books/about/The_Case_of_Labourers_in_Husbandry.html?id=awrnAAAAMAAJ.

Day, David. 2008. *Conquest: How Societies Overwhelm Others*. Oxford: Oxford University Press.

Defoe, Daniel. 1719. *Robinson Crusoe*. Edited by John Richetti. London: Penguin Books, 2003.

———. 1723. *A Tour through the Whole Island of Great Britain*. New Haven, CT: Yale University Press, 1991.

de Jong, Jan. 2007. "Between Optimism and Pessimism: A Look at the Demography and Geography in the Occupied Palestinian Territory." In *40 Years after the 1967 War: The Impact of a Prolonged Occupation*, 21–25. Washington, DC: The Palestine Center. www.thejerusalemfund.org/wp-content/uploads/2016/06/40-Years-after-the-1967-War-The-Impact-of-a-Prolonged-Occupation.pdf.

Delano-Smith, Catherine, and Roger J. P. Kain. 1999. *English Maps: A History*. Toronto: University of Toronto Press.

De Moor, Martina, Leigh Shaw-Taylor, and Paul Warde, eds. 2002. *The Management of Common Land in North West Europe, c. 1500–1850*. Turnhout, Bel.: Brepols.

Denevan, William M., ed. 1992a. *The Native Population in the Americas in 1492*. Madison: University of Wisconsin Press.

———. 1992b. "The Pristine Myth: The Landscape of the Americas in 1492." *Annals of the Association of American Geographers* 82 (3): 369–85.

De Tocqueville, Alexis. 1835. *Democracy in America*. Vol. 1. New York: Vintage Books.

De Vorsey, Louis, Jr. 1989. "Oglethorpe and the Earliest Maps of Georgia." In *Oglethorpe in Perspective: Georgia's Founder after Two Hundred Years*, edited by Phinizy Spalding and Harvey H. Jackson, 22–43. Tuscaloosa: University of Alabama Press.

Dieckhoff, Alain. 2003. *The Invention of a Nation: Zionist Thought and the Making of Modern Israel*. New York: Columbia University Press.

Dinur, Ben Zion. 1969. *Israel and the Diaspora*. Philadelphia: Jewish Publication Society of America.

Di Palma, Vittoria. 2014. *Wasteland*. New Haven, CT: Yale University Press.

Divine, Donna Robinson. 2009. *Exiled in the Homeland: Zionism and the Return to Mandate Palestine*. Austin: University of Texas Press.

Dobbs, G. Rebecca. 2009. "Frontier Settlement Development and 'Initial Conditions': The Case of the North Caroline Piedmont and the Indian Trading Path." *Historical Geography* 37: 114–37.

Dodgshon, Robert A. 1975. "The Landholding Foundations of the Open Field System." *Past & Present* 67 (1): 3–29.

————. 1980. *The Origins of British Field Systems: An Interpretation.* New York: Academic Press.

————. 1990. "The Changing Evaluation of Space, 1500–1914." In *A New Historical Geography of England and Wales,* edited by R. A. Dodghshon and R. A. Butlin, 255–83. San Diego: Academic Press.

Doolittle, William E. 1992. "Agriculture in North America on the Eve of Contact: A Reassessment." *Annals of the Association of American Geographers* 82 (3): 386–401.

————. 2000. *Cultivated Landscapes of Native North America.* Oxford: Oxford University Press.

Doukhan, Moses J. 1938. "Land Tenure." In *Economic Organization of Palestine,* edited by Sa'id B. Himadeh, 73–107. Beirut: American University of Beirut.

Doumani, Beshara. 1992. "Rediscovering Ottoman Palestine: Writing Palestinians into History." *Journal of Palestine Studies* 21 (2): 5–28.

————. 1995. *Rediscovering Palestine: Merchants and Peasants in Jabal Nablus, 1700–1900.* Berkeley: University of California Press.

Dowson, Sir Ernest. 1931. *An Inquiry into Land Tenure and Related Questions: Proposals for the Initiation of Reform.* London.

Dowty, Alan. 2000. "Much Ado About Little: Ahad Ha'am's 'Truth from Eretz Israel: Zionism and the Arabs.'" *Israel Studies* 5 (2): 154–81.

Drinnon, Richard. 1990. *Facing West: The Metaphysics of Indian Hating and Empire Building.* 2nd ed. New York: Schocken Books.

DuVal, Kathleen. 2006. *The Native Ground: Indians and Colonists in the Heart of the Continent.* Philadelphia: University of Pennsylvania Press.

Dymock, Cressey. 1653. *A Discoverie for Division or Setting Out Land as to the Best Form. . . .* London: Samuel Hartlib. http://gateway.proquest.com/openurl?ctx_ver=Z39.88–2003&res_id=xri:eebo&rft_id=xri:eebo:image:49516:5.

Dyer, Christopher. 2006. "Conflict in the Landscape: The Enclosure Movement in England, 1220–1349." *Landscape History* 28: 21–33.

Earle, Carville. 1992. "Pioneers of Providence: The Anglo-American Experience, 1492–1792." *Annals of the Association of American Geographers* 82 (3): 478–99.

Edelson, S. Max. 2012. Comments on the Catawba Map of 1721. Podcast interview. http://backstoryradio.org/shows/here-to-there-a-history-of-mapping-2.

————. 2013. "Defining Carolina: Cartography and Colonization in the American Southeast, 1657–1733." In *Creating and Contesting Carolina: Proprietary-Era Histories,* edited by Michelle LeMaster and Bradford J. Wood, 27–48. Columbia: University of South Carolina Press.

Eden, Peter. 1983. "Three Elizabethan Estate Surveyors: Peter Kempe, Thomas Clerke, and Thomas Langdon." In *English Map-Making, 1500–1650,* edited by Sarah Tyacke, 68–84. London: British Library.

Edney, Mathew H. 1992. "Mapping the Early Modern State: The Intellectual Nexus of Late Tudor and Early Stuart Cartography." *Cartographica* 29 (3–4): 89–93.

————. 1993. "Cartography without 'Progress': Reinterpreting the Nature and Historical Development of Mapmaking." *Cartographica* 30 (2–3): 54–68.

————. 2005. "The Origins and Development of J. B. Harley's Cartographic Theories." *Cartographica* 40 (1–2). Cartographica Monograph no. 54. Toronto: University of Toronto Press.

————. 2007. "A Publishing History of John Mitchell's Map of North America, 1755–1775." *Cartographic Perspectives,* no. 58: 4–27.

————. 2008. "John Mitchell's Map of North America (1755): A Study of the Use and Publication of Official Maps in Eighteenth-Century Britain." *Imago Mundi* 60 (1): 63–85.

Edwards, Jess. 2005. "Between 'Plain Wilderness' and 'Godly Corn Fields': Representing Land Use in Early Virgina." In *Envisioning an Empire: Jamestown and the Making of the North Atlantic World,* edited by Robert Appelbaum and John Wood Sweet, 217–35. Philadelphia: University of Pennsylvania Press.

————. 2006. *Writing, Geometry, and Space in Seventeenth-Century England and America.* London: Routledge.

————. 2011. "A Compass to Steer By: John Locke, Carolina, and the Politics of Restoration Geography." In *Early American Cartographies,* edited by Martin Bruckner, 93–115. Chapel Hill: University of North Carolina Press.

Efrat, Elisha. 1988. *Geography and Politics in Israel since 1967.* London: Frank Cass.

Eisenzweig, Uri. 1981. "An Imaginary Territory: The Problematic of Space in Zionist Discourse." *Dialectical Anthropology* 5 (4): 261–86.

Elazari-Volcani, Issac Avigdor. 1925. *The Transition from Primitive to Modern Agriculture in Palestine.* Publications of the Palestine Economic Society, 4. Tel-Aviv: Palestine Economic Society.

El-Eini, Roza I. M. 1997. "Government Fiscal Policy in Mandatory Palestine in the 1930s." *Middle Eastern Studies* 33 (3): 570–96.

————. 2006. *Mandated Landscape: British Imperial Rule in Palestine, 1929–1948.* New York: Routledge.

Ellickson, Robert C. 1993. "Property in Land." *Yale Law Journal* 102 : 1315–45.

Emerson, Thomas E. 1997. *Cahokia and the Archaeology of Power.* Tuscaloosa: University of Alabama Press.

Epstein, Izhak. 1907. "A Hidden Question." *Israel Studies* 6 (1): 39–54.

Essaid, Aida. 2014. *Zionism and Land Tenure in Mandate Palestine.* London: Routledge.

Ethridge, Robbie 2003. *Creek Country: The Creek Indians and Their World.* Chapel Hill: University of North Carolina Press.

Etkes, Dror, and Hagit Ofran. 2006. "One Violation Leads to Another: Israeli Settlement Building on Private Palestinian Property." A Report of Peace Now's Settlement Watch Team. http://peacenow.org.il/wp-content/uploads/2009/01/Breaking_The_Law_in_WB_nov06Eng.pdf.

Everitt, Alan. 2000. "Common Land." In *The English Rural Landscape,* edited by Joan Thirsk, 210–35. Oxford: Oxford University Press.

Ezrahi, Sidra DeKoven. 2000. *Booking Passage: Exile and Homecoming in the Modern Jewish Imagination.* Berkeley: University of California Press.

Faith, Rosamond. 1997. *The English Peasantry and the Growth of Lordship*. London: Leicester University Press.

Falah, Ghazi Walid. 1983. "The Development of the 'Planned Bedouin Settlement' in Israel 1964–1982: Evaluation and Characteristics." *GeoForum* 14 (3): 311–23.

———. 1985a. "Planned Bedouin Settlement in Israel: The Reply." *Geoforum* 16 (4): 440–51.

———. 1985b. "How Israel Controls the Bedouin in Israel." *Journal of Palestine Studies* 14 (2): 35–51.

———. 1985c. "The Spatial Pattern of Bedouin Sedentarization in Israel." *GeoJournal* 11 (4): 361–68.

———. 1989a. "Israeli State Policy toward Bedouin Sedentarization in the Negev." *Journal of Palestine Studies* 18 (2): 71–91.

———. 1989b. "Israelization of Palestine Human Geography." *Progress in Human Geography* 13 (4): 535–50.

———. 1991. "Israeli 'Judaization' Policy in Galilee." *Journal of Palestine Studies* 20 (4): 69–85.

———. 1996. "The 1948 Israeli-Palestinian War and Its Aftermath: The Transformation and Designification of Palestine's Cultural Landscape." *Annals of the Association of American Geographers* 86 (2): 256–85.

Falvey, Heather. 2001. "Crown Policy and Local Economic Context in the Berkhamsted Common Enclosure Dispute, 1618–42." *Rural History* 12 (2): 123–58.

———. 2007. "Custom, Resistance, and Politics: Local Experiences of Improvement in Early Modern England." PhD thesis, University of Warwick. http://wrap.warwick.ac.uk/1143/1/WRAP_THESIS_Falvay1_2007.pdf.

Feige, Michael. 2001. "Jewish Settlement of Hebron: The Place and the Other." *GeoJournal* 53 (3): 323–33.

Feiner, Shmuel. 2011. *The Origins of Jewish Secularization in Eighteenth-Century Europe*. Philadelphia: University of Pennsylvania Press.

Fellman, Jack. 1973. *The Revival of a Classical Tongue: Eliezer Ben Yehuda and the Modern Hebrew Language*. The Hague: Mouton.

Fenster, Tovi. 2004. "Belonging, Memory, and the Politics of Planning in Israel." *Social and Cultural Geography* 5 (3): 403–17.

Fields, Gary. 2007. "Landscapes of Power: British Enclosure and the Palestinian Geography." *Arab World Geographer* 10 (3–4): 189–211.

———. 2012. "This Is Our Land: Collective Violence, Property Law, and Imagining the Geography of Palestine." *Journal of Cultural Geography* 29 (3): 267–91.

———. 2016. "Excavating Palestine: Documenting Occupation Landscapes in the Village of Jayyous." *Arab World Geographer* 19 (3–4): 256–71.

Finch, Jonathan, and Kate Giles, eds. 2008. *Estate Landscapes: Design, Improvement, and Power in the Post-Medieval Landscape*. Woodbridge, UK: Boydell and Brewer.

Fine, Steven. 2005. *Art and Judaism in the Greco-Roman World: Toward a New Jewish Archaeology*. Cambridge: Cambridge University Press.

Firestone, Ya'akov. 1975. "Crop-sharing Economics in Mandatory Palestine." *Middle Eastern Studies* 11 (2): 175–95.

———. 1990. "The Land-Equalizing Musha' Village: A Reassessment." In *Ottoman Palestine, 1880–1914: Studies in Economic and Social History,* edited by Gad G. Gilbar, 91–130. Leiden: E. J. Brill

Fischbach, Michael R. 2000. *State, Society, and Land in Jordan.* Leiden: Brill.

———. 2003. *Records of Dispossession: Palestinian Refugee Property and the Arab-Israeli Conflict.* New York: Columbia University Press.

———. 2013. "British and Zionist Data Gathering on Palestinian Arab Landownership and Population during the Mandate." In *Surveillance and Control in Israel/Palestine: Population, Territory, and Power,* edited by Elia Zureik, David Lyon, and Yasmeen Abu-Laban, 297–312. London: Routledge.

Fischel, Roy S., and Ruth Kark. 2008. "Sultan Abdülhamid II and Palestine: Private Lands and Imperial Policy." *New Perspectives on Turkey,* no. 39: 129–66.

Fitzherbert, Master [John]. 1523. *The Book of Husbandry.* London: Trubner and Co., 1882. [Reprinted from the edition of 1534.] https://archive.org/stream/bookof husbandryoofitzuoft#page/n3/mode/2up.

Fitzmaurice, Andrew. 1999. "The Civic Solution to the Crisis of English Colonization, 1609–1625." *Historical Journal* 42 (1): 25–51.

———. 2000. "'Every Man That Prints, Adventures': The Rhetoric of the Virginia Company Sermons." In *The English Sermon Revised: Religion, Literature, and History, 1600–1750,* edited by Lori Anne Ferrell and Peter McCullough, 24–42. Manchester: University of Manchester Press.

———. 2003. *Humanism and America: An Intellectual History of English Colonisation, 1500–1625.* Cambridge: Cambridge University Press.

———. 2007a. "The Commercial Ideology of Colonization in Jacobean England: Robert Johnson, Giovanni Botero, and the Pursuit of Greatness." *William and Mary Quarterly* 64 (4): 791–820.

———. 2007b. "The Genealogy of *Terra Nullius.*" *Australian Historical Studies* 38 (129): 1–15.

Fixico, Donald, ed. 1997. *Rethinking American Indian History.* Albuquerque: University of New Mexico Press.

———. 1996. "Ethics and Responsibility in Writing American Indian History." *American Indian Quarterly* 20 (1): 29–39.

Fletcher, David. 1995. *The Emergence of Estate Maps: Christ Church, Oxford, 1600–1840.* Oxford: Oxford University Press.

———. 1998. "Map or Terrier? The Example of Christ Church, Oxford, Estate Management, 1600–1840." *Transactions of the Institute of British Geographers* 23 (2): 221–37.

———. 2003. "The Parish Boundary: A Social Phenomenon in Hanoverian England." *Rural History* 14 (2): 177–96.

Forman, Geremy. 2002. "Settlement of the Title in the Galilee: Dowson's Colonial Guiding Principles." *Israel Studies* 7 (3): 61–83.

———. 2005. "Israeli Settlement of Title in Arab Areas: 'The Special Land Settlement Operation' in Northern Israel (1955–1967)." PhD diss., University of Haifa.

———. 2006. "Law and the Historical Geography of the Galilee: Israel's Litigatory Advantages during the Special Operation of Land Settlement." *Journal of Historical Geography* 32 (4): 796–817.

———. 2009. "A Tale of Two Regions: Diffusion of the Israeli '50 Percent Rule' from the Galilee to the Occupied West Bank." *Law and Social Inquiry* 34 (3): 671–711.

———. 2011. "Israeli Supreme Court Doctrine and the Battle over Arab Land in Galilee: A Vertical Assessment." *Journal of Palestine Studies* 40 (4): 24–44.

Forman, Geremy, and Alexandre Kedar. 2003. "Colonialism, Colonization, and Land Law in Mandate Palestine: The Zor al-Zarqa and Barrat Qisarya Land Disputes in Historical Perspective." *Theoretical Inquiries in Law* 4 (2): 491–539.

———. 2004. "From Arab Land to 'Israeli Lands': The Legal Dispossession of Palestinians Displaced by Israel in the Wake of 1948." *Environment and Planning D* 22 (6): 809–30.

Fortrey, Samuel. 1663. *England's Interest and Improvement.* Edited by Jacob Hollander. Baltimore: The Lord Baltimore Press, 1907. https://tinyurl.com/hrnwnk9.

Foucault, Michel. 1977. *Discipline and Punish: The Birth of the Prison.* New York: Pantheon Books.

———. 1984. "Space, Knowledge, and Power." In *The Foucault Reader,* edited by Paul Rabinow, 239–57. New York: Pantheon Books.

Franklin, Benjamin. 1751. "Observations Concerning the Increase of Mankind." National Archives. https://founders.archives.gov/documents/Franklin/01–04–02–0080.

Frantzman, Jonathan, Noam Levin, and Ruth Kark. 2014. "Counting Nomads: British Census Attempts and Tent Counts of the Negev Bedouin, 1917 to1948." *Population, Space, and Place* 20 (6): 552–68.

Frazer, Bill. 1999. "Common Recollections: Resisting Enclosure 'by Agreement' in Seventeenth-Century England." *International Journal of Historical Archeology* 3 (2): 75–99.

Friedman, Lara 2005. "Gush Etzion." *Settlements in Focus* 1, no. 14. https://peacenow.org/entry.php?id=10152#.WLPCPYozWM8.

Fulford, Tim. 1996. *Landscape, Liberty, and Authority; Poetry, Criticism, and Politics from Thomson to Wordsworth.* Cambridge: Cambridge University Press.

Galloway, Patricia. 1995. *Chocktaw Genesis, 1500–1700.* Lincoln: University of Nebraska Press.

Ganev, Robin. 2004. "Popular Ballads and Rural Identity in Britain, 1700–1830." PhD diss., York University.

Garrett, Leah. 2003. "Landscape in the Jewish Imagination." In *Studying Cultural Landscapes,* edited by I. Robertson and P. Richards, 108–20. London: Arnold.

Gaudiosi, Monica M. 1988. "The Influence of the Islamic Law of Waqf on the Development of the Trust in England: The Case of Merton College." *University of Pennsylvania Law Review* 136 (4): 1231–61.

Gavish, Dov. 2005. *A Survey of Palestine under the British Mandate, 1920–1948.* London: Routledge.

Gavish, Dov, and Ruth Kark. 1993. "The Cadastral Mapping of Palestine, 1858–1928." *Geographical Journal* 159 (1): 70–80.

Gerber, Haim. 1987. *The Social Origins of the Modern Middle East.* Boulder, CO: Lynne Rienner, 1987.

Gilbar, Gad G. 1984. "The Growing Economic Involvement of Palestine with the West." In *Palestine in the Late Ottoman Period: Political, Social, and Economic Transformation,* edited by David Kushner, 188–210. Leiden: E.J. Brill.

———, ed. 1990. *Ottoman Palestine, 1800–1914: Studies in Economic and Social History.* Leiden: E.J. Brill.

Ginsberg, Mitch. 2014. "Israel's Next Major Land Dispute Brews in the Negev." *Times of Israel.* www.timesofisrael.com/israels-next-major-land-dispute-seethes-in-the-negev-desert.

Glover, Susan P. 2006. "The Incomplete Tradesman: Daniel Defoe and the Lay of the Land." In Engendering Legitimacy: Law, Property, and Early Eighteenth-Century Fiction. Lewisburg, PA: Bucknell University Press.

Goadby, Fredric, and Moses Doukhan. 1935. *The Land Law of Palestine.* Jerusalem: Shoshany Printing Co.

———. 2002. "Israeli Historical Geography and the Holocaust: Reconsidering the Research Agenda." *Journal of Historical Geography* 28 (4): 554–65.

Golan, Arnon. 1995. "The Transfer to Jewish Control of Abandoned Arab Land during the War of Independence." In *Israel, the First Decade of Independence,* edited by S. Ilan Troen and Noah Lucas, 403–40. Albany: State University of New York Press.

Goldberg Commission. 2011. "Goldberg Commission's Recommendations." www.landpedia.org/landdoc/Analytical_materials/Goldberg_recommendations-english.pdf.

Goldman, Shalom. 2009. *Zeal for Zion: Christians, Jews, and the Idea of the Promised Land.* Chapel Hill: University of North Carolina Press.

Gordon, A.D. 1911a. "Some Observations." In *The Zionist Idea: An Historical Analysis and Reader,* edited by Arthur Hertzberg, 375–79. Philadelphia: Jewish Publication Society, 1997.

———. 1911b. "People and Labor." In *The Zionist Idea: An Historical Analysis and Reader,* edited by Arthur Hertzberg, 372–74. Philadelphia: Jewish Publication Society, 1997.

———. 1911c. "Labor: The Core of the Matter." In *A.D. Gordon: Selected Essays,* translated by Frances Burnce, 50–91. New York: League for Labor Palestine, 1938.

———. 1920. "Our Tasks Ahead." In *The Zionist Idea: An Historical Analysis and Reader,* edited by Arthur Hertzberg, 379–83. Philadelphia: Jewish Publication Society, 1997.

———. 1938. *A.D. Gordon: Selected Essays,* translated by Frances Burnce. New York: League for Labor Palestine, 1938.

Gorney, Joseph. 1987. *Zionism and the Arabs, 1882–1948: A Study of Ideology.* Oxford: Clarendon Press.

Government of Palestine. 1922. *Report and General Abstracts of the Census of 1922 Taken on 23rd of October 1922.* Compiled by J. B. Barron. Jerusalem. http://users .cecs.anu.edu.au/~bdm/yabber/census/PalestineCensus1922.pdf.

———. Department of Statistics. 1947. *Survey of Social and Economic Conditions in Arab Villages, 1944.*

Granott [Granovsky], A. 1952. *The Land System in Palestine: History and Structure.* London: Eyre and Spottiswoode.

Graymont, Barbara, ed. 2001. "Treaty of Peace: Six Nations, Seven Nations of Canada, and Cherokees (Johnson Hall, 3/4/1768)." In *Early American Indian Documents: Treaties and Laws, 1607–1789,* edited by Alden T. Vaughan, vol. 10: *New York and New Jersey Treaties, 1754–1775,* edited by Barabara Graymont. Washington, DC: University Publications of America.

Green, Michael D. 1985. *The Politics of Indian Removal: Creek Government and Society in Crisis.* Lincoln: University of Nebraska Press.

Greer, Allan. 2012. "Commons and Enclosure in the Colonization of North America." *American Historical Review* 117 (2): 365–86.

———. 2014. "Dispossession in a Commercial Idiom: From Indian Deeds to Land Cession Treaties." In *Contested Spaces of Early America,* edited by Julianna Barr and Edward Countryman, 69–92. Philadelphia: University of Pennsylvania Press.

Gregory, Derek. 1995. "Imaginative Geographies." *Progress in Human Geography* 19 (4): 447–85.

———. 2004. *The Colonial Present: Afghanistan, Palestine, Iraq.* Oxford: Blackwell.

Gregory, Jon. 2005. "Mapping Improvement: Reshaping Rural Landscapes in the Eighteenth Century." *Landscapes* 6 (1): 62–82.

Greven, Philip J., Jr. 1970. *Four Generations: Population, Land, and Family in Colonial Andover, Massachusetts.* Ithaca, NY: Cornell University Press.

Griffin, Carl J. 2010. "Becoming Private Property: Custom, Law, and Geographies of Ownership in Eighteenth- and Nineteenth-Century England." *Environment and Planning A* 42 (3): 747–62.

Groag, Shmuel. 2006. "The Politics of Roads in Jerusalem." In *City of Collision: Jerusalem and the Politics of Conflict Urbanism,* edited by Phillip Misselwitz and Tim Rieniets, 176–84. Basel: Birkhauser.

Grossman, David. 2011. *Rural Arab Demography and Early Jewish Settlement in Palestine: Distribution and Population Density during the Late Ottoman Period.* New Brunswick, NJ: Transaction Press.

Grove, Richard. 1981. "Cressey Dymock and the Draining of the Fens: An Early Agricultural Model." *Geographical Journal* 147 (1): 27–37.

Hablos, Farouk. 2010. "Public Services and Tax Revenues in Ottoman Tripoli (1516–1918)." In *Syria and Bilad al-Sham under Ottoman Rule: Essays in Honour of Abdul-Karim Rafeq,* edited by Peter Sluglett and Stefan Weber, 115–35. Leiden: E.J. Brill.

Hadawi, Sami. 1970. *Village Statistics: A Classification of Land and Ownership in Palestine.* Beirut: Palestine Liberation Organization Research Center.

HAGAR: Studies in Culture, Polity, and Identities. 2008. Special Issue on Bedouins. Vol. 8 (2).

Hajjar, Lisa. 2017. "Lawfare and Armed Conflict." In *Living in the Age of Drones,* edited by Lisa Parks and Caren Kaplan. Durham, NC: Duke University Press.

Hakluyt, Richard. 1584. *A Particuler Discourse Concerninge the Greate Necessitie and Manifolde Commodyties That Are Like to Growe to This Realme of Englande by the Westerne Discoueries Lately Attempted, Written in the Yere 1584,... Known as Discourse of Western Planting.* Edited by David B. Quinn and Alison M. Quinn. London: Hakluyt Society, 1993.

Halabi, Usamah, Aron Turner, and Meron Benvenisti. 1985. *Land Alienation in the West Bank: A Legal and Spatial Analysis.* Jerusalem: The West Bank Data Project.

Halkin, Hillel. 2010a. *Yehuda Halevi.* New York: Schocken Books.

———. 2010b. *On Yehuda Halevi.* http://vimeo.com/7690308.

Halper, Jeff. 2002. "The Three Jerusalems: Planning and Colonial Control. *Jerusalem Quarterly,* no. 15: 6–17.

Hamalainen, Pekka. 2003. "The Rise and Fall of Plains Indian Horse Cultures." *Journal of American History* 90 (3): 833–62.

———. 2008. *The Comanche Empire.* New Haven, CT: Yale University Press.

Hanafi, Sari. 2009. "Spacio-cide: Colonial Politics, Invisibility, and Rezoning in Palestinian Territory." *Contemporary Arab Affairs* 2 (1): 106–21.

———. 2013. "Explaining Spacio-cide in the Palestinian Territory: Colonization, Separation, and State of Exception." *Current Sociology* 61 (2): 190–205.

Harcourt, Hugh. 1975. "Review: The Zionist Outlook." *Journal of Palestine Studies* 4 (3): 110–13.

Harel, Israel. 2015. "An Israeli Answer to Palestinian Terror: Annexation—And Let It Begin in Judea and Samaria with Gush Etzion." *Haaretz.* www.haaretz.com /opinion/.premium-1.688418.

Hariot, Thomas. 1588. *A Brief and True Report of the New Found Land of Virginia.* Edited by Paul Royster. Lincoln: University of Nebraska. http://digitalcommons .unl.edu/cgi/viewcontent.cgi?article=1020@context=etas.

Harley, J. B. 1965. "The Re-Mapping of England, 1750–1800." *Imago Mundi* 19 (1): 56–67.

———. 1983. "Meaning and Ambiguity in Tudor Cartography." In *English Mapmaking, 1500–1650,* edited by Sarah Tyacke, 22–45. London: British Library.

———. 1988. "Maps, Knowledge, and Power." In *The Iconography of Landscape: Essays on the Symbolic Representation, Design, and Use of Past Environments,* edited by Denis Cosgrove and Stephen Daniels, 277–312. Cambridge: Cambridge University Press.

———. 1989. "Deconstructing the Map." *Cartographica* 26 (2): 1–20.

———. 2001. "New England Cartography and the Native Americans." In *The New Nature of Maps,* 169–95. Baltimore: Johns Hopkins University Press.

Harley, J. B., and David Woodward. 1987. "Concluding Remarks." In *The History of Cartography,* vol. 1: *Cartography in Prehistoric, Ancient, and Medieval Europe and the Mediterranean,* edited by J. B. Harley and David Woodward, 502–9. Chicago: University of Chicago Press. www.press.uchicago.edu/books/HOC/HOC_V1 /HOC_VOLUME1_chapter21.pdf.

Harris, Cole. 2004. "How Did Colonialism Dispossess? Comments from an Edge of Empire." *Annals of the Association of American Geographers* 94 (1): 165–82.

Harris, William Wilson. 1980. *Taking Root: Israeli Settlement in the West Bank, the Golan, and Gaza-Sinai, 1967–1980.* Chicester, UK: Research Studies Press.

Harrison, Christopher. 1997. "Manor Courts and the Governance of Tudor England." In *Communities and Courts in Britain, 1150–1900,* edited by Christopher W. Brooks and Michael Lobban, 43–59. London: Hambledon Press.

Harvey, P. D. A., ed. 1984. *The Peasant Land Market in Medieval England.* Oxford: Oxford University Press.

———. 1993a. *Maps in Tudor England.* Chicago: University of Chicago Press.

———. 1993b. "Estate Surveyors and the Spread of the Scale-Map in England." *Landscape History* 15: 37–49.

———. 1996a. "English Estate Maps: Their Early History and Their Use as Historical Evidence." In *Rural Images: Estate Maps in the Old and New Worlds,* edited by David Buisseret, 27–61. Chicago: University of Chicago Press.

———. 1996b. "The Peasant Land Market in Medieval England—and Beyond." In *Medieval Society and the Manor Court,* edited by Zvi Razi and Richard M. Smith, 392–407. Oxford: Clarendon Press.

———. 2010a. *Manors and Maps in Rural England, from the Tenth Century to the Seventeenth.* Farnham, UK: Ashgate/Variorum.

———. 2010b. "The Peasant Land Market and the Winchester Pipe Rolls." In *Land and Family: Trends and Local Variations in the Peasant Land Market on the Winchester Bishopric Estates, 1263–1415,* edited by John Mullen and Richard Britnell, 1–10. Hatfield, UK: University of Hertfordshire Press.

Hayfield, Colin, and Andrew Watkins. 2012. "A Seventeenth-Century Warwickshire Estate Map." *Landscape History* 33 (2): 29–48.

Haynes, Joshua 2013. "Patrolling the Border: Theft and Violence on the Creek-Georgia Frontier, 1770–1796." PhD diss., University of Georgia.

Hegel, Georg Wilhelm Friedrich. 1833. *The Philosophy of History.* New York: Dover, 1956.

Helgerson, Richard. 1992. *Forms of Nationhood: The Elizabethan Writing of England.* Chicago: University of Chicago Press.

———. 1993. "Nation or Estate? Ideological Conflict in the Early Modern Mapping of England." *Cartographica* 30 (1): 68–74.

Helmholz, R. H. 2003. "Christopher St. German and the Law of Custom." *University of Chicago Law Review* 70 (1): 129–39.

Henige, David P. 1998. *Numbers from Nowhere: The American Indian Contact Population Debate.* Norman: University of Oklahoma Press.

Herodotus. Ca. 440 B.C.E. *The Histories.* New York: Penguin Books, 1976.

Hershberger, Mary. 1999. "Mobilizing Women, Anticipating Abolition: The Struggle against Indian Removal in the 1830s." *Journal of American History* 86 (1): 15–40.

Hertz, Deborah, 2007. *How Jews Became Germans. The History of Conversion and Assimilation in Berlin.* New Haven, CT: Yale University Press.

Herzl, Theodor. 1896. *The Jewish State: An Attempt at a Modern Solution to the Jewish Question.* 2nd ed. London: Central Office of the Zionist Organization, 1934.

———. 1902. *Altneuland* [Old New Land]. Translated from the German by Lotta Levinsohn. Princeton, NJ: M. Wiener, 1997.

———. 1958. *The Diaries of Theodor Herzl.* Edited and translated by Marvin Lowenthal. London: Victor Gollancz.

———. 1973. *Zionist Writings.* Translated by Harry Zohn. New York: Herzl Press.

Hinderaker, Eric, and Peter C. Mancall. 2003. *At the Edge of Empire: The Back Country in British North America.* Baltimore: Johns Hopkins University Press.

Hindle, Steve. 1998. "Persuasion and Protest in the Caddington Common Enclosure Dispute 1635–1639." *Past & Present,* no. 158: 37–78.

———. 2000. "A Sense of Place? Becoming and Belonging in the Rural Parish, 1550–1650." In *Communities in Early Modern England: Networks, Places, Rhetoric,* edited by Alexandra Shepard and Phil Withington, 96–114. Manchester: Manchester University Press.

———. 2006. "The Battle of Newton-field and the Midland Rising of 1607." www.newtonrebels.org.uk/rebels/academic.htm.

———. 2008. "Imagining Insurrection in Seventeenth-Century England: Representations of the Midland Rising of 1607." *History Workshop Journal,* no. 66: 21–61.

Hipkin, Stephen. 2000. "'Sitting on his Penny Rent': Conflict and Right of Common in Faversham Blean, 1595–1610." *Rural History* 11 (1): 1–35.

Hoblos, Farouk. 2010. "Public Services and Tax Revenues in Ottoman Tripoli (1516–1918)." In *Syria and Bilad al-Sham under Ottoman Rule: Essays in Honour of Abdul-Karim Rafeq,* edited by Peter Sluglett and Stefan Weber, 115–30. Leiden: E.J. Brill.

Hollowell, Steven. 2000. *Enclosure Records for Historians.* Chichester, UK: Phillmore & Co.

Holzman-Gavit, Yifat. 2007. *Land Expropriation in Israel: Law, Culture, and Society.* London: Aldershot.

Home, Robert. 2003. "An Irreversible Conquest: Colonial and Postcolonial Land Law in Israel/Palestine." *Social and Legal Studies* 12 (3): 291–310.

Home, R. K., and J. Kavanagh. 2001. *Mapping the Refugee Camps of Gaza: The Surveyor in a Political Environment.* London: Royal Institution of Chartered Surveyors.

Homer, Henry Sacheverell. 1769. *An Essay on the Nature and Method of Ascertaining the Specifick Shares of Proprietors, upon the Inclosure of Common Fields. With Observations upon the Inconveniencies of Open Fields, and upon the Objections to Their Inclosure, Particularly as Far as They Relate to the Publick and the Poor.* 2nd ed. Oxford: Printed for S. Parker. http://find.galegroup.com/ecco/infomark.do?&source=gale&prodId=ECCO&userGroupName=ucsandiego&tabID=T001

&docId=CW3305211776&type=multipage&contentSet=ECCOArticles&versi
on=1.0&docLevel=FASCIMILE.

Hooke, Della, ed. 2000. *Landscape: The Richest Historical Record*. London: Society
for Landscape Studies.

———. 2010. "'The Past in the Present'—Remnant Open Field Patterns in England." *Landscape History* 31 (2): 73–75.

Hope Simpson, John, 1930. *Palestine. Report on Immigration, Land Settlement and
Development*. London: His Majesty's Stationery Office.

Hoppit, Julian. 1996. "Patterns of Parliamentary Legislation, 1660–1800." *Historical
Journal* 39 (1): 109–31.

Horn, James. 1994. *Adapting to a New World: English Society in the Seventeenth-
Century Chesapeake*. Chapel Hill: University of North Carolina Press.

———. 2005. "The Conquest of Eden." In *Envisioning an Empire: Jamestown an the
Making of the North Atlantic World*, edited by Robert Appelbaum and John
Wood Sweet, 25–47. Philadelphia: University of Pennsylvania Press.

Horn, Pamela. 1982. "An Eighteenth-Century Land Agent: The Career of
Nathaniel Kent (1737–1810)." *Agricultural History Review* 30 (1): 1–16.

Horovitz, David. 2012. "Talia Sasson: We Had No State for 2,000 years. Why Are
We Now Jeopardizing Its Jewish, Democratic Essence?" *Times of Israel*, April 15.
www.timesofisrael.com/talia-sasson-we-had-no-state-for-2000-years-why-are-we-
now-jeopardizing-its-jewish-democratic-essence.

Horsman, Reginald. 1981. *Race and Manifest Destiny: The Origins of American
Racial Anglo-Saxonism*. Cambridge, MA: Harvard University Press.

Hoskins, W. G. 1957. *The Midland Peasant: The Economic and Social History of a
Leicestershire Village*. London: Macmillan.

———. 1977. *The Making of the English Landscape*. London: Hodder and
Stoughton.

Hourani, Albert, 1994. "Ottoman Reform and the Politics of Notables." In *The
Modern Middle East: A Reader,* edited by Albert Hourani, Philip Khoury, and
Marcy C. Wilson, 83–109. London: I. B. Tauris.

Howlett, John. 1787. *Enclosures, A Cause of Improved Agriculture of Plenty and
Cheapness of Provisions, of Population, and of Both Private and National Wealth*.
London: Printed for W. Richardson. http://find.galegroup.com/mome/infomark
.do?&source=gale&prodId=MOME&userGroupName=ucsandiego&tabID=
Tool&docId=U3608048743&type=multipage&contentSet=MOMEArticles&
version=1.0&docLevel=FASCIMILE.

Hoyle, R. W. 1990. "Tenure and the Land Market in Early Modern England: or a Late
Contribution to the Brenner debate." *Economic History Review,* 2nd ser., 43 (1):
1–20.

———, ed. 2004. *People, Landscape, and Alternative Agriculture: Essays for Joan
Thirsk*. Exeter, UK: Agricultural History Society.

———, ed. 2011. *Custom, Improvement, and the Landscape in Early Modern Britain*. Burlington, VT: Ashgate.

Hull, Edward. 1885. *Mount Seir, Sinai, and Western Palestine.* London: Richard Bentley and Son. https://archive.org/stream/mountseirsinaiweoohull#page/n7/mode/2up.

Hulton, Paul, and David Beers Quinn. 1964. *American Drawings of John White, 1577–1590.* Chapel Hill: University of North Carolina Press.

Human Rights Watch. 2008. *Off the Map: Land and Housing Rights Violations in Israel's Unrecognized Bedouin Villages.* www.hrw.org/reports/2008/iopt0308/iopt0308webwcover.pdf.

Humphries, Jane. 1990. "Enclosures, Common Rights, and Women: The Proletarianization of Families in the Late Eighteenth and Early Nineteenth Centuries." *Journal of Economic History* 50 (1): 17–42.

Hurt, R. Douglas. 1987. *Indian Agriculture in America: Prehistory to the Present.* Lawrence: University of Kansas Press.

———. 2002. *American Agriculture: A Brief History.* Lafayette, IN: Purdue University Press.

Hurtado, Albert L., and Peter Iverson. 2001. *Major Problems in American Indian History.* Boston: Houghton Mifflin.

Hutson, James H. 1973. "Benjamin Franklin and the West." *Western Historical Quarterly* 4 (4): 425–34.

Hütteroth, Wolf-Dieter. 1973. "The Pattern of Settlement in Palestine in the Sixteenth Century: Geographical Research on Turkish Defter-I Mufassal." In *Studies on Palestine during the Ottoman period,* edited by Moshe Ma-oz, 3–10. Jerusalem: Magnes Press.

Hütteroth, Wolf-Dieter, and Kamal Abdulfattah. 1977. *Historical Geography of Palestine, Transjordan, and Southern Syria in the Late Sixteenth Century.* Erlangen: Fränkische Geographische Gesellschaft.

Ibn Khaldun, Mohammed. 1381. *The Muqaddimah: An Introduction to History.* Translated by Franz Rosenthal; edited by N.J. Dawood. Princeton: Princeton University Press, 1974.

Imber, Colin. 1996. "The Status of Orchards and Fruit Trees in Ottoman Law." In *Studies in Ottoman History and Law,* 207–16. Istanbul: Isis.

Inalcik, Halil. 1954. "Ottoman Methods of Conquest." *Studia Islamica* 2: 103–29.

———. 1994. "The Ottoman State: Economy and Society, 1300–1600." In *An Economic and Social History of the Ottoman Empire, 1300–1914,* edited by Halil Inalcik and Donald Quataert, 9–154. Cambridge: Cambridge University Press.

———. 2002. "Foundations of Ottoman-Jewish Cooperation." In *Jews, Turks, Ottomans: A Shared History, Fifteenth through the Twentieth Century,* edited by Avigdor Levy, 3–14. Syracuse, NY: Syracuse University Press.

Isenberg, Andrew C. 2000. *The Destruction of the Bison.* Cambridge: Cambridge University Press.

Islamoglu[-Inan], Huri. 1994. *State and Peasant in the Ottoman Empire: Agrarian Power Relations and Regional Economic Development in Ottoman Anatolia during the Sixteenth Century.* Leiden: E.J. Brill.

———. 2000. "Property as a Contested Domain: A Reevaluation of the Ottoman Land Code of 1858." In *New Perspectives on Property and Land in the Middle East,* edited by Roger Owen, 3–61. Cambridge, MA: Harvard University Press.

———, ed. 2004. *Constituting Modernity: Private Property in the East and West.* New York: Palgrave Macmillan.

Israel & Palestine (I & P) Monthly Review. 1980. No. 79.

Issawi, Charles. 1982. *An Economic History of the Middle East and North Africa.* New York: Columbia University Press.

Jabareen, Yosef Rafeq. 2010. "The Politics of State Planning in Achieving Geopolitical Ends: The Case of the Recent Master Plan for Jerusalem." *International Development Planning Review* 32 (1): 27–43.

Jabotinsky, Vladimir Ze'ev. 1923. "The Iron Wall." www.jewishvirtuallibrary.org /quot-the-iron-wall-quot.

Jackson, John Brinkerhoff. 1984. *Discovering the Vernacular Landscape.* New Haven, CT: Yale University Press.

Jewish National Fund. "Our History." www.kkl-jnf.org/about-kkl-jnf/our-history /fifth-decade-1941–1950.

Jiryis, Sabri. 1973. "The Legal Structure for the Expropriation and Absorption of Arab Lands in Israel." *Journal of Palestine Studies* 2 (4): 82–104.

———. 1976a. "The Land Question in Israel." *MERIP Reports,* no. 47: 5–20, 24–26.

———. 1976b. *The Arabs in Israel.* New York: Monthly Review Press.

Johansen, Bruce E. 2000. *Shapers of the Great Debate on Native Americans—Land, Spirit, and Power.* New York: Greenwood.

Johnson, Hildegard B. 1976. *Order upon the Land: The U.S. Rectangular Land Survey and the Upper Mississippi Country.* New York: Oxford University Press.

Johnson, Mathew 1996. *An Archaeology of Capitalism.* Oxford: Blackwell.

Jones, David S. 2003. "Virgin Soils Revisited." *William and Mary Quarterly* 60 (4): 703–42.

Jones, P. M. 2012. "Arthur Young (1741–1820): For and Against." *English Historical Review* 127 (528): 1100–1120.

Joseph, Sabrina. 1995. "Britain's Social, Moral, and Cultural Penetration of Palestine: British Travelers in Nineteenth- and Early Twentieth-Century Palestine and Their Perception of the Jews." *Arab Studies Journal* 3 (1): 45–67.

———. 1998–99. "An Analysis of Khayr al-Din al-Ramli's Fatawa on Peasant Land Tenure in Seventeenth-Century Palestine." *Arab Studies Journal* 6/7 (2/1): 112–27.

———. 2007. "The Legal Status of Tenants and Sharecroppers in Seventeenth- and Eighteenth-Century France and Ottoman Syria." *Rural History* 18 (1): 23–46.

———. 2012. *Islamic Law on Peasant Usufruct in Ottoman Syria: Seventeenth to Early Nineteenth Century.* Leiden: E. J. Brill.

Kades, Eric. 2001. "History and Interpretation of the Great Case of *Johnson v. M'Intosh*." *Law and History Review* 19 (1): 67–116.

———. 2008. "The 'Middle Ground' Perspective on the Expropriation of Indian Lands." *Law and Social Inquiry* 33 (3): 827–39.

Kadman, Noga. 2015. *Erased from Space and Consciousness: Israel and the Depopulated Palestinian Villages of 1948.* Indianapolis: Indiana University Press.

Kain, Roger J. P. 2007. "Maps and Rural Land Management in Early Modern Europe." In *The History of Cartography,* vol. 3, pt. 1, edited by David Woodward, 705–18. Chicago: University of Chicago Press.

Kain, Roger, and Elizabeth Baigent. 1992. *The Cadastral Map in the Service of the State: A History of Property Mapping.* Chicago: University of Chicago Press.

Kain, Roger J. P., John Chapman, and Richard R. Oliver. 2004. *The Enclosure Maps of England and Wales, 1594–1918.* Cambridge: Cambridge University Press.

Kalischer, Zvi Hirsch. 1862. "Seeking Zion." In *The Zionist Idea: An Historical Analysis and Reader,* edited by Arthur Hertzberg, 112–14. Philadelphia: Jewish Publication Society, 1997.

Kamaisi, Rassam. 1995. "Land Ownership as a Determinant in the Formation of Residential Areas in Arab Localities." *GeoForum* 26 (2): 195–211.

Kamen, Charles S. 1991. *Little Common Ground: Arab Agriculture and Jewish Settlement in Palestine, 1920–1948.* Pittsburgh: University of Pittsburgh Press.

Kaplan, Moti. 2011. "National Outline Plan for Forests and Afforestation, NOP 22." Jerusalem: Jewish National Fund. www.kkl-jnf.org/files/forests/tma/TAMA22_eng.pdf.

Kark, Ruth. 1981. "Jewish Frontier Settlement in the Negev, 1880–1948: Perception and Realization." *Middle Eastern Studies* 17 (3): 334–56.

———. 1983a. "Landownership and Spatial Change in Nineteenth-Century Palestine: An Overview." In *Seminar on Historical Types of Spatial Organizations: The Transition from Spontaneous to Regulated Spatial Organisation.* Warsaw.

———. 1983b. "Millenarism and Agricultural Settlement in the Holy Land in the Nineteenth Century." *Journal of Historical Geography* 9 (1): 47–62.

———. 1984. "Changing Patterns of Landownership in Nineteenth-Century Palestine: The European Influence." *Journal of Historical Geography* 10 (4): 357–84.

———. 1997. "Mamlūk and Ottoman Cadastral Surveys and Early Mapping of Landed Properties in Palestine." *Agricultural History* 71 (1): 46–70.

Kark, Ruth, and Seth J. Frantzman. 2012. "The Negev: Land, Settlement, the Bedouin, and Ottoman and British Policy, 1871–1948." *British Journal of Middle Eastern Studies* 39 (1): 53–77.

Karsten, Peter. 2002. *Between Law and Custom: High and Low Legal Cultures in the Land of the British Diaspora: The United States, Canada, Australia, and New Zealand, 1600–1900.* Cambridge: Cambridge University Press.

Katz, Jacob. 1978. "The Forerunners of Zionism." *Jerusalem Quarterly* 7: 10–21.

Katz, Y. 1992. "Transfer of Population as a Solution to International Disputes." *Political Geography* 11 (1): 55–72.

Kaveh, Yoav. 2005. "The Game of the Names." *Haaretz,* March 3. www.haaretz.com/the-game-of-the-names-1.151874.

Kedar, Alexandre. 2001. "The Legal Transformation of Ethnic Geography: Israeli Law and the Palestinian Landholder, 1948–1967." *New York University Journal of International Law and Politics* 33 (4): 923–1000.

Kellerman, Ahron. 1993. *Society and Settlement: Jewish Land of Israel in the Twentieth Century.* Albany: State University of New York Press.

Kemp, Adriana. 2001. "Borders, Space, and National Identity in Israel." *Theory and Criticism* 18: 13–43.

Kent, Nathaniel. 1793. *Hints to Gentlemen of Landed Property.* 2nd ed. London: J. Dodsley. https://archive.org/stream/hintstogentlemookent#page/n5/mode/2up.

Kerridge, Eric. 1992. *The Common Fields of England.* Manchester: Manchester University Press.

Kestler-D'Amours, Jillian. 2012. "The End of the Bedouin." *Le Monde Diplomatique,* August. http://mondediplo.com/2012/08/06bedouin.

Keydar, Caglar, and Faruk Tabak, eds. 1991. *Landholding and Commercial Agriculture in the Middle East.* Albany: State University of New York Press.

Keys, Eric. 2003. Review of *Cultivated Landscapes of Native North America* by William E. Doolittle. *Journal of Latin American Geography* 2 (1): 115–17.

Khalaf, Issa. 1997. "The Effect of Socioeconomic Change on Arab Societal Collapse in Mandate Palestine." *International Journal of Middle East Studies* 29: 93–112.

Khalidi, Rashid. 1997. *Palestinian Identity: The Construction of Modern National Consciousness.* New York: Columbia University Press.

Khalidi, Tarif, ed. 1984. *Land Tenure and Social Transformation in the Middle East.* Beirut: American University of Beirut.

Khalidi, Walid. 1971. *From Haven to Conquest: Readings in Zionism and the Palestine Problem until 1948.* Beirut: Institute for Palestine Studies.

———. 1993. "The Jewish-Ottoman Land Company: Herzl's Blueprint for the Colonization of Palestine." *Journal of Palestine Studies* 22 (2): 30–47.

Khamaisi, Rassem. 2006. "Villages under Siege: Adaptation, Resistance, Imposed Modernization, and Urbanization in Jerusalem's Eastern Villages." In *City of Collision: Jerusalem and the Principles of Conflict Urbanism,* edited by Phillipp Misselwitz and Tim Rieniets, 121–29. Basel: Birkhauser.

Khurshid, Imam. 2008. "Hebrew Language Policy of Israel: An Assessment, 1948–2000." PhD diss., Jawaharlal Nehru University, New Delhi. http://shodhganga.inflibnet.ac.in//handle/10603/14515.

King, Peter. 1989. "Gleaners, Farmers, and the Failure of Legal Sanctions in England, 1750–1850." *Past & Present,* no. 125: 116–50

———. 1992. "Legal Change, Customary Right, and Social Conflict in Late Eighteenth-Century England: The Origins of the Great Gleaning Case of 1788." *Law and History Review* 10 (1): 1–31.

Kitchen, Frank. 1997. "John Norden (c. 1547–1625): Estate Surveyor, Topographer, County Mapmaker, and Devotional Writer." *Imago Mundi* 49: 43–61.

Klein, Bernhard. 2001. *Maps and the Writing of Space in Early Modern England and Ireland.* London: Macmillan.

Klein, Menahem. 2008. "Jerusalem as an Israeli Problem—A Review of Forty Years of Israeli Rule over Arab Jerusalem." *Israel Studies* 13 (2): 54–72.

Klinefelter, Walter. 1970. "Surveyor General Thomas Holme's 'Map of the Improved Part of the Province of Pennsilvania.'" *Winterthur Portfolio* 6 : 41–74.

Knittl, Margaret Albright. 2007. "The Design for the Initial Drainage of the Great Level of the Fens: An Historical Whodunit in Three Parts." *Agricultural History Review* 55 (1): 23–50.

Konkle, Maureen. 2008. "Indigenous Ownership and the Emergence of U.S. Liberal Imperialism." *American Indian Quarterly* 32 (3): 297–323.

Kram, Noa. 2012. "Legal Struggles for Land Ownership Rights in Israel." In *Indigenous (In)Justice: Human Rights Law and Bedouin Arabs in the Naqab/Negev*, edited by Ahmad Amara, Ismael Abu-Saad, and Oren Yiftachel, 127–56. Cambridge, MA: Harvard University Press.

Kulikoff, Allan. 2000. *From British Peasants to Colonial American Farmers*. Chapel Hill: University of North Carolina Press.

Kupperman, Karen. 2000. *Indians and English: Facing Off in Early America*. Ithaca, NY: Cornell University Press.

Kuran, Timur. 2001. "The Provision of Public Goods under Islamic Law: Origins, Impact, and Limitations of the Waqf System." *Law and Society Review* 35 (4): 841–98.

Kushner, David, ed. 1984. *Palestine in the Late Ottoman Period*. Leiden: E.J. Brill.

Kuzar, Ron. 2001. *Hebrew and Zionism: A Discourse Analytic Cultural Study*. Berlin: Mouton de Gruyter.

Lachmann, Richard. 1987. *From Manor to Market: Structural Change in England, 1536—1640*. Madison: University of Wisconsin Press.

Larsen, C.S., and G.R. Milner, eds. 1994. *In the Wake of Contact: Biological Responses to Conquest*. New York: Wiley Liss.

Laurence, Edward. 1727. *The Duty and Office of a Land Steward: Represented under Several Plain and Distinct Articles. . . .* 3rd ed. London: Printed for J. and P. Knapton, T. Longman, H. Lintot, and J. and H. Pemberton, 1743.

Lee, Joseph. 1653. *Considerations Concerning Common Fields and Enclosures*. London: Abel Roper.

Lemon, James T. 1987. "Agriculture and Society in Early America." *Agricultural History Review* 35 (1): 76–94.

Lesch, Ann M. 2001. "Zionism and Its Impact." www.palestineremembered.com /Acre/Palestine-Remembered/Story452.html.

Leuenberger, Christine, and Izak Schnell. 2010. "The Politics of Maps: Constructing National Territories in Israel." *Social Studies of Science* 40 (6): 803–42.

Levin, Noam, Ruth Kark, and Emir Galilee. 2010. "Maps and the Settlement of Southern Palestine, 1799–1948: An Historical/GIS Analysis." *Journal of Historical Geography* 36 (1): 1–18.

LeVine, Mark. 2005. *Overthrowing Geography: Jaffa, Tel Aviv, and the Struggle for Palestine, 1880–1948*. Berkeley: University of California Press.

Levinson, Chaim, and Jack Koury. 2014. "Israel Appropriates Massive Tract of West Bank Land." *Haaretz*, August 31. www.haaretz.com/israel-news/.premium-1.613319.

Levy, Avigdor, ed. 1994. *The Jews of the Ottoman Empire*. Princeton, NJ: Darwin Press.

————. 2002. *Jews, Turks, Ottomans: A Shared History, Fifteenth through the Twentieth Century*. Syracuse, NY: Syracuse University Press.

Lewis, Bernard. 1979. "Ottoman Land Tenure and Taxation in Syria." *Studia Islamica*, no. 50: 109–24.

Lewis, G. Malcolm. 1998a. "Maps, Mapmaking, and Map Use by Native North Americans." In *The History of Cartography*, vol. 2, pt. 3, edited by David Woodward and G. Malcom Lewis, 51–182. Chicago: University of Chicago Press.

————. 1998b. "Frontier Encounters in the Field: 1511–1925." In *Cartographic Encounters: Perspectives on Native American Mapmaking and Map Use*, edited by G. Malcolm Lewis, 9–34. Chicago: University of Chicago Press.

Library of Virginia. 2007. *Virginia Discovered and Described: John Smith's Map and Its Derivatives*. Research Notes No. 28. www.lva.virginia.gov/public/guides/rn28_johnsmith.pdf.

Linebaugh, Peter. 2008. *The Magna Carta Manifesto: Liberties and Commons for All*. Berkeley: University of California Press.

————. 2010. "Enclosures from the Bottom Up." *Radical History Review* 2010 (108): 11–27.

Linebaugh, Peter, and Markus Rediker. 2012. *The Many-Headed Hydra: Sailors, Slaves, Commoners, and the Hidden History of the Revolutionary Atlantic*. London: Verso.

Linklater, Andro. 2002. *Measuring America: How an Untamed Wilderness Shaped the United States and Fulfilled the Promise of Democracy*. New York: Walker and Co..

Litvak, Olga. 2012. *Haskalah: The Romantic Movement in Judaism*. New Brunswick, NJ: Rutgers University Press.

Livingston, Robert. 1979. *The Livingston History Records, 1666–1723*. Edited by Lawrence H. Leder. Stanfordville, NY: E. M. Coleman.

Locke, John. 1690. *The Second Treatise of Civil Government*. Edited by Peter Laslett. Cambridge: Cambridge University Press, 1999.

Lockman, Zachary. 1996. *Comrades and Enemies: Arab and Jewish Workers in Palestine, 1906–1948*. Berkeley: University of California Press.

Long, Burke O. 2003. *Imagining the Holy Land: Maps, Models, and Fantasy Travels*. Bloomington: Indiana University Press.

Long, Joanna C. 2009. "Rooting Diaspora, Reviving Nation: Zionist Landscapes of Palestine-Israel." *Transactions of the Institute of British Geographers* 34 (1): 61–77.

————. 2011. "Geographies of Palestine-Israel." *Geography Compass* 5 (5): 262–74.

Lori, Aviva. 2010. "Reclaiming the Desert." *Haaretz*, August 27. www.haaretz.com/israel-news/reclaiming-the-desert-1.310558.

Loux, Andrea C. 1993. "The Persistence of the Ancient Regime: Custom, Utility, and the Common Law in the Nineteenth Century." *Cornell Law Review* 79 (1): 183–218.

Low, Anthony. 1992. "Agricultural Reform and the Love Poems of Thomas Carew; with an Instance from Lovelace." In *Culture and Cultivation in Early Modern England: Writing and the Land*, edited by Michael Leslie and Timothy Raylor, 83–80. Leicester: University of Leicester Press.

Lowry, S. Todd. 2003. "The Agricultural Foundations of the Seventeenth-Century English Oeconomy." In *Oeconomies in the Age of Newton,* edited by Margaret Schabas and Neil De Marchi, 74–100. Durham, NC: Duke University Press. [Annual supplement to *History of Political Economy,* vol. 35.]

Mackenthun, Gesa. 1997. *Metaphors of Dispossession: American Beginnings and the Translation of Empire, 1492–1637.* Norman: University of Oklahoma Press.

MacLean, Gerald, Donna Landry, and Joseph P. Ward. 1999. *The Country and the City Revisited: England and the Politics of Culture, 1550–1850.* Cambridge: Cambridge University Press.

MacMillan, Ken. 2003. "Sovereignty 'More Plainly Described': Early English Maps of North America, 1580–1625." *Journal of British Studies* 42: 413–47.

———. 2006. *Sovereignty and Possession in the English New World: The Legal Foundations of Empire, 1576–1640.* Cambridge: Cambridge University Press.

Makdisi, Saree. 2008. *Palestine Inside Out: An Everyday Occupation.* New York: W. W. Norton.

Manahan, Karen B. N.d. "Robert Gray's *A Good Speed to Virginia.*" http://digital .lib.lehigh.edu/trial/justification/jamestown/essay/4.

Mancall, Peter C., ed. 1995. *Envisioning America: English Plans for the Colonization of North America, 1580–1640.* Boston: Bedford Books of St. Martin's Press.

———. 2007. *Hakluyt's Promise: An Elizabethan's Obsession for an English America.* New Haven, CT: Yale University Press.

Mancall, Peter C., and James H. Merrell, eds. 2007. *American Encounters: Natives and Newcomers from European Contact to Indian Removal, 1500–1850.* 2nd ed. London: Routledge.

Mancke, Elizabeth. 2002. "Negotiating an Empire: Britain and Its Overseas Peripheries, c. 1550–1780." In *Negotiated Empires: Centers and Peripheries in the Americas, 1500–1820,* edited by Christine Daniels and Michael V. Kennedy, 235–66. New York: Routledge.

Manna, Adel. 1994. "Eighteenth- and Nineteenth-Century Rebellions in Palestine." *Journal of Palestine Studies* 24 (1): 51–66.

———. 2009. "Rereading the 1834 Revolt against Muhammad 'Ali in Palestine and Rethinking Ottoman Rule." In *Transformed Landscapes: Essays on Palestine and the Middle East in Honor of Walid Khalidi,* edited by Camille Mansour and Leila Tarazi Fawaz, 83–104. Cairo: American University in Cairo Press.

Manor, Dalia. 2003. "Imagined Homeland: Landscape Painting in Palestine in the 1920s." *Nations and Nationalism* 9 (4): 533–54.

Manski, Rebecca. 2010. "Blueprint Negev." *Middle East Report,* no. 256: 2–7. www .jstor.org/stable/pdf/40985232.pdf.

Mansour, Camille, and Leila Tarazi Fawaz, eds. 2009. *Transformed Landscapes: Essays on Palestine and the Middle East in Honor of Walid Khalidi.* Cairo: American University in Cairo Press.

Ma'oz, Moshe. 1968. *Ottoman Reform in Syria and Palestine, 1840–1861.* Oxford: Clarendon Press.

———. 1975. "Changes in the Position of the Jewish Communities of Palestine and Syria in Mid-Nineteenth Century." In *Studies on Palestine during the Ottoman Period,* edited by Moshe Ma'oz, 142–63. Jerusalem: Magnes Press.

Marshall, William. 1804. *On the Landed Property of England: An Elementary and Practical Treatise; Containing the Purchase, the Improvement, and the Management of Landed Estates.* London.

Martin, John E. 1983a. *Feudalism to Capitalism: Peasant and Landlord in English Agrarian Development.* London: Macmillan.

———. 1983b. "The Midland Revolt of 1607." *In An Atlas of Rural Protest in Britain, 1548–1900,* edited by Andrew Charlesworth, 33–36. Philadelphia: University of Pennsylvania Press.

Marx, Karl. 1867. *Capital: A Critical Analysis of Capitalist Production.* Vol. 1. Edited by Frederick Engels. London: Lawrence and Wishart, 1974.

Marx, Karl, and Engels, Frederick. 1846. "The German Ideology." In *Selected Works in Three Volumes,* 1:16–80. Moscow: Progress Publishers, 1969.

Marzec, Robert P. 2002. "Enclosures, Colonization, and the *Robinson Crusoe* Syndrome: A Genealogy of Land in a Global Context." *Boundary 2* 29 (2): 129–56.

Masalha, Nur. 1992. *Expulsion of the Palestinians: The Concept of "Transfer" in Zionist Political Thought, 1882–1948.* Washington, DC: Institute for Palestine Studies.

———. 2007. *The Bible and Zionism: Invented Traditions, Archaeology, and Post-Colonialism in Palestine-Israel.* London: Zed Books.

———. 2013. *The Zionist Bible: Biblical Precedent, Colonialism, and the Erasure of Memory.* Durham, UK: Acumen.

Matless, David. 1993. "One Man's England: W. G. Hoskins and the English Culture of Landscape." *Rural History* 4: 187–207.

Mazie, Aaron. 1925. "The Tomb of Jehoshaphat in Relation to Hebrew Art." *Proceedings of the Jewish Palestine Exploration Society* 1 (2–4): 68–71.

McCarthy, Justin. 1990. *The Population of Palestine: Population History and Statistics of the Late Ottoman Period and the Mandate.* New York: Columbia University Press.

McCloskey, Donald N. 1975a. "The Economics of Enclosure: A Market Analysis." In *European Peasants and Their Markets,* edited by W. N. Parker and E. L. Jones, 123–60. Princeton, NJ: Princeton University Press.

———. 1975b. "The Persistence of English Common Fields." In *European Peasants and Their Markets,* edited by W. N. Parker and E. L. Jones, 73–119. Princeton, NJ: Princeton University Press.

McClure, David. 1772. *Diary of David McClure.* New York: Knickerbocker Press, 1899.

McDonagh, Briony. 2013. "Making and Breaking Property: Negotiating Enclosure and Common Rights in Sixteenth-Century England." *History Workshop Journal,* no. 76: 32–56.

McKee, Emily. 2014. "Performing Rootedness in the Negev/Naqab: Possibilities and Perils of Competitive Planting." *Antipode* 46 (5): 1172–89.

McMillan, Ken. 2006. *Sovereignty and Possession in the English New World: The Legal Foundations of Empire, 1570–1640.* Cambridge: Cambridge University Press.

McRae, Andrew. 1992. "Husbandry Manuals and the Language of Agrarian Improvement." In *Culture and Cultivation in Early Modern England: Writing and the Land,* edited by Michael Leslie and Timothy Raylor, 35–62. Leicester: University of Leicester Press.

———. 1993. "To Know One's Own: Estate Surveying and the Representation of the Land in Early Modern England." *Huntington Library Quarterly* 56 (4): 333–57.

———. 1994–95. "Landscape and Property in Seventeenth-Century Poetry." *Sydney Studies in English* 20: 36–62.

———. 1996. *God Speed the Plough: The Representation of Agrarian England, 1500–1660.* Cambridge: Cambridge University Press.

Meinig, D. W. 1979. "The Beholding Eye: Ten Versions of the Same Scene." In *The Interpretation of Ordinary Landscapes: Geographical Essays,* edited by D. W. Meinig and John Brinckerhoff Jackson, 33–48. New York: Oxford University Press.

Merchant, Carolyn. 2007. *American Environmental History: An Introduction.* New York: Columbia University Press.

MERIP Reports. 1979. "A Settler Looks at Autonomy." *MERIP Reports,* no. 78: 20–21. www.jstor.org/stable/3011691.

Merrell, James H. 1999. *Into the American Woods: Negotiators on the Pennsylvania Frontier.* New York: W. W. Norton.

———. 2007. "The Indians' New World: The Catawba Experience." In *American Encounters: Natives and Newcomers from European Contact to Indian Removal, 1500–1850,* 2nd ed., edited by Peter C. Mancall and James H. Merrell, 25–48. London: Routledge.

Metzer, Jacob. 1998. *The Divided Economy of Mandatory Palestine.* Cambridge: Cambridge University Press.

Miller, Christopher L., and George R. Hamel. 1986. "New Perspective on Indian-White Contact: Cultural Symbols and Colonial Trade." *Journal of American History* 73 (2): 311–28.

Miller, Robert J. 2006. *Native America Discovered and Conquered: Thomas Jefferson, Lewis and Clark, and Manifest Destiny.* Westport, CT: Praeger.

Mills, Dennis. 2006. "Canwick (Lincolnshire) and Melbourn (Cambridgeshire) in Comparative Perspective within the Open-Closed Village Model." *Rural History* 17 (1): 1–22.

Mingay, Gordon E. 1968. *Enclosure and the Small Farmer in the Age of the Industrial Revolution.* London: Macmillan.

Mingay, G. E., ed. 1975. *Arthur Young and His Times.* London: Macmillan Press.

Mitchell, Don. 2000. *Cultural Geography: A Critical Introduction.* Oxford: Blackwell.

———. 2012. *They Saved the Crops: Labor, Landscape, and the Struggle over Industrial Farming in Bracero-Era California.* Athens: University of Georgia Press.

Mitchell, W. J. T., ed. 2002. *Landscape and Power.* Chicago: University of Chicago Press.

Mohammed, Zakariyeh. 2005. "Maqdisi: An 11th-Century Palestinian Consciousness." *Jerusalem Quarterly*, nos. 22–23: 86–92.

Monk, Daniel Bertrand. 2002. *An Aesthetic Occupation: The Immediacy of Architecture and the Palestine Conflict.* Durham, NC: Duke University Press.

Moore, Adam. 1653. *Bread for the Poor and Advancement of the English Nation Promised by Enclosure of the Wastes and Common Grounds of England.* London: R. and W. Leybourn. http://gateway.proquest.com/openurl?ctx_ver=Z39.88–2003&res_id=xri:eebo&rft_id=xri:eebo:image:60084.

Moors, Annelies, and Steven Machlin. 1987. "Postcards of Palestine: Interpreting Images." *Critique of Anthropology* 7: 61–77.

Morgan, Victor. 1979. "The Cartographic Image of 'The Country' in Early Modern England." *Transactions of the Royal Historical Society* 29: 129–54.

Morris, Benny. 1986. "Yosef Weitz and the Transfer Committees, 1948–49." *Middle Eastern Studies* 22 (4): 522–61.

———. 2001. *Righteous Victims: A History of the Zionist-Arab Conflict, 1881–2001.* New York: Vintage Books.

———. 2002. "Revisiting the Palestinian Exodus of 1948." In *The War for Palestine*, edited by Eugene L. Rogan and Avi Shlaim, 37–59. Cambridge: Cambridge University Press.

Mukerji, Chandra. 1997. *Territorial Ambitions and the Gardens of Versailles.* Cambridge: Cambridge University Press.

Muldoon, James. 1977. *The Expansion of Europe: The First Phase.* Philadelphia: University of Pennsylvania Press.

———. 1979. *Popes, Lawyers, and Infidels: The Church and the Non-Christian World, 1250–1550.* Philadelphia: University of Pennsylvania Press.

———. 1980. "John Wyclif and the Rights of Infidels: The Requerimiento Re-Examined." *The Americas* 36 (3): 301–16.

Munayyer, Yousef. 2012. "When Settlers Attack." The Palestine Center, Washington, DC. www.thejerusalemfund.org/wp-content/uploads/2016/06/WhenSettlersAttack-1329158069-document-32677.pdf.

Mundy, Martha. 1994. "Village Land and Individual Title: Musha' and Ottoman Land Registration in the 'Ajlun District." In *Village, Steppe, and State: The Social Origins of Modern Jordan*, edited by Eugene L. Rogan and Tariq Tell, 58–79. London: British Academic Press.

———. 2010. "Islamic Law and the Order of State: The Legal Status of the Cultivator." In *Syria and Bilad al-Sham under Ottoman Rule: Essays in Honour of Abdul-Karim Rafeq*, edited by Peter Sluglett and Stefan Weber, 399–420. Leiden: E. J. Brill.

Mundy, Martha, and Richard Saumarez Smith. 2007. *Governing Property, Making the Modern State: Law, Administration, and Production in Ottoman Syria.* New York: I. B. Tauris.

Myers, David. 1988. "History as Ideology: The Case of Ben Zion Dinur, Zionist Historian 'Par Excellence.'" *Modern Judaism,* May, 167–93. www.sscnet.ucla.edu/history/myers/CV/History_as_Ideology.pdf.

———. 1995. *Re-inventing the Jewish Past: European Jewish Intellectuals and the Zionist Return to History.* New York: Oxford University Press.

Myers, Jody. 1991. "The Messianic Idea and Zionist Ideologies." In *Jews and Messianism in the Early Modern Era: Metaphor and Meaning,* edited by Jonathan Frankel, 3–13. Oxford: Oxford University Press.

———. 2003. *Seeking Zion: Modernity and Messianic Activism in the Writings of Tsevi Hirsch Kalischer.* Oxford: Littman Library of Jewish Civilization.

Nabokov, Peter. 1998. "Orientations from their Side: Dimensions of Native American Cartographic Discourse." In *Cartographic Encounters: Perspectives on Native American Mapmaking and Map Use,* edited by G. Malcolm Lewis, 241–69. Chicago: University of Chicago Press.

Nadan, Amos. 2003. "Colonial Misunderstanding of an Efficient Peasant Institution: Land Settlement and Mushā Tenure in Mandate Palestine, 1921–47." *Journal of the Economic and Social History of the Orient* 46 (3): 320–54.

Naff, Thomas, and Roger Owen, eds. 1977. *Studies in Eighteenth- Century Islamic History.* Carbondale: Southern Illinois University Press.

Nash, Gary B. 1972. "The Image of the Indian in the Southern Colonial Mind." *William and Mary Quarterly* 29 (2): 198–230.

Nasrallah, Rami. 2014. "Planning the Divide: Israel's 2020 Master Plan and Its Impact on East Jerusalem." In *Decolonizaing Palestinian Political Economy: Dedevelopment and Beyond,* edited by Mandy Turner and Omar Shweiki, 158–75. New York: Palgrave Macmillan.

Nassar, Issam. 2009. "Photography as Source Material for Jerusalem's Social History." In *Transformed Landscapes: Essays on Palestine and the Middle East in Honor of Walid Khalidi,* edited by Camille Mansour and Leila Tarazi Fawaz, 137–57. Cairo: The American University in Cairo Press.

National Library of Israel. N.d. "War of the Languages." http://web.nli.org.il/sites/NLI/English/collections/israel-collection/language_war/Pages/default.aspx.

Neeson, Jeanette M. 1984. "The Opponents of Enclosure in Eighteenth-Century Northamptonshire." *Past & Present,* no. 105: 114–39.

———. 1993. *Commoners: Common Right, Enclosure, and Social Change in England, 1700–1820.* Cambridge: Cambridge University Press.

Negev Coexistence Forum for Civil Equality. 2011. *The Demolition of Arab Bedouin Homes in the Negev-Naqab.* www.dukium.org/wp-content/uploads/2011/06/Demolitions_Report_2011-for-print.pdf.

———. 2014. *The House Demolition Policy in the Negev-Naqab.* www.dukium.org/wp-content/uploads/2014/12/HDR_2014_Egnlish_web.pdf.

———. 2015. *Community Under Attack: The Situation of the Human Rights of the Bedouin Community in the Negev-Naqab 2015.* www.dukium.org/wp-content/uploads/2015/12/HRDR_2015_ENG.pdf.

————. 2016. "Segregated Spaces: The Spatial Discrimination Policies among Jewish and Arab Citizens in the Negev-Naqab." www.dukium.org/wp-content/uploads/2016/03/IDARD_ENG_WEB-1.pdf.

————. 2017. *Discrimination in Numbers: Collection of Statistical Data – The Bedouin of the Negev-Naqab.* www.dukium.org/wp-content/uploads/2014/07/DINSC_JAN_2017_ENG.pdf.

Nelson Limerick, Patricia. 1987. *The Legacy of Conquest: The Unbroken Past of the American West.* New York: W. W. Norton.

Netzloff, Mark, ed. 2010. *John Norden's "The Surveyor's Dialogue" (1618): A Critical Edition.* Farnham, UK: Ashgate.

Neumann, Boaz. 2011. *Land and Desire in Early Zionism.* Waltham, MA: Brandeis University Press.

Nevo, Issac. 2003. "The Politics of Un-recognition: Bedouin Villages in the Israeli Negev." *HAGAR: Studies in Culture, Polity, and Identities* 4 (1–2): 183–201.

Newman, David. 2001. "From National to Post-National Territorial Identities in Israel-Palestine." *GeoJournal* 53 (3): 235–46.

Nichols, Roger L. 2003. *American Indians in U.S. History.* Norman: University of Oklahoma Press.

Noach, Haia. 2014. "The Government's Plan for the Dispossession of the Bedouin from Its Lands, the Demolition of Its Historic Villages, and Its Forced Resettlement in Townships." *Negev Coexistence Forum Newsletter,* no. 20: 1–2.

Nobles, Gregory. 1993. "Straight Lines and Stability: Mapping the Political Order of the Anglo-American Frontier." *Journal of American History* 80 (1): 9–35.

Norden, John. 1607a. *The Surveyor's Dialogue.* 2nd ed. London: Thomas Snodham, 1610. http://gateway.proquest.com/openurl?ctx_ver=Z39.88-2003&res_id=xri:eebo&rft_id=xri:eebo:image:13664.

————. 1607b. *The Surveyor's Dialogue.* 4th ed., 1738. http://find.galegroup.com/ecco/infomark.do?&source=gale&prodId=ECCO&userGroupName=ucsandiego&tabID=T001&docId=CW3309364822&type=multipage&contentSet=ECCOArticles&version=1.0&docLevel=FASCIMILE.

O'Brien, Jean M. 1997. *Dispossession by Degrees: Indian Land and Identity in Natick, Massachusetts.* Cambridge: Cambridge University Press.

Ofran, Hagit. 2009. "Despite Promises—Land Confiscation Continues throughout 2008–2009." [Document in author's possession.]

Ogborn, Miles. 1998. *Spaces of Modernity: London's Geographies, 1600–1811.* London: Guilford Press.

Ogborn, Miles, and Charles W. J. Withers. 2004. *Georgian Geographies: Essays on Space, Place, and Landscape in the Eighteenth Century.* Manchester: Manchester University Press.

Oliver, Lisi. 2012. *The Beginnings of English Law.* Toronto: University of Toronto Press.

Ornan, Uzzi. 1984. "Hebrew and Palestine before and after 1882." *Journal of Semitic Studies* 29 (2): 225–54.

Orwin, C. S. 1938. "Observations on the Open Fields." *Economic History Review* 8 (2): 125–35.

Ostler, Jeffrey. 2004. *The Plains Sioux and U.S. Colonialism from Lewis and Clark to Wounded Knee.* Cambridge: Cambridge University Press.

Ottoman Land Code. 1892. Translated from the Turkish by F. Ongley. London: William F. Clowes and Sons. https://ia902605.us.archive.org/4/items/ottoman-landcodeooturkuoft/ottomanlandcodeooturkuoft.pdf.

Outhwaite, R. B. 1986. "Progress and Backwardness in English Agriculture, 1055–1650." *Economic History Review* 39 (1): 1–18.

Overton, Mark. 2004. *Agricultural Revolution in England: The Transformation of the Agrarian Economy, 1500—1850.* Cambridge: Cambridge University Press.

Owen, Roger. 1982. *Studies in the Economic and Social History of Palestine in the Nineteenth and Twentieth Centuries.* Carbondale: Southern Illinois University Press.

———. 2000. *New Perspectives on Property and Land in the Middle East.* Cambridge, MA: Harvard University Press.

Pagden, Anthony. 1995. *Lords of All the World: Ideologies of Empire in Spain, Britain, and France, c. 1500–c. 1800.* New Haven, CT: Yale University Press.

Palmer, E. H. 1871. *The Desert of the Exodus: Journeys on Foot in the Wilderness of the Forty Years' Wanderings.* Pt. 2. Cambridge: Deighton, Bell, and Co.

———. 1881. *The Survey of Western Palestine: Arabic and English Names List.* Transliterated and explained by E. H. Palmer. London: Committee of the Palestine Exploration Fund. http://babel.hathitrust.org/cgi/pt?id=ien.3555603474891 3;view=1up;seq=7;size=175.

Pamuk, Sevket. 2004. "The Evolution of Financial Institutions in the Ottoman Empire, 1600–1914." *Financial History Review* 11 (1): 7–32.

Pappe, Ilan. 2004. *A History of Modern Palestine: One Land, Two Peoples.* Cambridge: Cambridge University Press.

———. 2010. "Zionizing the Palestinian Space: Historical and Historiographical Perspectives." *Makan* 2: 9–21. www.academia.edu/1392987/Makan_Adalah_s_Journal_for_Land_Planning_and_Justice.

———. 2015. "The Forgotten Victims of Palestine Ethnic Cleansing." In *The Naqab Bedouin and Colonialism: New Perspectives,* edited by Mansour Nasasra et al., 57–68. London: Routledge.

Parfitt, T. V. 1972. "The Use of Hebrew in Palestine, 1800–1882." *Journal of Semitic Studies* 17 (2): 237–52.

———. 1984. "The Contribution of the Old Yishuv to the Revival of Hebrew." *Journal of Semitic Studies* 29 (2): 255–65.

Parker, Linda Sue. 1989. *Native American Estate: The Struggle over Indian and Hawaiian Land.* Honolulu: University of Hawai'i Press.

Patai, Raphael. 1949. "Musha'a Land Tenure and Cooperation in Palestine." *American Anthropologist* 51 (1): 436–45.

Patriquin, Larry. 2004. "The Agrarian Origins of the Industrial Revolution in England." *Review of Radical Political Economy* 36 (2): 196–216.

Patterson, David. 1964. *Abraham Mapu.* London: East and West Library.

———. 1981. "The Influence of Hebrew Literature on the Growth of Jewish Nationalism in the Nineteenth Century." *Hebrew Studies* 21: 103–12.

———. 2004. "Avraham Mapu." In *Encyclopedia of the Romantic Era, 1760–1850,* edited by Christopher John Murray, 710–11. New York: Fitzroy Dearborn.

———. 2006. Introduction to Abraham Mapu, *The Love of Zion and Other Writings.* New Milford, CT: Toby Press.

Pattison, William D. 1979. *The Beginnings of the Rectangular Survey System, 1784–1800.* New York: Arno Press.

Pauketat, Timothy R. 2004. *Ancient Cahokia and the Mississippians.* Cambridge: Cambridge University Press.

Payne, Christina. 1993. *Images of the Agricultural Landscape in England, 1780–1890.* New Haven, CT: Yale University Press.

Pearce, Margaret Wickens. 1998. "Native Mapping in Southern New England Indian Deeds." In *Cartographic Encounters: Perspectives on Native American Mapmaking and Map Use,* edited by G. Malcolm Lewis, 157–86. Chicago: University of Chicago Press.

Pearce, Roy Harvey. 1988. *Savagism and Civilization: A Study of the Indian and the American Mind.* Berkeley: University of California Press.

Pelli, Moshe. 2010. *Haskalah and Beyond: The Reception of the Hebrew Enlightenment and the Emergence of Haskalah Judaism.* Lanham, MD: Rowman and Littlefield.

Penslar, Derek. 1991. *Zionism and Technocracy: The Engineering of Jewish Settlement in Palestine, 1870–1918.* Bloomington: Indiana University Press.

———. 2001. "Zionism, Colonialism, and Postcolonialism." *Journal of Israeli History: Politics, Society, Culture* 20 (2–3): 84–98.

———. 2005. "Herzl and the Palestinian Arabs: Myth and Counter-Myth." *Journal of Israeli History* 24 (1): 65–77.

Perdue, Theda, and Michael D. Green. 2008. *The Cherokee Nation and the Trail of Tears.* New York: Penguin Books.

Perelman, Michael. 2000. *The Invention of Capitalism: Classical Political Economy and the Secret of Primitive Accumulation.* Durham, NC: Duke University Press.

Perreault, Melanie. 2007. "American Wilderness and First Contact." In *American Wilderness: A New History,* edited by Michael Lewis, 15–33. Oxford: Oxford University Press.

Peteet, Julie. 2005. "Words as Interventions: Naming in the Palestine/Israeli Conflict." *Third World Quarterly* 26 (1): 153–72.

Pfeffer, Anshel. 2010. "Bil'in Protesters Dismantle Section of West Bank Separation Barrier." *Haaretz,* February 19. www.haaretz.com/news/bil-in-protesters-dismantle-section-of-west-bank-separation-barrier-1.263651.

Philo, Chris. 2011. "Michel Foucault." In *Key Thinkers on Space and Place,* edited by Phil Hubbard et al., 162–70. London: Sage.

Piker, Joshua A. 2003. "'White & Clean & Contested': Creek Towns and Trading Paths in the Aftermath of the Seven Years War." *Ethnohistory* 50 (2): 315–47.

Pinsker, Leo. 1882. "Auto-Emancipation: An Appeal to His People by a Russian Jew." In *The Zionist Idea: An Historical Analysis and Reader,* edited by Arthur Hertzberg, 181–98. Philadelphia: Jewish Publication Society, 1997.

Pirinoli, Christiane. 2005. "Erasing Palestine to Build Israel: Landscape Transformation and the Rooting of National Identities." *Etudes Rurales,* no. 173/174: 67–85. www.cairn-int.info/article-E_ETRU_173_0067-erasing-palestine-to-build-israel.htm.

POICA. 2013. "Increased Attacks on Nahhalin." April 23. http://poica.org/2013/04/increased-attacks-on-nahhalin.

Postgate, M. R. 1973. "Field Systems of East Anglia." In *Studies of Field Systems in the British Isles,* edited by Aland R. H. Baker and Robin Butlin, 281–324. Cambridge: Cambridge University Press.

Press, I. 1925. "Arbel in the Valley of Jezreel." *Proceedings of the Jewish Palestine Exploration Society* 1 (2–4): 87–91.

Prucha, Francis Paul, ed. 2000. *Documents of United States Indian Policy.* Lincoln: University of Nebraska Press.

Quataert, Donald, 1994. "The Age of Reforms, 1812–1914." In *An Economic and Social History of the Ottoman Empire, 1300–1914,* edited by Halil Inalcik and Donald Quataert, 759–985. Cambridge: Cambridge University Press.

Quitt, Martin H. 1995. "Trade and Acculturation at Jamestown, 1607–1609: The Limits of Understanding." *William and Mary Quarterly* 52 (2): 227–58.

Raanan, Yeela. 2010. "The JNF in the Naqab." *al-Majdal,* no. 43: 34–38. www.badil.org/phocadownload/Badil_docs/publications/al-majdal-43.pdf.

Raban, Sandra. 2004. *A Second Domesday? The Hundred Rolls of 1279–80.* Oxford: Oxford University Press.

Rackham, Oliver. 1986. *The History of the Countryside.* London: J. M. Dent.

Rafeq, Abdel Karim. 1981. "Economic Relations between Damascus and the Dependent Countryside." In *The Islamic Middle East, 700–1900: Studies in Economic and Social History,* edited by A. L. Udovititch, 653–96. Princeton, NJ: Darwin Press.

———. 2008. "The Economic Organization of Cities in Ottoman Syria." In *The Urban Social History of the Middle East, 1750–1950,* edited by Peter Sluglett, 104–40. Syracuse, NY: Syracuse University Press.

Ram, Uri. 1995. "Zionist Historiography and the Invention of Modern Jewish Nationhood: The Case of Ben-Zion Dinur." *History and Memory* 7 (1): 91–124.

———. 2009. "Ways of Forgetting: Israel and the Obliterated Memory of the Palestinian Nakba." *Journal of Historical Sociology* 22 (3): 366–95.

———. 2011. *Israeli Nationalism: Social Conflicts and the Politics of Knowledge.* London: Routledge.

Randall, Adrian, and Andrew Charlesworth, eds. 2000. *Moral Economy and Popular Protest: Crowds, Conflict and Authority.* New York: St. Martin's Press.

Ravenhill, William, ed. 1992. *Christopher Saxton's Sixteenth-Century Maps : The Counties of England and Wales.* Shrewsbury, UK: Chatsworth Library.

Raylor, Timothy. 1992. "Samuel Hartlib and the Commonwealth of Bees." In *Culture and Cultivation in Early Modern England: Writing and the Land,* edited by Michael Leslie and Timothy Raylor, 91–129. Leicester: University of Leicester Press.

RCUV (Regional Council for Unrecognized Villages)/BIMKOM (Planners for Planning Rights). 2012. "Alternative Master Plan for the Unrecognized Bedouin Villages in the Negev." http://bimkom.org/eng/wp-content/uploads/Bedouin-Negev-Alternative-Master-Plan.pdf.

———. 2014. "A Master Plan for the Unrecognized Bedouin Villages in the Negev. Selected Sections Updated 2014." Planning Team: Oren Yiftachel, Nili Baruch, Said Abu Sammur, Nava Sheer, Ronen Ben Arie. [Document in author's possession.]

Reed, Michael, ed. 1984. *Discovering Past Landscapes.* London: Croom Helm.

———. 1987. "Enclosure in North Buckinghamshire, 1500–1750." *Agricultural History Review* 32 (2): 133–44.

———. 1990. *The Landscape of Britain: From the Beginnings to 1914.* London: Routledge.

Reid, Charles J., Jr. 1995. "The Seventeenth-Century Revolution in the English Land Law." *Cleveland State Law Review* 43: 221–302.

Reilly, James. 1981. "The Peasantry of Late Ottoman Palestine." *Journal of Palestine Studies* 10 (4): 82–97.

Reiter, Yitzhak. 2009. *National Minority, Regional Majority: Palestinian Arabs versus Jews in Israel.* Syracuse, NY: Syracuse University Press.

Richter, Daniel K. 2001. *Facing East from Indian Country: A Native History of Early America.* Cambridge, MA: Harvard University Press.

Ridner, Judith. 2011. "Building Urban Spaces for the Interior: Thomas Penn and the Colonization of Eighteenth-Century Pennsylvania." In *Early American Cartographies,* edited by Martin Brückner, 306–38. Chapel Hill: University of North Carolina Press.

Roberts, B. K. 1973. "Field Systems of the West Midlands." *Studies of Field Systems in the British Isles,* edited by Alan R. H. Baker and Robin Butlin, 188–231. Cambridge: Cambridge University Press.

Roberts, Jo. 2013. *Contested Land, Contested Memory: Israel's Jews and Arabs and the Ghosts of Catastrophe.* Toronto: Dundurn.

Robertson, Lindsay G. 2005. *Conquest by Law: How the Discovery of America Dispossessed Indigenous Peoples of Their Lands.* Oxford: Oxford University Press.

Robertson, William. 1800. *The History of America.* 8th ed. Edinburgh: A. Strahan.

Robinson, Nicola. 2013. "Utopian Zionist Development in Theodor Herzl's *Altneuland.*" *Green Letters: Studies in Ecocriticism* 17 (3): 223–35.

Rollison, David. 1984. "Property, Ideology, and Popular Culture in a Gloucestershire Village, 1660–1740." In *Rebellion, Popular Protest, and the Social Order in Early Modern England,* edited by Paul Slack, 294–321. Cambridge: Cambridge University Press.

Rosen-Zvi, Issachar. 2004. *Taking Space Seriously: Law, Space, and Society in Contemporary Israel.* Burlington, VT: Ashgate.

Rotberg, Robert I. 2006. *Israeli and Palestinian Narratives of Conflict: History's Double Helix.* Bloomington: Indiana University Press.

Rotem, Guy, Amos Bouskila, and Alon Rothschild. 2014. *Ecological Effects of Afforestation in the Northern Negev.* Translated by Zev Labinger. [Tel Aviv:] Society for the Protection of Nature in Israel. www.teva.org.il/GetFile.asp?CategoryID =1698&ArticleID=19415&ID=7679

Rountree, Helen C. 1989. *The Powhatan Indians: Their Traditional Culture.* Norman: University of Oklahoma Press.

Rowley, Trevor. 1982. "Medieval Field Systems." In *The English Medieval Landscape,* edited by Leonard Cantor, 25–55. Philadelphia: University of Pennsylvania Press.

Rubies, Joan-Pau. 2009. "Text, Images and the Perception of 'Savages' in Early Modern Europe: What We Can Learn from White and Harriot." In *European Visions, American Voices,* edited by Kim Sloan, 120–30. London: British Museum Press.

Rubin, G. R., and David Sugarman, eds. 1984. *Law, Economy, and Society, 1750–1914: Essays in the History of English Law.* Abingdon, UK: Professional Books.

Sack, Robert David. 1986. *Human Territoriality: Its Theory and History.* Cambridge: Cambridge University Press.

Saenz-Badillos, Angel. 1993. *A History of the Hebrew Language.* Cambridge: Cambridge University Press.

Safran, William. 2005. "Language and Nation Building in Israel: Hebrew and Its Rivals." *Nations and Nationalism* 11 (1): 43–63.

Said, Edward. 1978. *Orientalism: Western Conceptions of the Orient.* London: Kegan Paul.

———. 1993. *Culture and Imperialism.* New York: Alfred A. Knopf.

———. 1995. "Projecting Jerusalem." *Journal of Palestine Studies* 25 (1): 5–14.

———. 2000. "Invention, Memory, and Place." *Critical Inquiry* 26 (2): 175–92.

Salisbury, Neil. 1998. "The Best Poor Man's Country as Middle Ground? Mainstreaming Indians in Early American Studies." *Reviews in American History* 26 (3): 497–503.

———. 2007. "The Indians' Old World: Native Americans and the Coming of Europeans." In *American Encounters: Natives and Newcomers from European Contact to Indian Removal, 1500–1850,* 2nd ed., edited by Peter C. Mancall and James H. Merrell, 3–25. London: Routledge. [Originally published in *William and Mary Quarterly* 53 (1996): 435–58.]

Saposnik, Arieh Bruce. 2008. *Becoming Hebrew: The Creation of a Jewish National Culture in Ottoman Palestine.* Oxford: Oxford University Press.

Sauer, Carl O. 1925. "The Morphology of Landscape." In *Land and Life: A Selection from the Writings of Carl Ortwin Sauer,* edited by John Leighly, 315–50. Berkeley: University of California Press, 1963.

Saulson, Scott B. 1979. *Institutionalized Language Planning: Documents and Analysis of the Revival of Hebrew.* The Hague: Mouton.

Saunt, Claudio. 1999. *A New Order of Things: Property, Power, and the Transformation of the Creek Indians, 1733–1816.* Cambridge: Cambridge University Press.

———. 2000. "Taking Account of Property: Stratification among the Creek Indians in the Early Nineteenth Century." *William and Mary Quarterly* 57 (4): 733–60.

Sayigh, Rosemary. 1979. *The Palestinians: From Peasants to Revolutionaries—A People's History.* London: Zed Press.

Schaebler, Birgit. 2000. "Practicing Musha': Common Lands and the Common Good in Southern Syria under the Ottomans and the French." In *New Perspectives on Property and Land in the Middle East,* edited by Roger Owen, 241–307. Cambridge, MA: Harvard University Press.

Schechter, Yitzhak. 1985. "Land Registration in Eretz-Israel in the Second Half of the Nineteenth Century." *Cathedra,* no. 45: 147–59.

Schein, Richard H. 1997. "The Place of Landscape: A Conceptual Framework for Interpreting an American Scene." *Annals of the Association of American Geographers* 87 (4): 660–80.

Schnell, Izhak. 1997. "Nature and Environment in the Socialist Pioneers' Perceptions: A Sense of Desolation." *Cultural Geographies* 4 (1): 69–85.

Schnell, Izhak, and Christine Leuenberger. 2014. "Mapping Genres and Geopolitics: The Case of Israel." *Transactions of the Institute of British Geographers* 39: 1–14.

Schölch, Alexander. 1982. "European Penetration and Economic Development of Palestine, 1856–1882." In *Studies in the Economic and Social History of Palestine in the Nineteenth and Twentieth Centuries,* edited by Roger Own, 10–87. London: Palgrave Macmillan.

———. 1984. "Was There a Feudal System in Ottoman Lebanon?" In *Palestine in the Late Ottoman Period: Political, Social, and Economic Transformation,* edited by David Kushner, 130–45. Leiden: E. J. Brill.

———. 1985. "The Demographic Development of Palestine, 1850–1882." *International Journal of Middle East Studies* 17 (4): 485–505.

———. 1988. "The Emergence of Modern Palestine (1856–1882)." In *Studia Palaestina: Studies in Honor of Constantine K. Zurayk,* edited by Hisham Nashabe, 69–82. Beirut: Institute for Palestine Studies.

Schorr, David B. 2014. "Forest Law in Mandate Palestine." In *Managing the Unknown: Essays on Environmental Ignorance,* edited by Frank Uekotter and Uwe Lübken, 71–90. New York: Berghahn Books.

Scott, James C. 1998. *Seeing Like a State: How Certain Schemes to Improve the Human Condition Have Failed.* New Haven, CT: Yale University Press.

Seed, Patricia. 1992. "Taking Possession and Reading Texts: Establishing the Authority of Overseas Empires." *William and Mary Quarterly* 49 (2): 183–209.

———. 1995. "Houses, Gardens, and Fences: Signs of English Possession in the New World." In *Ceremonies of Possession in Europe's Conquest of the New World, 1492–1640,* 16–40. Cambridge: Cambridge University Press.

———. 2001. *American Pentimento: The Invention of Indians and the Pursuit of Riches.* Minneapolis: University of Minnesota Press.

Segev, Tom. 1986. *1949: The First Israelis.* New York: Free Press.

————. 2001. *One Palestine, Complete: Jews and Arabs under the British Mandate.* New York: Henry Holt.

Seikaly, Samir M, 1984. "Land Tenure in Seventeenth-Century Palestine: The Evidence from the al-Fatâwâ al-Khairiyya." In *Land Tenure and Social Transformation in the Middle East,* edited by Tarif Khalidi, 397–408. Beirut: American University of Beirut.

Seipp, David. J. 1994. "The Concept of Property in the Early Common Law." *Law and History Review* 12 (1): 29–91.

Selwyn, Tom. 2001. "Landscapes of Separation: Reflections on the Symbolism of By-pass Roads in Palestine." In *Contested Landscapes,* edited by Barbara Bender and Margot Winer, 225–40. Oxford: Berg.

Shachar, Ari. 1998. "Reshaping the Map of Israel: A New National Planning Doctrine." *Annals of the Academy of Political and Social Sciences* 555 (1): 209–18.

Shafir, Gershon. 1996. *Land, Labor, and the Origins of the Israeli-Palestinian Conflict, 1882–1914.* Berkeley: University of California Press.

Shafir, Gershon, and Yoav Peled. 2002. *Being Israeli: The Dynamics of Multiple Citizenship.* Cambridge: Cambridge University Press.

Shahak, Israel. 1989. "A History of the Concept of 'Transfer' in Zionism." *Journal of Palestine Studies* 18 (3): 22–37.

Shamir, Ronen. 1990. "Landmark Cases and the Reproduction of Legitimacy: The Case of Israel's High Court of Justice." *Law and Society Review* 24 (3): 781–806.

————. 1996. "Suspended in Space: Bedouins under the Law of Israel." *Law and Society Review* 30 (2): 231–58.

————. 2000. *The Colonies of Law: Colonialism, Zionism, and Law in Early Mandate Palestine.* Cambridge: Cambridge University Press.

————. 2002. "The Comrades Law of Hebrew Workers in Palestine: A Study in Socialist Justice." *Law and History Review* 20 (2): 279–305.

Shannon, Bill. 2011. "Approvement and Improvement in Lowland Wastes of Early Modern Lancashire." In *Custom, Improvement, and the Landscape in Early Modern Britain,* edited by R. W. Hoyle, 175–202. Burlington, VT: Ashgate.

Shapira, Anita. 1992. *Land and Power: The Zionist Resort to Force.* New York: Oxford University Press.

Sharp, Buchanan. 2000. "The Food Riots of 1347 and the Medieval Moral Economy." In *Moral Economy and Popular Protest: Crowds, Conflict, and Authority,* edited by Andrew Charlesworth and Adrian Randall. London: Macmillan.

Shaw, Stanford J. 1975. "The Nineteenth-Century Ottoman Tax Reforms and Revenue System." *International Journal of Middle East Studies* 6 (4): 421–59.

Shaw-Taylor, Leigh. 2001. "Labourers, Cows, Common Rights, and Parliamentary Enclosure: The Evidence of Contemporary Comment, c. 1760–1810." *Past & Present,* no. 171: 95–126.

Shehadeh, Raja. 1982. "The Land Law of Palestine: An Analysis of the Definition of State Lands." *Journal of Palestine Studies* 11 (2): 82–99.

————. 1997. *From Occupation to Interim Accords: Israel and the Palestinian Territories.* Cambridge: Kluwer Law.

————. 2008. *Palestinian Walks: Forays into a Vanishing Landscape.* New York: Scribner.

Shlay, Anne B., and Gillad Rosen. 2010. "Making Place: The Shifting Green Line and the Development of 'Greater' Metropolitan Jerusalem." *City and Community* 9 (4): 358–89.

Shmuelevitz, Aryeh. 1984. *The Jews of the Ottoman Empire in the Late Fifteenth and the Sixteenth Centuries: Administrative, Economic, Legal, and Social Relations as Reflected in the Responsa.* Leiden: E. J. Brill.

Shmueli, Deborah F., and Rassem Khamaisi. 2015. *Israel's Invisible Negev Bedouin: Issues of Land and Spatial Planning.* New York: Springer.

Short, Brian, ed. 1992. *The English Rural Community: Image and Analysis.* Cambridge: Cambridge University Press.

Short, John Rennie. 2004. *Making Space: Revisioning the World, 1475–1600.* Syracuse, NY: Syracuse University Press.

Shragai, Nadav. 2010. "Demography, Geopolitics, and the Future of Israel's Capital: Jerusalem's Proposed Master Plan." Jerusalem Center for Public Affairs. http://jcpa.org/text/jerusalem-master-plan.pdf.

Singer, Amy. 1994. *Palestinian Peasants and Ottoman Officials: Rural Administration around Sixteenth-Century Jerusalem.* Cambridge: Cambridge University Press.

Skelton, R. A. 1970. "The Military Surveyor's Contribution to British Cartography in the Sixteenth Century." *Imago Mundi* 24: 77–83.

Skelton, R. A., and P. D. A. Harvey. 1986. *Local Maps and Plans from Medieval England.* Oxford: Clarendon Press.

Skocpol, Theda, ed. 1984. *Vision and Method in Historical Sociology.* Cambridge: Cambridge University Press.

————. 2003. "Doubly Engaged Social Science: The Promise of Comparative Historical Analysis." In *Comparative Historical Analysis in the Social Sciences,* edited by James Mahoney and Dietrich Rueschemeyer, 407–27. Cambridge: Cambridge University Press.

Sloan, Kim. 2007. *A New World: England's First View of America.* Chapel Hill: University of North Carolina Press.

Sluglett, Peter, and Marion Farouk-Sluglett. 1984. "The Application of the 1858 Land Code in Greater Syria: Some Preliminary Observations." In *Land Tenure and Social Transformation in the Middle East,* edited by Tarif Khalidi, 409–21. Beirut: American University of Beirut.

Smit-Marais, Susan. 2011. "Converted Spaces, Contained Places: Robinson Crusoe's Monologic World." *Journal of Literary Studies* 27 (1): 102–14.

Smith, Adam. 1776. *An Inquiry into the Causes of the Wealth of Nations.* Oxford: Clarendon Press, 1976.

Smith, D. K. 2008. *The Cartographic Imagination in Early Modern England: Rewriting the World in Marlowe, Spenser, Raleigh, and Marvell.* London: Ashgate.

Smith, Henry E. 2000. "Semicommon Property Rights and Scattering in the Open Fields." *Journal of Legal Studies* 29 (1): 131–69.

Smolett, Tobias George. 1771. *The Expedition of Humphrey Clinker*. Vol. 3. London: W. Johnston.

Snell, K. D. M. 1985. *Annals of the Labouring Poor: Social Change and Agrarian England, 1660–1900*. Cambridge: Cambridge University Press.

———. 2006. *Parish and Belonging: Community, Identity, and Welfare in England and Wales, 1700–1950*. Cambridge: Cambridge University Press.

Soffer, Arnon, and Yoram Bar-Gal. 1985. "Planned Sedentarization of Bedouins in Israel." *Geoforum* 16 (4): 425–28.

Spence, Mark David. 2000. *Dispossessing the Wilderness: Indian Removal and the Making of the National Parks*. New York: Oxford University Press, 2000.

Stein, Kenneth. 1984. *The Land Question in Palestine, 1917–1939*. Chapel Hill: University of North Carolina Press.

———. 1987. "Palestine's Rural Economy, 1917–1939." *Studies in Zionism* 8 (1): 25–49.

Stein, Rebecca L. 2009. "Travelling Zion: Hiking and Settler-Nationalism in Pre-1948 Palestine." *Interventions: International Journal of Postcolonial Studies* 11 (3): 334–51.

Sternhell, Zeev. 1998. *The Founding Myths of Israel: Nationalism, Socialism, and the Making of the Jewish State*. Princeton: Princeton University Press.

Strachey, William. 1612. *The Historie of Travaile into Virgina Britannia; Expressing the Cosmographie and Commodities of the Country Together with the Manners and Customes of the People*. Edited by R. H. Major. London: Hakluyt Society, 1849.

Stuart, David E. 2000. *Anasazi America*. Albuquerque: University of New Mexico Press.

Sufian, Sandy. 2005. "Re-imagining Palestine: Scientific Knowledge and Malaria Control in Mandatory Palestine." *DYNAMIS: Acta Hispanica ad Medicinae Scientiarumque Historiam Illustrandam* 25: 351–82. http://ddd.uab.cat/pub/dynamis/02119536v25p351.pdf.

Sullivan, James. 1801. *The History of Land Titles in Massachusetts*. Boston: I. Thomas and E. T. Andrews.

Sutton, Imre. 1975. *Indian Land Tenure: Bibliographical Essays and a Guide to the Literature*. New York: Clearwater.

Swedenburg, Ted. 1990. "The Palestinian Peasant as National Signifier." *Anthropological Quarterly* 63 (1): 18–30.

———. *Memories of Revolt: The 1936–1939 Rebellion and the Palestinian National Past*. Minneapolis: University of Minnesota Press.

Swirski, Shlomo. 2008. "Transparent Citizens: Israeli Government Policy toward the Negev Bedouins." *HAGAR: Studies in Culture, Polity, and Identities* 8 (2): 25–45.

Tabak, Faruk. 2009. "Agriculture in the Ottoman Empire." In *Encyclopedia of the Ottoman Empire*, edited by Gábor Ágoston and Bruce Masters, 19–21. New York: Facts on File. http://psi424.cankaya.edu.tr/uploads/files/Agoston and Masters, Enc of Ott Empire.PDF.

Tal, Alon. 2013. *All the Trees of the Forest: Israel's Woodlands from the Bible to the Present*. New Haven, CT: Yale University Press.

Tamari, Salim. 2002. "The Last Feudal Lord in Palestine." *Jerusalem Quarterly*, no. 16: 27–42.

———. 2004. "Ishaq al-Shami and the Predicament of the Arab Jew in Palestine." *Jerusalem Quarterly*, no. 21: 10–26.

———. 2005. "Heard Nothing, Seen Nothing." *Journal of Palestine Studies* 34 (3): 89–91.

———. 2006. "Jerusalem between Urban Area and Apparition: A Conversation on Jerusalem with Meron Benvenisti and Salim Tamari." In *City of Collision: Jerusalem and the Politics of Conflict Urbanism,* edited by Phillip Misselwitz and Tim Rieniets, 34–47. Basel: Birkhauser.

Tanner, Helen Hornbeck. 1995. *The Settling of North America: The Atlas of the Great Migrations into North America from the Ice Age to the Present.* New York: Macmillan.

Taraki, Lisa, ed. 2006. *Living Palestine: Family Survival, Resistance, and Mobility under Occupation.* Syracuse, NY: Syracuse University Press.

Tarlow, Sarah. 2007. *The Archeology of Improvement in Britain, 1750–1850.* Cambridge: Cambridge University Press.

Taub, Gadi. 2010. *The Settlers: And the Struggle over the Meaning of Zionism.* New Haven, CT: Yale University Press.

Taylor, Alan. 2001. *American Colonies: The Settling of North America.* New York: Penguin Books.

———. 2006. *The Divided Ground: Indians, Settlers, and the Northern Borderland of the American Revolution.* New York: Alfred A. Knopf.

Taylor, Alan R. 1974. *The Zionist Mind: The Origins and Development of Zionist Thought.* Beirut: Institute for Palestine Studies.

Taylor, Christopher. 1997. "Dorset and Beyond." In *Making English Landscapes: Changing Perspectives,* edited by Katherine Barker and Timothy Darvill, 9–25. Oxford: Oxbow Books.

Thirsk, Joan 1964. "The Common Fields." *Past and Present,* no. 29 (1): 3–25.

———. 1967a. "The Farming Regions of England." In *The Agrarian History of England and Wales,* vol. 4: *1500–1640,* edited by Joan Thirsk, 1–112. Cambridge: Cambridge University Press.

———. 1967b. "Enclosing and Engrossing." In *The Agrarian History of England and Wales,* vol. 4: *1500–1640,* edited by Joan Thirsk, 200–255. Cambridge: Cambridge University Press.

———. 1973. "Field Systems of the East Midlands." In *Studies of Field Systems in the British Isles,* edited by Alan R.H. Baker and Robin A. Butlin, 232–80. Cambridge: Cambridge University Press.

———. 1983. "Plough and Pen: Agricultural Writers in the Seventeenth Century." In *Social Relations and Ideas: Essays in Honour of R.H. Hilton,* edited by T.H. Aston, P.R. Coss, Christopher Dyer, and Joan Thirsk, 295–318. Cambridge: Cambridge University Press.

———. 1984. *The Rural Economy of England.* London: Hambledon Press.

———. 1985. "Agricultural Innovations and Their Diffusion." In *The Agrarian History of England and Wales,* vol. 5: *1640–1750,* pt. 2, edited by Joan Thirsk, 533–89. Cambridge: Cambridge University Press.

————. 1992a. "Making a Fresh Start: Sixteenth-Century Agriculture and the Classical Inspiration." In *Culture and Cultivation in Early Modern England: Writing and the Land,* edited by Michael Leslie and Timothy Raylor, 15–34. Leicester: University of Leicester Press.

————. 1992b. "English Rural Communities: Structures, Regularities, and Change in the Sixteenth and Seventeenth Centuries." In *The English Rural Community: Image and Analysis,* edited by Brian Short, 44–61. Cambridge: Cambridge University Press.

Thompson, E. P. 1963. *The Making of the English Working Class.* New York: Vintage Books.

————. 1971. "The Moral Economy of the English Crowd in the Eighteenth Century." *Past & Present,* no. 50: 76–136.

————. 1975. *Whigs and Hunters: The Origins of the Black Act.* London: Allen Lane.

————. 1991. *Customs in Common.* London: Merlin.

Thompson, F. M. L. 1966. "The Social Distribution of Landed Property." *Economic History Review.* Second Series. 19 (3): 505–17.

————. 1968. *Chartered Surveyors: The Growth of a Profession.* London: Routledge.

Thornton, Russell. 1987. *American Indian Holocaust and Survival: A Population History since 1492.* Norman: University of Oklahoma Press.

Tilly, Charles. 1984. *Big Structures, Large Processes, Huge Comparisons.* New York: Russell Sage.

Tishby, Ariel, ed. 2001. *Holy Land in Maps.* New York: St. Martin's Press.

Tomlins, Christopher. 2001. "The Legal Cartography of Colonization, the Legal Polyphony of Settlement: English Intrusions on the American Mainland in the Seventeenth Century." *Law and Social Inquiry* 26 (2): 315–72.

Tomlins, Christopher, and Bruce H. Mann, eds. 2001. *The Many Legalities of Early America.* Chapel Hill: University of North Carolina Press.

Townshend, Charles. 1989. "The First Intifada: Rebellion in Palestine 1936–39." *History Today* 39 (7). www.historytoday.com/charles-townshed/first-intifada-rebellion-palestine-1936-39.

Trigger, Bruce G., and William R. Swagerty. 1996. "Entertaining Strangers: North America in the Sixteenth Century." In *The Cambridge History of the Native Peoples of the Americas,* vol. 1: *North America,* edited by Bruce G. Trigger and Wilcomb E. Washburn, 325–98. Cambridge: Cambridge University Press.

Trigger, Bruce G., and Wilcomb E. Washburn, eds. 1996. *The Cambridge History of the Native Peoples of the Americas,* vol. 1: *North America.* Cambridge: Cambridge University Press.

Tripp, Charles. 2006. *Islam and the Moral Economy: The Challenge of Capitalism.* Cambridge: Cambridge University Press.

Tristam, H. B. 1865. *The Land of Israel: A Journal of Travels in Palestine.* London: Society for Promoting Christian Knowledge.

Troen, S. Ilan. 2003. *Imagining Zion: Dreams, Designs, and Realities in a Century of Jewish Settlement.* New Haven, CT: Yale University Press.

———. 2007. "De-Judaizing the Homeland: Academic Politics in Rewriting the History of Palestine." *Israel Affairs* 13 (4): 872–84.

Tuan, Yi-Fu. 2013. *Landscapes of Fear.* Minneapolis: University of Minnesota Press.

Tully, James. 1993. *An Approach to Political Philosophy: Locke in Contexts.* Cambridge: Cambridge University Press.

Turner, Michael E. 1976. "Parliamentary Enclosure and Population Change in England, 1750–1830." *Explorations in Economic History* 13 (4): 463–68.

———. 1980. *English Parliamentary Enclosure: Its Historical Geography and Economic History.* Folkestone, UK: William Dawson.

———. 1984a. *Enclosures in Britain, 1750–1830.* London: Macmillan.

———. 1984b. "The Landscape of Parliamentary Enclosure." In *Discovering Past Landscapes,* edited by Michael Reed, 132–66. London: Croom Helm.

———. 1988. "Economic Protest in a Rural Society: Opposition to Parliamentary Enclosure in Buckinghamshire." *Southern History* 10: 94–128.

Turner, G. L. E. 1983. "Mathematical Instrument-Making in London in the Sixteenth Century." In *English Map-Making, 1500–1650,* edited by Sarah Tyacke, 93–106. London: British Library.

———. 1991. "Introduction: Some Notes on the Development of Surveying and the Instruments Used." *Annals of Science* 48 (4): 313–17.

Tute, R. C. 1927. *The Ottoman Land Laws, with a Commentary on the Ottoman Land Code.* Jerusalem: Greek Convent Press.

Tyacke, Sarah. 1988. "Intersections or Disputed Territory." *Word and Image* 4 (2): 571–79.

Tyler, Warwick P. N. 2001. *State Lands and Rural Development in Mandatory Palestine, 1920–1948.* Brighton: Sussex Academic Press.

United Nations—Office for the Coordination of Humanitarian Affairs (OCHA). 2007. *The Humanitarian Impact on Palestinians of Israeli Settlements and Other Infrastructure in the West Bank.* https://unispal.un.org/pdfs/OchaRpt_Update-30July2007.pdf.

———. Occupied Palestinian Territory. 2009. *Restricting Space: The Planning Regime Applied in Area C of the West Bank.* Jerusalem.

———. 2011. *Restricting Space in the OPT: Area C Map.* www.ochaopt.org/documents/ochaopt_atlas_restricting_space_december2011.pdf.

Usner, Daniel H., Jr. 1987. "The Frontier Exchange Economy of the Lower Mississippi Valley in the Eighteenth Century." *William and Mary Quarterly* 44 (2): 165–92.

Vilnay, Zev. 1944. *The Hebrew Maps of Palestine: A Research in Hebrew Cartography.* Jerusalem: Jewish Palestine Exploration Society.

Wallach, Yair. 2011. "Trapped in Mirror-Images: The Rhetoric of Maps in Israel/Palestine." *Political Geography* 30 (7): 258–69.

Walton, J. R. 1990a. "Agriculture and Rural Society, 1730–1914." In *An Historical Geography of England and Wales,* edited by R. A. Dodgshon and R. A. Butlin, 323–50. London: Academic Press.

————. 1990b. "On Estimating the Extent of Parliamentary Enclosure." *Agricultural History Review* 38: 79–82.

Warde, Paul. 2011. "The Idea of Improvement, c. 1520–1700." In *Custom, Improvement, and the Landscape in Early Modern Britain,* edited by Richard W. Hoyle, 127–48. Burlington, VT: Ashgate.

Warhus, Mark. 1997. *Another America: Native American Maps and the History of Our Land.* New York: St. Martin's Press.

Warner, Debra Jean. 2005. "True North—and Why It Mattered in Eighteenth-Century America." *Proceedings of the American Philosophical Society* 149 (3): 372–85.

Warren, Louis S. 2004. "The Nature of Conquest: Indians, Americans, and Environmental History." In *A Companion to American Indian History,* edited by Philip J. Deloria and Neal Salisbury, 287–306. London: Blackwell.

Warriner, Doreen. 1948. *Land and Poverty in the Middle East.* London: Royal Institute of International Affairs.

Waselkov, Gregory A. 2006. "Indian Maps of the Colonial Southeast." In *Powhatan's Mantle: Indians in the Colonial Southeast,* edited by Gregory A. Waselkov et al., 435–502. Lincoln: University of Nebraska Press.

Waselkov, Gregory A., et al., eds. 2006. *Powhatan's Mantle: Indians in the Colonial Southeast.* Lincoln: University of Nebraska Press.

Waterman, Stanley. 1979. "Ideology and Events in Israeli Human Landscapes." *Geography* 64 (2): 171–81.

Weber, Max. 1904–5. *The Protestant Ethic and the Spirit of Capitalism.* Upper Saddle River, NJ: Prentice Hall, 1976.

Webster, Sarah. 2007. "Estate Improvement and the Professionalisation of Land Agents on the Egremont Estates in Sussex and Yorkshire, 1770–1835." *Rural History* 18 (1): 47–69.

Weitz, Joseph, 1974. *Forests and Afforestation in Israel.* Jerusalem: Masada Press.

Weizman, Eyal. 2007. *Hollow Land: Israel's Architecture of Occupation.* London: Verso.

Weizman, Eyal, and Fazal Sheikh. 2015. *The Conflict Shoreline: Colonization as Climate Change in the Negev Desert.* Brooklyn, NY: Steidl.

Wells, R. A. E. 1979. "The Development of the English Rural Proletariat and Social Protest, 1700–1850." *Journal of Peasant Studies* 7: 115–39.

Wessel, Thomas R. 1976. "Agriculture, Indians, and American History." *Agricultural History* 50 (1): 9–20.

White, Richard. 1983. *The Roots of Dependency: Subsistence, Environment, and Social Change among the Choctaws, Pawnees, and Navajos.* Lincoln: University of Nebraska Press.

————. 1991. *"It's Your Misfortune and None of My Own": A New History of the American West.* Norman: University of Oklahoma Press.

White, C. Albert. 1983. *A History of the Rectangular Survey System.* Washington DC: Federal Bureau of Land Management.

Whitney, Gordon G. 1994. *From Coastal Wilderness to Fruited Plain: A History of Environmental Change in Temperate North America, 1500 to the Present.* New York: Cambridge University Press.

Whittle, Jane. 2010. "Lords and Tenants in Kett's Rebellion." *Past & Present,* no. 207: 3–52.

Whyte, Ian. 2003. *Transforming Fell and Valley: Landscape and Parliamentary Enclosure in North West England.* Lancaster: University of Lancaster Center for North-West Regional Studies.

———. 2006a. "The Costs of Parliamentary Enclosure in an Upland Setting: South and East Cumbria, ca. 1760–1860." *Northern History* 43 (1): 97–115.

———. 2006b. "Parliamentary Enclosure and Changes in Landownership in an Upland Environment: Westmorland, c. 1770–1860." *Agricultural History Review* 54 (2): 240–56.

Whyte, Nicola. 2007. "Landscape, Memory, and Custom: Parish Identities ca. 1550–1700." *Social History* 32 (2): 166–86.

———. 2009. *Inhabiting the Landscape: Place, Custom, and Memory, 1500–1800.* Oxford: Windgather Press.

———. 2011. "Contested Pasts: Custom, Conflict, and Landscape in West Norfolk, 1550–1650." In *Custom, Improvement, and the Landscape in Early Modern Britain,* edited by Richard W. Hoyle, 101–25. Burlington, VT: Ashgate.

Widgren, Mats. 2006. "Reading Property into the Landscape." *Norwegian Journal of Geography* 60 (1): 57–64.

Wilkens, David E. 1993. "Modernization, Colonialism, Dependency: How Appropriate Are These Models for Providing an Explanation for North American Indian Underdevelopment?" *Ethnic and Racial Studies* 16 (3): 390–419.

Williams, Michael. 1989. *Americans and Their Forests: A Historical Geography.* Cambridge: Cambridge University Press.

Williams, Robert A. 1990. *The American Indian in Western Legal Thought: The Discourses of Conquest.* New York: Oxford University Press.

Williamson, Tom. 1992. "Enclosure and the English Hedgerow." In *The Cambridge Cultural History of Britain,* vol. 6: *The Romantic Age in Britain,* edited by Boris Ford, 263–71. Cambridge: Cambridge University Press.

———. 2000. "The Rural Landscape: 1500–1900, the Neglected Centuries." In *Landscape: The Richest Historical Record,* edited by Della Hooke, 111–17. London: Society for Landscape Studies.

———. 2002. *The Transformation of Rural England: Farming and the Landscape, 1700–1870.* Exeter: University of Exeter Press.

———. 2011. "Estate Landscapes in England: Interpretive Archaeologies." In *Interpreting the Early Modern World: Transatlantic Perspectives,* edited by Mary C. Beaudry and James Symonds, 25–44. New York: Springer.

Williamson, Tom, and Liz Bellamy. 1987. *Property and Landscape: A Social History of Land Ownership and the English Countryside.* London: George Philip.

Wilson, Nigel. 2016. "Israel Destroys Palestinian Village for 100th Time." *al-Jazeera,* July 3. www.aljazeera.com/news/2016/07/israel-destroys-palestinian-village-100th-time-160703091747401.html.

Winchester, Angus J. L. 2005. "Statute and Local Custom: Village Byelaws and the Governance of Common Land in Medieval and Early-Modern England." http://

dlc.dlib.indiana.edu/dlc/bitstream/handle/10535/1418/Winchester_145301
.pdf.

Winichakul, Thongchai, 1994. *Siam Mapped: A History of the Geo-body of a Nation.*
Honolulu: University of Hawai'i Press.

Wishart, David. 1994. *An Unspeakable Sadness: The Dispossession of the Nebraska
Indians.* Lincoln: University of Nebraska Press.

Withers, Charles W.J. 2007. *Placing the Enlightenment: Thinking Geographically
about the Age of Reason.* Chicago: University of Chicago Press.

Wordie, J.R. 1983. "The Chronology of English Enclosure." *Economic History
Review,* 2nd ser., 36 (4): 483–505.

Wright, John K. 1947. "Terrae Incognitae: The Place of the Imagination in Geography." *Annals of the Association of American Geographers* 37 (1): 1–15.

Wrightson, Keith. 2000. *Earthly Necessities: Economic Lives in Early Modern Britain.* New Haven, CT: Yale University Press.

Wrigley, E.A. 1989. "Urban Growth and Agricultural Change: England and the
Continent in the Early Modern Period." In *People, Cities, and Wealth: The Transformation of Traditional Society,* 157–93. Oxford: Basil Blackwell.

Wrigley, E.A., and R.S. Schofield. 1981. *The Population History of England, 1541–
1871: A Reconstruction.* London: Edward Arnold.

Yagna, Yanir. 2010. "Bedouin Blamed after 1,600 Trees in Negev Vandalized."
Haaretz, September 16. www.haaretz.com/bedouin-blamed-after-1–600-trees-
in-negev-vandalized-1.314045.

Yazbak, Mahmoud. 2000. "From Poverty to Revolt: Economic Factors in the Outbreak of the 1936 Rebellion in Palestine." *Middle Eastern Studies* 36 (3): 93–113.

Yelling, J.A. 1977. *Common Field and Enclosure in England, 1450–1850.* London:
Macmillan.

Yiftachel, Oren. 2006. *Ethnocracy: Land and Identity Politics in Israel/Palestine.*
Philadelphia: University of Pennsylvania Press.

———. 2013. "Naqab/Negev Bedouins and (Internal) Colonial Paradigm." In
*Indigenous (In)Justice: Human Rights Law and Bedouin Arabs in the Naqab/
Negev,* edited by Ahmad Amara, Ismael Abu-Saad, and Oren Yiftachel, 289–318.
Cambridge, MA: Harvard University Press.

Yiftachel, Oren, Ahmad Amara, and Sandy Kedar. 2013. "Debunking the 'Dead
Negev Doctrine.'" *Haaretz,* December 31. http://nomadicpeoples.info/pdf
/Debunking_the_Dead_Negev_Doctrine_Haaretz.pdf.

Yiftachel, Oren, Alexandre Kedar, and Ahmad Amara. 2012. "Questioning the
'Dead *(Mewat)* Negev Doctrine': Property Rights in Arab Bedouin Space."
Unpublished translation of "Rethinking the Dead Negev Doctrine: Property
Rights in Bedouin Regions," *Mishpat u-mimshal* [Law and Government] 14 (1):
7–147 (Hebrew). Used and quoted with permission.

Yiftachel, Oren, and Haim Yacobi. 2006. "Barriers, Walls, and Urban Ethnocracy
in Jerusalem." In *City of Collision: Jerusalem and the Principles of Conflict
Urbanism,* edited by Phillipp Misselwitz and Tim Rieniets, 170–75. Basel:
Birkhauser.

Yiftachel, Oren, Batya Roded, and Alexandre Kedar. 2016. "Between Rights and Denials: Bedouin Indigeneity in the Negev/Naqab." *Environment and Planning A* 48 (11): 2129–61. http://epn.sagepub.com/content/early/2016/07/20/03085 18X16653404.full.pdf.

Young, Arthur. 1768. *A Six Week Tour, through the Southern Counties of England and Wales.* London: W. Nicoll.

———. 1770. *A Six Months Tour through the North of England.* Vol. 4. London: W. Strahan.

———. 1771. *The Farmer's Tour through the East of England.* Vol. 2. London: W. Strahan and W. Nicoll.

———. 1774. *Political Arithmetic: Containing Observations on the Present State of Great Britain and the Principles of Her Policy in the Encouragement of Agriculture.* London: W. Nicoll.

———. 1792. *Travels during the Years 1787, 1788, and 1789.* Bury St. Edmund's: J. Rackham.

———. 1799. *General View of the Agriculture of the County of Lincoln.* London: W. Bulmer and Co.

———. 1801. *An Inquiry into the Propriety of Applying Wastes to the Better Maintenance and Support of the Poor.* Bury St. Edmund's: J. Rackham.

———. 1809. *General View of the Agriculture of Oxfordshire.* London: Sherwood, Neely, and Jones.

———. 1813. *General View of the Agriculture of Lincolnshire.* London: Sherwood, Neely, and Jones.

Zakai, Avihu. 1992. *Exile and Kingdom: History and Apocalypse in the Puritan Migration to America.* Cambridge: Cambridge University Press.

Zakim, Eric. 2006. *To Build and Be Built: Landscape, Literature, and the Construction of Zionist Identity.* Philadelphia: University of Pennsylvania Press.

Ze'evi, Dror. 1996. *An Ottoman Century: The District of Jerusalem in the 1600s.* Albany: State University of New York Press.

———. 2008. "Clans and Militias in Palestinian Politics." Crown Center for Middle East Studies, Brandeis University. www.brandeis.edu/crown/publications /meb/MEB26a.pdf.

Zerubavel, Yael. 1995. *Recovered Roots: Collective Memory and the Making of Israeli National Tradition.* Chicago: University of Chicago Press.

———. 2002. "The 'Mythological Sabra' and Jewish Past: Trauma, Memory, and Contested Identities." *Israel Studies* 7 (2): 115–44.

———. 2008. "Desert and Settlement: Space Metaphors and Symbolic Landscapes in the *Yishuv* and Early Israeli Culture." In *Jewish Topographies: Visions of Space, Traditions of Place,* edited by Julia Brauch, Anna Lippharadt, and Alexandra Nocke, 201–22. Burlington, VT: Ashgate.

———. 2009. "The Conquest of the Desert and the Settlement Ethos." In *The Desert Experience in Israel: Communities, Arts, Science, and Education in the Negev,* edited by A. Paul Hare and Gideon M. Kressel, 33–44. Lanham, MD: University Press of America.

Zu'bi, Nahla. 1984. "The Development of Capitalism in Palestine: The Expropria-tion of the Palestinian Direct Producers." *Journal of Palestine Studies* 13 (4): 88–109.

Zvielli, Alexander. 2013. "Happy Anniversary Israel Exploration Society." *Jerusalem Post,* August 14. www.jpost.com/Opinion/Columnists/Happy-anniversary-Israel-Exploration-Society-323064.

INDEX

Abdul Hamid II, Sultan, 208
absentee land owners, Palestinian, 15,
   184–85, 196, 239–48, 251, 266, 268, 288;
   Custodian of Absentee Property
   (CAP), 239–41; Israeli Absentee Prop-
   erty Law, 239–43, 266; Israeli Ministerial Committee on Abandoned Property, 239; present absentees, 240–43
Abu Dis, 2, 296
Abu-Freih tribe, 279, 280
Abu Madigem, Hameq, 282
Adams, John Quincy, 139, 143
Addington, Stephen, 67
adverse possession, rights of, 246–47, 262
aerial photography, Mandate Palestine,
   249–50
afforestation, Israeli, 258–67, 270–71,
   277–82, 281 fig
Agas, Ralph, 51–53, 52 fig; "A Preparative to
   Platting of Landes and Tenements for
   Surveigh," 53
Age of Reason, 200
agriculturalist perspective, on entitlement
   to land, 116–17, 127–30, 151–53, 155,
   177–78, 210
agriculture, 320n2; Amerindian, xii, 1,
   97–106, 100 fig, 124, 128–29, 151–53,
   160–62, 311, 322n18; Anglo-American,
   xii, 118–19, 139, 156–64; beans, 102;
   corn, 99–101, 100 fig, 160–62; cotton,
   322nn18,19; domestication, 98–99,
   159–64; England, xii, 27–91, 309, 319;
   environmentally sustainable, 172;

irrigation, 48, 99; Jewish settlers, 202,
   206–7, 209–10; labor, 18, 60, 63–64, 71,
   73, 84, 160, 209–10, 320n2, 322nn18,19;
   monoculture, 162; Ottoman, 180–92;
   Palestinian, 172, 176–77, 185–92, 259,
   268–69, 298–99; rent-maximizing
   farms, 16–18, 26, 63, 71–72, 80, 84,
   86–87, 311, 316; squash, 102. See also
   cultivation; farmsteads; pastoralism
Ahad Ha'am, 216; "Truth from the Land of
   Israel," 208–9
Aharoni, Reuven, 249
Ahmed Nimr Badran v. State of Israel
   (1961), 249–50
al-Araqib, 279–82, 281 fig
Albeck, Plia: Commission on Bedouin
   Lands, 267–68, 270, 291; *Elon Moreh*
   (1979), 291–92; "Summary Report of
   the Experts Team on Land Settlement
   on the Siyag and the Northern Negev"
   (Albeck Committee), 267–68, 270
Alexander II, assassination (1881), 202
Alexander VI, Pope, 116, 120
al-Hawashlah v. State of Israel (1984), 267,
   269
Aliya, 211, 212
al-Khalidi, Yusuf, 205
al-Khatib v. State of Israel (1962), 250
Allon, Yigal/Allon Plan, 285–87
al-Muqaddasi, *The Best Divisions for
   Knowledge of the Regions*, 175, 259–60
Alon Shvut, 299, 304
Al-Quds daily newspaper, 302

cartographic revolution: England, 14, 50.
See also mapping
cartouche, map, 131, 136–37, 138 fig, 228
Catawba map, 107–9, 108 fig
Catholic Church: England, 118. See also
Popes
Catlin, George, 153
census: British Mandate, 223, 265 fig;
Ottoman, 190, 193, 194, 269; U.S., 170.
See also population
chancery courts, 31, 43, 78
Charles, Prince, 134
Charles II, 136
Cheny, Lord, 51
Cherokees, removal, 165–68, 170, 322n18
Choctaws, 170, 321n3
Christianity: egalitarianism vs. English
enclosure, 41, 42, 45; English colonial-
ism, 115–24; missionaries to Amerindi-
ans, 104, 116–24, 153; Palestinian arche-
ology, 220; Palestinian population, 217,
310; Protestant English, 117–20. See also
Catholic Church
cities. See urban areas
Clare, John, xiv
Clark, John, Agriculture of the County of
Hereford, 76
"clearing" landscape, 6, 18–19, 313
Cobb, Thomas, 165
Cohen, Haim, 250
Coke, Edward: Chief Justice, 56, 76; The
Second Part of the Institutes of the Laws
of England, 47
collective/cooperative control: Amerindian
lands, 98, 103–6; English common fields,
28, 36, 186; kibbutzim and moshavim,
271; Palestinian mushā, 186–97. See also
"sharing the land"; use rights
colonialism, 73, 81, 309–10; early English
efforts, 121; English entitlement to,
116–70, 309, 314; mapping and, 50–51,
131–43; planting colonies, 118–26, 129;
Second Aliya (1904–14), 211; Yishuv, 209;
Zionist, 259, 310. See also Anglo-American colonialism; settler colonialism
Columbus, Christopher, 121, 122
Committee for a National Hebrew Education, 215

commoners. See English common fields
common good, land improvement as, 44,
56, 59, 60, 196, 309
comparative analysis, ix, xiv, 2, 3–6, 11,
20–21, 313
Conder, Claude R., 234–35, 284 fig, 298
Congress, U.S.: Indian removal, 16, 19, 144,
155, 165, 168; Trade and Intercourse Act
(1790), 150
conifer trees, 262, 263, 270, 277–78, 282,
316
Conoghquieson, Oneida chief, 159, 308
conquest: Anglo-American colonial, 73,
119, 129, 139, 152, 154–56; Arab (c. 638),
198; discovery equivalent to, 154–55;
Norman (1066), 28, 34; Ottoman, 172,
175–79, 183, 210–11; and reclamation,
177–79, 182; sovereignty and land rights
through, 176–79, 183, 210–11; William
the Conqueror, 28. See also military;
subduing the earth; taking possession of
land
"The Conquest of the Desert" exhibition,
257–58
Continental Congress, 148
contracts, with Amerindians, 145–47
control, 4–5, 8–11, 21, 25, 313–14, 317; of
Amerindian territory, x, 21, 95, 98–99,
103–6, 131–37, 143, 145–47, 311, 319n2;
collective/cooperative, 36, 98, 103–6,
186–88; of English landscape, 14, 16, 21,
25, 28, 34, 36, 40, 41, 81, 186, 319n2;
individual, 34, 36, 88; instruments of, ix,
5–6, 9–11, 81, 131, 277, 315; lordship, 64,
74–75, 188–89; of Palestinian land, ix, x,
xvi, 16, 21, 175, 186–97, 210, 230–306,
319n2. See also boundaries; colonialism;
dispossession; land ownership; power;
taking possession of land; technologies
of force; territoriality
Cooper, William, 156–57
cooperative management. See collective/
cooperative control
co-ownership, 186, 322n2
copyholders, 30–33, 38–47, 76; enclosure
ending tenancies of, 63, 81–82; evicted,
40–41, 42–43, 45, 47, 53–54; improvement writers vs., 46–47, 51, 53–54; of

inheritance, 31; legal revolution and, 74;
   for lives, 31, 32
corn: Amerindian, 99–101, 100 *fig*, 160–61;
   Anglo-American, 162
cosmology: Amerindian, 106–9, 321n4. *See*
   also religion; spirit worlds
costs: parliamentary enclosure, 80. *See also*
   fees; rents
cottagers, 32, 41, 59, 68, 83, 86
cotton economy, 322nn18,19
courts: Anglo-American, 160–61; Israeli,
   171, 249–52, 289; Mandate Palestine,
   250, 254. *See also* English courts;
   Supreme Court
covetousness, 4, 7; Anglo-American colonists, xi, 314–15; English enclosure, 44,
   61, 314–15; imaginative geography
   justifying, 9, 11, 314–15; improvement
   discourse supporting, 45, 61; Jewish
   land, 201–4, 232, 243, 291, 314–15; moral
   economy condemning, 42, 45, 56;
   technologies of force enlisted for, 10–11,
   14. *See also* land hunger
Cowper, John, 66, 67
Cox, David, 83
Crashaw, William, 122, 124–25, 126
Creek Indians, 112, 165, 166, 168, 307, 321n3
criminalization: English land law, 77–78.
   See also police power; trespassers
Crown: Anglo-American colonialization,
   143, 144, 145, 147–50; Charles II, 136;
   commission to grant exemptions from
   earlier anti-enclosure statutes (1618), 56;
   Commission Report on Depopulation
   (1517), 41, 43; confiscated royalist
   estates, 58; Crown courts, 42; Crown
   law, 37, 56; Edward I, 30, 319n3; Elizabeth I, 49, 50, 51, 117–20; empire-building, 50; enclosure opposition, 42–43, 56,
   76; enclosure support, 56, 76; George
   III, 88, 147; Henry VII, 42, 117, 118;
   Henry VIII, 117; James I, 121–22; King
   Philip's War (1775–76), 145–46; land
   owned by, 179; Prince Charles, 134;
   Royal Proclamation (1763), 144, 147–
   49; Stuarts, 121; taxes, 182–83; Tudors,
   42–43, 56, 76, 121
Crusades (1096–1271), 115

cultivation, 319n1, 320n2; Amerindian, xii,
   97–106, 100 *fig*, 128–29, 151–53, 213;
   Anglo-American, 118–19, 139, 156–64;
   English common fields, 18, 26–38, 41,
   45, 51, 58–75, 311; entitlement to land
   based on (agriculturalist perspective),
   116–17, 127–30, 151–53, 155, 177–78, 210;
   Jewish settlement, 207, 231, 259, 311, 316;
   land improvement characterized by, xi,
   xii, 11–12, 23, 47–48, 61–63, 66, 116–17,
   127–30, 151, 155–64, 177–78, 210; Palestinian small cultivators, 13, 171, 176–98,
   204, 209, 211–12, 231, 249–63, 268–70,
   292–94, 301, 303, 323n8; "reasonable
   cultivation," 250. *See also* agriculture
culture: difference, 268–69, 274–75, 277,
   314, 318; Jewish, 210; Palestinian *mushā*,
   187–88. *See also* education; language;
   names; religion
Cushman, Robert, 161
customary rights, 315–16; criminalization
   of, 77–78; easement, 37–38; English
   common fields, 36–42, 45, 46, 54,
   58–59, 75, 77–78; improvement writers
   and, 54, 58–59; Ottoman Palestine, 178,
   180–81; *profit-à-prendre*, 37–38

Damascus, Ottoman reforms and, 175–76
David, Paul, 3
dead land, Palestinian, 242–43, 251–55;
   "Dead Negev" doctrine, 267–70, 281,
   289, 315; Negev/Naqab, 243, 258–59,
   266–70; Ottoman Land Code, 192;
   West Bank, 288. *See also* empty land
   (terra nullius); *mawat* land
de Bry, Theodore, 124, 133
declaration, of state land, 291–94, 299–300,
   303, 304 *fig*, 305
Declaration of Independence, U.S., 147
Defoe, Daniel: *Robinson Crusoe*, 66, 205;
   Tour of Great Britain, 66
deforestation, Anglo-American, 155–59
de Grey, Thomas, 79, 89, 90 *fig*
dei Fieschi, Sinibaldo, 115
Deir Hanna, 250, 256
de Lamberville, Father Jean, 102
de Lery, Jean, 123
demesne land, 28–29, 30

demography. *See* population; redistribution of populations

demolitions, house: Bedouin, 276–82; English smallholders, 41; West Bank, 293, 295–96, 302

Denevan, William M., 320n1

desert: improving, 258–61, 264–67, 270–71, 277, 278 *fig*, 315. *See also* Negev/Naqab

de Tocqueville, Alexis, 166

Development Authority (DA), Israeli, 240–42, 247, 248, 266

Development Authority Law, Israeli, 239–43, 257–58

diaspora, Jewish, 198–204, 209–10, 217, 259

difference, cultural, 268–69, 274–75, 277, 314, 318

discourse of improvement. *See* land improvement discourse

discovery doctrine, 116–18, 120–21, 154–55

diseases: Amerindian, 109–10, 321n5; Black Death plague, 30–33, 38–41, 110

dispossession, x, 4, 20, 21, 308–17; Amerindian, 13, 16–21, 95, 112–70, 309; English smallholders into wage earners, 18, 19, 41, 60–76, 81–85, 257, 311–12, 316, 320n7; of infidels (Crusades), 115–17; Jordan, 288, 291. *See also* English enclosure; erasure; evictions; exclusion; lawfare of dispossession; Palestinian dispossession; removal; settler colonialism; taking possession of land

Domesday survey (1086), 319n3

domestication, agricultural, 98–99, 159–64

dominium: Arab Palestinian, 177, 211; English law, 116–18, 122, 128–30, 133, 137, 139, 144, 154–55, 160; Ottoman *(raqaba)*, 177; Roman law, 116; Zionist, 199, 202, 207, 244, 315

Dowson, Sir Ernest, "Preliminary Study of Land Tenure in Palestine," 196–97

Drake, Francis, 121

Dweikat, Mustafa/*Dweikat et al. v. Government of Israel/Elon Moreh* (1979), 290–94

Dymock, Cressy, *A Discoverie for Division or Setting Out Land*, 60

Earle, Robert, 83

Ebussuud, Sheikh ul-Islam, 180

economy: Amerindian food, 102, 158–59; Anglo-American, 155, 157–64; colonialism motivated by, 120, 122; costs of parliamentary enclosure, 80; of deforestation, 157–58; English agrarian, 28–45, 309, 311; *fellaheen*, 183–84; JNF fundraising, 15, 229–30, 229 *fig*; livestock, 159–64; moral, 41–44, 45, 187–88; Palestinian, 176, 187–88, 191–92; political economy, 18, 24–25; *waqf* (Islamic trust), 178–79, 182. *See also* agriculture; capitalism; land markets; modernization; profit; rents; taxes; trade

Ecton, Hertfordshire, 69 *fig*

education, Israel, 215, 216–17

Edward I, 30, 319n3

egalitarianism, Christian, 41, 42, 45

El'azar, 299, 304, 305

Elizabeth I, 49, 50, 51, 117–20

Elon Moreh, Jewish settlement, 290–94

Elon Moreh/Dweikat et al. v. Government of Israel (1979), Israeli Supreme Court, 290–94

empire-building: English, 50, 117–30. *See also* colonialism; conquest

empty land *(terra nullius)*, 12–13, 14, 46–47; Amerindian, xi, 12, 14, 97, 105, 113, 118, 121–43; blank slate, 129, 230, 234–35; *res nullius*, 127–28; *vacuum domicilium*, 14, 128, 130–31. *See also* dead land; Palestinian empty land; waste land

enclosure, 2, 3, 6, 13, 20–21, 307–18; "clearing" landscape, 6, 18–19, 313; in historical mirror, 313–18; improved land characterized by, 11, 23, 45–91, 314–15; Negev enclosure zone (Siyag), 234, 257–59, 264–82, 265 *fig*, 272 *fig*, 323n8; "proto-enclosed," 41. *See also* boundaries; English enclosure; exclusion rights; fences; modernization

England: agriculture, xii, 27–91, 309, 319; early modern landscapes, 27–44, 319; mapping, 14–15, 49–53, 55, 57 *fig*, 89, 90 *fig*, 95–96; Norman Conquest (1066),

English land tenure, 21, 27–44, 98, 312, 319;
customary rights, 36–42, 45, 46, 54,
58–59, 75, 77–78; hierarchical system,
28–30; Hundred Rolls (1279), 28, 29,
319n3; land improvement effects, 45–91,
309; manorial, 28–34, 82, 86–87; plague
affecting, 30–33, 38–41, 110; smallholders, 18, 19, 41, 60–75, 81–85, 311–12, 316,
320n7. *See also* copyholders
English law: contract, 145–47; Crown,
37, 56; estate acts, 76–77; fugitive serf,
30; *Quia Emptores* (Third Statute of
Westminster), 30. *See also* English
common law; English land law;
Parliament
engrossment, land, 40, 42, 68, 81
Enlightenment: European, 61, 151–52, 200;
Jewish *Haskalah*, 199–201, 203, 215
entitlement. *See* land rights; taking possession of land
environmental sustainability: agriculture,
172; forests, 158
Epstein, Yitzhak, "A Hidden Question,"
230, 231
erasure: Amerindian, 131–43, 151–52; Palestinian, 18, 228, 234, 237, 264, 280. *See
also* dispossession
Eretz Yisrael (Zion), 14–15, 198–231, 226 *fig*,
229 *fig*
estates: Palestinian large privately owned,
184–85, 194–96, 208. *See also* English
estates
evictions: English enclosure, 40–43, 45, 47,
53–54, 56, 76, 78–79; English opposition to, 42–43; Palestinian, 63, 231,
233–38. *See also* dispossession;
removal
excavating landscape, 218–21. *See also*
archeology
exclusion rights, xii–xiv, 4, 5–6, 10, 62, 75,
311–17; Anglo-American colonial view,
xii–xiii, 5, 6, 153, 155, 311, 316; English
enclosure, xii–xiii, 5, 6, 24, 26, 36, 43,
62, 74–75, 77, 88, 311, 316; Israeli, xiii,
xiv, 5, 6, 231, 316, 317. *See also* boundaries; dispossession; individual landed
property rights; landscape architecture;
trespassers

factories, labor, 24–25, 64–65
Faculty for Israeli/Palestinian Peace
(FFIPP), 1–2
Falah, Ghazi-Walid, xiv, 15, 245, 256–57,
264, 266, 270, 271, 273, 274, 323n8
families: Amerindian, 99, 103–5, 113; English family farms, 32–34, 80–84; Hussein family of Transjordan, 225; Jewish
settlement, 299–300. *See also* Crown;
Palestinian families
farmsteads: Anglo-American, 162–64. *See
also* agriculture; cultivation; English
farms; homesteads; tax farming
fear, power and, ix
fees: fee-simple title, 150, 155; fee for use
right to Ottoman-owned land, 182–83;
manorial economy, 29. *See also* costs;
rents
Felix, Menachem, 292
fellaheen, Palestinian, 182–92, 195, 196–98
fences, 128, 312, 317; Anglo-American, 96,
156–70, 316; English enclosure, xi–xiii,
16–17, 46, 47, 65, 79–80, 83, 88, 307, 316;
Iroquois deer fences, 113; Israeli, 308,
312; resistance action against, 26, 47,
55–56, 83, 88, 307–8, 317–18; *Robinson
Crusoe*, 66. *See also* walls
field systems, English, 27–28, 319n1;
regional, 27, 68–70, 319n2. *See also*
English common fields
Fifty Percent Rule, Israeli, 250, 292–94
fishing, Amerindian, 98–99, 102, 105, 311
Fitzherbert, John, 45, 48–49, 50, 53, 74, 118;
Boke of Husbandrye, 48–49; *Boke of
Surveying and Improvement*, 48–49;
"Howe to Make a Townshippe Worth
20 Marke a yere worthe 20 .xx. li.
[pounds]," 48
fixity, spatial: Amerindians and, 101–4,
113–14. *See also* boundaries
food economy: Amerindian, 102, 158–59.
See also agriculture; subsistence systems
footpaths, English common field, 38, 39 *fig*,
79
force. *See* evictions; military; technologies
of force; violence
forest management: afforestation by Zionists, 258–67, 270–71, 277–82, 281 *fig*;

Haifa, 184, 206, 216
Hakluyt, Richard, *Discourse of Western Planting*, 118–21, 122, 123, 125
Halevi, Yehuda, 199–200
Halima, Eliyahu, 268, 269
Hanafi, Sari, 319n2
Hapoel Hatzair (The Young Worker) organization, 211, 216
Hapoel Hatzair (The Young Worker) publication, 211
Harel, Israel, 298
Har Gilo, 287, 297 *fig*, 299
Harriot, Thomas, *Briefe and True Report of the New Found Land of Virginia*, 123–24, 125, 153
Hartlib, Samuel, 59–60
Haselbech village, 56, 57 *fig*
Ha-Shahar Hebrew monthly, 203–4
Hashiloach journal, 219–20
Haskalah (Jewish Enlightenment), 199–201, 203, 215
Hebrew Bible, 222, 236, 261–62
Hebrew language, 15, 203–4, 214–30; names, 203, 217–18; place-names/ hebraicization of landscape, 15, 203, 213–14, 221–37, 260. *See also* Judaization
Hebrew Language College, Jerusalem, 217
Hebrew schools, 215, 217
Hebrew Teachers Association, 215
Hebrew University, Jerusalem, 216
Hebron, 176, 227–28
hedges, xii, 88, 128, 317; English enclosure, 16–17, 27–28, 46, 65, 79–80, 87–88, 316; resistance action against, 26, 44, 47, 55–56, 88
Henry, Lord Stafford, 49
Henry VII, 42, 117, 118
Henry VIII, 117
heritable land rights, 31, 181, 195
Herodotus, *The Histories*, 175
Herzl, Theodor, xiii, 13, 202, 209, 214, 310, 315; *Altneuland*, 204, 207–8, 209, 218, 220; *Jewish State*, 199, 204–8, 209; World Zionist Congress, 215; "The Zionist Deputation in Palestine: A Travel Report," 206
Higher Planning Council (HPC), Israeli, 289

Hillhouse, James, 150
history, 4, 20, 312; archeology, 218–21, 282; comparative, ix, xiv, 2, 3–6, 11, 20–21, 313; enclosure in mirror of, 313–18; Foucault's *History of Sexuality* on power and resistance, 308; Hebrew in Palestine, 213; Herodotus, 175; Jewish antiquities, 213, 218–21, 322n4; land linearity, 94; Palestinian landscape, 175–97, 210–11, 218–21; Robertson and Sullivan texts on Amerindians, 151–54
Hockney, David, 24, 24 *fig*, 91
Holland, James, 150
Holme, Thomas, 14, 134–37, 135 *fig*
Holmes, Thomas, 69 *fig*
homesteads: Anglo-American settler, 17, 18, 137–39, 311, 316. *See also* farmsteads
Hope Simpson, John, "Report on Immigration, Land Settlement, and Development," 230–31
Houghton, Mary, 78
Hull, Edward, 269
human actors: landscape and, 7, 8, 22; society and, 7; "territoriality," 8–9, 313. *See also* covetousness; imaginative geography
Hundred Rolls (1279), 28, 29, 319n3
hunting, Amerindian, 98–99, 102, 105, 111–13, 152–54, 156, 161, 308, 311
Hura, 273, 274
Hussein family, Transjordan, 225

identity: Jewish, 219; Palestinians, 175
imaginative geography, x–xi, 4–13, 17, 20–21, 314–15; Amerindian, 94, 107–9; Anglo-American colonists, xi, 13, 14, 17, 95, 106–9, 117–70, 314; desert, 258–61; England, 12, 14, 26, 51–53, 89, 91, 117–30; of improvement, 11–13, 46, 47–53, 89, 91, 314; Jewish land, xiii, 13, 14–16, 198–261, 294, 296–98, 306; mapping, 10–11, 14, 89, 106–9, 130–43, 132–42 *figs*, 213–31; "performative," 9; Said on, x, 8–9, 20, 314. *See also* land improvement discourse; reimagining and remaking landscapes
imagined economic order, moral economy, 42

enclosed," 41; reinventions of, x–xi, 9, 12, 130–43, 150–53; savage, 128–29. *See also* agriculture; empty land *(terra nullius)*; linearity; reimagining and remaking landscapes

landscape architecture, 8–11, 14, 16–17, 298, 310, 315–17. *See also* fences; hedges; reimagining and remaking landscapes; walls

Land Settlement Ordinance (1928), Mandate Palestine, 245

land speculators, Anglo-American, 139, 145, 147, 149, 156–57

land tenure, 4–6, 310–11, 315–16; Amerindian, 97–114, 144, 311; Anglo-American colonial, 312; collective/cooperative, 28, 36, 98, 103–6, 186–87; Jewish, 242, 312; Palestine historic, 175–97. *See also* customary rights; *dominium*; English land tenure; freeholders; landed property rights; land ownership; land rights; Palestinian land tenure; possession; tenancy

language: Amerindian and old Welsh and English, 121; British-ruled Palestine, 217; German, 214, 216; Jewish nationalism based on, 216; *Yishuv*, 214–18. *See also* Arabic; Hebrew

las Casas, Bartolomé de, *A Short Account of the Destruction of the Indies*, 120

Laurence, Edward, 67

law: canon, 115, 126; Mandate Palestine ordinances, 245, 252- 53, 255, 262, 267–68; natural, 61–62, 117, 125–26; Ottoman, 176–79, 187–97, 244–48, 251–54, 261, 263, 267–68, 290, 292, 322n2; Roman, 116, 127–28, 182; U.S. Indian Removal Act (1830), 16, 19, 144, 168; U.S. Land Ordinance (1785), 139–40; U.S. Trade and Intercourse Act (1790), 148–49, 150. *See also* courts; English law; Israeli law; lawfare of dispossession; Parliament; rights; treaties

lawfare of dispossession, 8, 10, 14, 315; Anglo-American, 16, 19, 95–96, 128–29, 143–55; English enclosure, 15–16, 33, 56, 63–91, 69 *fig*, 316, 320n4; Zionist, 232–58, 266–79, 291–94

Laxton, 35 *fig*, 39 *fig*

legal revolution, 15–16, 31–32, 47, 74–78. *See also* lawfare of dispossession

Lehavim, 271, 280

Levens, George, 57 *fig*

Levin, Moshe, 247

Lewis and Clark expedition, 153

Lifshitz, Zalman, 234, 239–40; Negev Names Committee, 234, 266; "Report on the Need for Legal Settlement of the Issue of Absentee Property," 240

linearity, xiii, 50, 94, 316; Anglo-American, 17, 93–95, 109, 113–14, 131, 134–35, 137–43, 141 *fig*, 155–70; English enclosure, 23–24, 60, 65, 79, 86, 88; Green Line, 1–2, 285, 291–98, 312; Jewish settlements, 172, 259. *See also* boundaries; fences; geometric order; grids; hedges; walls

Linebaugh, Peter, with Markus Rediker, *The Many-Headed Hyrda*, xii

livestock, 159–64. *See also* pastoralism

Locke, John, 61–63, 66, 250; and Amerindians, 61, 62, 129–30, 151, 213, 259; Anglo-American colonial official, 61, 309, 321n3; enclosure advocate, 23, 61–63, 75, 268, 309; labor-driven theory of landed property rights, xii, 1, 23, 61–63, 181, 206, 211, 213; land improvement discourse, xii, 1, 12, 13, 61–63, 75, 129–30, 151, 213, 259, 268, 314; *Second Treatise*, 63, 129–30; subduing the earth, 12, 61, 62, 153

London Gazette, 136

lordship: England, 64, 74–75; Palestinian, 188–89

Loughborough, Lord, 78

Louisiana Purchase (1803), 165

Magnes, Judah, 219

malikane, Ottoman reform, 184

Malthus, Thomas, *Essay on the Principle of Population*, 65

Mandate Palestine, 175, 222–27, 231, 232; absentees, 239; aerial photography, 249–50; census, 223, 265 *fig*; courts, 250, 254; end (1947), 245; Hebrew, 215, 216–17, 221–24, 234–36; Jerusalem, 254,

Occupied Palestinian Territories, ix, xiv, 16; land taken for Jewish settlements, 16–18, 172–73, 172 *fig*, 282–95, 298–306, 301 *fig*, 311–12, 315. *See also* Gaza/Gaza Strip; West Bank

OED. See *Oxford English Dictionary (OED)*

Oklahoma, Amerindians relocated to, 170

olive trees, 260–62

Oneida Indians, 153, 159, 308

open fields, England, 27–28, 34, 38, 46, 64

opponents: to English enclosure, 41–47, 56, 66–67, 76, 84–85; to Israeli expropriation of Palestinian land, 241, 291. *See also* resistance

Ordinance for Regulation of Forest Lands and the Protection of Trees (1920), Mandate Palestine, 262

Oslo peace process, 293, 300, 301, 302

O'Sullivan, John L., 321n6

Ottomans, 171–98; Bedouin rights to land, 269–70; cadastral system, 194–95, 244; conquest (1516), 172, 175–79, 183, 210–11; defeat (1916–17), 196; Land Code (1858), 177, 189–97, 244–48, 251–54, 261, 263, 267–68, 290, 292, 322n2; mapping, 194–95, 244, 322n1; Palestine, 171–72, 175–97, 215, 244–48, 251–54, 261, 263, 267–68, 290, 292, 294, 322n1; state land, 176–98, 251–53; Sultanate, 179, 180, 195, 208; *Tanzimat* reforms, 175–77, 189–97, 244; taxes, 176–77, 180, 182–84, 188–94, 196, 246, 252, 269

Outline Plan (2000), "Report Number 4: The Proposed Plan and the Main Planning Policies," 295, 323n12

ownership. *See* control; land ownership; possession; property

Oxford English Dictionary (OED): on land improvement, 47–48; to plant, 118–19; on surveying, 50

Page, William, 83

painting, landscape, 24

Pakistan, expropriation of Hindu and Sikh property, 240

Palestine, 171–318; Arab conquest (c. 638), 198; historic, 175–97, 210–11, 218–21;

imaginative geography, 14–15; Ottoman, 171–72, 175–97, 215, 244–48, 251–54, 261, 263, 267–68, 290, 292, 294, 322n1; settler colonialism, 14–19, 206–13, 302; *Yishuv* prevailing in (1948–49), 17. *See also* Israeli state; Jewish settlements; Mandate Palestine; Occupied Palestinian Territories; Palestinians; Zion *(Eretz Yisrael)*; Zionists

Palestine Exploration Fund (PEF), 194, 234–35, 260, 284 *fig*

Palestine Land Development Company, 270

Palestinian dispossession, x, xiii–xiv, 6, 19–21, 230–306, 308–9, 310, 312; as absentee land owners, 15, 184–85, 196, 239–48, 251, 266, 268, 288; Bedouin, 233–37, 257–79, 290, 315; *Elon Moreh* and, 290–94; Galilee, 238, 243, 245–48, 251, 255–57, 266, 290; Hope Simpson report on, 230–31; improvement discourse justifying, 5, 12, 13, 21, 205, 207, 209–13, 314–15; for Jewish settlements, 16–19, 171–73, 172 *fig*, 219–21, 230–306, 310–12, 315; Knesset opposition, 241; lawfare of, 232–58, 266–79, 291–94; by mapping, 14–15, 213–37, 226 *fig*, 229 *fig*, 244, 315; Negev/Naqab, 233–35, 238, 257–59, 264–82, 272 *fig*, 275, 277, 290; reallocations of land rights, 4, 16, 22, 186–87, 232, 240–41, 245, 303; to resettlement outside Palestine, 208; settlement of title, 238–57, 266–67, 290; tree-planting and, 258–82. *See also* Palestinian resistance

Palestinian empty land, 12, 209, 310; absentee land owners, 15, 184–85, 196, 239–48, 251, 266, 268, 288; Ariel, 1, 171; blank slate, 230, 234–35; Brawer map, 228, 229 *fig*; dead land, 192, 242–43, 251–55, 258–59, 266–70, 281, 288, 289, 315; *mawat* land, 181–82, 246, 251–55, 267–70; Naḥḥālīn, 300; Naqab/Negev, 234–35, 243, 258–59, 266–70, 281

Palestinian families: absentee land owners, 246; estate owners, 184–85; *hamula*, 187; *mushā*, 186–87; Naḥḥālīn, 300, 302; Nassar, 171–72, 305

Palestinian land ownership, 15, 18, 238–48, 268–70; absentee, 15, 184–85, 196, 239–48, 251, 266, 268, 288; Mandate Palestine, 290–91; Ottoman state, 176–98, 246, 248

Palestinian land tenure, x, 18, 21, 175–98, 243–48; Mandate Palestine, 290–91; *miri*, 176–85, 191–92, 246, 248, 251–55, 290, 292; *mülk*, 179–80; *mushā*, 177, 185–97, 311; registration, 194–97, 246, 251, 253, 255, 270, 290–94, 300. *See also* Palestinian empty land; Palestinian land ownership

Palestinian resistance, 199, 205, 207, 318; Arab Revolt (1936–39), 262, 263; Bedouin, 266–70, 274–75, 280–82; fence breaking, 308, 318; Intifada, 283; to Jewish settlements, 171–72, 199, 205, 207, 263, 283, 305, 308, 318; Nassar family, 171–72, 305; rioting between Jews and Palestinians (1929), 230

Palestinians: agriculture, 172, 176–77, 185–92, 259, 268–69, 298–99; Arab, 198, 205–11, 231, 233–34; identity, 175; land rights, 176–97, 209, 210–13, 244, 267–70, 285, 292, 311; Revolt vs. Zionists and Mandate (1936–39), 262, 263; small cultivators, 13, 171, 176–98, 204, 209, 211–12, 231, 249–63, 268–70, 292–94, 301, 303, 323n8; trespassers, 246–49, 253, 255, 275–76, 283–84; use rights, 176–92, 261, 292. *See also* Palestine; Palestinian . . . ; population

Palestinian villages, 18; *mushā*, 185–88, 193, 197; Naḥḥālīn, 298–306; Ottoman, 176, 183–84, 193; Palestinian dead land, 242–43; rents, 188–89; *Saleh Badran* and, 254. *See also* Bedouin villages

Palmer, Edward Henry, 234–35, 260, 268, 269

Parliament, English: Black Act (1723), 77; enclosure laws, 15–16, 33, 56, 63–91, 69 *fig*, 316, 320n4. *See also* English law

"participant observation," 21–22

partition plan, Mandate Palestine, 225, 233

Paspehay, Indian king, 144–45

pastoralism: Amerindian, 122; Anglo-American livestock, 159–64; Bedouin,

323n8; English common fields, 12, 33–36, 35 *fig*, 42–43, 57 *fig*, 71, 82, 319n5

patent rights, 116

patronage, mapping, 50, 51

peace process: Faculty for Israeli/Palestinian Peace (FFIPP), 1–2; Oslo, 293, 300, 301, 302; San Remo Peace Conference (1920), 217

"peasant land market," in medieval England, 32

Penn, William, 136–37

Pennsylvania, map, 134–36, 135 *fig*

"Permanent Arrangement of the Bedouins of the Siyag in the Negev" (Israeli military), 271–72

Petah Tikva, 222

petition: *Elon Moreh* (1979), 291–92; for parliamentary enclosure, 78–81; vs. West Haddon enclosure (1765), 307

Philadelphia, in map, 136–37

photography, aerial, Mandate Palestine, 249–50

piecemeal enclosure, 40–41

Pierce, Mark, 35 *fig*, 39 *fig*

pigs, Anglo-American settlement, 159, 160, 161

Pindruss, Yitzhak, 298, 299–300

Pinhasovitch, Yosef, 247

Pinsker, Leo, "Auto-Emancipation: An Appeal to His People by a Russian Jew," 202–3

"pious activities," Islamic land category, 178–79

place-names: Amerindian, 107, 133, 134; Anglo-American, 131, 133, 134; Arabic, 15, 221–22, 233–36, 266; Hebrew/hebraicization of landscape, 15, 203, 213–14, 221–37, 260, 266

plague, Black Death, 30–33, 38–41, 110

Planning and Building Law (1965), Israeli, 276

planting, 118–26, 129, 258–82. *See also* colonialism; cultivation; trees

Plat of the Seven Ranges of Townships, 140, 141 *fig*

pogroms, in Russia, 202

rack-rent tenant, 84
Raleigh, Walter, 121, 123
raqaba, 177, 180. *See also dominium*
Rauch, Jim, xiv
reallocations of land rights, 4; cultivator to
  lordship, 188–89; English commons to
  enclosure, 25, 60, 63, 79–80, 83, 187;
  Palestinian to Jewish, 4, 16, 22, 186–87,
  232, 240–41, 245, 303. *See also* taking
  possession of land
"reasonable cultivation," Mandate Palestine, 250
reciprocity: Amerindian trade principle,
  109, 110, 111. *See also* "sharing the land"
reclamation: land rights through, 177–78,
  179, 182. *See also* cultivation;
  improvement
redemption: afforestation as, 258–60,
  270–71; deforestation as, 157; Jewish
  land, xiii, 198–99, 201–5, 214, 219, 228,
  238, 243, 258, 259–60
Rediker, Markus, with Peter Linebaugh,
  The Many-Headed Hyrda, xii
redistribution of land, 25, 60, 83, 186–89.
  See also reallocations of land rights;
  taking possession of land
redistribution of populations, 18–19; disinherited, 6, 10, 310, 312, 317; English
  smallholders into wage earners, 18, 19,
  41, 60–76, 81–85, 257, 311–12, 316,
  320n7; undesirables, 120. *See also* dispossession; removal; trespassers
referees, parliamentary enclosure, 320n4
reformers: of Amerindians, 153–54, 164;
  writers, 43
refugees: Jewish, 198; Palestinian, 17, 19,
  238–40, 243, 245, 312, 317. *See also*
  immigration
Regional Council for the Unrecognized
  Villages in the Negev (RCUV), 275
regionalism, English agriculture, 27, 68–70,
  319n2
registration, Palestinian land, 194–97, 246,
  251, 253, 255, 270, 290–94, 300
reimagining and remaking landscapes,
  314–15; Amerindian, 115–70; English
  common fields, 45–91; Palestinian,
  198–306. *See also* empty land *(terra*

nullius); imaginative geography; land
  improvement; technologies of force
reinventions: of landscape, x–xi, 9, 12,
  130–43, 150–53. *See also* reimagining
  and remaking landscapes
religion, 310, 312. *See also* Christianity;
  cosmology; Hebrew Bible; Islam; spirit
  worlds
removal, 310, 313–14, 317; Amerindians, 16,
  19, 144, 164–70, 258, 312, 322nn18,19;
  Bedouins, 233, 235–36, 258, 264, 266–71,
  274–75, 279, 290. *See also* dispossession;
  evictions
rents: English rent-maximizing farms,
  16–18, 26, 63, 71–72, 80, 84, 86–87, 311,
  316; on Palestinian villages, 188–89;
  rack-rent, 84. *See also* fees; tenancy
"Report Number 4: The Proposed Plan and
  the Main Planning Policies," Outline
  Plan (2000), 295, 323n12
reservations, Amerindian, 17, 96, 144, 169
  fig, 170, 258, 312, 316–17
resistance, 317–18; Amerindian, 307–8,
  317–18; to English enclosure, 26, 43–44,
  47, 55–56, 76, 78, 82–83, 88, 307, 312;
  fence and hedge breaking, 26, 44, 47,
  55–56, 83, 88, 307–8, 317–18; poaching,
  44; power arousing, 19, 21, 308, 318. *See
  also* opponents; Palestinian resistance
res nullius, 127–28. *See also* empty land
  (terra nullius)
return, Jewish concept of, 218, 219, 220
Revolutionary War, American, 13, 144, 147,
  148, 149, 164
Rhode Island, Roger Williams, 103, 161
rights: Israeli state, 232; patent, 116; possession, 125–26; property distinguished
  from, 74; states vs. federal, 165. *See also*
  customary rights; land rights; law; use
  rights
rioting, between Jews and Palestinians
  (1929), 230
Rishon LeZion, 206, 215, 222
roads: Anglo-American, 163; English
  landscape transformed by, 88–89, 90 *fig*;
  Naḥḥālīn, 298. *See also* footpaths;
  tracks
Roanoke, 121, 123

Robertson, Thomas, 73
Robertson, William, 314; *History of America*, 151–54
Robinson Crusoe (Defoe), 66, 205
Roman law, 116, 127–28, 182
Romanticism, 200–201
Rosh Tzurim (Zurim), 283, 285, 299, 303–5
Royal Geographical Society, Names Committee, 222–24
Royal Proclamation (1763), England, 144, 147–49
royalty, English. *See* Crown
rural geography: English, 23–24, 24 *fig*, 27; Palestinian, 197. *See also* agriculture; empty land *(terra nullius)*; English common fields; pastoralism; villages

Saban, Moshe, 250
sachem (Amerindian chief), 103–6, 133, 158–59, 168, 308
Said, Edward, 8–9, 20, 314; *Culture and Imperialism*, x
Sakhnin, 256–57, 256 *fig*
Saleh Badran (1962), 253–55
Samuel, Sir Herbert, 217
San Diego/Tijuana, ix, 2, 3
San Remo Peace Conference (1920), 217
Sasquesahanough Indian, 133
Sasson, Talia, 300
Sauer, Carl, 7
Sauk nation, 97
savages: Amerindians as, 54, 93, 121–30, 134, 150–53, 155, 170; Arabs as, 209; benevolent, 123–25; contemptible, 125–27, 150–52; English commoners as, 54
Saxton, Christopher, *Atlas of the Counties of England and Wales*, 51
schools, Israel, 215, 216–17
Schuyler, Phillip, 148
seasonality: and Amerindian land rights, 105; Amerindian mobility, 102, 105
Second Aliya (1904–14), 211
Secoton, 100 *fig*, 124, 153
security: Jewish settlements for, 286, 288, 289, 291–92. *See also* military; national interest
Segev Shalom, 273, 274

selions, arable fields, 33–34
Seminoles, removal, 165, 170
Seneca Indians, 153
settlement: cultural differences over meaning of, 268–69; "strict settlement" rules, 77. *See also* Jewish settlements; settler colonialism
settlement of title: British Mandate, 245; Israeli, 238–57, 266–67, 290
settler colonialism, x–xiii, 5; Anglo-American homesteads, 17–18, 137–39, 311, 316; Palestine, 14–19, 206–13, 302. *See also* Jewish settlements; taking possession of land
severalty: Amerindian losing land to, 95, 146; English enclosure turning common land to, 15–16, 45–46, 63, 76, 78, 79–80, 84, 95, 180; *mülk* land right like, 180. *See also* subdivided spaces
"sharing the land": Amerindian, 104. *See also* collective/cooperative control; use rights
Sharon, Ariel, 277
Shehadeh, Raja, xiv, 177, 178, 179, 283, 286
sheikh, village, 183–84
Shilo settlement, 289
Sinclair, John, 73
Six-Day War (June 1967), 267, 283, 285–86, 288, 294
Six Nation Indians, council, 148
Siyag (enclosure zone), 234, 257–59, 264–82, 265 *fig*, 272 *fig*, 323n8
slave labor, 322nn18,19
Slouschz, Nahum, 218, 219–20
small cultivators, Palestinian, 13, 171, 176–98, 204, 209, 211–12, 231, 249–63, 268–70, 292–94, 301, 303, 323n8
smallholders, English enclosure displacing, 18, 19, 41, 60–75, 81–85, 311–12, 316, 320n7
Smith, Adam: division of labor, 24–25, 64, 87; *Wealth of Nations*, 24–25, 64, 68
Smith, John, 105; *Description of the Country, the Commodities, People, Government, and Religion*, 131–33; maps, 14, 131–34, 132 *fig*, 133 *fig*
Smith, Richard, 113
Smolenskin, Peretz, 203

Smollet, Tobias, *Humphrey Clinker*, 72
socage use right, 28–29, 30
social undesirables: colonies for, 120. *See also* savages
Society for the Reclamation of Antiquities initiative, 218
socioeconomic effects: Amerindian contact with colonists, 18–19, 111–12; English enclosure, 18–19, 32–33, 84–86; moral economy, 42. *See also* dispossession; labor; land ownership; poor; wage earners
sovereignty: Amerindian chief *(sachem)*, 103–6; Anglo-American colonial mapping, 137; British Mandate in Palestine, 223, 232, 235; through conquest (Ottoman), 176–79, 183, 210–11; English *imperium*, 116–18, 121; European sovereignty in North America, 154–55; Jewish land/Israel, 197, 202, 205, 232, 233–34, 238, 244, 286; monarchical, 116
space: of belonging, 5–6; fixity, 101–4, 113–14; power and, ix, 2, 20–21, 313; "spacio-cide," 319n2. *See also* land; subdivided spaces; territoriality
Spain: English entitlement compared with, 119–21, 123; territory of non-Christians, 116
speculators, land, 139, 145, 147, 149, 156–57
spirit worlds, Amerindian, 97–98, 106–9, 110–11, 321n4
springs, Naḥḥālīn, 283
standard of living, moral economy standard of living, 42
state land: declaration of, 291–94, 299–300, 303, 304 *fig*, 305; Israeli, 16, 17–18, 171, 182, 232, 237–57, 266–70, 278, 285–94, 299–306, 304 *fig*; Mandate Palestine state domain, 290–91; Ottoman, 176–98, 251–53
State of Israel v. Khatib and Da'ash (1960), 250
State of Israel v. Saleh Badran (1962), 253–55
states. *See* British; Crown; Israeli state; nation-state; United States
Statute of Limitation (1958), Israeli, 248
Steel, James, 78

Steel v. Houghton et Uxor (1788), 77–78
St. German, Christopher, *Doctor and Student*, 74
Stoddard, Solomon, 146
Strachey, William, xi, 127, 128
Stretton Baskerville (Warwickshire), enclosure, 41
"strict settlement" rules, 77
Stuarts, English, 121
subdivided spaces: Amerindian, 113; English landscape, 24, 25, 63, 65, 79, 86, 88, 89; Israeli, 244–45; Palestine partition plan, 225, 233. *See also* boundaries; enclosure; fences; hedges; walls; zones of impassable space
subduing the earth: commandment, 12, 61, 62, 117, 153, 156. *See also* conquest
subsistence systems: Amerindian, 97, 98–106, 111–13, 158–59, 161; English, 159; Palestinian, 177, 187–88. *See also* agriculture; fishing; gathering; hunting
Sukenik, Eleazar, 219
Suleyman I, Sultan, 180
Sullivan, James, 314; *The History of Land Titles in Massachusetts* (1801), 151–54
Sultanate, Ottoman, 179, 180, 195, 208
"Summary Report of the Experts Team on Land Settlement on the Siyag and the Northern Negev" (Albeck Committee), 267–68, 270
Supreme Court: Israeli, 249–50, 252–55, 267–69, 288, 290–94; U.S., 16, 144, 154–55, 167; Virginia, 150
Supreme Land Settlement Committee (SLSC), 247
surveying, 316; British Mandate in Palestine, 245, 249, 290–91; for English enclosure, 48–50, 53–56, 58, 79; Israeli, 171, 244–45, 251, 289–91, 300; U.S., 140, 150
sustainability: agriculture, 172; forests, 158
Symonds, William, 122, 128; "Virginia: A Sermon Preached at White Chapel," 126
Syria: Golan Heights taken from, 285; Ottoman, 175–76, 183, 186, 193